Unequal
Partnerships

DATE DUE

OCT 26 1991		
JAN 8 1992		

DEMCO NO. 38-298

Unequal Partnerships

The Political Economy of Urban Redevelopment in Postwar America

Edited by Gregory D. Squires

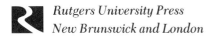*Rutgers University Press*
New Brunswick and London

Library of Congress Cataloging-in-Publication Data

Unequal partnerships.

    Bibliography: p.
    Includes index.
    1. Urban renewal—United States—Case studies.
  2. Urban policy—United States—Case studies.
  3. Business and politics—United States—Case studies.
  I. Squires, Gregory D.
  HT175.U56   1989   307.7'6'0973   88-32534
  ISBN 0-8135-1451-7 (cloth)
  ISBN 0-8135-1452-5 (pbk.)

British Cataloging-in-Publication information available

Hirsch

Contents

DAVID W. BARTELT is an Associate Professor of Geography and Urban Studies and Director of the Institute for Public Policy Studies at Temple University. His research has focused on the historical, economic, and political factors of urban structure, particularly as it affects neighborhood stability and change and the distribution of housing opportunities across neighborhoods. He is the coauthor of a recent theoretical review of urban sociospatial structures ("Islands in the Stream: Neighborhoods in the Political Economy of Cities," published in Altman and Wandersman's *Neighborhood and Community Environments*) and the forthcoming Philadelphia volume in the Temple University Press Comparative American Cities Series. He has an ongoing consulting relationship with a wide variety of community organizations in Philadelphia regarding housing and economic revitalization efforts.

LARRY BENNETT is a member of the Political Science Department of DePaul University. He is coauthor of *Chicago: Race, Class, and the Response to Urban Decline* 1987) and has contributed articles to several urban affairs and public policy journals. His principal research interest is the politics of downtown and neighborhood redevelopment.

SCOTT CUMMINGS is Associate Dean of Urban Affairs at the School of Urban Policy, University of Louisville. He has published numerous books and articles dealing with urban policy, minority relations, and urban education. He is the editor of the *Journal of Urban Affairs*, and is currently completing a new book dealing with racial transition in declining neighborhoods.

PETER DREIER is Director of Housing at the Boston Redevelopment Authority and housing policy advisor to Boston mayor Ray Flynn. Before joining Mayor Flynn's administration, he was Assistant Professor at Tufts University (1977–1983). He is the coauthor of *Who Rules Boston?* (1984), a study of that city's corporate power structure, and coeditor of *Jewish Radicalism* (1973). His articles on urban politics, housing, and social movements have appeared in many journals, including *Social Problems, Social Policy,* the *International Journal of Urban and Regional Research,* the *Harvard Business Review,* the *Columbia Journalism Review,* and elsewhere. He has worked closely with a variety of grassroots organizations, such as Massachusetts Fair Share, the Massachusetts Tenants Organization, Citizen Action, and others. He is currently on the board of the National Low-Income Housing Coalition and a member of the Institute for Policy Studies' housing task force.

NORMAN I. FAINSTEIN is Dean of Liberal Arts and Sciences and Professor of Sociology at Baruch College of the City University of New York. He has written extensively on urban political economy and policy, and is coauthor of *Restructuring the City* (revised edition, 1986).

SUSAN S. FAINSTEIN is Professor of Urban Planning and Policy Development at Rutgers University. She is author of numerous books and articles on urban political economy and urban redevelopment, and coauthor of *Restructuring the City* (revised edition, 1986).

JOE R. FEAGIN is Professor of Sociology at the University of Texas at Austin. Author of twenty books and several dozen scholarly articles, he does research on public policy and inequality issues, particularly race and gender discrimination, and urban political-economic development, including comparative studies of European and American cities. A major product of this research on urban economic development is a recent book, *Free Enterprise City: Houston in Political-Economic Perspective* (1988). Some of his comparative urban research has appeared in *The Capitalist City* (1987), edited with Michael P. Smith.

JOHN I. GILDERBLOOM is Associate Professor of Urban Policy at the University of Louisville. Gilderbloom's work includes fifteen journal articles, thirteen chapters in edited books, four monographs, six syndicated newspaper opinion pieces, and six government reports. He is editor of *Rent Control: A Source Book*, coauthor (with Richard Appelbaum) of *Rethinking Rental Housing*, and coauthor of the forthcoming books, *Community Versus Commodity: Tenants and the American City* (with Stella Capek) and *The Invisible Jail: The Disabled in the Urban Environment* (with Mark Rosentraub). Gilderbloom's research on urban problems has received numerous awards, including honors from the American Planning Association, the Douglas McGregor Memorial Award, and the American Institute of Architects. In 1987 he received the University of Houston's College of Social Science Teaching Excellence award.

GREGORY A. GUAGNANO is a lecturer at the University of California, Davis. He has a joint appointment in the Department of Applied Behavioral Sciences and the Department of Sociology with research interests in the areas of natural resource sociology and network analysis. He currently serves on the board of directors of several community organizations within the city of Sacramento.

W. DENNIS KEATING is an Associate Professor in the College of Urban Affairs and the College of Law at Cleveland State University. His research includes urban and neighborhood development, housing, and urban policy and politics. His most recent published work includes a chapter in the *Handbook of Housing and the Built Environment in the United States* (1988) and *Housing and Community Development Law* (1989). His evaluation research on housing and community development has been sponsored by the Ford, Cleveland, and Gund foundations.

C. THEODORE KOEBEL is the Associate Director of the University of Louisville's Urban Studies Center and the deputy editor of the *Journal of Urban Affairs*. He conducts research in the areas of housing and economic development. He is a member of the board of directors of several nonprofit development corporations, some of which he helped create. He received his Ph.D. in Urban Planning and Policy Development from Rutgers University.

NORMAN KRUMHOLZ, Professor at Cleveland State University's College of Urban Affairs, was Assistant Planning Director for the City of Pittsburgh (1965–1969) and Planning Director for the city of Cleveland (1969–1979). He is writing a book on planning theory with John Forester.

MARC V. LEVINE is an Assistant Professor of History and Urban Affairs, and Coordinator of the Urban Affairs Program, at the University of Wisconsin-Milwaukee. His research and publications have focused on urban redevelopment and economic change, as well as the policy implications of urban multiculturalism. He is the coauthor of *The State and Democracy: Revitalizing America's Government*, and has completed a book-length study on the impact of language policy on Montreal. A former Congressional Fellow and economic policy advisor to Senator Edward M. Kennedy, he has worked with numerous government agencies and community organizations on matters of economic development and urban revitalization.

JOHN T. METZGER is Economic Development Specialist with the Oakland Planning and Development Corporation, a nonprofit community development corporation in Pittsburgh, Pennsylvania. He formerly worked with the Center for Neighborhood Development at Cleveland State University. He has coauthored an article on local economic development in Pittsburgh for the *Journal of the American Planning Association,* and has coauthored two studies of neighborhood reinvestment initiatives in Chicago, for Northwestern University and the Lincoln Institute of Land Policy.

JACK NORMAN is a reporter for the *Milwaukee Journal,* covering economics and Wisconsin's manufacturing sector.

CATH POSEHN is currently an undergraduate student in Applied Behavioral Sciences at the University of California, Davis. Active for over ten years with nonprofit social service organizations, her emphasis is organizational effectiveness for nonprofits. She is a contributing author and coeditor of *A Sampler: Applying Semiotics to Contemporary Myths* (forthcoming).

NESTOR P. RODRIGUEZ is an Assistant Professor in Sociology at the University of Houston. He has done research and published in the areas of urban sociology, world-systems and U.S. immigration. In 1988–1989 he directed an ethnographic investigation of social and political relations between long-term residents and new Latino immigrants in Houston, as part of a Ford Foundation study of evolving relations between established residents and newcomers in the United States.

ALBERTA SBRAGIA is an Associate Professor of Political Science at the University of Pittsburgh and Director of the West European Studies Program. Her research has focused on the comparative politics of local borrowing and capital investment in Italy, France, Great Britain, and the United States. She has taught at the Harvard Business School, is affiliated with the Brookings Institution and edited *The Municipal Money Chase: The Politics of Local Government Finance.*

DEREK SHEARER is Director of the Public Policy Program at Occidental College in Los Angeles. He served for six years as a member of the Planning Commission of Santa Monica, California, and played a leading role in the formulation and implementation of innovative development and housing policies. During the Carter administration, he served on the board of the National Consumer Cooperative Bank. He is the coauthor of *Economic Democracy, A New Social Contract,* and other works. His articles have appeared in the *Los Angeles Times*, the *New York Times*, *The New Republic*, and other publications.

MICHAEL PETER SMITH is Professor of Community Studies and Development and Chair, Department of Applied Behavioral Sciences at the University of California, Davis, a position he has held since 1986. Smith is a theorist whose work focuses on urban political economy, social theory, and cultural criticism. His empirical research has focused on the processes of urbanization, bureaucratization, immigration, and state policy formation. His most important books are: *The City and Social Theory* and *City, State, and Market*. He is coauthor of *Restructuring the City* and editor of *Cities in Transformation*, and *The Capitalist City*, which he recently coedited with Joe R. Feagin. In 1986, he accepted the position of editor-in-chief of *Comparative Urban and Community Research*, an annual serial publication in the field of urban studies. He is currently directing a group research project using ethnographic methods to study the agency of new Asian and Latino immigrants to California cities and beginning an interpretive study of the implications of postmodern discourse in the aesthetic domain for social science theory and practice.

GREGORY D. SQUIRES is an Associate Professor of Sociology and a member of the Urban Studies Program faculty at the University of Wisconsin-Milwaukee. His research has focused on the process of urban development and the implications for minority communities in major metropolitan areas. His recent publications include the coauthored book *Chicago: Race, Class, and the Response to Urban Decline*. He served as a research analyst with the U.S. Commission on Civil Rights for seven years and has worked with several neighborhood organizations, civil rights groups, and other government agencies throughout the United States.

JUNE MANNING THOMAS, an associate professor of the Urban Planning and Urban Affairs Programs at Michigan State University, has published other works on Detroit. A recent effort was a book coauthored with Joe Darden, Richard C. Hill, and Richard Thomas: *Detroit: Race and Uneven Development* (1987). She has published other articles on redevelopment and planning for social equity, and is currently focusing on a study of the postwar history of planning in Detroit. Thomas has worked with the Michigan Department of Commerce and the Michigan Governor's Urban Affairs Advisor as a consultant.

ROBERT K. WHELAN is a Professor in the School of Urban and Regional Studies at the University of New Orleans. He is coauthor of *Urban Policy and Politics in a Bureaucratic Age*, and author of numerous articles and papers. His major current research interest is urban economic development, focusing on the New Orleans and Montreal metropolitan areas.

J. ALLEN WHITT is a Professor of Sociology at the University of Louisville. He is the author of *Urban Elites and Mass Transportation*, and coauthor of *The Cooperative Workplace* (cowinner of the 1986 C. Wright Mills Award). Dr. Whitt is currently investigating the role of the performing arts in urban development strategies.

*Unequal
Partnerships*

Gregory D. Squires

1. Public-Private Partnerships: Who Gets What and Why

Leaders may call these deals "public-private partnerships" and attempt to fold them under the ideological umbrella of laissez-faire. But they must be seen for what they are: the reallocation of public resources to fit a new agenda. That agenda is no longer redistribution, or even economic growth as conventionally defined. Rather, that agenda entails nothing less than the restructuring of the relations of production and the balance of power in the American economy. In the pursuit of these dubious goals, the public sector continues to play a crucial role.

Bluestone and Harrison 1988:107–108

In 1983 a contributor to *Reader's Digest* declared Cleveland to be the nation's "comeback city" largely on the strength of what he perceived to be the emergence of a set of productive partnerships involving politicians, businessmen, and neighborhood groups (Methvin 1984). The Urban Land Institute assembled 3,500 developers, architects, planners, and lenders in Milwaukee in 1987 in part to examine what was presumed to be landmark success by local public-private partnerships in generating slow growth in a no-growth area (*Milwaukee Journal* 1987). Indeed, Milwaukee's commissioner of city development stated: "Partnership. That word seems to apply to nearly every significant accomplishment of the Department of City Development during the period 1980 through 1985" (City of Milwaukee, Department of City Development 1986:2). "Public-private partnership" has become a leading buzzword in economic development circles.

Yet, as Keating, Krumholz, and Metzger observe in Chapter 7, poverty in Cleveland increased by one-third between 1980 and 1986. In three all-black East Side neighborhoods, the poverty rate now exceeds 65 percent. Citywide, 19 percent of one- to four-unit housing structures were substandard in 1985. Jack Norman notes (Chapter 10) that between 1979 and 1985, Milwaukee lost 22 percent of its manufacturing jobs; in 1986 the disparity between black and white unemployment was greater in Milwaukee than in any other metropolitan area; and the proportion of the city's households spending over half their income on rent doubled

1

between 1980 and 1985. Clearly, partnerships are not working for everyone.

In fact, most partnerships are firmly rooted in the historically unequal relationship between the public and private sectors—an inequality that has given rise to the uneven development of communities so characteristic of U.S. cities. Redevelopment initiatives throughout the nation have historically shared an ideological commitment to private-sector growth and to the notion of the public sector as a junior partner in efforts to stimulate that growth. Since World War II, those efforts have focused on downtown development predicated on expected but rarely materialized trickle down benefits, at great cost to urban neighborhoods. The increasing integration of the United States in the world economy, coupled with the restructuring of the national economy in the past two decades, has placed constraints on public resources while at the same time reinforcing traditional relationships between the public and private sectors. Today's partnerships represent as much continuity with the past as they do new efforts to rejuvenate urban economies. Important differences do exist among regions of the nation and among individual cities, but in a context of nationwide constraints and a shared but flawed ideological commitment to growth.

This book is an examination of how diverse cities have attempted to deal with the post–World War II urban crisis. Focusing on contemporary public private partnerships, it reveals how emerging constraints, the commitment to growth, and long-standing inequalties between the public and private sectors have frustrated efforts to resolve the economic and related problems plaguing urban areas. At the same time, promising movements have been organized to challenge the dominant ideology and actors. Their impact, and the potential for future initiatives, are also explored.

The Privileged Position of Business

The celebration of public-private partnerships has occurred in cities around the nation, at all levels of government, and among prestigious business organizations. Mayors and prominent business leaders from such diverse cities as Cleveland, Milwaukee, Pittsburgh, New York, Oakland, and Salt Lake City have testified to the "success" achieved in their communities. In 1978 President Carter made public a new urban policy entitled "A New Partnership to Conserve America's Communities." President Reagan's Task Force on Private-Sector Initiatives endorsed joint public and private efforts to solve local problems. The Committee for Economic Development issued a study entitled *Public-Private Partnerships: An Opportunity for Urban Communities* (Porter and Sweet 1984:203–204,

230–232). In describing such partnerships, the Committee for Economic Development stated: "The linchpins of public-private partnerships are negotiation and cooperation. . . . Partnerships, almost by definition, require equitable commitment of capacity and investment" (Porter and Sweet 1984:204).

What has frequently been overlooked, however, is the inherently unequal nature of most partnerships. Frequently they exclude altogether the neighborhood residents most affected by development decisions (Spiegel 1981; Langton 1983). Public goals often go unmet and democratic processes are undermined (De Neufville and Barton 1987). Public support for public goals can dissipate if it is perceived (incorrectly) that the private sector is picking up the slack (Woodside 1986). The principal beneficiaries are often large corporations, developers, and institutions because the tax burden and other costs are shifted to consumers. And perhaps the most important public benefits—jobs—are either temporary and lowpaying or, in the case of good jobs, go to suburbanites or other out-of-towners recruited by local businesses. As Norman Krumholz has argued, "A nagging doubt arises. Does the publicly subsidized splendor of downtown and the institutional parts of our cities really have much to do with a city's recovery? The answer must be no. The recovery of cities is far more than brick and mortar projects. The city is people, and unless most of them are employed, self-respecting, and respected, the new towers of downtown are a mockery and a delusion" (Krumholz 1984:179).

At the same time Krumholz observes that such relationships between the public and private sectors are hardly new. In documenting what he refers to as the nation's "rich history" of public-private partnerships (Krumholz 1984:182), he quotes Alexander Hamilton's endorsement of public assistance for private enterprise and notes the long-standing subsidization of water, rail, and highway transportation; tariff and trade policies; and use of the military to protect overseas investment, along with tax abatements and low-interest loans.

Contemporary partnerships take many forms. Coalitions of business leaders have been organized, sometimes including prominent public officials, to generate local economic growth. Redevelopment authorities have been created that give selected private developers rights and responsibilities traditionally vested in the public sector, such as land clearance, administration of governmental grants, and approval of public subsidies. In the name of public-private partnership, public officials have provided an array of subsidies in efforts to stimulate private business development. Every state has issued industrial revenue bonds—tax-exempt bonds that make loans available to selected private businesses at below-market rates. Tax increment finance districts have been declared in several cities where public investments are made in selected areas, and the increased tax revenues generated by appreciating property values are retained in those areas for designated periods. Some states have established enterprise zones in which various regulations are waived or taxes are reduced. Urban Development Action Grants (UDAGs), whereby the federal government offers what amounts to seed funding for cities to leverage private investment for depressed areas, have financed several developments in many cities. Subsidies for training have been provided. Tax abatements and even cash grants have been offered in efforts to attract and retain private businesses (Pinsky 1988). Partnerships have been organized around single projects and also as a part of ongoing redevelopment efforts. Community organizations have sometimes been invited to join. In virtually all cases, the traditionally unequal relationship between the private and public sectors has prevailed.

Business has indeed enjoyed a privileged position in the political economy of the United States. As Lindblom has observed, in a market economy it is business that decides what goods and services are to be produced, in what quantities, and how that production will be allocated. Because of the central role business plays in determining the standard of living, governments feel compelled to defer to the conditions business deems necessary in order to ensure that such vital functions are performed. Consequently, business assumes public functions and business people frequently act as unelected public officials (Lindblom 1977:170–188). At the national, state, and local levels this unequal relationship between the public and private sectors has traditionally relegated to the public sector those tasks deemed necessary to stimulate private growth (Judd 1984).

This fundamental traditional inequality—what Marc V. Levine describes in Chapter 2 as "the ideology of privatism"—helps explain why the Fainsteins found, in their study of New York (Chapter 4), that Mayor Ed Koch is beholden to big developers for campaign contributions; hence, his commitment to major development projects. It also explains the frustration David Bartelt (Chapter 5) reports on the part of a former director of Philadelphia's Redevelopment Authority, who claimed the city never had much power to direct development but rather could only package redevelopment options for the private sector. Larry Bennett (Chapter 9) observes that even in those city administrations that publicly take a more progressive approach to development, public officials frequently find themselves acquiescing to the demands of capital, as Harold Washington did in Chicago.

The power of private capital has been enhanced by several myths that have evolved pertaining to the roles and behaviors of the public and private actors. As De Neufville and Barton (1987) note, it is widely assumed that government lacks the private sector's expertise in solving urban problems. Unfortunately, it is argued, government burdens private industry with regulations that impede its ability to exercise its initiative in meeting the challenge. Government is inflexible, bureaucratic, and unresponsive to community needs, whereas the private sector is more flexible and efficient and, therefore, better positioned (if allowed to do so) to address urban problems. Promulgation of these myths impedes the very progress partnerships are purportedly organized to pursue.

The dynamics of market forces, the dominance of private capital, and the myths surrounding public- and private-sector behavior are powerful factors that have exacerbated the unequal relationship between the public and private sectors. The deindustrialization that struck many cities beginning in the late 1960s and the corporate response to the declining profits that ensued have reinforced these myths, while laying the groundwork for the current versions of public-private partnerships.

Between 1960 and 1980, the U.S. share of world economic output declined from 35 percent to 22 percent (Reich 1987:44). The subsequent declining rate of profit generated several responses on the part of U.S. corporations. A central objective of the emerging strategy has been to secure larger subsidies and financial incentives from the public sector and to reduce corporate taxes and other contributions to the array of social welfare programs that Bluestone and Harrison (1982) refer to as the social wage. Tax cuts and a decrease in regulations at the federal level have been complemented by demands for incentives from state and local governments to stimulate private-sector growth as corporations have played off capital-starved communities against each other in efforts to create a more attractive business climate (Goodman 1979; Bluestone and Harrison 1982; Bowles et al. 1983). As cities throughout the country, and particularly in the rustbelt region, have continued to decline, the demand for further incentives as the solution to economic and related ills has become louder.

Prominent actors in the public sector joined in this call to "grow out of" the urban crisis in particular and the economic crisis in general. President Carter's Commission for a National Agenda for the Eighties (1980) said that economic growth was essential to a solution of the social problems facing cities and called for a range of incentives to facilitate private capital accumulation. Arguing that cities were simply going through a natural transformation, it called for policies to facilitate the relocation of people from declining to growing areas. President Carter's successor took these policies to heart, exacerbating the uneven development of urban areas and the hardships faced by residents of declining communities.

In recent years private capital accumulation has increasingly been viewed as a legitimate end in its own right, rather than a means to some broader public good. The dominance of private capital in both private and public life has been strengthened. And democratic processes and safeguards have been weakened (Smith and Judd 1984). As William E. Connolly (1983) has cogently argued,

> at every turn barriers to growth become occasions to tighten social control, to build new hedges around citizen rights, to insulate bureaucracies from popular pressures while opening them to corporate influence, to rationalize work processes, to impose austerity on vulnerable constituencies, to delay programs for environmental safety, to legitimize military adventures abroad. Growth, previously seen as the means to realization of the good life, has become a system imperative to which elements of the good life are sacrificed. (Pp. 23–24)

Market dynamics, the dominance of private capital, and the myths that mystify the nature of public- and private-sector behavior continue to shape urban policy. As these forces strengthen the unequal relationship between the public and private sectors, the role and behavior of contemporary public-private partnerships are more expressly revealed.

Public-private partnerships have a long history. The relationships and objectives of today's partnerships were established during the postwar urban renewal. Businessmen took the lead, through such organizations as Pittsburgh's Allegheny Conference on Community Development and the Greater Milwaukee Committee, in securing public assistance for massive land clearance and redevelopment projects. These two organizations, and many others formed in the 1950s, continue to shape the corporate strategy for development of downtown areas. As in the 1950s, the focus today is on office complexes, convention centers, shopping malls, and related downtown real estate investments.

Among the more visible symbols of such efforts are Milwaukee's Grand Avenue Mall and Boston's Faneuil Hall Marketplace. Although they have perhaps been profitable for selected investors, as Peter Dreier (Chapter 3) and Jack Norman (Chapter 10) observe. these developments, like their urban renewal predecessors, have failed to generate the presumed spillover benefits to neighborhoods surrounding the central business district.

Indeed, the renaissance that several downtowns may be experiencing today simply reflects what *Business Week* (1985) characterized as a "Casino Society," where, as Bluestone and Harrison (1988) have demonstrated, investment is shifting from productive uses (new plants and equipment) to speculative ventures (real estate, futures trading, conglomerate mergers). Such redirection of national and international investment practices by U.S. corporations contributes to the shaping of an "hourglass economy": one that creates a few technically demanding, highly paid professional positions (predominantly for white males) at the top and many unskilled, low-paying jobs (disproportionately for racial minorities) at the bottom, while squeezing the middle class downward. Occupationally, geographically, and racially, these inequalities are drawn most sharply in the nation's major cities. The growth of downtown areas and the suburbs, coupled with the decline of the residential, industrial, and commercial districts of major cities, has contributed to what *Chicago Tribune* columnist Clarence Page (1987) has appropriately labeled a "dumbbell economy."

The downtown area remains the focus in many cities including Philadelphia, New York, Cleveland, and Chicago, which are analyzed in this book and elsewhere. Massive subsidies for downtown projects continue to be justified in terms of the benefits that presumably will trickle down (but raerly do) throughout the city. And downtown is not just seen as a local savior. In perhaps the boldest defense, one business association official referred to downtown New York as "the heart pump of the capital blood that sustains the free world" (Chapter 4).

Important differences among U.S. cities exist despite fundamental commonalities in partnership activities. New York and Boston have been more successful than most cities in transforming their economies to accommodate the rising demand for financial services and high-technology products. Rustbelt cities like Pittsburgh, Cleveland, Detroit, and Milwaukee still suffer from the decline of their manufacturing base, even though manufacturing employment has stabilized somewhat in recent years and efforts are being made to diversify the industrial base. Philadelphia, too, is struggling to develop commercial, tourist, and other industries to counterbalance its manufacturing job loss. Although Chicago was also hurt by the region's decline in manufacturing, that city has long had a more diversified economy, which has cushioned its residents from the vagaries of uneven development more effectively than the economies of its Midwestern neighbors. Public-private partnerships in their contemporary forms came later to Houston than to most cities, but even in that "free enterprise city," the public sector has long subsidized private profits. The cases of Louisville and New Orleans demonstrate that public-private partnerships are Southern as well as rustbelt developments. Growing cities like Sacramento have looked to such partnerships as a key to their prosperity. Despite important differences, fundamental structural and ideological constraints remain that have generated patterns of uneven development in virtually every U.S. city. Severe racial disparities persist. Increasing polarization between rich and poor appears to be a national trend. And the corporate center downtown strategy is a nationwide phenomenon.

At the same time, forces have emerged that have challenged urban "growth machines" (Logan and Molotch 1987) and the traditional politics of redevelopment. Boston has implemented linked development programs to increase the number of low-income housing units and related jobs policies in efforts to distribute the benefits of resurgence to all areas of the city. In Louisville, city officials have aggressively negotiated to maximize the return to the city from recent development projects, rather than passively acquiescing to private-sector demands for incentives. Community development corporations in several cities, including Milwaukee, Pittsburgh, and Cleveland, are beginning to respond successfully to the needs of neighborhoods outside the central business district. Community-based organizations in Chicago have successfully pressured lenders and insurers to implement reinvestment programs in their neighborhoods and, at least under Harold Washington, have worked with local officials to achieve more balanced growth throughout the city. In Sacramento a citywide coalition of environmental activists and other middle-income constituency groups has utilized existing laws and regulatory requirements to extract important public concessions from private developers. In some cities, the privileged position of business is being challenged.

Public-Private Partnerships: Twelve Case Studies

The twelve case studies presented in this book are representative of trends occurring in urban areas of the United States today. In Chapter 2 Marc V. Levine provides an overview of the political economy of urban development in the postwar years. In describing the history of public-private partnerships, he identifies the central actors and delineates the consequences of these redevelopment efforts.

The twelve chapters that follow trace the patterns of urban development in large and medium-sized cities in all regions of the country. The authors analyze structural changes in the local economy, review redevelopment strategies, identify key individual and institutional actors, assess the consequences of partnership and related development initiatives, and discuss oppositional approaches to traditional redevelopment practices that are being attempted. In the final chapter Derek Shearer discusses the many progressive policy initiatives that have emerged in these and other cities and offers some optimistic yet realistic proposals for the future.

Whose City?

Systematic quantitative data are not widely available to enable us precisely to measure the net public and private returns (in terms of finances, quality of life, and other criteria) of most partnerships. Anecdotal case studies frequently provide the best available evidence for assessing their impact. Sufficient quantitative and qualitative evidence is available, however, to allow us to conclude that the costs and benefits of public-private partnerships are not uniformly distributed within or among U.S. cities. Changing national and international economic realities shape redevelopment at the local level. Market forces are very real; some of the most intense competition occurs among the cities themselves as they attempt to attract and create jobs. The fundamental long-standing inequality that has always prevailed in joint public-private ventures has also informed the activities of contemporary partnerships. A key question that is explicit in the following studies of Philadelphia and Sacramento, but implicit in the analysis of redevelopment efforts in other cities, is, "For whom are we saving the cities?"

Despite the broad social forces that both shape and constrain redevelopment initiatives, the diversity of responses to urban decine documented in the following chapters reveals that people still make choices, and those choices significantly affect community life. As Clarence Stone simply but appropriately states, "urban politics still matters" (1987:4). Obviously, not all participants enter these debates on an equal footing. But if it is realistic to view the city as "an arena of growing competition where pressure, counter-pressure and bargaining are the processes that work" (Cunningham 1981:526), then the future of cities is not economically predetermined. Indeed, it is not unreasonable to at least strive to achieve the heavenly city.

References

Bluestone, Barry, and Bennett Harrison. 1982. *The Deindustrialization of America: Plant Closings, Community Abandonment, and the Dismantling of Basic Industry*. New York: Basic Books.

———. 1988. *The Great U-Turn: Corporate Restructuring and the Polarizing of America*. New York: Basic Books.

Bowles, Samuel, David M. Gordon, and Thomas E. Weisskopf. 1983. *Beyond the*

Wasteland: A Democratic Alternative to Economic Decline. New York: Anchor Press.

Business Week. 1985. "Playing with Fire: Games the Casino Society Plays" (September 16):78–86.

City of Milwaukee. Department of City Development. 1986. "Report of Activities 1980–1985."

Connolly, William E. 1983. "Progress, Growth, and Pessimism in America." *democracy* 3 (Fall):22–31.

Cunningham, James V. 1981. "Assessing the Urban Partnership: Do Community Forces Fit?" *National Civic Review* 70 (November):521–526.

De Neufville, Judith, and Stephen E. Barton. 1987. "Myths and the Definition of Policy Problems: An Exploration of Home Ownership and Public-Private Partnerships." *Policy Sciences* 20:181–206.

Goodman, Robert. 1979. *The Last Entrepreneurs: America's Regional Wars for Jobs and Dollars*. New York: Simon and Schuster.

Judd, Dennis R. 1984. *The Politics of American Cities: Private Power and Public Policy*. Boston: Little, Brown.

Krumholz, Norman. 1984. "Recovery of Cities: An Alternate View." In *Rebuilding America's Cities: Roads to Recovery*, ed. Paul R. Porter and David Sweet. New Brunswick, N.J.: Rutgers University, Center for Urban Policy Research.

Langton, Stuart. 1983. "Public-Private Partnerships: Hope or Hoax?" *National Civic Review* 72 (May):256–261.

Lindblom, Charles E. 1977. *Politics and Markets: The World's Political Economic Systems*. New York: Basic Books.

Logan, John R., and Harvey L. Molotch. 1987. *Urban Fortunes: The Political Economy of Place*. Berkeley: University of California Press.

Methvin, Eugene H. 1984. "Cleveland Comes Back." In *Rebuilding America's Cities: Roads to Recovery*, ed. Paul R. Porter and David C. Sweet. New Brunswick, N.J.: Rutgers University, Center for Urban Policy Research. (Reprinted from the March 1983 *Reader's Digest*.)

Milwaukee Journal. 1987. "Developers' Conference to Look at City's Success" (September 3).

Page, Clarence. 1987. Personal interview with Gregory D. Squires.

Pinsky, Paul G. 1988. "A Costly Way to Woo Business." *New York Times* (April 20).

Porter, Paul R., and David C. Sweet. 1984. *Rebuilding America's Cities: Roads to Recovery*. New Brunswick, N.J.: Rutgers University, Center for Urban Policy Research.

President's Commission for a National Agenda for the Eighties. 1980. *A National Agenda for the Eighties*. Washington, D.C.: Government Printing Office.

Reich, Robert B. 1987. *Tales of a New America*. New York: Times Books.

Smith, Michael Peter, and Dennis R. Judd. 1984. "American Cities: The Production of Ideology." In *Cities in Transformation: Class, Capital, and the State*, ed. Michael Peter Smith. Beverly Hills: Sage.

Spiegel, Hans B. C. 1981. "The Neighborhood Partnerships: Who's In It? Why?" *National Civic Review* 70 (November):513–520.

Stone, Clarence N. 1987. "The Study of the Politics of Urban Development." In *The Politics of Urban Development,* ed. Clarence N. Stone and Heywood T. Sanders. Lawrence: University Press of Kansas.

Woodside, William S. 1986. "The Future of Public-Private Partnerships." in *Public-Private Partnerships: Improving Urban Life,* ed. Perry Davis. New York: Academy of Political Science.

Marc V. Levine

2. The Politics of Partnership: Urban Redevelopment Since 1945

Public-private partnerships have become an increasingly important force shaping the politics and economics of U.S. cities. Municipal boosterism, an approach to urban political economy that equates the success of a city's leading private interests with the public good, has long been a part of the nation's urban life. After World War II, however, facing growing blight in downtown areas and enticed by the federal incentives of the urban renewal program, city governments across the United States joined forces with private developers in more formal and systematic collaborative enterprises than had heretofore existed. New political institutions—"quasi-public" redevelopment corporations—were created to sidestep the cumbersome instruments of conventional municipal policymaking and implement the redevelopment policies of the cities' corporate elite. By the 1960s, these business-government "partnerships" had produced an impressive roster of redevelopment projects: Pittsburgh's Golden Triangle, Baltimore's Charles Center, Minneapolis's Nicollet Mall, and San Francisco's Yerba Buena Gardens, to name just a few.

In the 1970s and 1980s, because of growing problems of deindustrialization and fiscal distress, city governments moved beyond the single-project collaborations with developers that had characterized urban renewal efforts in the 1950s. In the context of heightened intercity competition for private investment, municipal governments became entrepreneurial, providing an extensive web of subsidies and incentives to developers, and often becoming codevelopers of risky redevelopment projects (Judd and Ready 1986:217–218; Levitt 1987:6–8). Public-private partnerships became the cornerstone of economic development strategies of virtually all U.S. cities—strategies that centered on the creation of a good business climate. As Baltimore's economic development chief commented in 1984, "I think corporations appreciate being able to work with us because we're here to smooth the way. It's not like trying to deal with a government agency. We're very entrepreneurial. We think government *is* a business" (*New York Times Magazine* 1984:74). By the 1980s, an apparent consensus had emerged among urban policymakers that "many of the goals of American society can best be realized by developing a system of incentives for private firms to do those social jobs which business can perform better and more economically than other institutions" (Committee for Economic Development 1982:42). Paying homage to partnerships became de rigeur for public officials and aspiring politicians.

Since the late 1970s, two sets of literature have emerged on the subject of public-private partnerships. The studies in one group, chiefly written by economic development practitioners, begin with the premise that public-private partnerships are an indispensable tool of urban revitalization. Such studies generally then detail how such partnerships are forged and what kinds of development tools they deploy (Fosler and Berger 1982; Levitt 1987; National Council on Urban Economic Development 1978a, 1978b). This literature contains little empirical research on the actual impact of public-private partnerships in specific cities. Public support for private development is assumed to generate public benefits and is viewed as a fundamental, accepted function of local government, in the same category as public safety and sanitation (Frieden and Sagalyn 1986; Peterson 1981).

But some urban political economists have begun to critically examine the dynamics of urban redevelopment and the role of public-private partnerships in promoting corporate-oriented redevelopment policies (Molotch 1976; Fainstein 1983; Mollenkopf 1983; Logan and Molotch 1987). Studies such as those presented in this volume suggest that the creation of formal public-private partnerships has often amounted to "corporations doing the planning while the city government facilitates corporate plans using municipal legal powers" (Carnoy et al., 1983:198). Municipal democracy is compromised, analysts suggest, as business control over public resource allocation is increased, and as economic development policy is removed from the normal channels of municipal governance and lodged in public-private development institutions. Moreover, political economists argue, because public-private partnerships reflect the agenda of urban business elites, they tend to have little impact on the central economic problems of urban areas: inner-city poverty, neighborhood decay, and the shrinking number of quality employment opportunities available to city residents.

In this chapter I examine, from a political economy perspective, the historical and theoretical contexts of contemporary public-private partnerships: how, why and when such partnerships emerged; the specific institutional arrangements established to implement the redevelopment priorities of partnerships; and the socioeconomic and political impacts of partnership activity. I conclude with an analysis of the challenges to traditional partnership programs that have emerged in various cities since the 1970s, and how such challenges may encourage the development of new, and ultimately more egalitarian, public-private partnerships in U.S. cities.

Historical and Ideological Basis of
Public-Private Partnerships

There has always been an ambiguous line separating public and private interests in the nation's urban economic development. Throughout the nineteenth century, as Charles N. Glaab and A. Theodore Brown have written, "the community's general interest crystallized around a project conceived to stimulate growth, and the community's character was cast in terms of the success of its businessmen" (Glaab and Brown 1976:36). Historian Sam Bass Warner has aptly characterized the urban center as a "private city"—a "community of private money makers" in which the proper role of local government was to "keep peace among the individual money makers and, if possible, help create an open and thriving setting where each citizen would have some substantial opportunity to prosper" (Warner 1968:x, 4).

This ideology of privatistic growth has continually shaped the relationship between the public and private sectors. Adhering to the tenets of privatism, nineteenth-century urban land speculators and commercial interests energetically promoted public investment in canals, railroads, and other internal improvements—investments explicitly justified as vital to the profitability of local businesses. State and municipal governments functioned as the public arm of urban capitalists. They provided subsidies and incentives to business interests to encourage private investment, and used public investment to help local speculators enhance the value of their real estate holdings, or industrial and commercial interests gain access to new markets. Major public works projects of the early nineteenth century, such as the Erie Canal and the Baltimore and Ohio Railroad, were explicitly conceived as projects to boost the economic fortunes of New York and Baltimore businessmen; later, developing cities such as Milwaukee, Chicago, and Cleveland utilized public infrastructure investments to help build market niches for local entrepreneurs. By mid-century, when a railroad line could create urban fortunes overnight, public treasuries opened up in efforts to entice railroad companies to build a spur in a particular community. The intercity competition to create partnerships by offering packages of subsidies and loans to private railroad companies in the nineteenth century presaged the kind of public entrepreneurialism that emerged in the 1970s as mobile capital began hunting for the most hospitable urban business climate (Goodman 1979).

During the Progressive era (roughly 1900–1920), the relationship between city governments and private enterprise altered somewhat. By the end of the nineteenth century, the deplorable social and economic conditions of industrialized cities had prompted an unavoidable reformulation of the ideology of privatism. "Civic-minded" businessmen, middle-class reformers, and, in some cases, politicians with large working-class constituencies argued for a more activist municipal government to alleviate the problems of urban industrialism. The widespread existence of slum housing and unsanitary health conditions in impoverished neighborhoods led to calls for greater public regulation of the private sector, resulting in housing codes, zoning ordinances, and public health laws. The corruption of privately owned utility companies in mass transit, water, gas, and electricity—coupled with persistent complaints about the high costs and poor performance of these companies—stimulated calls for greater municipal regulation of these franchises and, in some areas, municipal ownership of utilities. Progressive mayors such as Tom Johnson in Cleveland and Hazen Pingree in Detroit were particularly energetic in asserting public power over such heretofore privately controlled spheres of urban economic activity.

By the early 1900s, an urban planning movement had emerged, based on the belief that "the process of city building was being determined by real estate speculation rather than by public policies based on the long-term interests of the community," and that a more activist urban government was necessary to prevent the public good from being abused by private developers (Fogelsong 1986:3). However, the apparent challenge to privatism attempted by this movement never fully materialized. Rather than surmount the ideology of privatism, the urban planning movement and other Progressive era initiatives were incorporated into a modified version of privatism that accommodated a more visible public presence in urban life while maintaining a vision of the city as a "community of private money-makers." Municipal policy would seek to alleviate some of the social costs of urban capitalism, as well as coordinate urban development in the interests of capital; but public planning would not contest the legitimacy of privately controlled markets or seek to establish public control over urban investment or land use.

Thus, even the timid public regulation of private land use and housing during the Progressive era was vigorously contested by developers and landlords; "land reform, American-style" has historically remained more respectful of the rights of property owners than attentive to the needs of tenants or community groups (Geisler and Popper 1986). Experiments in municipal ownership of dynamic sectors of the economy were generally short-lived, and public enterprise was generally limited to those activities, such as mass transit, that capital had written off as unprofitable. As Richard Fogelsong has argued, despite the public interventionist beginnings of urban planning, the profession has historically "served to identify, organize, and legitimate the interests of capital in the sphere of urban development" (Fogelsong 1986:6). As a result, although city governments took on significantly greater powers in the twentieth century, the ideology of privatism remained the dominant force shaping public-private interaction.

Why Privatism Dominates Public-Private Partnerships

Contemporary political analysts have given three main explanations for the historically privatistic tilt of urban development policy and the prominence of public-private partnerships. Paul E. Peterson, in his influential study *City Limits*, argues that public policies that increase returns to private capital advance the interests of the city as a whole and therefore reflect a community *consensus* with regard to economic development. In Peterson's analysis, the city is treated as a "unitary" organization in which the community as a whole objectively benefits from "developmental policies" that promote local business interests and thereby "strengthen the local economy, enhance the local tax base, and generate additional resources that can be used for the community's welfare" (Peterson 1981: 131). Peterson maintains that such growth policies are "praised by the many and opposed only by those few whose partial interests stand in conflict with community interests." He contrasts development policies with "redistributive policies," which, in targeting urban resources for the most disadvantaged members of the community, "negatively affect the local economy" and generate intense political conflict (Peterson 1981:132).

Some elements of Peterson's analysis are helpful. The dynamics of the capital accumulation process are such that cities clearly face limits on their ability to pursue policies other than private profit–driven growth programs. All things being equal, cities whose development policies have encouraged a healthy rate of private investment will have a stronger local economy and tax base than other cities.

However, Peterson's theory about the public benefits of procapital "developmental policies"—his label for what I describe in this chapter as public-private partnerships—is based on three questionable assumptions: (1) that the benefits of pro-capital growth policies are not disproportionately reaped by developers, corporate elites, or upper-income residents; (2) that an urban consensus exists regarding issues of economic development and that cities do not have geographic, racial, and class divisions that reflect conflicting development priorities; (3) that there are limited social costs as a result of pro-capital development policies.

But Peterson provides no evidence to support these assumptions, and there is now ample evidence from the case study literature on urban redevelopment that the entire community does not benefit from "developmental policies": the benefits of privatistic growth are disproportionately received by developers and upper-income groups, and substantial social costs often accompany such policies. In addition, by accepting the premise of "city limits"—essentially, market-based constraints on public policy—Peterson unduly overestimates the community consensus about development policy and underestimates the role of *politics* in shaping municipal policy (Stone 1987). Public-private partnerships need not invariably reflect the priorities of capital, and it is certainly unclear that partnerships benefit the entire community. The emergence of what John Mollenkopf calls "contested cities" in the 1960s clearly calls into question Peterson's assumption that cities reached a consensus on the subject of public-private development programs (Mollenkopf 1983).

A second theoretical explanation for the private business orientation of urban economic development policy is what may be called the urban "fiscal imperative." Like Peterson, these political analysts start with the assumption that cities are hostages to the policy demands of the businessmen upon whom cities depend for investment and for creating a local revenue base. Public support of private enterprise is seen as a way of demonstrating to capital the "political worthiness" of a city. This is particularly important because cities are at the mercy of credit markets, steady access to which they require to support urban capital budgets; that is, funds for infrastructure construction and maintenance, public buildings, schools, and so forth.

Martin Shefter has argued that the restraints placed on urban policy by credit markets "are one of the uncontested boundaries within which democratic politics is conducted in American cities, and the great majority of all participants in urban politics regard them as no more subject to challenge or change than are the laws of physics" (Shefter 1985:233). Shefter concludes that the need for access to credit markets means that city politics is "weighted toward the concerns of creditors—and against the democratic impulse" (p. 233). Shefter's analysis appears to suggest that, because of the urban fiscal imperative, public-private partnerships weighted toward the interests of capital are inevitable in U.S. cities.

The reality of fiscal distress was unquestionably an important factor generating the surge of partnership activity that began in the 1970s, particularly in financially strapped frostbelt cities. As Shefter argues, "patterns of public expenditure and public policy in New York have been more favorable to business since 1975 than they had been prior to the fiscal crisis" (Shefter 1985:142). Shefter's historical analysis is persuasive, especially the connection he draws between the onset of fiscal crises (with the subsequent emergence of explicitly pro-capital municipal policy) and historical moments when capital has decided that urban politicians have become too responsive to the voters. Fiscal crisis presents an opportunity for capital to discipline an "unruly" electorate in an urban democracy.

But accepting the inevitability of the power of capital that flows from the dynamics of urban bond markets and equating it to "laws of physics" is a case of neoclassical economics masquerading as political science. Shefter underestimates forces that have historically been mobilized to contest these constraints on urban policy (Clavel 1985; Mollenkopf 1983) and fails to acknowledge how *politics* can fundamentally alter the economic "rules of the game" according to which such phenomena as public-private partnerships operate.

A third explanation for the prominence of partnerships is offered in writings on urban "growth machines" (Logan and Molotch 1987). Speculators and investors in urban land have historically looked to the local state to promote growth "that can increase aggregate rents and trap related wealth for those in the right position to benefit" (Logan and Molotch 1987:50). In this model, public support for private development is vital to property holders, developers, the local real estate community, and other interests in a position to profit from favorable patterns of urban land use. In recent years, local growth coalitions have been augmented by multinational corporations seeking to establish "command centers" in urban downtowns and a national industry of urban redevelopers—such as the Rouse Corporation and Trammel-Crow—with a major economic interest in how city governments control land use. Politicians are eager to promote such growth partnerships because they receive financial support from elements of the local growth coalition, and usually receive public acclaim since development projects produce an image of urban economic progress.

In cities experiencing more disinvestment than unbridled growth, the local government is viewed by capital as a crucial partner whose chief role is to transcend the "anarchy of the market" and to coordinate investment and development in a way that maximizes the profits of urban land use. The corporatist Committee for Economic Development explains how, working through public-private partnerships, the local government plays this coordinating role: "An important attribute of public-private partnerships is that they provide a means for *reducing uncertainty*. . . . Collaboration may be essential to the revitalization of downtown commercial centers. *Small, uncoordinated, and fragmented* investments are rarely sufficient to reverse the cumulative effects of economic decline" (Committee for Economic Development 1982:36–40).

In short, capital needs the local government to coordinate the actions of individual developers, lower the risks for individual investors by establishing stable, predictable land use patterns, and provide planned profit opportunities for investors. In this sense, public-private partnerships represent an urban form of state capitalism in which city governments help underwrite important components of the capital accumulation process.

The Emergence of Formal Public-Private Partnerships, 1945–1970

The ideology of privatism, the dynamics of urban credit markets, and local capital's need for public coordination are the crucial factors that caused the emergence of more systematic public-private partnerships in the years following World War II. City governments, facing decaying downtowns, spreading slums, and a shrinking local revenue base, joined forces with leading businessmen to promote single, dramatic projects — such as Pittsburgh's Gateway Center, the first public-private urban renewal program in the United States—designed to boost investor confidence in downtowns and stimulate urban revitalization.

These postwar public-private redevelopment partnerships had four main characteristics. First, they were governed by local corporate committees, composed of the city's leading private-sector elites, whose chief goal was to revitalize downtown business districts rather than target investment in deteriorating inner-city neighborhoods. (Hartman 1984; Mollenkopf 1983; Stone 1976). The first of these committees was the Allegheny Conference on Community Development, formed in Pittsburgh in 1943 by industrialist and financier Richard K. Mellon and composed of the chief executive officers of the city's major corporations. The Allegheny Conference was designed to bring Pittsburgh's leading corporate interests together to develop a coherent, corporate-oriented redevelopment strategy for the city, and this model served as the explicit prototype for similar organizations in Milwaukee and Baltimore. Throughout the 1950s, corporate organizations such as the Blythe-Zellerbach Committee in San Francisco, the "Vault" in Boston, and the Dallas Citizens Council took the lead in shaping urban redevelopment agendas. Invariably, these corporate committees called for public involvement in the process, to partially fund revitalization projects as well as to use municipal powers (such as eminent domain) to coordinate the process. But control over the content of redevelopment policy rested clearly with these corporate committees; the city role was to *facilitate* corporate plans.

Second, postwar partnerships were stimulated by federal dollars, made available through the urban renewal program. This program, established in Title I of the 1949 Housing Act, amended in 1954, represented a crucial federal underwriting of local public-private partnerships. It offered developers new profit opportunities and provided a financial incentive for them to work with city governments in redeveloping blighted areas (Wilson 1966). Urban renewal was not a program of direct public investment for revitalization. Cities were to use the power of eminent domain to obtain land and then sell it to private developers; federal dollars would pay for land clearance expenses and partially subsidize redevelopment costs. Unlike public housing, which was seen as a direct challenge to privately controlled markets, urban renewal was supported by developers who recognized that federal dollars might now create urban profit opportunities. This approach—using public dollars to "leverage" private investment—became a cardinal principle of public-private partnerships, and helps explain why partnership activities tended to be "limited to those [projects] which developers initiated and would cooperate with" (Hartman 1984:321). The upshot was that urban renewal investment was rarely targeted to cities' most distressed neighborhoods.

Third, partnerships were controlled by new instruments of urban governance: virtually autonomous redevelopment authorities that could deploy vast public powers of land disposal and resource allocation to implement the redevelopment plans of the city's corporate elite. These authorities, established in the 1950s generally to funnel federal urban renewal funds into local redevelopment projects, resembled Robert Moses's Triborough Bridge Authority in New York: "clothed with the powers of government but possessed of the flexibility and initiative of a private enterprise" (Lines et al. 1986:236)

Such authorities were explicitly designed to sidestep regular channels of municipal governance and to use enormous municipal financial and land use powers to expedite private development projects. Pittsburgh's Urban Redevelopment Authority was set up as a separate entity so that redevelopment "was not subject to political whims or elections" (Economou 1987:119). Redevelopment authority heads such as Ed Logue in Boston and New Haven, and Justin Herman in San Francisco became notorious as a result of summarily using public land use powers to implement the corporate community's redevelopment agenda.

Some cities went even further, conferring upon private corporations some of the key powers normally reserved for city government. Chapter 353 of the Missouri Urban Redevelopment Corporation Law, passed in 1949, permits the city of St. Louis to pass on its powers of eminent domain and tax abatement to private, for-profit redevelopment corporations "formed to implement a private redevelopment plan for an area legislatively designated as blighted" (Ward et al. 1987:159). According to a careful study of redeveloment in St. Louis, "Chapter 353 encourages the private sector to take the initiative in selecting targets for development and, in so doing, to take much stronger control of the risks to be borne. As a result, a redevelopment industry emerged to take advantage of the myriad urban redevelopment opportunities in the city rather than relying on public initiatives, planning, and implementation" (Ward et al. 1987:160). The city of St. Louis retained broad control over redevelopment, through its powers to designate blighted areas and approve specific redevelopment plans. Nevertheless, the intent and impact of Chapter 353—and of analogous arrangements in other cities—were to create formal institutions that enhanced the control of private developers over the direction of urban redevelopment policy.

Fourth, partnerships were promoted by boosterish, pro-development mayors. John Collins in Boston, David Lawrence in Pittsburgh, and George Christopher in San Francisco were all elected in the 1940s and 1950s with strong support from their city's business communities, and all took a leading role in promoting the redevelopment agendas of their city's corporate committees. John Mollenkopf has documented that "innovative mayors saw redevelopment as a way to overcome [central city stagnation] and reap political benefits along the way" (Mollenkopf 1983:6). Becoming identified with flashy redevelopment projects increasingly became a sine qua non for aspiring urban politicians. Although Mollenkopf may exaggerate the extent to which "public entrepreneurship" rather than corporate planning drove this first phase of partnership activity, his analysis is useful because it points to the political interests, as well as economic interests, that were served by the promotion of public-private partnerships after 1945.

The Proliferation of Public-Private Partnerships, 1970–1985

The patterns of redevelopment between 1945 and 1970 established the basic ingredients of public-private partnerships: corporate control, federal leveraging, autonomous redevelopment authorities, and entrepreneurial mayors. In the early 1970s, a second phase of partnership building began, marked by more complex and sophisticated versions of the arrangements developed in the early 1950s. Changes in the U.S. political and economic climate—rapid deindustrialization and fiscal distress in the frostbelt; rapid growth in the sunbelt; and politicization of the business community with its conservative policy agenda—made cities increasingly anxious to increase partnerships with the private sector. In frostbelt cities, partnerships were seen as crucial to economic revitalization; in sunbelt cities, partnerships were seen as an integral component of rapid growth.

The partnerships that emerged after 1970 differed from the earlier versions mainly in the expanded scope and complexity of their activity, and in the increased public resources and power that were made available to support private development and create a good business climate. Partnerships were based on the notion that the chief role of city government was "to establish and maintain an economic climate in which the private developer is willing to take risks" (Ward et al. 1987:160), and a wide range of sophisticated public tools was developed to leverage such private risk-taking. An industry of megadevelopers — Rouse, Trump, Trammel-Crow — emerged to take advantage of the profit opportunities presented by the new urban entrepreneurialism.

Specifically, cities drew upon the 1950s partnership pattern in three main ways:

1. *Financial inducements*. Helped by federal programs such as the 1977 Urban Development Action Grant (UDAG) program, as well as "creative financing" techniques that comingled public and private investments, cities began offering a dazzling array of subsidies, loans, and loan guarantees to promote private, primarily downtown, redevelopment. The Broadway Renaissance project in Louisville, for example, was funded by UDAGs, state economic development bonds, loans from the Kentucky Industrial Finance Authority and the city of Louisville, city equity participation, and industrial revenue bonds (Yater 1987:78). By the 1980s, virtually all major cities had significant financial "exposure" in public-private redevelopment, either through loans or loan guarantees, or as a result of equity involvement in a redevelopment project.

Cities increasingly relied on intricate and extensive manipulation of the tax code to stimulate private investment. Tax-exempt municipal bonds, heretofore issued for "public purpose" projects such as school construction and sewers, were increasingly used to subsidize private development (Squires 1984). Cities such as New York, Cleveland, and St. Louis offered extensive tax abatements (Tabb 1982; Swanstrom 1985, Ward et al. 1987). Some cities, such as Baltimore, tried to encourage private investment by erecting tax shelters for private developers, through gimmicky arrangements in which public buildings would be sold and then leased back to the city, effectively conferring the city's tax-exempt status on a private developer.

Finally, changes in the federal tax code provided a major incentive for real estate development and office construction in urban areas. The 1976 Tax Reform Act, which extended an investment tax credit for building rehabilitation expenses, and the 1981 tax bill, which dramatically increased investment tax credit for the rehabilitation of historic properties and non-residential structures, helped unleash a frenzied effort to build downtown offices and gentrify historic neighborhoods (Levitt 1987:7).

2. *Quasi-public redevelopment corporations.* The number of these entities, and the scope of the development powers accorded them, increased significantly in the 1970s. In city after city, these corporations became central institutions wherein public-private deal-making could take place, thus avoiding the harsh glare of conventional political arenas. In some cities, these corporations now wield extraordinary powers historically reserved for institutions of representative government: they can condemn and assemble land parcels, issue tax-exempt bonds, receive and administer grants and loans from other levels of government, and offer investment inducements such as tax abatements. As the National Council for Urban Economic Development points out, quasi-public corporations are ideal instruments for rapidly allocating municipal resources to private developers with minimal public discussion. Often staffed by individuals who move freely between the public and private sectors, such redevelopment corporations offer the following advantages to private developers:

Structural independence from city government

Expansion of public powers because such institutions are not constrained by city charters

Privacy of negotiations: "negotiations for the sale or lease of public property can occur without constant public scrutiny or bidding procedures"

Coordination of public and private resources

Continuous access to public officials by private developers

(National Council on Urban Economic Development 1978a:3)

Although the council recognizes a certain public accountability problem with these development corporations, it explains the logic behind these institutions when it warns: "Too much public control . . . may discourage effective private participation" (1978a:3). In short, quasi-public redevelopment corporations represented an important *formalization* of private control over key areas of municipal policy.

3. *Public entrepreneurialism.* By the 1970s and 1980s, city mayors had assumed a much more visible role as promoters of public-private redevelopment. Mayors such as William Donald Schaefer in Baltimore, Kevin White in Boston, Richard Caliguiri in Pittsburgh, George Voinovich in Cleveland, and Edward Koch in New York took active roles in bringing

public and private resources together to promote extensive redevelopment programs favored by each city's corporate elite. Not so coincidentally, all of these "entrepreneurial" mayors had close connections to local developers and other important business interests. In an era when competitive mayoral races in cities such as Baltimore, Philadelphia, and Milwaukee were costing between $750 thousand and $1 million, the poltical economy of urban campaign finance made it logical that mayors and would-be mayors should continue to be unusually attentive to the redevelopment agendas of the business community.

Public-Private Partnerships in Action: The Rouse Company and the Redevelopment of Downtowns

No trend better exemplifies the policies and politics of post-1970 public-private collaboration than the "Rouse-ification" of downtowns across the United States. With its "festival marketplaces" in Boston (Faneuil Hall Marketplace), New York (South Street Seaport), Baltimore (Harborplace), Milwaukee (Grand Avenue Mall), Philadelphia (the Gallery at Market East), and St. Louis (Union Station), to name a few, the Rouse Company has become the leading downtown developer in the country. Rouse projects, with their distinctive architecture and innovative linkage of entertainment and retailing, have been credited with changing the image of center cities, stimulating spin-off downtown redevelopment, and rekindling investor confidence in downtown areas—all factors that have made mayors, anxious to promote growth and claim political credit for it, line up to coax Rouse to their cities (Gunts 1985a:16A–17A).

A hallmark of Rouse urban operations has been their insistence that their projects function within a public-private partnership framework. As company chairman Matthias DeVito puts it, "We won't do a project that a city wants us to do unless we see that the city government is terribly committed to it, and ready to be our partners in it to make it work" (Gunts 1985b:13B).

For the Rouse company, the "city as a partner" means land assemblage and project coordination. Says DeVito: "Building a shopping center, we can go out to the suburbs and buy a tract of land. But in order for an urban project to be done there has to be condemnation, relocation of tenants, building of parking structures, changes in streets—all the things that a developer can't do" (Gunts 1985b:13B). It also means financial support. The Rouse company requires municipal financial involvement—to make their projects economically feasible, but also to encourage cities "to think of themselves as entrepreneurs and partners in the redevelopment process" (Gunts 1985b:13B) For example, the $70 million Grand Avenue Mall in Milwaukee was funded in three ways: (1) $15 million from a consortium of local firms assembled by the Milwaukee Redevelopment Corporation; (2) $35 million from the city of Milwaukee (including a $12.6 million UDAG); and (3) $20 million from Rouse.

Aside from assisting in financing, the partnership approach helps Rouse market its projects. By highlighting their collaboration with cities, Rouse officials make their private projects seem like civic ventures that people should patronize out of civic duty (Gunts 1985a:17A).

Nothing could more clearly illustrate the unequal nature of public-private partnerships. Not only is there little evidence that public officials systematically weigh how best to deploy public resources to maximize public benefits (was the $35 million allocated by Milwaukee to underwrite Grand Avenue the best way to meet the city's employment and spinoff development needs?), but private and public interests have become so blurred by the partnership concept that private development projects are praised as the epitome of civic achievement.

Economic Development Results of Public-Private Partnerships

Research on urban redevelopment clearly suggests that the traditional public-private partnership approach has done little to improve living conditions for the majority of urban dwellers and, in fact, has exacerbated inequality and urban dualism. In city after city, redevelopment has been associated with a "tale of two cities": pockets of revitalization surrounded by areas that experience growing hardship. For example, more jobs were created in New York in 1983 than in any year since 1950; however, the city's poverty rate increased 20 percent between 1979 and 1985 (*New York Times* 1985). Boston has emerged as a "renaissance city" in the 1980s; yet conditions in Roxbury, Dorchester, and other poor areas of the city continue to deteriorate (Ganz 1986). Baltimore's Inner Harbor is a national model of public-private waterfront reclamation; during the 1970s, however, the poverty rate increased in 90 percent of the city's black neighborhoods (Levine 1987a). Redeveloped downtowns, in Brian Berry's phrase, tend to be "islands of renewal in seas of decay" (Berry 1985:69).

Why has the public-private approach to urban economic development produced such uneven results? The evidence suggests that both the *content* and the *process* of typical local efforts are deeply flawed.

First, downtown corporate centers based on advanced services and tourism—the focus of most partnership efforts—are deficient anchors of a local economy. As Stanback and Noyelle point out, the income distribution in such economies tends to be two-tiered, with few occupational ladders and middle-income jobs bridging the tiers. The downtown services sector tends to be isolated from the local component of a city economy; limited linkages to small and medium-sized local firms mean that there are few ripple effects in neighborhood economic development (Stanback and Noyelle 1982:140–142). What is more, the kinds of jobs created in downtown corporate centers are unlikely to provide employment opportunities for urban poor and minorities. New York, for example, lost 492,000 jobs requiring less than a high school diploma between 1970 and 1984; in those years, the city added 239,000 jobs requiring at least some college education. The same trend occurred in Philadelphia, Boston, Baltimore, St. Louis, and Atlanta (Kasarda 1986:24).

This jobs mismatch helps explain why poverty rates rose and neighborhoods deteriorated in all urban areas, despite the proliferation of public-private redevelopment projects. The loss of entry-level employment in basic manufacturing has not been adequately replaced by redeveloped corporate centers. Moreover, the entry-level service jobs that have been created pay substantially less than the manufacturing positions being replaced. Finally, the cities' overall conditions remain distressed because many of the benefits of redevelopment have been transmitted to the suburbs. Studies of Boston, Baltimore, New York, and Cleveland all show that over 60 percent of the "good" jobs created by downtown revitalization—those paying over $25,000 a year—have gone to suburban commuters. Such transfer does little to shore up the urban revenue base and support local public services, and it suggests that city residents are not the main beneficiaries of their governments' redevelopment policies (Ganz 1986; Levine 1987a; *New York Times* 1985; Swanstrom 1985).

The displacement of urban manufacturing positions and the increase in downtown services are national and international trends virtually impossible for individual cities to alter. But, in embracing a corporate center strategy, urban officials have done little to mitigate the deficiencies just noted by attempting to channel downtown growth so that it spurs economic development in distressed neighborhoods. In sum, the corporate center approach appears flawed because it ignores such issues as the quality of jobs created and the linkage between development in one sector and development needs in another, while relying on the trickle down effect rather than public targeting to encourage economic development in the most distressed urban neighborhoods.

Second, the public-private redevelopment *process* helped promote policies that favor developers and the wealthy at the expense of the majority of city residents. Billed as a model of how government and business can cooperate to revitalize a city, these partnerships have in effect meant corporate domination of municipal policy. Having abandoned any serious "concept of themselves as stewards of the public interest," to borrow Hartman's phrase, public planning agencies merely identify investment opportunities for private developers, or work out the details on projects initiated by developers (Hartman 1984:219).

The modus operandi of most partnerships—concentrating redevelopment decision-making in quasi-public development entities—has also had negative consequences. Purposely insulated from public influence and dominated by downtown-oriented interests, these institutions have emphasized deal-making and profit opportunities, rather than systematic planning of how best to deploy public resources to create good jobs and meet pressing neighborhood needs. Peterson argues that such undemocratic institutions flourish because development is a consensual issue. Because everyone agrees that the entire city benefits from policies designed to improve the city's attractiveness to business, going through normal political institutions would be unnecessarily cumbersome (Peterson 1981: 133–134).

A more plausible explanation, however, is that quasi-public corporations are insulated from public control in order to keep those groups deriving few benefits from partnership activity from interfering with the deal-making process. The *depoliticization* of redevelopment decision-making effectively stymies groups supporting alternative strategies; it insulates a crucial area of urban policy from democratic impulses. In Baltimore, for example, a quasi-public redevelopment bank, which disbursed or guaranteed over $500 million of public moneys for city redevelopment projects between 1976 and 1986, was run "by men and women whose names never appear on the ballot, whose decisions are not public, and whose actions are obscured through a string of corporations that operate outside the established system of government" (Smith 1980:1; Smith 1986:1) One of the bank's directors was surprisingly candid in describing the antidemocratic aspects of the bank's operations: "[We] have the responsibility of determining priorities for the community, deciding what projects come above something else. This is, in my view, far better than what happens in most cities, where operations are based on who gets there first and who yells the loudest" (United States Conference of Mayors 1984:70).

Under these circumstances, it is not surprising that the chief beneficiaries of urban economic development have been developers and advanced services professionals; it has been these groups, along with pro-business policy entrepreneurs, who have dominated typical public-private "partnerships." *Uneven* growth has been the logical outcome of *unequal* partnerships and closed decision-making processes. As Franklin James points out, "Public-private partnership efforts cannot be expected to have the same commitment to social equity as endeavors can have when the initiative lies in the public sector. . . . Such partnerships are likely to focus on traditional types of activities offering few direct benefits to disadvantaged persons" (James 1984:170). The perverse role of partnerships in allocating public resources is graphically demonstrated in St. Louis; a recent study shows that Chapter 353 tax abatements have cost the city's public schools almost $6 million a year (Jones 1987:150). Taking resources away from public education to fund tourist attractions and yuppie housing is hardly a way to meet the needs of the city's most disadvantaged residents; nor is such a strategy likely to improve the long-term redevelopment prospects in a community.

A major argument in favor of downtown-centered partnership projects has been that, although such projects may not produce immediate, tangible gains for distressed urban neighborhoods, the increased city revenue base created by downtown revitalization provides funds that cities can use to more directly address social neeeds. Yet, as research on Baltimore's celebrated redevelopment program has revealed, between 1980 and 1985 the downtown absorbed almost $17 million *more* in annual city expenditures for infrastructure, servicing, and so forth than it generated in increased local property taxes (Levine 1987b:136). As the boom continues downtown, receipts should eventually exceed expenditures, but there is little evidence, in Baltimore or other similarly austerity-minded cities, that local governments are inclined to use downtown revitalization as a "cash cow" for social programs; the returns from downtown growth are generally recycled into further redevelopment activity.

In sum, based on a pro-business growth ideology, the redevelopment strategies of U.S. cities have succeeded mainly in creating a "profit machine" for developers and investors. Downtowns have been revitalized and transformed into centers of corporate services and tourism, but the great majority using these facilities are not city residents. Neighborhood distress and shrinking economic opportunities remain serious problems for large numbers of urban dwellers. Urban democracy has been compromised by a partnership approach that views city government as a hindrance to "fast track" redevelopment deal-making, rather than as a genuine redevelopment partner representing the public interest.

New Directions in Public-Private Partnerships

Although traditional public-private partnership remains the dominant approach to urban economic development, the 1980s have seen the emergence of new conceptions of urban partnerships that hold the promise of focusing redevelopment priorities on the needs of the truly disadvantaged. The election of populist mayors such as Harold Washington in Chicago, Raymond Flynn in Boston, and Art Agnos in San Francisco—all of whom ran on platforms of neighborhood revitalization, balanced growth, and a more democratic development process—reflected public concern over precisely who benefits from urban redevelopment policy. Even New York Mayor Ed Koch, heretofore unswervingly loyal to the agenda of his city's powerful developers, joined the public bandwagon in criticizing the West Side megaprojects of Mortimer Zuckerman and Donald Trump. In New York, Chicago, Baltimore, and elsewhere, pressures from community groups have resulted in new redevelopment decision-making processes designed to augment community influence over the terms of redevelopment deals and the size and density of redevelopment projects. Movements have emerged throughout the country aimed at increasing public scrutiny of how public subsidies are used. And in cities such as Chicago, Hartford, and Burlington, public officials have begun to reorient local planning efforts, from working out the details of development deals to delineating *public* economic priorities and pursuing economic development projects strategically targeted to meet the city's basic needs (Clavel 1985; Mier et al. 1986).

Clearly, the high tide of privatistic redevelopment is ebbing. Cities no longer tell investors that "we'll let you write your own terms." The new concepts of partnership emerging in several cities include not only greater public control of the redevelopment process but also more equitable distribution of benefits and burdens in local partnership activities. These concepts are exemplified by three important trends.

1. *Strategic and democratic planning of economic development*. Several cities have recognized that throwing incentives at developers may not be the most rational approach to urban economic development and have begun to insist on a more active public planning presence in redevelopment policy. In Chicago, for example, economic development planning under Mayor Washington sought to "identify economic sectors that have promise for providing high-quality, lasting employment locally" (Mier et al. 1986:306). Instead of indiscriminately offering public incentives for any private investment, city officials assembled public-private task forces to develop coherent industry revitalization plans. In addition, the city established a number of mechanisms, based on the assumption that "planning cannot be a 'top down' process" (City of Chicago 1984:14), to encourage wider public participation in city planning. They include funding for the development of neighborhood organizations to engage in strategic

planning and deliver development services, public workshops on city resource allocation, and increased public access to information necessary for
informed decision-making. The upshot of these trends, driven by the concepts of political reform and social equity, was to create genuine partnerships for development, rather than merely using public subsidies for
private profit.

2. *Linkage policies*. The recent adoption of so-called linkage policies in
several cities is an encouraging sign of genuine partnership activity. In return for lucrative development rights, primarily in downtown areas, cities
such as Boston and San Francisco require developers to contribute to special funds to meet community needs in such areas as housing, job training, public transportation, and child care (Porter 1985; Keating 1986).
Chicago has operated a de facto linkage policy in which developers of
prime real estate have worked out development agreements with the city.
In these agreements, in return for development rights, a given investor
also helps meet a specified public objective such as building a factory elsewhere in the city.

Linkage policies are not a panacea for the uneven growth typical of
U.S. cities. Nevertheless, they do provide a way for public planning to
influence market trends somewhat, to the benefit of the entire community. Perhaps more important, the concept of linkage inscribes in government policy a profoundly different concept of partnership than has
heretofore existed in U.S. cities, by specifying that profit-making opportunities for developers carry social obligations.

3. *Community economic development*. A growing element in urban redevelopment activity are community development corporations (CDCs).
Targeting their efforts on low-income areas, CDCs engage in "hard" and
"soft" development activities: constructing or rehabilitating housing,
starting small businesses, providing child care, or offering skills training.
"Whatever the development mix," write Peirce and Stanbach, "the goal
of every CDC is the immediate relief of severe economic, social, and
physical distress—and eventually, wider regeneration of the community
(Peirce and Steinbach 1987:13) Unlike traditional urban redevelopment
methods, CDCs do not rely on the trickle down theory to provide economic benefits to distressed neighborhoods; rather, they seek to channel
direct investment into low-income areas that have fallen outside conventional market processes. The record of CDCs so far has been uneven,
in part because they have been woefully underfunded, and in part because they have been relatively unsuccessful in moving beyond small business and real estate development to communitywide strategic planning.
Moreover, CDCs have not been successful in linking housing issues with

economic development planning, nor have they succeeded in blending traditional community organizing with issues of economic development. Nevertheless, CDCs appear to hold promise for promoting revitalization in the most distressed urban areas (Barbe and Sekera 1983; Duncan 1986).

CDCs have received most of their funding from local and state agencies, as well as from organizations such as the Ford Foundation, which has invested $170 million since the 1960s. Increasingly, however, some private corporations and banks have become investors in CDC projects. Although private-sector support of CDCs remains low—especially compared with the billions going toward profitable downtown ventures around the country—corporate participation in CDC activity does represent a new form of partnership that promises greater social benefits than traditional redevelopment activities.

City governments cannot make redevelopment policy exactly as they please. They cannot repeal "laws of value" by ignoring national and international market trends. Moreover, the phenomenon of capital mobility, coupled with the tight fiscal constraints felt by most city governments, means that cities will continue to experience strong pressures to engage in traditional programs of privatistic growth. In the absence of regional or national policies regulating the velocity of capital movements, or providing an infusion of resources for direct investment in distressed communities, it is difficult to imagine radical, new departures in urban redevelopment policy.

But recent trends have demonstrated that cities are capable of altering the rules of the game under which public-private partnerships operate. Cities can extract better deals from developers, assert greater control over the redevelopment process, and better target resources to meet the needs of the disadvantaged. If these trends continue, then public-private collaboration may indeed become a *partnership* and contribute to the improvement of life in U.S. cities.

Note

I wish to thank Chester Hartman, Clarence Stone, Todd Swanstrom, and Sam Bass Warner for critical readings of earlier drafts of this chapter and for their many useful suggestions.

References

Barbe, Nancy, and June Sekera. 1983. *States and Communities: The Challenge for Economic Action*. Washington, D.C.: National Congress for Community Economic Development.

Berry, Brian. 1985. "Islands of Renewal in Seas of Decay." In *The New Urban Reality*, ed. Paul E. Peterson, pp. 69–98. Washington, D.C.: Brookings Institution.

Carnoy, Martin, Derek Shearer, and Russell Rumberger. 1983. *A New Social Contract: The Economy and Government after Reagan*. New York: Harper and Row.

City of Chicago. 1984. *Chicago Works Together*.

Clavel, Pierre. 1985. *The Progressive City: Planning and Participation, 1969–1984*. New Brunswick, N.J.: Rutgers University Press.

Committee for Economic Development. 1982. *Public-Private Partnership: An Opportunity for Urban Communities*. New York: Committee for Economic Development.

Duncan, William. 1986. "An Economic Development Strategy." *Social Policy* (Spring):117–124.

Economou, Bessie S. 1987. "Pittsburgh." In *Cities Reborn*, ed. Rachelle Levitt, pp. 110–146. Washington, D.C.: Urban Land Institute.

Fainstein, Norman I., and Susan S. Fainstein. 1983. *Restructuring the City: The Political Economy of Urban Redevelopment*. New York: Longman.

Fogelsong, Richard. 1986. *Planning the Capitalist City: The Colonial Era to the 1920s*. Princeton, N.J.: Princeton University Press.

Fosler, R. Scott, and Renee Berger, eds. 1982. *Public-Private Partnership in American Cities*. Lexington, Mass.: D. C. Heath.

Frieden, Bernard, and Lynn Sagalyn. 1986. "Downtown Shopping Malls and the New Public-Private Strategy." In *The Great Society and Its Legacy: Twenty Years of U.S. Social Policy*, ed. Marshall Kaplan and P. Cuciti, pp. 120–137. Durham, N.C.: Duke University Press.

Ganz, André. 1986. "Where Has the Urban Crisis Gone? How Boston and Other Large Cities Stemmed Economic Decline." In *Cities in Stress*, ed. M. Gottdiener. Beverly Hills: Sage.

Geisler, Charles, and Frank Popper, eds. 1986. *Land Reform, American Style*. Totowa, N.J.: Littlefield and Adams.

Glaab, Charles N., and A. Theodore Brown. 1976. *A History of Urban America*. New York: Macmillan.

Goodman, Robert. 1979. *The Last Entrepreneurs*. Boston: South End Press.

Gunts, Edward. 1985a. "Rouse Projects Stand Out as Symbol of Rejuvenation of U.S. Downtowns." Baltimore *Sun* (May 26).

———. 1985b. "Rouse Works with Cities as Partners—or Not at All." Baltimore *Sun* (May 27).

Hartman, Chester. 1984. *The Transformation of San Francisco*. Totowa, N.J.: Rowman and Allanheld.

James, Franklin. 1984. "Urban Economic Development: A Zero-Sum Game? In *Urban Economic Development*, ed. Richard Bingham and John Blair, pp. 157–174. Beverly Hills: Sage.

Jones, E. Terrence. 1987. "St. Louis: A Commentary." In *Cities Reborn*, ed. Rachelle Levitt, pp. 148–151. Washington, D.C.: Urban Land Institute.

Judd, Dennis, and Randy Ready. 1986. "Entrepreneurial Cities and the New Politics of Economic Development." In *Reagan and the Cities*, ed. George Peterson and Carol Lewis, pp. 209–248. Washington, D.C.: Urban Institute Press.

Kasarda, John D. 1986. "The Regional and Urban Redistribution of People and Jobs in the U.S." Paper prepared for the National Research Council Committee on National Urban Policy, National Academy of Sciences.

Keating, W. Dennis. 1986. "Linking Downtown Development to Broader Community Goals: An Analysis of Linkage Policy in Three Cities." *Journal of the American Planning Association* (Spring): 133–141.

Levine, Marc V. 1987a. "Downtown Redevelopment as an Urban Growth Strategy: A Critical Appraisal of the Baltimore Renaissance." *Journal of Urban Affairs* 9(2):103–123.

———. 1987b. "Economic Development in Baltimore: Some Additional Perspectives." *Journal of Urban Affairs* 9(2):133–138.

Levitt, Rachelle L., ed. 1987. *Cities Reborn*. Washington, D.C.: Urban Land Institute.

Lines, Jon J., Ellen L. Parker, and David C. Perry. 1986. "Building the Twentieth-Century Public Works Machine: Robert Moses and the Public Authority." In *Reindustrializing New York State: Strategies, Implications, Challenges*, ed. Morton Schoolman and Alvin Magid, pp. 231–256. Albany: State University of New York Press.

Logan, John R., and Harvey Molotch. 1987. *Urban Fortunes: The Political Economy of Place*. Berkeley: University of California Press.

Mier, Robert, Kari J. Moe, and Irene Sherr. 1986. "Strategic Planning and the Pursuit of Reform, Economic Development, and Equity." *Journal of the American Planning Association* 52 (Summer):299–309.

Mollenkopf, John. 1983. *The Contested City*. Princeton, N.J.: Princeton University Press.

Molotch, Harvey. 1976. "The City as a Growth Machine: Towards a Political Economy of Place." *American Journal of Sociology* 82 (September):309–330.

National Council on Urban Economic Development. 1978a. *Coordinated Urban Economic Development: Development Finance*. Washington, D.C.: NCUED.

———. 1978b. *Coordinated Urban Economic Development: Public/Private Development Institutions*. Washington, D.C.: NCUED.

New York Times. 1985. "A Symposium: A City Divided" (January 20).

New York Times Magazine. 1984. "Baltimore Advertisement" (May 17):72–74.

Peirce, Neal R., and Carol F. Steinbach. 1987. *Corrective Capitalism: The Rise of America's Community Development Corporations*. New York: Ford Foundation.

Peterson, Paul E. 1981. *City Limits*. Chicago: University of Chicago Press.

Porter, Douglas. 1985. *Downtown Linkages*. Washington, D.C.: Urban Land Institute.

Shefter, Martin. 1985. *Political Crisis/Fiscal Crisis: The Collapse and Revival of New York City*. New York: Basic Books.

Smith, C. Fraser. 1980. "Two Trustees and a $100 Million 'Bank' Skirt Restrictions of City Government." Baltimore *Sun* (April 13).

———. 1986. "Trustee Process Was Controversial within Small Circle." Baltimore *Sun* (March 16).

Squires, Gregory D. 1984. "Industrial Revenue Bonds and the Deindustrialization of America." *Urbanism: Past and Present* 9(1):1–9.

Stanback, Thomas, and Thierry Noyelle. 1982. *Cities in Transition*. Totowa, N.J.: Allanheld-Osmun.

Stone, Clarence N. 1976. *Economic Growth and Neighborhood Discontent*. Chapel Hill: University of North Carolina Press.

———. 1987. "The Study of the Politics of Urban Development." In *The Politics of Urban Development*, ed. Clarence N. Stone and Heywood T. Sanders, pp. 3–21. Lawrence: University Press of Kansas.

Swanstrom, Todd. 1985. *The Crisis of Growth Politics: Cleveland, Kucinich, and the Challenge of Urban Populism*. Philadelphia: Temple University Press.

Tabb, William. 1982. *The Long Default: New York City and the Urban Fiscal Crisis*. Monthly Review Press.

United States Conference of Mayors. 1984. *The Baltimore City Loan and Guarantee Program: A Trustee System*. Washington, D.C.: U.S. Conference of Mayors.

Ward, Richard, Robert M. Lewis, and S. Jerome Prater. 1987. "St. Louis." in *Cities Reborn*, ed. Rachelle Levitt, pp. 152–201. Washington, D.C.: Urban Land Institute.

Warner, Sam Bass. 1968. *The Private City: Philadelphia in Three Periods of Its Growth*. Philadelphia: University of Pennsylvania Press.

Wilson, James Q., ed. 1966. *Urban Renewal*. Cambridge, Mass.: Harvard University Press.

Yater, George H. 1987. "Louisville." In *Cities Reborn*, ed. Rachelle Levitt, pp. 60–104. Washington, D.C.: Urban Land Institute.

Peter Dreier

3. Economic Growth and Economic Justice in Boston: Populist Housing and Jobs Policies

The key dilemma for progressive local politicians is deciding to what extent city government can intervene in the private economy before business either pulls up stakes or mobilizes politically to oppose elected officials. Since most decisions affecting a city's business climate are made by national corporations and the federal government, there are limits to what a city government can do to improve the business climate *or* social conditions. Still, all local government officials are concerned about the business climate, because the city's tax base and jobs base depend on whether businesses stay and expand. A major difference between conservative, liberal, and progressive city governments is their willingness to constantly test how far government can go before business acts on its threats to leave, cut back, expand elsewhere, or organize political opposition.

If progressive elected officials are to challenge business perogatives, they need to have a strong political constituency that will support them despite the potential threats of local businesses. They also have to know when and how to compromise. Progressive city officials, in other words, must have a clear sense of economics (i.e., when the threats of business are real and when they are not), as well as a strong political base. Of course, much depends on the nature of the particular business or industry, the relative mobility of the firms, and the overall health of the local and regional economy at the time.

Raymond L. Flynn was elected mayor of Boston in November 1983 with a popular mandate to "share the prosperity" of Boston's downtown economic boom—particularly in terms of jobs and housing—with the city's poor and working-class residents. Taking office at a time of dramatic federal cutbacks in housing, job training, and economic development programs, the Flynn administration developed policies that looked to Boston's booming private economy to carry out these redistributive goals. Some of these policies took the form of so-called public-private partnerships; others involved government regulation (zoning, rent control, hiring quotas) of the private sector. These policies assumed that the benefits of

35

the private economy's growth would not automatically trickle down to Boston's nonaffluent residents; they had to be steered in that direction by government action.

Housing and *jobs* policies, the major focus of this chapter, were clearly Boston's biggest problems and were the issues that had most galvanized support for Flynn's election. The theme he had articulated was that "neighborhood residents" had been "left behind" by the "downtown boom." They are also the programs that have been cut mostly severely by the Reagan government, thus forcing local governments to deal with the consequences.

Flynn inherited a city of striking contrasts. Although Boston had experienced a shift from a manufacturing-based to a service-oriented economy, it had never been as dependent on industry as many rustbelt cities were. By 1984, when he took office, Boston had experienced almost a decade of steady economic prosperity, symbolized by tall new office buildings in the downtown area. But the benefits of Boston's economic resurgence had not been broadly distributed. Neighborhoods close to downtown, or near colleges, were experiencing rapid gentrification, while other low-income and working-class neighborhoods were facing disinvestment and were still scarred with abandoned buildings. Over 10,000 families were on the waiting list for public housing and homelessness was becoming a serious problem. The city's total unemployment rate was among the nation's lowest and its average wages among the nation's highest. But unemployment in the minity community was double the city's rate. Many of the jobs in Boston's service-oriented economy, especially those held by Boston residents, were low-paying and dead end; suburbanites held most of the better jobs. These contrasts set the stage for Flynn's election and provided his popular mandate to share the prosperity more equitably.

The Early Growth Coalition and Urban Renewal, 1949–1967

The problems Boston faced in 1984 were very different from those it had faced in the 1950s, when the first growth coalition of business, government, and labor emerged.

In the eighteenth century, Boston was a maritime center. In the nineteenth century, it was the cradle of the nation's industrial revolution. By the early twentieth century, however, Boston's economy was collapsing. Even before the Depression, New England's manufacturing sector (particularly textiles) faced disinvestment and capital flight. Boston's banks and insurance companies, dominated by old Yankee families, refused to invest in the city. Only one private office building was constructed in Boston between 1929 and 1960. Business leaders blamed the Irish politicians who were running (particularly Mayor James Michael Curley) for Boston's high real estate taxes, uneven and questionable assessment practices, and corruption. Their hostility was a mixture of Brahmin snobbery and opposition to New Deal–style government programs for the poor. Some institutions simply found more profitable investments outside the region, especially in the Southern states and Latin America (Levitt 1987; O'Connor 1984; Trout 1977).

Thus the Yankee capitalists had, by the end of World War II, turned Boston into an economic wasteland. Events following the war exacerbated the city's economic plight. Between 1950 and 1960, the city's population decreased by 13 percent (801,000 to 697,000), and its employment rate fell by 10 percent (558,000 to 500,000). Meanwhile, suburban population and employment grew, by 9 percent and 22 percent, respectively (Levitt 1987).

In addition to the city's high tax rate and assessment practices, its antiquated infrastructure, aging residential buildings, and inadequate transportation system (particularly between the suburbs and downtown) stifled new investment. Boston was at a crossroads. Business leaders— particularly the large corporations, banks, and insurance companies that owned much of the downtown real estate and held mortgages on property throughout the city—had a choice to make. They could either write off their investments and continue to abandon the city, or they could seek to rebuild it to protect and enhance their investments. The newly enacted federal urban renewal program, initiated by the nation's major corporate and real estate leaders to revitalize downtown business districts, offered the resources to carry out a rebuilding strategy in Boston. To realize this potential, however, Boston's business leaders believed they had to exert more direct influence on the political system.

In 1949 Boston's business leaders began mobilizing to change the city's political and economic climate. They helped elect two pro-business mayors (John Hynes, who defeatd Curley in 1949, and John Collins, who served 1959–1968) and helped shape their fiscal and development agendas.

Business leaders also created a number of organizations to coordinate their efforts. The New Boston Committee, headed by Henry L. Shattuck, a well-connected Brahmin Republican lawyer, and Jerome L. Rappaport, a young Jewish Harvard Law School graduate, helped Hynes defeat Curley and worked with Hynes to implement the federally funded urban renewal program in 1952.

In 1954, with a grant from the Ford Foundation, the Boston College School of Business started a series of Citizen Seminars in an attempt to initiate a new partnership between the city's closely knit Yankee business elite and its upwardly mobil Irish politicians. The business leaders saw themselves spearheading Boston's economic recovery, but their rhetoric suggests that they also viewed their mission as having a higher purpose: restoring the public's confidence in its own leadership and vision. The early seminars served as pep rallies for Boston's business elite. Robert Ryan, vice president of Cabot, Cabot & Forbes, the giant real estate firm, addressed the seminar in 1957 in almost missionary terms: "Gentlemen, we are marked men, Bostonians at mid-century! The most significant idea which has come out of these seminars is that Boston is crying for leadership. We have been tapped by fate, for which we should be very grateful and give thanks." Ryan made it clear what kind of leadership he had in mind: "Boston has reached the point where private funds cannot be invested in Boston in any amount equal to filling the need until those funds can be assured a chance of return on investment."

In 1957 a small group of prominent businessmen, led by John Hancock's Paul F. Clark, founded the Greater Boston Economic Study Committee, which produced a series of reports that emphasized the importance of turning Boston's downtown into a center for retail and service businesses and for corporate headquarters. The study committee was closely linked to the Committee for Economic Development (Clark was its vice chairman), a national business group that had promoted the federal urban renewal legislation of the late 1940s. One of the study committee's recommendations was to create a superagency to coordinate downtown redevelopment.

The activities of the New Boston Committee, the Citizen Seminars, and the Greater Boston Economic Study Committee suggest that Boston's business elite was becoming increasingly politically cohesive. What finally emerged, in 1959, was a group of fourteen corporate leaders— mostly Yankees with close business, civic, and social connections—who formed the Coordinating Committee (soon nicknamed "the Vault," reportedly because of their mystery-shrouded meetings held at a bank). The first item on the Vault's agenda was to help Suffolk County Registrar John Collins defeat highly favored State Senate President John Powers in the 1959 mayoral race. The Vault's members and connections helped fill Collins's campaign war chest, gave him advice on issues, and ultimately helped him win the election.

Between 1959 and 1968, the Vault (which gradually increased its membership) met regularly and worked closely with Collins. It was instrumental in catalyzing what came to be known as the "New Boston" downtown redevelopment. It also provided experts for studies (including many from the Massachusetts Institute of Technology, where Collins later taught) and mobilized business support for Collins's projects. Collins embarked on a program of budget cuts sought by the Vault. His first step was to lay off 1,200 city employees and to reduce city services. He then offered tax concessions to developers to attract investment, beginning in 1960 with Prudential's massive office-residental complex, the first major private office investment in decades (Dreier 1983; Levin 1960; Meyerson and Banfield 1966; Mollenkopf 1983).

The Vault persuaded the state legislature and city leaders to create a "superagency," the Boston Redevelopment Authority (BRA), to oversee development, thus combining the city's planning and urban renewal functions. Stung by the bad publicity aroused by Hynes's earlier urban renewal efforts, particularly the razing of the West End neighborhood (Gans 1982), Collins and Ralph Lowell (a founder of the Vault) persuaded planner Edward Logue to leave New Haven and head the BRA.

Logue undertook an ambitious urban renewal program that included more than one-fourth of the city's land area. Boston received more federal urban renewal funds, per capita, than any other city, in part because Boston's John F. Kennedy was in the White House and Congressman John McCormack was Speaker of the House. The downtown core underwent a dramatic physical change. Residential neighborhoods experienced both demolition and rehabilitation efforts; the net effect was to reduce the overall number of housing units in the city.

This "partnership" between the public and private sectors was precisely what the drafters of the federal urban renewal legislation had intended. The federal government provided funds to purchase and clear land, rehabilitate existing housing, construct subsidized housing, and improve the infrastructure, while the private sector invested capital in the city, particularly the downtown area. The Collins-Logue effort was closely coordinated with that of the Vault and business leaders. For example, the waterfront plant was initially drafted by the staff of the Chamber of Commerce. The Committee for the Central Business District, a group formed to support the downtown renewal plan, was chaired by Charles Coolidge, chairman of the Vault. The Hynes-Collins period saw the first large-scale office towers and luxury housing erected downtown and public housing constructed in the outlying neighborhoods.

During this period, the economy and the work force underwent a change. Crafts and production jobs declined from 33.4 percent in 1950 to 24 percent in 1970; professional, technical, and managerial employment grew from 18.2 percent to 22.5 percent; clerical and sales jobs increased from 28 percent to 32.6 percent. Still, the population of Boston continued to decrease—from 697,000 in 1960 to 641,000 in 1970—while the suburbs grew. Boston's minority population grew from 5.3 percent of the population in 1950, to 9.8 percent in 1960, to 18.2 percent in 1970. (Boston Redevelopment Authority 1986; Ganz 1985; Levitt 1987).

The Kevin White Years, 1968–1983

Collins decided not to run for reelection in 1967. Secretary of State Kevin White defeated a large field of candidates, including Ed Logue, who had the backing of the business community. White was mayor for four terms (sixteen years), during which federal urban policy, local fiscal conditions, and his own political goals changed significantly.

White inherited the development momentum from Collins and Logue. The amount of new office space completed averaged more than 800,000 square feet annually between 1965 and 1974 and reached a high of 5.2 million square feet in 1975. The national recession in the mid-1970s slowed the pace of Boston's recovery. Between 1976 and 1983, an annual average of only 360,000 square feet of office space was added. The local office vacancy rate rose. The city's unemployment rate increased from 4.9 percent in 1970 to 12.8 percent in 1975, while the national rate went from 4.9 percent to 8.5 percent (Boston Redevelopment Authority 1986; Ganz 1985).

By the late 1970s, Boston's private-sector economy had recovered, reflecting international, national, and regional economic changes. The urban renewal program had paved the way for Boston to become a headquarters city for financial services, insurance, and high-technology industries, as well as a center for educational and medical institutions, and for tourism. This led to an increased demand for office space; the Class A office vacancy rate fell to less than 1 percent in 1981. Real estate developers again flocked to Boston to assemble parcels and seek the city government's approval. A dramatic boom in the city's office and hotel construction began about 1979. The revitalization of Fanueil Hall and the Quincy Market symbolized Boston's downtown rebirth as well as its gentrification. By the early 1980s, Boston's real estate market was the strongest in the country (Levitt 1987).

Despite this development boom, the White years, particularly his last two terms, were a period of political, economic, and demographic turmoil. White began his reign in 1968 with neighborhood-oriented policies: A Little City Hall program to advocate the cause of neighborhood residents; a rent control program to protect the city's large tenant (70 percent) population; and an aggressive effort to build public and subsidized housing with federal funds.

By the mid-1970s, White began shifting his political and development priorities toward downtown revitalization. The controversy over court-ordered busing that began in 1974 caused the middle-class "white flight" from Boston to continue and exacerbated racial tensions. White almost lost his 1975 reelection bid. To cultivate the white middle class, he targeted Community Development Block Grant (CDBG) funds for homeowner improvements. To cultivate the real estate industry, he began dismantling rent control in 1975 by the introduction of vacancy decontrol. He also terminated the Little City Hall program and increasingly used City Hall jobs as part of his political patronage machine. White expected campaign contributions from housing developers who received property tax breaks, from landlords whose anti–rent control views were reflected in the new policy, and particularly from office developers (Ferman 1985; Lucas 1985; Lupo 1977).

Boston also faced an unprecedented *fiscal crisis*. In 1980, Massachusetts voters passed Proposition 2 1/2, which dramatically cut property taxes, local governments' major revenue source. Within a few years, revenues from the local property tax had declined by one-third. Boston's tax base was already a narrow one; about half of its land (churches, government buildings, hospitals, museums, universities, and parks) was exempt from property taxes. In addition, under the Reagan administration, federal aid to Boston ($167.4 million in 1981) declined by 36 percent in 1982 and 24 percent between 1982 and 1985.

Boston was plunged into near bankruptcy. White turned to the Vault to help the city out of its fiscal crisis. The Vault's corporate leaders used their influence with investment banks and bond-rating firms to avoid bankruptcy. They also lobbied the state legislature to allow Boston to raise revenues by imposing additional taxes on condominium conversions and hotel occupancies. In exchange, the Vault assigned the corporate-sponsored Municipal Research Bureau to monitor the city's layoffs, reduction of municipal services, and negotiations with public-sector unions. Thus, while the city was booming as a result of new private real estate investment, the city was closing schools, fire stations, and police stations, and laying off workers. In 1981 alone the city government laid off 3,820 employees—19 percent of the total work force. Because Boston was unable to increase property tax revenues despite the investment boom, its bond rating dropped, limiting its ability to make much-needed capital improvements. By 1984 the city still had a $40 million deficit in its operating budget (Kahn 1981; Slavet and Torto 1985).

The shutting down of vital public services and the layoffs alienated voters. More middle-class families moved outside the city or sent their children to private and parochial schools; angry residents organized demonstrations directed against Mayor White. This disaffection on the part of neighborhood residents led White to focus even more attention on downtown projects and to cultivate Boston's image as a "world class city." He spent more time lavishly entertaining national and foreign dignitaries and traveling abroad, and less time attending neighborhood meetings and groundbreaking ceremonies. One columnist nicknamed White "Mayor Deluxe." No longer able to depend on the delivery of basic municipal services or the visible results of neighborhood improvement programs to bolster his electoral support, White increasingly attempted to build a political "machine" composed of municipal employees. In the early 1980s, the U.S. attorney began investigating the White administration, focusing on campaign contribution irregularities and other forms of corruption. Several close White aides were indicted.

From 1970 to 1980, Boston's population declined another 12 percent, from 641,000 to 563,000. During that period, the minority population grew from 18.2 percent to 30 percent. It was not until the early 1980s that, as a result of downtown development and the job boom, Boston's population began to climb—for the first time since 1950 (Boston Redevelopment Authority 1986; Ganz 1985).

White realized that the city's changing demographics, the fiscal crisis, the corruption investigations, and the growing disparity between the downtown's affluence and the neighborhoods' decline made his reelection in 1983 difficult at best. In May 1983, urged to do so by the powerful *Boston Globe*, he announced he would not seek a fifth term.

Flynn Takes Office

White's announcement triggered a fierce competition for the post of mayor. Eventually, seven men were serious candidates in the nonpartisan preliminary election. The two top vote-getters, Raymond Flynn (a city councillor and former state representative) and Mel King (a former state representative and the first black to make it to a final election), were also the most progressive, neighborhood-oriented candidates, with the least support among the business community and real estate industry. They shared similar views on housing, the most prominent issue in the campaign. Both supported strong tenant protection laws, a strong "linkage" policy (to require downtown developers to contribute funds for affordable housing), and a stronger neighborhood voice in development decisions. Flynn beat King in November 1983 by a two-to-one margin and took office the following January. (Flynn was reelected four years later, when he defeated conservative City Councilor Joseph Tierney by an even wider margin.)

Flynn's core political coalition had three sources. The first consisted of progressive community organizers, activists, and policy specialists (from groups such as Massachusetts Fair Share, the Massachusetts Tenants Organization, Nine-to-Five, and the hotel workers union) who had played key roles in the campaign. A second was drawn from the city's Irish working-class neighborhoods and included neighborhood activists, union members, and others angered by the White administration's attitude and policies. The third was composed of friends and admirers whom he had gained as a star athlete at South Boston High School and an All-American basketball player at Providence College (class of 1963)—accomplishments that helped propel his political career. Each group was rewarded with positions in City Hall. The first (which the press came to label the "Sandinistas") gained significant influence over the new mayor's policy agenda.

The business community was initially suspicious of Flynn; the real estate industry was openly hostile. Developers, landlords, and corporate leaders strongly supported Flynn's opponents. They opposed linkage and rent control and generally viewed Flynn as "anti-development." Yet the key to Flynn's campaign rhetoric and electoral support had been his pledge to "share the prosperity" of Boston's economic growth, not to halt it.

Housing and Economic Conditions

The inconsistency between Boston's booming economy and the socioeconomic conditions of its working class provided the Flynn administration with a mandate for a "populist" policy agenda. The nation's media have focused considerable attention on the "Massachusetts miracle" and the effect of Governor Michael Dukakis's policies in promoting economic prosperity during his three terms in office. From 1976 to 1986, Massachusetts gained 853,000 jobs, a 31 percent increase (surpassing the national figure of 26 percent). In December 1987, the state's jobless rate was 2.9 percent. Per capita income in Massachusetts rose from 5 percent above the national average in 1976 to 21 percent above it in 1986. Boston is the state's economic, political, and cultural capital. Its ratio of jobs to population is second only to that of Washington, D.C. Three-quarters of all the jobs created in the state between 1975 and 1986 were located in metropolitan Boston. The city's jobs gain since and the more than doubling of its average annual wage during that decade helped to spur the state's prosperity (Harrison and Kluver 1988). Private development and several major state and federally funded public works projects in Boston are expected to generate many construction jobs as well as permanent employment. As Harrison and Kluver (1988) observe, "In reality, the Massachusetts miracle remains largely a Boston miracle" (see also Ferguson and Ladd 1986).

With the exception of the construction industry, the jobs created in the growth sectors tended to be divided between well-paid professional and managerial positions, on the one hand, and poorly paid clerical, service, sales, and related positions on the other. Most of the economic growth was concentrated in a few sectors: business and legal services, finance, insurance, higher education and medicine, real estate and construction. Manufacturing jobs have steadily declined since the mid-1970s. A significant portion of the state's poverty population consists of the so-called working poor. The low unemployment rates are due, in part, to slow labor force growth tied to several other factors, particularly high housing costs.

In several ways, Boston residents did not share proportionately in the region's economic prosperity. In 1950, Boston residents held 54 percent of Boston's 523,171 jobs. By 1980, the share had dropped to 35 percent of 548,497 jobs; three years later, it was down to 31 percent of 587,000 jobs. Furthermore, suburban commuters held most of the well-paying jobs, whereas Boston residents (and disproportionately minorities and women) held primarily lower-rung jobs without career ladders (Boston Redevelopment Authority 1986).

Boston's demographic and labor market trends were reflected in its school system. From 1972 to 1987, the number of students in public schools declined from 110,000 to 58,000, while the percentage of minorities in public schools increased from 25 percent to 75 percent. (Approximately 23,000 school-age children live in Boston but do not attend Boston's public schools.) By 1987, 60 percent of Boston's public schools came from families receiving Aid to Families with Dependent Children (AFDC); three-quarters lived in single-parent or foster homes; half lived in public housing. Indicators of school system performance—reading scores, attendance records, dropout rates—were consistently below the national average and also below those of other large-city school systems. A school system that could only hold out the promise of dead-end, low-paying jobs for students who stayed in school had little to offer (Boston School Department 1988).

The city's economic prosperity and population growth (as well as a new subway line) fueled a strong housing market, which threatened to displace many of the city's poor and working-class residents. By 1983, Boston had already experienced several years of sustained real estate appreciation, leading to gentrification (Achtenburg, 1984; Boston Redevelopment Authority 1988). This trend had begun in the late 1970s in the areas closest to downtown; by the early 1980s it had spread to outlying working-class neighborhoods. The magnitude of the housing problem is reflected by the following statistics (Boston Redevelopment Authority 1988).

> Housing prices more than tripled between1975 and 1984. The average price of a single family house increased from $25,000 to $81,300. By 1985, the Boston area had the highest housing prices in the nation.

> Private-sector rents increased dramatically. Between 1977 and 1981, rents rose 48 percent while renters' incomes rose only 35 percent. By the first quarter of 1984, the median rent (of dwellings advertised in the *Boston Globe*) was $528—a 16 percent increase in one year. By 1980, almost half of Boston renters were spending more than one-quarter of their income for rent. In 1983, the rental vacany rate was 2.5 percent, and 10,000 families were on the waiting list for public housing.

> Condominium conversions began in the late 1970s. In 1975, Boston had only 1,568 condominiums out of approximately 240,000 housing units. By the end of 1983, the number of condominiums had reached 14,377. Only one-fifth of Boston renters could afford the average condominium.

> In 1983, the city's Emergency Shelter Commission estimated the homeless population to be 2,700.

When it took office in January 1984, the Flynn administration inherited these economic conditions, which had been created primarily by private-sector market forces, but were exacerbated by both federal cutbacks and the White administration's policies. The dilemma was succinctly stated by Ed Logue, when comparing his reign as BRA director with that of Flynn's BRA chief, Steve Coyle: "I had one thing Steve doesn't have—federal money, but a very limp market. Steve has very limp federal money, and a very strong market" (Pantridge 1988).

Housing and Jobs Policies

The local government had very limited tools and resouces at its disposal (primarily regulatory powers, earmarked funds, and public property) with which to address this housing and jobs crisis. What follows is a brief description of five key housing and jobs policies that involved government regulation of, or partnership with, business.

Linkage and Inclusionary Housing

Boston's strong real estate market, and the severe decrease in federal housing funds, led advocates of affordable housing to seek new revenues and techniques to create such housing by extracting additional "public benefits" from developers. Linkage and inclusionary zoning became two hotly contested mechanisms for achieving this goal.

Linkage is a fee on downtown development projects targeted for the construction or rehabilitation of low-income and moderate-income housing (Keating 1986). It was first proposed in Boston in early 1983 (by Massachusetts Fair Share, a confrontational community group based in working-class neighborhoods, and by a *Boston Globe* columnist) as a way to mitigate some of the pressure on Boston's housing market caused by the increase in jobs and population spurred by the downtown redevelopment. It became a major issue during the mayoral contest. All but one of the seven major contenders endorsed some version of linkage; Flynn and King advocated the versions with the highest fee. When it looked like the eventual winner would seek to enact some form of linkage, White decided that he wanted the credit. In October 1983, White's advisory committee —heavily weighted with developers and City Hall staff—issued its report, which recommended a linkage policy requiring downtown office developers to pay $5/per square foot, over a twelve-year period, exempting the first 100,000 square feet. This formula, in real terms, actually amounted to only $2.40/per square foot. Flynn, Fair Share, and other advocates criticized the advisory committee's recommendation, calling for a a full $5/per square foot formula. The Greater Boston Real Estate Board (GBREB) warned that any linkage policy would destroy Boston's favorable development climate.

A few weeks before Flynn took office, White pushed his advisory committee's proposal through the BRA and the Zoning Commission. As mayor, Flynn accepted this compromise linkage formula for a year and a half, during which he waited to see if the real estate industry's dire predictions would come true. When it became clear that developers viewed the linkage fee as simply another cost of doing business in Boston's hot real estate market, Flynn proposed increasing the linkage fee to $6/per square foot, paid over seven years instead of twelve—in effect, doubling the linkage formula. Despite GBREB opposition, Flynn (with support from housing activists) got the BRA and the Zoning Commission to pass his linkage amendment to the city's zoning code in early 1986.

By the end of 1987, more than $45 million in linkage funds had been committed by downtown developers. At least another $20 million was projected to come from projects in the development pipeline. As of the end of 1987, $17 million had been approved for allocation, primarily for "gap financing" of housing developments, encompassing about 2,000 units. A Neighborhood Housing Trust now allocates the funds, with priority given to nonprofit developers.

The different segments of the growth coalition have learned to live with linkage. The lowest office vacancy rate in the country (8 percent in mid-1987) allows Boston developers simply to pass on the fee to commercial tenants. Unions do not mind it so long as the office projects provide jobs. Nonprofit housing groups support it and compete for the limited supply of linkage funds.

In 1986, housing activists and the Flynn administration began to push for another policy, *inclusionary zoning*, which required housing developers to set aside affordable housing units in market-rate projects. Flynn's housing staff pointed out that 98 percent of the affordable housing built in Boston was on publicly owned property; private developers were not creating affordable units. Housing activists, encouraged by a long Sunday *Boston Globe* article, joined together to form a Linkage Action Coalition, staffed by Fair Share, to advocate strengthening of the linkage policy and introduction of inclusionary zoning.

The opposition to inclusionary zoning was expected to be even broader than the opposition to linkage. Whereas linkage affected a small number of downtown office towers, inclusionary zoning would affect a much larger and more diverse group of housing developers. It was also not at all clear that many neighborhood associations, which in the past had opposed subsidized housing, would support a policy that would bring more low-income housing to their neighborhoods.

In July 1986, Flynn submitted an inclusionary zoning policy to the BRA. It called for private developers to set aside 10 percent of all housing units (in projects of ten units or more) for low- and moderate-income residents. The GBREB voiced the only opposition, claiming that the policy would slow the housing boom and was an unfair tax on housing developers. Speaking in favor of the policy at a public hearing were housing activists, state housing officials (Governor Dukakis endorsed it a few days later), a leader of the city's building trades unions, and a number of developers with projects in the pipeline who wished to curry favor with the

Flynn administration. The support of this latter group helped to undermine the GBREB's argument that the policy was financially unworkable. City housing officials argued that developers could afford, in effect, to internally skew prices—that is, use some of the profits from market-rate units to subsidize the low-income (5 percent) and moderate-income (5 percent) housing.

To prove their point, city officials began to encourage housing developers to voluntarily comply with the inclusionary zoning guidelines while the policy was being publicly debated. This period of "voluntary" compliance was extended by several factors. Most housing developments in Boston require extensive design review, variances (due to the outdated zoning code, few developments are as-of-right), and community review. Few projects get approved by city agencies without substantial neighborhood support, involving meetings and compromises between residents and developers. After Flynn announced his inclusionary zoning policy, neighborhood associations began demanding that housing developers include affordable housing as well as meet their concerns about design, density, and parking. During the next year and a half, almost every private housing development requiring the city's approval incorporated affordable housing; alternatively, the developer paid an "in lieu of" fee to be added to the city's linkage fund. After the Supreme Court rendered the *Nolan* v. *California Coastal Commission* decision in April 1987, limiting the "social" uses of zoning, the Flynn administration continued to negotiate "voluntary" agreements rather than risk a legal challenge by officially enacting the inclusionary zoning amendment.

Support for NonProfit Housing:
The Boston Housing Partnership

Key resources available to local government for housing development include the inventory of publicly owned buildings and land, as well as discretionary funds (including CDBG and linkage moneys). In the allocation of these scarce resources, the city government gave priority to nonprofit housing developers.

When Flynn took office, Boston already had a fledgling network of community development corporations (CDCs), church groups, unions, and other nonprofit housing advocates. The Flynn administration decided to nurture and expand this network. By late 1987, Boston had more than thirty nonprofit housing groups. The Flynn administration provided grants (to hire staff and consultants) as well as city properties. It also provided funds to help CDCs and tenant groups hire consultants and buy occupied buildings (both private rental buildings and HUD-subsidized developments) in order to transform them into limited-equity cooperatives. City agencies developed an inventory of city-owned properties. Whereas the White administration had auctioned city parcels to the highest bidders, the Flynn administration sold city property for a nominal amount—often as little as a dollar—to reduce development costs, with priority given to nonprofit housing developers. The CDBG and linkage funds were targeted for affordable housing developments on city-owned property; city funds were often attached to state and federal housing funds.

To expand the capacity of CDCs to undertake large-scale projects, the Boston Housing Partnership (BHP) was formed in 1983. The BHP was an outgrowth of discussions between city officials, the director of the Greater Boston Community Development Corporation (a support agency for CDCs), and the chairman of the State Street Bank, who also served as head of Goals for Boston, a business group tied to the Committee for Economic Development. The BHP's board includes the top executives of the city's major banks, utility companies, and insurance firms; the top housing officials of city and state governments; and the directors of ten neighborhood-based CDCs. Working through the BHP, the CDCs rehabilitate, own, and manage the housing.

The BHP's role is to help the CDCs improve their development capacity by taking advantages of economies of scale. Its first project was the rehabilitation of 700 vacant or substandard units in 69 buildings, many of them city-owned—all for low-income residents. The BHP completed its first project early in 1987 and began work on its second (900-unit) project later that year.

The BHP's core staff arranged subsidies from city, state, federal, and private foundation sources; provided funds to the CDCs to hire staff, architects, and consultants; arranged the syndication of tax losses to investors; worked with city agencies to obtain tax abatements and permits; got the utility companies to forgive unpaid bills inherited from prior owners; and worked with the banks and state agencies to provide private and public financing of the $38 million project. Business leaders on the BHP board also lobbied in Washington for low-income tax credit legislation, persuaded Boston businesses to use the tax credit to invest in BHP projects, and worked with the Flynn administration, state officials, and Boston's congressional delegation to persuade HUD to sell 900 HUD-foreclosed apartments to BHP-affiliated CDCs instead of carrying out its intention of auctioning them to the highest bidders. Several local foundations and the United Way, as well as the national Local Initiatives Support Corporation (a Ford Foundation spin-off), also provided funds for the hiring of core and CDC staff.

Tenants' Rights: Rent Control and Condominium Conversion

Since the mid-1960s, Boston's major housing battleground has been the regulation of rents, evictions, and condominium conversions. It has become the key litmus test for identifying political candidates as conservative or liberal.

Boston enacted a strong rent control law in 1969, covering all private (unsubsidized) rental housing, except owner-occupied two- and three-unit buildings. By 1975, rent control had become a scapegoat for housing abandonment and the high property taxes levied on homeowners, and political support for it eroded. In that year Mayor White and the City Council adopted vacancy decontrol, which permanently removed an apartment from regulation after a tenant left. As a result, by 1983 a vast majority of the once-regulated apartments were gradually eliminated from rent control—the number decreased from more than 100,000 units to less than 25,000 units. White appointed members to the five-person Rent Control Board who opposed rent control (including Boston's largest landlord) and understaffed the agency, leading to administrative confusion and inefficiency (Achtenburg 1984).

Flynn had been the strongest (and often the only) tenants' rights advocate on the City Council. When he was elected mayor in 1983 (with Massachusetts Tenants Organization's endorsement), a cornerstone of his platform was to overhaul and strengthen tenants' rights laws. In April 1984, Flynn proposed a comprehensive tenant protection ordinance, but the council rejected his plan. This reflected the balance of political forces at that time, particularly the influence of the real estate lobby on the council as a result of its campaign contributions.

During its first five years, the Flynn administration substantially changed the city's tenants' rights laws. Rather than the dramatic sweeping change Flynn sought in his first year in office, however, the improvements came incrementally—through amendments to the existing law strengthening tenant protection against rising rents, evictions, and condominium conversions. For example, the city enacted an eviction ban with regard to condominium conversions as well as a law giving the Rent Board authority to regulate condominium conversions by requiring landlords to obtain a permit—and support of at least half of the tenants—before a conversion could take place. Although Flynn could not get council support for full restoration of rent control, he forged a compromise to limit rent increases (and grounds for eviction) for most tenants. In 1988, Boston became the first city to impose rent control on privately owned, federally subsidized developments facing conversion to market-rate housing due to "expiring use restrictions." Flynn also doubled the Rent Board's budget.

Tenants' rights laws involve government regulation of private property. Opposition from landlords and from the GBREB, and support from tenant groups, are expected. The Flynn administration helped shift the balance of political forces by enlisting the support of labor unions, religious leaders, and some neighborhood leaders who had previously been neutral on the issue (or opposed it). Flynn's staff worked closely with tenant groups to mobilize support at press conferences, neighborhood meetings, and public hearings. The Flynn administration also issued a series of reports documenting the housing crisis, to keep the issue "hot" and to rebut GBREB propaganda. In addition, in 1987, assured of reelection, Flynn used his political influence to elect a more progressive council by helping candidate Rosaria Salerno (a former nun and a neighborhood activist) win an at-large seat, thus setting the stage for several tenants' rights victories in the council.

Flynn also sought to enlist the Vault and major employers to support his tenants' rights agenda. He sent letters to business leaders, wrote articles for business publications, and issued a major study, all arguing that the Boston area's economic growth could be stymied by the shortage of affordable housing (Greiner 1987). Flynn argued that stronger tenants' rights laws (along with new housing production) would help alleviate the region's deepening labor shortage. The GBREB sent a strongly worded letter to the Vault in May 1988 opposing what it viewed as Flynn's efforts to divide the business community. Flynn was unable to get any major business leaders to support his tenants' rights legislation. On that issue, there was no "partnership" between the business community and the city government.

Boston Residents Jobs Policy

The Boston Residents Job Policy requires developers of private commercial buildings to hire Boston residents (50 percent), minorities (25 percent) and women (10 percent) for construction jobs. (These figures apply on a craft-by-craft basis.) The city had already adopted this policy (in 1983) for publicly funded projects; the Flynn administration extended it in 1986 to the much larger number of private projects. (In 1987, for example, public projects accounted for 604,046 work hours, compared with

3.5 million work hours spent on private projects.) The goal is to provide these groups with the high-paying building trades jobs to allow them to benefit from the construction boom (Boston School Department 1988).

The expanded policy was hammered out by the mayor's staff, the Greater Boston Real Estate Board, the Building Trades Council, and leaders of the minority community during months of discussions. The latter three groups are typically at odds over a number of issues, including hiring practices, workplace safety issues, and union membership practices, but the strong economy provided an opportunity to forge a political growth coalition on the basis of this redistributive policy.

The chief obstacle to its implementation was the lack of skilled construction workers, and union members, in the three overlapping groups (Boston residents, minorities, women). Obtaining the cooperation of the building trades unions in admitting and training such individuals was a critical step in making it work. The city government and the building trades unions developed a union apprenticeship training program for Boston residents, minorities, and women. The program was paid for, in part, by funds generated from the additional $1 per square foot linkage fee that Flynn added in 1986 for job training programs.

After two years, none of the major developments had totally complied with the policy, primarily because of the lag in availability of a pool of trained workers. Each year, however, compliance improved, as new workers were trained for building trades jobs.

The Flynn administration also sought to increase the percentage of Boston residents, minorities, and women holding the permanent jobs created by the building boom. This goal was more difficult to achieve, since each office building would potentially have hundreds of tenants, whose hiring practices would be difficult to monitor by either the initial developer or the city government. In 1987, Flynn created a committee to implement a policy regarding such permanent jobs. Compliance would be voluntary, based on negotiations with developers and building tenants, while the administration reviewed the legal and administrative mechanisms necessary to make it mandatory.

The Boston Compact

The Boston Compact is an agreement reached in 1982 between the business community and the Boston public schools. School officials agreed to improve the school system's performance as a quid pro quo for the business community's promise to give hiring preference to Boston high school students and graduates. The Compact has been expanded to include agreements with local colleges to increase the enrollment of Boston public school graduates and with labor unions to place graduates in their apprenticeship programs. According to two observers, "The Compact was based on a simple idea—that if every student was assured a job after graduation, younsters would remain in school, teachers would work harder to teach them, and the district would launch efforts to improve the quality of education in the high schools" (Farrar and Cipollone 1988)

The Compact was initiated by leaders of the Private Industry Council (PIC), an organization of large employers that was created to implement federal job training programs. Business leaders had worried about the failure of the public schools to train students, their potential labor force, for jobs (with regard to both specific skills and "work-ready" attitudes). They regularly reviewed statistics about the Boston schools' dropout rates, reading scores, and other measures. Said one PIC members, "CEOs sitting on the PIC Board heard about the demographics on a regular basis, heard and understood that the people out there are our future employees and that we have to be more involved in their training and preparation" (Farrar and Cipolone 1988).

The Compact was an effort to encourage students to remain in school and learn the skills needed for the job market. The PIC pledged to work with the schools to forecast the job market skills needed. The city, concerned that the jobs offered would be unskilled, low-paying, dead end work, exacted an agreement from business leaders that the jobs offered under the Compact would pay subtantially more than the minimum wage and would offer a ladder of mobility. Under the Compact, the PIC would monitor school performance indicators such as attendance, dropout rates, reading scores, and computer literacy. The hiring preferences pertained to both summer jobs and permanent, post-graduation jobs. The PIC staffers—whose salary is paid out of funds contributed by business and government—would find jobs and work with students on job-readiness skills, résumés, stage mock interviews, and give them other forms of advice.

From the standpoint of business community cooperation, the Compact has been successful. Whereas 202 companies hired 852 students for summer jobs in 1983, 669 companies hired 3,010 students for them in 1987. Average summer wages increased from $3.86 per hour in 1982 to $5.39 in 1987. The year-round program (which helps students find part-time work during the school year) grew from a total of 274 students in 3 high schools in 1982 to 1,200 students in 14 high schools in 1987. Boston high school graduates were increasingly given priority in hiring for permanent, post-graduation jobs: 415 students were hired in 1983; 1,007 were hired in 1987. The average wage per hour increased from $4.28 in 1983 to $6.18 in 1987.

With regard to the schools' performance, the Compact has been less successful. Attendance rates and students' performance on standardized reading and math scores have risen slightly. The high school dropout rate has not declined, however. Some observers explain that five years (1983–1988) is not enough time for the Compact's influence to be felt in the schools; others note that the elected School Committee and the school system bureaucracy—both of which are independent of the mayor—have resisted making the administrative changes necessary to achieve reform.

A PIC survey of 1985 graduates found that half were going on to further schooling; 59 percent were employed, including 60 percent of the black graduates—double the national average. These employment figures cannot be attributed entirely to Boston's overall low jobless rate; they are, in part, a result of the Compact.

The Compact's agreements with local colleges to increase their enrollment of Boston public high school graduates had shown modest success, but college costs still posed a major obstacle, even for students who gained college entry. A logical next step was to help Boston public school students attend college. The ACCESS program was created to achieve this aim. The catalyst for the program, which was announced in September 1986 by Flynn and a group of business leaders, was a contribution of $1 million by the Boston-based New England Mutual Life Insurance Company. another $4 million was raised from other private sources, including $1 million from the firms represented on the Vault, and $1 million from the Boston Foundation. The goal of ACCESS was to guarantee financial aid to all public high school graduates who are accepted by a college and then to guarantee them with jobs when they finish their educations. John McElwee, chairman of both John Hancock and the PIC, said that "what business is saying (to students) is, 'finish high school and go to college, and we'll help you with your tuition expenses and your employment at graduation.' It's that simple" (Farrar and Cipollone 1988).

Similar programs have been created in other cities—typically by individual philanthropists. Boston's ACCESS program was the first to be funded by a consortium of corporations. It is governed by an eleven-member board drawn from Boston corporations and a twenty-member advisory group composed of community and school representatives. Advisers visit all Boston high schools and counsel students as part of the college admissions and financial aid processes. They also offer further counseling to graduates once they are in college, concerning study habits, work-study opportunities, finances, and even the social demands of college. During its first three years, ACCESS has distributed $620,000 to

408 students, meeting their needs by filling the gap left by other scholarship programs. In 1988, the average award was $1,606; awards that year ranged from a low of $200 to a high of $3,500. It is too early to evalutate the ACCESS program on the basis of whether public school graduates *remain* in college through graduation.

These and other programs allow businesses to provide high-visibility assistance to the public schools by giving benefits directly to students, thus circumventing the school bureaucracy. The benefits are measurable and thus allow business to assess the programs' success in bottom-line terms. Business has not sought to directly influence curriculum, teaching methods, or other classroom activities; its influence on the school budget is indirect, through the watchdog Boston Municipal Research Bureau.

Conclusion

The resources available to local governments to solve housing and unemployment problems are very limited. During a period of drastic federal housing and job training cutbacks, local governments lack the revenue base to address the needs of their low- and moderate-income residents. For a variety of political, fiscal, and administrative reasons, when federal largesse is withdrawn, most city government officials throw up their hands in frustration and await a new change of priorities in Washington.

The Flynn administration has been an exception to this rule. Perhaps more than any other major U.S. city, Boston under Flynn's leadership has sought actively to address these problems. Using existing tools and resources—and seeking to invent new ones—it has made an aggressive effort to develop housing and jobs policies that benefit poor and working-class residents. This effort has met political resistance and legal challenge, but it nevertheless reflects a strong commitment to serve the needs of Boston's poor and working class. After developers and the GBREB successfully challenged both linkage and the condominium permit system in court, Flynn got enabling authority from the legislature to enact these regulations.

As a skillfull politician, Flynn has been able to promote this agenda and still remain extremely popular (indicated by his overwhelming reelection). As a result of his popular appeal and his policies, he has been able to broaden and redefine the growth coalition. He has accommodated the development community (if not the landlords), the business community, and the building trades unions by promoting "managed growth" and "balanced development." Flynn has walked a tightrope between confrontation and compromise with the powerful business and real estate community, while promoting a progressive policy agenda that has helped unite all racial and ethnic communities around common interests, as reflected in the electoral support he has received in every area of the city, including the minority neighborhoods.

It is possible to find other cities that have some of Boston's policies, but no other city has sought to pull all these policies together into a comprehensive program. Clearly, these efforts have not solved the housing and employment problems confronting Boston's lower class and working class. But significant progress has been made in several areas. First, the Flynn administration redefined the politics of growth and the relationship between the public and private sectors. It used both partnerships and regulations to get private firms to further the "public interest"—defined in terms of benefits to poor and working-class residents. It did not accept the private sector's terms concerning what was reasonable or feasible, nor did it back down when business leaders claimed that policies like linkage, rent control, and the resident jobs policy would undermine the city's economic growth. Second, by providing activist groups with legitimacy, funding, and a voice in development decisions, the city government helped mobilize poor and working-class residents, and thus helped shift the balance of power relations. The Flynn administration will thus leave a legacy of *empowerment*. Third, the Flynn administration became a vocal advocate of housing and jobs programs to benefit the poor at both the state and federal levels. As chairman of the housing committee of the National League of Cities and of the homelessness and hunger task force of the U.S. Conference of Mayors, he worked with various advocacy groups to promote federal legislation to benefit the poor. He became the recognized spokesman for the nation's local officials on poverty issues, spoke at conferences around the country, testified before Congress, wrote articles for national publications, and appeared on television shows ("Today" and "Nightline"), critizing Reagan's policies and calling for progressive federal policies. Finally, the Flynn's administration's programs provide models both for other cities and for the federal government. For example, the Boston Housing Partnership and the Boston Compact have been replicated in at least a dozen other cities. Furthermore, Flynn's staff drafted federal legislation (the Community Housing Partnership Act) to provide support for nonprofit housing development. Introduced by Congressman Joseph Kennedy of Boston in February 1988, the bill was supported by major housing activist groups, the U.S. Conference of Mayors, and more than a hundred cosponsors (Dreier 1987). The Boston experience demonstrates that even in the face of declining federal revenues and a frequently unfriendly private sector, cities can develop "redistributive" housing and economic development policies.

References

Achtenburg, Emily, P. 1984. "Preserving Affordable Rental Housing in Boston." Report prepared for the Rent Equity Board (August).

Boston Redevelopment Authority. 1986. "Boston: Economic and Demographic Information."

———. 1988. "Boston Housing: Facts and Figures" (March).

Boston School Department. 1988. Unpublished data.

Dreier, Peter. 1983. "The Vault Comes Out of the Darkness." *Boston Business Journal* (October 10–16).

———. 1987. "Community-based Housing: A Progressive Approach to a New Federal Policy. *Social Policy* (Fall).

Dreier, Peter, David Schwartz, and Ann Greiner. 1988. "What Every Business Can Do about Housing." *Harvard Business Review* 88 (September/October).

Farrar, Eleanor, and Anthony Cipollone. 1988. "The Business Community and School Reform: The Boston Compact at Five Years." State University of New York at Buffalo. Unpublished manuscript.

Ferguson, Ronald F., and Helen F. Ladd. 1986. "Economic Performance and Economic Development Policy in Massachusetts." Cambridge, Mass.: John F. Kennedy School of Government. Working paper.

Ferman, Barbara. 1985. *Governing the Ungovernable City*. Philadelphia: Temple University Press.

Gans, Herbert J. 1982. *The Urban Villagers*. Rev. ed. New York: Free Press.

Ganz, Alexander. 1985. "Where Has the Urban Crisis Gone?" *Urban Affairs Quarterly* 20 (June).

Greiner, Ann. 1987. "The Housing Affordability Gap and Boston's Economic Growth." Boston Redevelopment Authority (October).

Harrison, Bennett, and Jean Kluver. 1988. "Re-Assessing the 'Massachusetts Miracle'" Massachusetts Institute of Technology, Department of Urban Studies and Planning (June).

Kahn, E. J. III. 1981. "The Day the Banks Saved Boston." *Boston* (November).

Keating, W. Dennis. 1986. "Linking Downtown Development to Broader Community Goals." *Journal of the American Planning Association* (Spring).

Levin, Murray. 1960. *The Alienated Voter: Politics in Boston*. New York: Holt, Rinehart and Winston.

Levitt, Rachel, ed. 1987. *Cities Reborn*. Washington, D.C.: Urban Land Institute.

Lucas, J. Anthony. 1985. *Common Ground*. New York: Knopf.

Lupo, Alan. 1977. *Liberty's Chosen Home*. Boston: Little, Brown.

Meyerson, Martin, and Edward Banfield. 1966. *Boston: The Job Ahead*. Cambridge, Mass.: Harvard University Press.

Mollenkopf, John. 1983. *The Contested City*. Princeton, N.J.: Princeton University Press.

O'Connor, Thomas H. 1984. *Bibles, Brahmins, and Bosses: A Short History of Boston*. Boston: Trustees of the Public Library.

Pantridge, Margaret. 1988. "'New Boston' Planner Comes Back for More." *Boston Herald* (January 12).

Slavet, Joseph S., and Raymond G. Torto. 1985. "Boston's Recurring Crises: Three Decades of Fiscal Policy." Boston: McCormack Institute (June).

Trout, Charles H. 1977. *Boston: The Great Depression and the New Deal*. New York: Oxford University Press.

Susan S. Fainstein
Norman Fainstein

4. New York City:
The Manhattan Business District,
1945–1988

New York City like many U.S. cities, has witnessed the departure of much of its manufacturing industry and a major augmentation of its service sector. Its government has actively participated in assisting this transformation, working closely with private developers and using a variety of subsidies and incentives to attract business investment. New York's size and its function as a global financial center have meant that the scale of change, the extent of public-sector activity, and the scope of spatial reallocation within the city exceed those of any other metropolis in the United States. The case of New York, therefore, is significant both as an example of a general process and as a description of what has happened in the country's biggest and richest city.

The postwar economic and social transformation of New York City as a whole profoundly influenced the character of its central business district—roughly speaking, the half of Manhattan south of Fifty-ninth Street. Forty years ago that area was a dense weave of manufacturing lofts, docks, and railroad sidings, but also office skyscrapers, shops, and giant department stores. Proletarian tenements abutted expensive townhouses and middle-class apartments. Office workers, factory operatives, and shoppers mixed daily on the streets and in the subways. By the 1980s, the social and functional heterogeneity of southern Manhattan was noticeably reduced. The portion devoted to office use had expanded enormously; 160 million square feet of competitive space was added to the existing 114 million square feet between 1960 and 1987 (Real Estate Board of New York 1985, Table 154).[1] An uncounted number of factories had disappeared or had been converted to other uses, and large expanses of proletarian tenements had been replaced by expensive apartment towers. Chic restaurants occupied abandoned factory showrooms. The fabric of the central business district had changed: many strands of its previous industrial woof had been exchanged for the golden threads of late capitalism. In this chapter we outline what happened, paying particular

59

Table 4.1. New York City Employment by Industry, 1950–1987 (thousands)

Industry	1950	1960	1970	1980	1987[a]
Manufacturing (incl. mining)	1,041	949	768	497	387
Contract construction	123	125	110	77	112
Transportation and utilities	332	318	323	257	216
Wholesale and retail trade	755	745	736	613	633
Finance, insurance, and real estate	336	386	460	448	532
Services	508	607	785	894	1,106
Government	374	408	563	516	589
Total	3,468	3,538	3,745	3,302	3,575

SOURCES: Temporary Commission on City Finances, *The Effect of Taxation on Manufacturing in New York City*, December 1976, Table 1; Real Estate Board of New York, *Fact Book 1983*, October 1982, Table 56; U.S. Bureau of Labor Statistics, *Employment and Earnings*, May 1987.
  [a]As of March 1987.

attention to market outcomes and government activities, and to the social consequences of the changes in the central business district. We then analyze the city's options for the future.

Economic and Social Restructuring, 1945–1987

In the four decades following World War II, the economic forces that battered the nation's older metropolitan areas caused sharp changes within the New York region. Nevertheless, New York City by 1987 could claim a level of total employment exceeding that of 1950 (Table 4.1).[2] A substantial restructuring of its economy permitted the city to hold its own as the nation's wealthiest metropolis.

The city government was an active agent in stimulating the investment that produced the glittering Manhattan of the 1980s. New York's public sector had traditionally played an unusually large role, compared with other U.S. municipal governments, in the development of the city; its activities ranged from fostering human capital formation in its unique municipal university system to pioneering public housing and urban renewal schemes. In the early postwar period, many of the city's redevelopment efforts involved private business participation, as will be discussed later, but the city and state governments were also willing to sponsor large housing, infrastructure, education, and social programs on their own. Increasingly, however, and especially after the 1975 fiscal crisis, the city relied on the private sector for capital spending, even for normally public-sector activities like mass transit improvements and low-income housing. To promote business investment, it developed new institutional frameworks that insulated project sponsors from popular inputs.

New York City was hurt by the postwar decentralization of manufacturing and goods distribution within the region and then by the shift of new production during the 1970s to the sunbelt and abroad. Also significant for employment and land use was the relative decline of the port of New York, and the transfer of activities from city piers to containerized facilities in New Jersey. The port's losses, and the concurrent movement of truck transport and warehousing firms to land-extensive suburban plants, reduced the city's importance as a distribution node. Before 1970 the erosion of its "goods" industries had been balanced by the expansion of its service industries (Table 4.1). During most of the 1970s, however, the service industries performed sluggishly, resulting in an aggregate economic downturn.

Nevertheless, in the 1980s New York City reestablished its dominance within a restructured national and world economy. New York had long been a national center for corporate services (e.g., law, advertising, and accounting), culture, health care, tourism, and specialized consumption. As these industries became more international in scope, the city established world dominance as well.[3] Most important, it became ever more prominent as a global headquarters of finance at a time when financial firms were establishing a more dominant position in the world economy. New York also prospered as a favored location for foreign surplus capital that could be invested in politically safe U.S. real estate, as well as a second home for an increasingly internationalized bourgeoisie. Collectively, these processes increased employment in the finance, insurance, real estate, and service industries; almost 300,000 jobs were added between 1980 and 1987, mainly during the booming half decade 1982–1987 (Table 4.1).[4]

The restructuring of the city's economy caused an equally significant social reorganization. As the nature of production changed, so too did that of work, and with it, the occupations of the resident work force. The tasks of manual labor changed from tending machines to tending people, from sewing garments to carrying bedpans and cleaning hotel rooms (Table 4.2).[5] A new white-collar proletariat of female clerical workers emerged. At the top, the number of middle-class technical and managerial jobs increased. The change in work and occupations altered the nature of class inequality, but overall it increased its extent. Relative to metropolitan and national figures, average incomes of the resident city population declined continuously after 1950, and economic inequality within the city

Table 4.2. Occupations of New York's Resident Population 1950–1980 (percentages)

Occupation	1950	1960	1970	1980
	New York City			
Professional, technical, managerial	22	21	24	28
Clerical and sales	27	28	34	34
Blue-collar and service	50	50	43	38
	Manhattan			
Professional, technical, managerial	24	25	35	44
Clerical and sales	23	23	30	37
Blue-collar and service	52	52	36	28

SOURCES: U.S. Bureau of the Census, *Census of Population, States and Areas, New York State*, 1950, 1960, 1970, 1980.

NOTE: Total for each year may deviate slightly from 100 percent due to rounding.

increased (Stegman 1988; Tobier and Stafford 1985; U.S. Bureau of the Census 1950).[6]

The ethnic composition of New York also changed profoundly, though only secondarily as a result of reorganization of the local economy. In 1950 New York was a white city, its lower classes still composed mainly of European immigrants. Thirty years later the city was approximately half black and Hispanic (Table 4.3). During the 1970s alone, the non-Hispanic

Table 4.3. New York City Population, 1940–1984 (thousands)

Borough	1940	1950	1960	1970	1980	1984
New York City	7,455 (94)	7,892 (90)	7,782 (85)	7,895 (62)	7,072 (51)	7,165
Manhattan	1,890 (83)	1,960 (79)	1,698 (74)	1,539 (54)	1,428 (50)	1,456
Brooklyn	2,698 (95)	2,738 (92)	2,627 (85)	2,602 (60)	2,231 (48)	2,254
Bronx	1,395 (98)	1,451 (93)	1,425 (88)	1,472 (50)	1,169 (34)	1,173
Queens	1,298 (97)	1,551 (96)	1,810 (91)	1,986 (78)	1,891 (62)	1,911
Staten Island	174 (98)	192 (96)	222 (95)	295 (90)	352 (85)	371

SOURCES: U.S. Bureau of the Census, *State and Metropolitan Area Data Book 1986*, p. 202, Table A; City of New York, Council on Economic Education, *1986 Fact Book on the New York Metropolitan Region*, p. 1; L. C. Rosenwaike, *Population History of New York City* (Syracuse, N.Y.: Syracuse University Press, 1972), pp. 121, 133, 136, 141, 197.

NOTE: Figures in parentheses are percentages of white residents. Prior to 1970, "white" includes individuals of Hispanic origin who are defined as Puerto Ricans.

white population declined by 1.2 million. As the enormous influx of black Americans and Puerto Ricans of the 1950s and 1960s began to slow, New York became the center of new waves of immigration from Central and South America and Asia. By the mid-1980s a quarter of the population was foreign born. In addition, at least 500,000 undocumented aliens lived in the city. Black Americans, Puerto Ricans, and immigrants filled most of the jobs at the lower end of the occupational structure.

The economic and social restructuring of the city played itself out geographically in this period. Despite the continued presence of a large low-income minority population, Manhattan's occupational profile became skewed upward relative to the rest of the city (Table 4.2). The borough was increasingly becoming the residential location for the city's professional and managerial households. In 1950 about 215,000 managers and professionals lived in Manhattan, compared with about 500,000 in the other boroughs, By 1980, Manhattan had added about 95,000 of these residents, but the other boroughs had gained only 12,000. As a result, Manhattan increased its share of the city's managerial and professional work force from 30 percent in 1950 to 38 percent in 1980. Thus, the uneven social development of New York was exhibited within Manhattan as well as between Manhattan and the rest of New York: Manhattan kept its share of the city's poor, but substantially increased its share of the city's rich.[7]

Government-Directed Redevelopment, 1945–1973

The economic and social changes occurring in southern Manhattan required and were in turn facilitated by physical redevelopment. Governmental officials and business leaders—such as Robert Moses and the Rockefellers—reshaped Manhattan's built environment. Even after the increase in effective community and minority group opposition in the 1960s, the city government and its business allies intervened to mediate and channel the forces created by the changing regional economy.[8]

From 1933 to 1960 Robert Moses was the czar of public development in New York City (see especially Caro 1974). He controlled the Triborough Bridge and Tunnel Authority, the Department of Parks, the urban renewal program, the Public Housing Authority, and the federal highway program. Moses opposed master planning, yet he was strongly influenced by the ideas of the 1929 regional plan. Like the business leaders associated with the Regional Plan Association (RPA), which pubished that document, Moses envisioned the decentralization of manufacturing from Manhattan and the continued expansion of office activities in the core. He deviated from the RPA, however, in his rejection of mass transit. Although Moses created a vast modern highway system for the city, his only transportation accomplishments in Manhattan were additions to the roads that circled the island. Had he gotten his way, he would also have bisected the central business district with expressways at Thirtieth Street in midtown and Grand Street in lower Manhattan. As an architect of the Manhattan transportation system, therefore, his main impacts were ones of omission — in the new transit lines that he blocked and in the highways that others prevented him from building.

Moses left his mark on the central business district by implementing the urban renewal program. Here his projects reflected two strategic considerations. First, he almost completely avoided nonresidential locations; for him, urban renewal was justified only by slum clearance. His projects razed large tracts of working-class housing in lower Manhattan, in the midtown West Side from south of Pennsylvania Station (Thirty-second Street) to Columbus Circle (Fifty-ninth Street), in Greenwich Village south of Washington Square, and near the East River between Twenty-third and Forty-second Streets. Tenements were replaced by middle- and upper-income apartments or by public facilities such as hospitals and college dormitories.[9] Whereas urban renewal in other cities was directed at commercial tracts within the central business district, in New York the program mainly affected residential areas on the periphery.[10]

Rejecting city planning on grounds of principle and practicality, Moses made a second strategic choice in implementing urban renewal. He devised a "New York method" of public-private partnership that anticipated the unplanned, capital-driven develoment programs of the Edward Koch–Ronald Reagan era. He privatized urban renewal by giving developers immediate title to occupied parcels of land and then allowing them to clear sites, relocate occupants, arrange financing, and erect new structures. Typically, institutional sponsors, developers, or political cronies identified desirable sites that were then found to be blighted and therefore legally qualified for urban renewal. This system guaranteed that urban renewal in New York reenforced the logic of the real estate market. As a result, projects were implemented much more rapidly than elsewhere, and the city received a disproportionate share of federal funds.

Redevelopment of lower Manhattan, in constrast to that of the midtown office district, was a product of planned and organized intervention by powerful segments of the business elite. The Rockefellers were the dominant actors. Throughout the 1950s and 1960s they (1) intervened directly in the real estate market of lower Manhattan, (2) sponsored a business planning group that organized a growth-oriented coalition, (3) encouraged the city to undertake supportive projects, and (4) mobilized enormous investments by a public agency — the Port Authority of New

York and New Jersey. The effort represented a response to the decline of lower Manhattan following World War II.[11] Although the financial institutions located there had plenty of investment capital, each viewed commitment to the area as too risky in the absence of large-scale redevelopment. Concerted action required the leadership of David Rockefeller and the Chase Manhattan Bank, which he controlled. Chase announced construction of a new headquarters building and helped finance the construction of several other skyscrapers. William Zeckendorf, the city's biggest developer in the 1950s, built modern facilities for five large banks. Within a decade of Chase's decision, private capital had erected thirty buildings downtown, comprising more than 11 million squre feet of office space (calculated from Robison 1976, map 7).

David Rockefeller also created a vehicle that helped define and unify the interests of big business—the Downtown–Lower Manhattan Association (DLMA). According to a high official, the association's objective was to create the physical environment necessary for the downtown area to remain "the heart pump of the capital blood that sustains the free world" (Collier and Horowitz 1976:315). The DLMA commissioned studies that culminated in a comprehensive plan for lower Manhattan and related proposals for government action. The plan called for urban renewal of economically blighted areas around the financial district, construction of the Lower Manhattan Expressway and of a new Second Avenue subway (to replace the ancient elevated line closed in 1940), and, most important, the development of a world trade center under the auspices of the Port Authority (see Robison 1976; Stein 1980).

The city began a series of projects around 1960 in response to the DLMA master plan. A wholesale food market was opened at Hunts Point in the Bronx to house firms previously located in lower Manhattan (City of New York 1960:38). In a related move, the city established the Washington Street urban renewal project to rebuild the site of the old markets (an area adjacent to what would become Battery Park City). The municipal government refashioned its plans for the tract along the East River south of the Brooklyn Bridge. Instead of developing low- and moderate-income housing, it let private capital redevelop the area for office skyscrapers, while it established additional urban renewal projects for government agencies and nonprofit institutions. The Port Authority, with the guidance of Governor Nelson Rockefeller, reshaped and expanded the concept of a world trade center. When the facility finally opened in 1972, its two gigantic skyscrapers and supporting structures added 10 million square feet of office space downtown at a public expenditure of more than $1 billion (Robison 1976; McClelland and Magdovitz 1981).

Planning by the DLMA had fully established the character of lower Manhattan by the time Mayor John Lindsay took office in 1966. His administration's commitment to the social and physical improvement of the city's worst ghettoes did not preclude it from supporting the DLMA's plans (which were officially incorporated in the New York City Master Plan of 1969). Except for the Lower Manhattan Expressway and the Second Avenue subway,[12] all the original elements of the DLMA strategy were implemented. Mayor Lindsay also encouraged the New York State Urban Development Corporation (UDC) to invest heavily in the urban core, building offices and housing for middle- and upper-income households. The Lindsay administration, however, outstripped its resources, as it attempted simultaneously to assist the lower classes and to establish the Manhattan infrastructure necessary for office-based production and managerial-class consumption.

The Decline and Rise of Large-Scale Development

The city's 1975 fiscal crisis, combined with retrenchment in Washington, brought significant capital expenditures virtually to a halt (Shefter 1985:138). Major construction projects such as the third water tunnel, the Second Avenue subway, and the expansion of the City University were aborted. The city deferred even routine maintenance functions as, under the direction of business-dominated agencies charged with restoring financial stability, it drastically cut its personnel budget (Hartman 1985).

At the same time, both commercial and residential private real estate investment almost ceased (Real Estate Board of New York 1982, Tables 128, 154). The Beame administration abandoned Lindsay's efforts to target very low income areas for concentrated action. In their stead the city formulated strategies to promote private development activity for the rehabilitation and conversion of existing structures in neighborhoods attractive to the middle class. The main stimulus was the J-51 tax abatement program, amended in 1975 to lift the restrictions limiting it to low-income dwellings. About 75 percent of the subsidy went to Manhattan; the benefits were enjoyed mostly by upper-income occupants (Parker 1982: 12).[13] New York did, however, maintain one important low-income housing program by allocating more than half of its $289 million Community Development Block Grant budget to rehabilitating and managing the 35,000 housing units whose control had reverted to the city due to tax delinquency (City of New York, Department of Housing Preservation and Development 1981:33).

The election of Edward Koch in 1977 reaffirmed the grip on political power of New York's older ethnic groups. Jews and homeowning Catholics united to support a candidate who declared himself the defender of the middle class (Koch 1984:200–221). Traumatized by fiscal crisis, an exodus of jobs from the city, and widespread perception of threat from drugs and crime, the electorate sought the reassurance of a candidate who rebelled against both the "bleeding-heart liberalism" attributed to John V. Lindsay and the pallid leadership of Abraham Beame. In his colorful style and assertiveness Koch contrasted sharply with his immediate predecessor. His strategy for economic development was based on the premise that Lindsay's social programs had bankrupted the city. Koch made little effort either to make appointments that symbolized the rise of minorities to political power or to pay much lip service to neighborhood interests. Although his programs typified the national trend, in which economic development and fiscal stringency replaced combating poverty as the urban goal of the 1980s, the absence of nonwhite minorities among his close advisors, as well as the mayor's own ethnicity, differentiated New York from other large cities.

Koch made the Public Development Corporation (PDC) the lead agency in development planning, thus relegating the Department of City Planning to a limited research and regulatory function. In order to free it from civil service requirements and various regulations concerning competitive bidding, the PDC was established as a quasi-independent local development corporation. Guided by a mayorally appointed board of prominent business people, it played an entrepreneurial role in spurring construction in a city suddenly revived by a vast expansion of the financial industry. With a staff of 200 and a $95 million annual budget obtained through a contract with the city, the PDC acted primarily as a financial intermediary, putting together packages of land improvements, tax abatements, and funding for specific development sites (Gottlieb 1986; City of New York, Public Development Corporation n.d.:i).

In its larger projects the PDC worked together with the state's UDC. The latter entity, originally established to develop housing for low- and moderate-income groups, was reconstituted after its financial insolvency as an economic development agency. Within New York City it retained its original power to override local zoning and citizen participation requirements (which had formerly been intended to enable it to build scattered-site, low-income housing); therefore, its involvement in a project permitted a streamlined process of regulatory approvals.

For most of the 1980s, New York was led by a mayor committed to major development projects and beholden to big developers for campaign contributions (Sleeper 1987). Koch's popularity with the electorate grew through two reelection campaigns; the local economy prospered, and dissident minority groups and liberal critics failed to reach agreement on opposing candidates. He had in place a powerful public agency insulated from popular control with development as its sole mission. The mayor's development team was acutely sensitive to criticisms of New York as a bureaucratically impossible and extraordinarily expensive place in which to do business, while it remained largely oblivious of the outcries of those fearing gentrification and environmental depredation.

Koch took credit for New York's powerful economic resurgence, but he became increasingly vulnerable to criticism that he was ignoring a housing crisis. Although the city's population grew by 78,000 between 1981 and 1984, the housing inventory increased by only 11,000 units (Stegman 1985, Table 9.1). Almost all the additions were in the luxury market; in 1983 the average cost of a new four-and-one-half-room cooperative or condominium was $340,000 (Real Estate Board of New York 1985, Table 125).[14] As homelessness increased, the initial criticisms of Koch's development policies came largely from low-income housing advocates. Ultimately, however, more conservative critics also predicted that the housing shortage would stifle economic growth because companies would no longer be able to attract needed workers (see, e.g., Regional Plan Association 1985; Sternlieb and Listokin 1985).

New York's development strategy during the 1980s represents a paradigmatic case of trickle down. This approach has brought some benefits to low-income people, as will be discussed later, but it has also been costly to them while proving massively profitable to developers. Examination of two projects—the Marriott Marquis Hotel in Times Square and Battery Park City—reveals the nature of the process more clearly.

The Marriott-Marquis Hotel

Times Square, in the heart of midtown Manhattan, had long been identified by city planners as an underutilized site. Theater and restaurant owners in the surrounding area had continuously complained that the drug, prostitution, and pornography trades were driving away their patrons. With the help of a federal Urban Development Action Grant (UDAG) and tax abatement, the PDC revived dormant plans for a giant atrium hotel, to be called the Marriott-Marquis, at the northern end of Times Square. Over the vehement objections of theater personnel, who protested the demolition of three legitimate theaters, the city used its rights of eminent domain and demolition to obtain cleared land for the building. A leasing arrangement whereby a public agency was the nominal owner of the site exempted construction materials from the sales tax; payments in lieu of the tax were reserved for improvements to the immediate area (City of New York, Public Development Corporation n.d.: M-15). The hotel, completed in 1985, is a megastructure that internalizes all services and presents an impenetrable wall to its neighbors.

This project, and the planned massive redevelopment of Forty-second Street three blocks away (Fainstein 1985), are classic examples of an effort to solve social problems through purely physical means. The development of a fortresslike tourist facility is a typical solution to the problem of economic and physical transformation of a site because of seemingly obsolete or undesirable land use (McCain 1985). In its own terms the Marriott is a success: it has attracted tourists and conventioneers; its restricted access and internal amenities protect its guests from its threatening environs. The deadening effect of the structure's bulk on the neighborhood, the project's tax abatements, and its limited economic spin-offs, however, raise significant questions concerning its benefits to the surrounding area and the city's overall economic well-being.

The design of the Marriott and the proposed Forty-second Street office towers nearby exemplify the use of zoning in New York today. Virtually no new building fits within the zoning limits; rather, the city trades additional floor space and other variances for on-site amenities such as plazas and neighborhood improvements like subway station renovations. Since most of this construction also involves tax abatement and in some instances loans raised by tax-exempt public bonds, the developer essentially receives a large financial bonus of which he then returns part to the city.[15] Physically, the outcome is ever increasing densities resulting in congestion, overtaxed services, and loss of sunlight in what is already by far the most intensely used central business district in the United States.

Battery Park City

Originally proposed in the late 1960s but begun more than fifteen years later, Battery Park City exemplifies a development for the wealthy that has produced direct benefits for the poor. Initially conceived as a new town to be constructed on a ninety-two-acre landfill in the Hudson River generated by excavation for the World Trade Center, it was to have both commercial and mixed-income residential uses. Its architectural forebear was Le Corbusier's radiant city; its planned high-rise structures arranged on superblocks would turn their backs on the adjacent city. Strong lobbying by low-income housing advocates produced an agreement in 1969 that two-thirds of the housing would be subsidized for low- and middle-income occupancy (Gottlieb 1985).

During the 1970s, however, the Battery Park City Authority (BPA), an agency established by the UDC with the power to issue moral obligation bonds, could not find a developer for the massive project. The fiscal crisis and office building glut of the period had thrown the whole enterprise in doubt; the BPA itself teetered on the edge of bankruptcy. The authority commissioned a new master plan aimed at integrating the project into the city rather than creating a self-contained new town; it called for staged development along a regular street grid and established design guidelines that would cause the new buildings to resemble traditional apartment blocks elsewhere in Manhattan (Ponte 1982:10–15). The BPA discarded its obligation to subsidize on-site housing and instead pledged part of the proceeds from the development to low-income housing in other parts of the city. The giant Canadian developer Olympia and York committed itself to the entire commercial portion of the venture, and a number of other major developers sponsored construction of luxury apartments expected to add 14,000 units to lower Manhattan. The BPA, which retains ownership of the project and pays no taxes, participates in profits from the enterprise; in 1987 it promised $1 billion for low-income housing throughout the city as well as $50 million for general revenues (Schmalz 1987).

Battery Park City has won virtually unanimous praise from architectural critics; it has attracted to its office towers such blue-ribbon tenants as Merrill Lynch, Dow Jones, and American Express; it has provided meaningful amenities to Wall Street's hundreds of thousands of workers, who throng its privately maintained and policed riverfront park and indoor botanical garden, brown bag lunches in hand. Its lively public esplanade and magnificent view of the harbor give New Yorkers a rare chance to enjoy the waterfront. It presents the optimum case of urban development for upper-class occupancy in that its construction involved no displacement. But except for diurnal visitors, it remains the domain of big business and of wealthy, mainly childless, households (Hinds 1986). Though vast, the sums it is turning over to the city are still less than would have been paid in the absence of a tax abatement.

Evaluating City Policy

New York City has unquestionably been riding a boom. The economic expansion of the 1980s occurred simultaneously with forceful governmental action in promoting private commercial investment and a decline in social and housing expenditures. Although the city has also sought to encourage the growth of manufacturing, at best its efforts slowed the rate of job loss. Tax incentives for housing production also had little effect except at the luxury end of the market. If, then, tax incentives and zoning business bonuses only stimulated development of very expensive office and residential space and had little consequence in the attainment of other development objectives, is it not likely that the growth that did occur would have happened anyway? In other words, can the government take credit for the city's renewed economic prosperity, or did that prosperity simply result from the rapid expansion of the financial industry, which would have stayed in New York regardless? And did the increase in economic activity benefit most city residents or only its upper-income inhabitants and suburban commuters?

The first of these questions is very difficult to answer in any scientific way. In his extensive survey of the literature on tax incentives, Netzer (1986:27) concludes that tax differentials matter if they are not capitalized into increased land values. If they are, then the developer's land acquisition costs increase by the amount taxes are reduced, because the enhanced potential rate of return makes the land more valuable. Unquestionably, New York land prices respond to both tax abatements and zoning bonuses. But no one knows to what extent the city's tax and regulatory relief programs simply produce cost shifts as opposed to genuine reductions.

Huge costs differentials within the metropolitan area seem to require that the city provide incentives for development. When Mayor Koch announced NBC's commitment to stay in Rockefeller Center in late 1987, NBC's chief executive indicated that despite nearly $100 million in tax incentives, the network would still have saved tens of millions of dollars a year by moving just across the Hudson River to New Jersey, where rents and utility costs are more than 50 percent lower (Finder 1987). Even if it were true that market forces would ultimately bring New York's costs into line as firms moved out, the exodus could prove irreversible since, by the time rental costs became competitive, New York might have lost the critical mass of industries that had initially caused its attractiveness. In the context of very strong intraregional competition and separate tax bases, New York City's government apparently has little choice but to pursue industry.

The equity issue therefore becomes more crucial than that of effectiveness for the city. Gains in production and tax revenues manifest the city's greater affluence. Drennan (1988, Table 1.10) shows that total private-sector value added increased by 110 percent between 1977 and 1986; this greater level of production was the engine causing employment growth. Simultaneously, total own-source tax revenues nearly doubled. Although the differential return to labor from various job categories raises questions concerning the distributional effects of employment growth, the jump in tax revenues did allow the city to balance its budget, increase services, improve its bond rating, and retire debt, therefore presumably improving life for all residents.

Measurements of geographical disparities and housing production, however, show the negative distributional aspects of current growth. Since 1980 little economic improvement has occurred in the outer boroughs, and housing production has been grossly inadequate. Manhattan accounted for about 75 percent of the city's total private employment growth from 1978 to 1985 and almost all of its new office construction (Real Estate Board of New York 1985, Table 165). The city's common tax base means that this geographical bipolarity does no fiscal harm to residents of the outer boroughs; however, it does exact costs from them in commuting time and access to employment opportunities. City residents, according to the 1980 Census, continued to hold about 80 percent of all New York City jobs (New York State Department of Labor 1984, Table 4). But survey data indicate that suburban commuters and Manhattan residents constituted a disproportionate and growing percentage of the better paid, professional and managerial work force (Tobier and Stafford 1985; Sassen-Koob 1986).

It is in the area of housing, however, that the trickle down development policy has had the most dire effects. Prosperity resulting from expansion in advanced services produces, on the one hand, a growing upper-income population and, on the other, a relatively poorly paid group of white-collar workers (Sassen-Koob 1986). These two groups have been bidding for a housing supply that has barely expanded in the last two decades; what growth has occurred has been entirely at the luxury end. As a consequence, median rents rose from 20 to 29 percent of household income between 1970 and 1987; three of every ten tenants spent at least 40 percent of their incomes on rent; and almost a quarter spent more than 50 percent (Stegman 1985, Table 5.14; Stegman 1988, Tables 5.25, 5.28).

The combined forces of abandonment and gentrification have produced the most glaringly obvious manifestation of housing crisis, as the homeless increasingly crowd the shelters, double up with friends and relatives, and occupy sidewalks, subways, and public spaces everywhere. On a typical day in 1987, the city housed nearly 10,000 single adults and over 17,000 children and their parents in dormitory-type shelters, lodging houses, and single-room occupancy hotels (Barbanel 1987). Although about 400 families a month were placed in permanent housing, about 450 simultaneously entered the emergency housing system. The city's low-income housing market had a turnover rate of less than 1 percent a month, and 200,000 names were on the public housing waiting list (Basler 1986). Thus, unless the city directly added to the low-income housing supply, in the face of virtually no available federal subsidies for low-income housing construction or renovation, the crisis could only get worse. During the post-1978 decade of economic expansion, however, there was no major city program for producing new low-income housing.

In December 1987, Mayor Koch announced an agreement for the financing of a plan to build or rehabilitate 252,000 low- and moderate-income housing units. The cost would be $4.2 billion over ten years, and the bulk of funding would come from $3 billion in city borrowing and $1 billion in Battery Park City revenues (Schmalz 1987). The plan represents a major increase in the city's commitment to solving the low-income housing problem; however, even with a net addition of 25,000 units a year to the housing stock, it would take many years to make a sizable dent in the shortfall. Since past experience has shown that the city's implementation rate has lagged far behind its targets in housing rehabilitation, it remains to be seen whether the present set of promises will translate into genuine housing improvement.

Political Constraints and Possibilities

Community politics in New York City has a long, complicated history. Opposition to bulldozer clearance caused modifications of the federal urban renewal program in the direction of rehabilitation and community participation much earlier in the city than elsewhere. Strong lobbying by unions and tenant groups kept the wartime system of rent control in place, whereas it was abolished in the rest of the country; most rental properties in New York continue to be regulated by the rent stabilization program, despite the unremitting efforts of landlords and real estate developers to prove that rent regulation is at the root of the housing shortage. A neighborhood coalition succeeded in blocking Westway, the planned superhighway and landfill scheme for the west side of Manhattan. And NBC indicated that it would not commit itself to moving to developer Donald Trump's Television City because of the strength of community opposition. Groups intent on saving New York's historic architecture mobilized after the destruction of Pennsylvania Station in 1964 and obtained protection for a number of specific sites, as well as whole neighborhoods, in the form of landmark and historic district designations.[16] The Municipal Art Society, one of several upper-class organizations devoted to architectural integrity, brought the lawsuit that halted the development of a huge mixed-use project on the site of the Coliseum, the old convention center.

The city government and real estate developers thus meet constant challenges in their attempts to foster economic growth and obtain the highest conceivable rate of return on every piece of land. Community boards, operating in each of the city's fifty-nine community planning districts, advise on all projects requiring City Planning Commission approval. The boards tend to be the principal forums for people in residential neighborhoods who fear gentrification or congestion from a project. District-based elected officials (borough presidents, City Council members, and state legislators) frequently act as advocates for their constituencies in opposing development. When political opposition fails, court suits sometimes block projects, as in the Westway and Coliseum instances.

New York's path of development, then, has not been the result of the uncontested or unmitigated triumph of capital with the government as its handmaiden. Nevertheless, the sums required for the creation of huge office and luxury apartment complexes dwarf the financial resources available for construction of low- and moderate-income housing or neighborhood commercial development. With enormous fortunes to be made, developers are not reluctant to spend a great deal of money seeking to influence officials and the public. And, in a city where the expenses and inconveniences of doing business are such as to discourage most manufacturers, city government has few alternatives to attracting and retaining tourist, entertainment, and financial enterprises.

For the city to follow a strategy that concentrates on providing economic diversity, middle-income jobs, and housing for those currently priced out of the market would require a willingness to counter market forces and to make very strong demands on private developers. Such action might nevertheless be in the long-run interests of the moneyed classes. New York is increasingly becoming a single-industry town; its dependence on the health of financial markets makes its economic future risky. Moreover, if limits are not placed on office development, New York may soon find itself in the same position as Houston or Denver, with millions of square feet of vacant space.

A reversal of emphasis, however, would depend on the replacement of the present governing regime with one that is more committed to meeting the demands of neighborhoods and minorities. The elements of a new electoral coalition do exist among those who are extremely disaffected by the housing situation, members of racial minority groups, and progressive business leaders who are distressed by the city's deteriorating infrastructure and educational system. Whether a political leader exists who can draw them together remains to be seen. Cities like Boston and San Francisco have elected mayors whose rhetoric has emphasized neighborhood empowerment. In early 1989 several aspirants for New York's mayoralty professed to have a more balanced program for development, and one black candidate seemed to have at least a reasonable chance to win the Democratic primary scheduled for later in the year. The mayor has been weakened by municipal scandal and adverse publicity concerning both his administative record and his abrasive personality. At the same time, a slowing of economic momentum—already indicated by revenue-raising difficulties, the growing number of office vacancies, reductions in transportation usage, and stagnation in the luxury housing market—might mean that even an administration pledged to achieve redistributional aims would have little leeway in which to press its program. New York's peak growth period for the last quarter of the twentieth century may well have occurred in the mid-1980s. Its principal beneficiaries were the developers and financiers, the attorneys and the accountants, not the needy.

Notes

1. "Competitive space" refers to space available for rental and excludes, for example, government-owned and -occupied buildings. Total office space in Manhattan in 1984 exceeded 300 million square feet. San Francisco and Washington were second and third after New York in total square feet of office space with 53 million square feet and 50 million square feet, respectively (Real Estate Board of New York 1985, Table 164).
2. The use of 1950 as a base year obscures the roller coaster nature of the city's aggregate employment figures. During New York's economic (and then fiscal) crisis from 1969 to 1977, the city lost 600,000 jobs; during the 1978–1987 expansion it gained back two-thirds of that number.
3. Drennan (1988) shows the increasing importance of multinational service and financial corporations in the export economy of the city.
4. A more detailed discussion is provided in Fainstein et al. (1989).
5. Almost all of the increase in the clerical and sales category of Table 4.2 was accounted for by clerical workers. The decrease in the proportion of blue-collar jobs was sharp, from 37 percent of the resident work force in 1950 to 23 percent in 1980. Were more recent data available, they would certainly show continuation of these trends in the 1980s.
6. The most recent data do show considerable improvement in the income status of the poorest New Yorkers in the period 1983–1986. Whereas the percentage of renter households living in poverty increased by nearly 25 percent (from 22.5 to 27.1 percent of the renter population) between 1977 and 1983, it declined by more than 10 percent (to 24.2 percent) between 1983 and 1986 (Stegman 1988, Table 2.21); 70 percent of the households were renters. Median income of all households (in constant dollars) also increased substantially between 1983 and 1986; after declining slightly between 1977 and 1980 and again between 1980 and 1983, real median income rose sharply by 18.5

percent between 1983 and 1986 (Stegman 1988, Table 5.1a). Some of these gains, however, were wiped out by increased shelter costs; whereas rents (in constant dollars) remained stable between 1978 and 1984, they increased by 9.3 percent in 1984–1987 (Stegman 1988, Table 4.1). Moreover, income inequality increased consistently during the period 1977–1986; the proportion encompassed by the bottom quintile decreased from 4.9 percent to 3.9 percent, and the proportion accruing to the top quintile grew from 45.2 percent to 47.3 percent (Stegman 1988, Table 5.11).

7. Moreover, these data do not reflect the major economic restructuring of 1982–1987.

8. A more detailed account is provided in Fainstein and Fainstein (1984, 1987) and Fainstein et al. (1989). Parts of this section are drawn from these sources.

9. Robert Moses also cleared a huge tract of land on the Lower East Side for public housing. Originally this housing was occupied by white, working-class families (though far fewer than lived in the more densely populated tenements it replaced). By the 1970s, its occupants were mainly Puerto Rican. This public housing occupies what is today prime land along a deindustrialized East River. It is well maintained and has long waiting lists. It is virtually the only "guaranteed" low-income housing in the central business district.

10. After Moses lost control of urban renewal in 1960, the program was used by Mayors Robert Wagner and John Lindsay to redevelop the manufacturing and business areas of the central business district.

11. More than 80 percent of its office space had been constructed prior to 1920, and nothing had been erected since the war (Real Estate Board of New York 1952, Table 4). Areas to the north and west were filled with manufacturing lofts and wholesale food markets, whose occupants were either going out of business or seeking modern quarters elsewhere.

12. When the DLMA championed Moses's plan for the expressway in the 1950s, it thought the road would become a barrier protecting the financial district from the incursion of manufacturing to the north. The plan for the Lower Manhattan Expressway was finally killed by community oppositin in the late 1960s despite strong support from both Mayor Wagner and Mayor Lindsay. The neighborhood it would have destroyed—SoHo—underwent gentrification in the 1970s and became a magnet for luxury consumption in the 1980s.

13. In 1982 much of Manhattan south of 96th Street was excluded from the Section J-51 rehabilitation program.

14. There was an usually large increase in new construction in 1986–1987, as builders rushed to put up more than 9,000 units before the deadline for receiving tax abatements in much of Manhattan under the Section 421 tax abatement for new construction (Hinds 1985).

15. Numerous private developers have used a variety of tax abatement programs. In 1982, the last year in which abatements were automatically provided in the Manhattan central business district, for example, twenty-seven office buildings were erected with the help of more than $42 million of Industrial and Commercial Incentive Board tax abatements (Mollenkopf 1983). By 1983 the

J-51 rehabilitation program was costing an annual $100 million in taxes sacrificed. The Section 421a residential new construction program cost more than $550 million in foregone property taxes between 1971 and 1987 (Hinds 1987).

16. In 1985 more than 700 of New York City's landmarks and almost 16,000 of its other structures were protected by virtue of their location within one of its forty-six historic districts (Barwick 1985).

References

Barbanel, Josh. 1987. "New York Shifts Debate on Homeless Problem." *New York Times* (November 23).

Barwick, Kent. 1985. "Foreword." *The Late, Great Pennsylvania Station*, ed. Lorraine B. Diehl, pp. 8–9. Lexington, Mass.: Stephen Greene Press.

Basler, Barbara. 1986. "City's Homeless: Portrait of a Growing and Varied Population." *New York Times* (November 17).

Caro, Robert. 1974. *The Power Broker*. New York: Knopf.

City of New York. 1960. *The Administration of Mayor Robert F. Wagner*.

City of New York. Department of Housing Preservation and Development. 1981. *The In Rem Housing Program, Third Annual Report*. New York: Department of Housing Preservation and Development.

City of New York. Public Development Corporation. n.d. *1984/1985 Development Projects*. New York: Public Development Corporation.

Collier, Peter, and David Horowitz. 1976. *The Rockefellers*. New York: Holt, Rinehart and Winston.

Drennan, Matthew. 1988. "Local Economy." Paper presented at a meeting of the Conference on Setting Municipal Priorities, sponsored by the Citizens Budget Commission, New York City.

Fainstein, Norman, and Susan S. Fainstein. 1984. "The Politics of Urban Development: New York City Since 1945." *City Almanac* 17:1–26.

———. 1987. "Economic Restructuring and the Politics of Land Use Planning in New York City." *Journal of the American Planning Association* 53 (Spring): 237–248.

Fainstein, Norman, Susan S. Fainstein, and Alex Schwartz. 1989. "Economic Shifts and Land Use in the Global City: New York, 1940–1987." In *Atop the Urban Hierarchy*, ed. Robert A. Beauregard, 45–85. Totowa, N.J.: Rowman and Littlefield.

Fainstein, Susan S. 1985. "The Redevelopment of 42nd Street: Clashing Viewpoints." *City Almanac* 18:2–12.

Finder, Alan. 1987. "New York City Prestige Outweighs Lower Costs in Jersey, NBC Chief Says." *New York Times* (December 9).

Gottlieb, Martin. 1985. "Battery Project Reflects Changing City Priorities." *New York Times* (October 18).

———. 1986. "A City Agency That Grew Rapidly Faces Scrutiny." *New York Times* (March 9).

Hartman, James M. 1985. "Capital Resources." In *Setting Municipal Priorities, 1986*, ed. Charles Brecher and Raymond Horton, pp. 139–169. New York: New York University Press.

Hinds, Michael deCourey. 1985. "A Building Boomlet Giving Manhattan 9,000 Apartments." *New York Times* (March 3).

———. 1986. "Battery Park City Is Finally Getting Shops and Services." *New York Times*, sec. 8 (March 23).

———. 1987. "421a: A Subsidy That Cost $551 Million." *New York Times*, sec. 8 (March 24).

Koch, Edward. 1984. *Mayor*. New York: Simon and Schuster.

McCain, Mark. 1985. " Architect Champions Marquis in Face of Ongoing Controversy." *Crain's New York Business* (October 21) 1,30.

McClelland, Peter, and Alan Mandovitz. 1981. *Crisis in the Making: The Political Economy of New York State Since 1945*. New York: Cambridge University Press.

Mollenkopf, John. 1983. "Economic Development." In *Setting Municipal Priorities, 1984*, ed. Charles Brecher and Raymond Horton, pp. 131–157. New York: New York University Press.

Netzer, Richard. 1986. "State Tax Policy and Economic Development: What Should Governors Do When Economists Tell Them Nothing Works?" *New York Affairs* 9:19–36.

New York State Department of Labor. Bureau of Labor Market Information. 1984. *Commuting in the New York City Metropolitan Area, 1970 and 1980*.

Parker, Andrew. 1982. "Local Tax Subsidies as a Stimulus for Development." *City Almanac* 16:8–15.

Ponte, Robert. 1982. "Building Battery Park City." *Urban Design International* 3:10–15.

Real Estate Board of New York. 1952. *Office Building Construction, Manhattan, 1901–1953*. New York: REBNY.

———. 1982. *Fact Book 1983*. New York: REBNY.

———. 1985. *Fact Book 1985*. New York: REBNY.

Regional Plan Association. 1985. "Prosperity Projected for New Jersey–New York–Connecticut Urban Region, Keeping Up with U.S. Growth by 1990—If Housing Is Built for Employees." *The Region's Agenda* 15 (August):1–4.

Robison, Maynard T. 1976. "Rebuilding Lower Manhattan: 1955–1974." Ph. D. thesis, City University of New York.

Sassen-Koob, Saskia. 1986. "New York City: Economic Restructuring and Immigration." *Development and Change* 17:85–119.

Schmalz, Jeffrey. 1987. "New York Reaches Accord on Housing." *New York Times* (December 27).

Shefter, Martin. 1985. *Political Crisis/Fiscal Crisis: The Collapse and Revival of New York City*. New York: Basic Books.

Sleeper, Jim. 1987. "Boodling, Bigotry, and Cosmopolitanism," *Dissent* 34:413–419.

Stegman, Michael. 1985. *Housing in New York: Study of a City, 1984*. New York: New York City Department of Housing Preservation and Development.

————. 1988. *Housing and Vacancy Report: New York City, 1987*. New York: New York City Department of Housing Preservation and Development.

Stein, Abraham. 1980. *The Port Authority of New York and New Jersey and the 1962 PATH-World Trade Center Project*. Ph.D. thesis, New York University.

Sternlieb, George, and David Listokin. 1985. "Housing." In *Setting Municipal Priorities, 1986*, ed. Charles Brecher and Raymond Horton, pp. 392–411. New York: New York University Press.

Tobier, Emanuel, and Walter Stafford. 1985. "People and Income." In *Setting Municipal Priorities, 1986*, ed. Charles Brecher and Raymond Horton, pp. 54–83. New York: New York University Press.

U.S. Bureau of the Census. 1950. *Census of Population, States and Areas, New York State*.

David W. Bartelt

5. Renewing Center City
Philadelphia: Whose City?
Which Public's Interests?

The revitalization of Center City Philadelphia, which began as a corollary of the political reforms sweeping the city after World War II, has often been cited as a model of how "rational" planning can control the destiny of a city and serve the public interest (Lowe 1967; Bacon 1976). During the first half of the 1960s, Philadelphia was nationally known as a model city for innovative planning, using a wide variety of public-private partnerships and quasi-public authorities to redraw the face of the city. So successful had this effort been that Edmund Bacon, executive director of the City Planning Commission, was featured in the cover story of an issue of *Time* magazine. Today, the city of Philadelphia is widely regarded as bankrupt (both financially and intellectually) when issues of planning for the future are discussed. In two decades, the action has clearly shifted to the private sector.

This drastic change in the city's fortunes is largely the result of broad-based changes in the nature of the nation's urban economy, rather than an outcome of the activities of Philadelphia's leadership group in either the public or the private sector. This study treats the city's planning efforts as if they were taking place on a constantly changing stage, over which the actors have little control. Philadelphia, which had been both a financial center and a booming industrial city throughout World War II, has been forced to cope with the deindustrialization and the simultaneous development of a postindustrial economy. Deindustrialization has meant loss of the majority of blue-collar jobs in the city and region, and the subsequent thinning out and abandonment of many of the neighborhoods that were linked to these jobs. As a consequence, both the city's population and its tax base have shrunk.

The development of a postindustrial economy has meant that most of the growth has been in the service sector, especially in the number of office jobs in the downtown area. Borchert (1978) has termed this new center of development a "command and control center"; its economy is linked to the coordination, control, and hierarchical command of geographically dispersed organizations. Attracting large organizations to the downtown area is the primary planning goal of cities that embark on this development path.

Philadelphia's efforts in this regard stressed three significant themes: (1) the importance of a distinctive and aesthetically appealing business district for the location of corporate headquarters; (2) facilitation of business services in the business district; and (3) a commitment to the primacy of office development for the city's transition to a significantly different employment and business base (City of Philadelphia, City Planning Commission 1985b:75–86).

The recent revitalization of the downtown area of Philadelphia has thus both occasioned and resulted from a civic boosterism of sorts; the city's new skyline has come to signify revival and growth. According to this new urban ethic, the exclusion of much of the city's population from both the residential revitalization and the limited job market of Center City is justified as both necessary and proper. Traditional ideologies of social justice and equal redistribution of benefits have been replaced with theories of "blaming the victim" and trickle down. Neighborhoods are either told to wait for the benefits of revitalization to spread throughout the entire city, or chided for being out of step, as it were, with the new realities of a postindustrial economy. In short, the revitalization of Center City Philadelphia, as physically and aesthetically pleasing as it is to many people, raises the same question one analyst saw being raised about one of the gentrified neighborhoods of this area, Queen Village: "For whom are we saving the cities?" (Levy 1979:191).

In some ways, this is not surprising. The "public interest" in the reshaping of downtown has, to some extent, always been a rhetorical pawn in discussions between private developers and the bureaucratically organized government and elected officials of Philadelphia. In this study I examine three distinctly different projects that reveal different facets of Philadelphia's Center City revival: the Society Hill/Independence Hall effort; the Market Street East retail, transportation, and convention center project; and the more recent Market Street West "skyscraper corridor," office space, and postindustrial service economy plan. These three projects were chosen because they are the areas most frequently mentioned in the current public debate over development in Philadelphia, or when people are asked to identify specific examples of the overdevelopment of downtown at the expense of neighborhoods, or the ways at which public dollars have enriched the private sector.

But they were also chosen for another, more significant reason. It would be a mistake to argue that Philadelphia's experience with public-private partnerships has included only one relationship between the public sector and the business community. In actuality, Philadelphia has experienced three forms of public-private partnership, each represented by one of these projects. A local government that was successful in its early efforts to assert control became a brokering, packaging entity whose role was ultimately merely to await instruction from the new generation of Center City developers. The central goal of each approach remained the same—to help downtown Philadelphia make a successful transition from its industrial past so that it can be a postindustrial command and control center, with an aesthetic identity and distinctive character that dramatically underscore this transition (City of Philadelphia, City Planning Commission 1951a; 1986). As will be seen, although this theme has remained constant, the mechanisms, and the control of the public and private sectors, have not.

If the effects of this revitalization were to trickle down to many of the city's neighborhoods, then public-sector support of private development might not generate substantial conflict. The information presented here indicates that these effects have been limited indeed. Recent conflicts over the city's development policy, in which the disputants have often been factually misinformed about the relative extent of expenditures for downtown and for neighborhood development, reflect all too well the symbolic importance attached to Center City revitalization. Neighborhood activists charge that neighborhood neglect yields developer profits. It is not that public dollars do not fuel private profits—they do. More to the point in Philadelphia is the impression that the public sector has abandoned any pretense of guiding or controlling development, and has surrendered responsibility for the downtown to a private-sector developers. Only the faintest of hopes remains that there will be citywide, beneficial effects. I elaborate on the nature of the resultant conflicts at the conclusion of the chapter.

Planning, Renewal, and Reform in Philadelphia

By the end of World War II, Philadelphia had regained much of the economic strength it had lost during the Great Depression. However, the forces of political change that had been forestalled during the war were about to sweep away the last vestiges of one hundred years of Republican party dominance. Philadelphia was run by a classic political machine; it had acquired the reputation of being "corrupt and contented." Both municipal jobs and contracts were either for sale or provided to a small group of regulars (Abernethy 1982:535).

Beginning in the early days of the Depression, a concerted voice for political reform had begun to be heard in the city. Disrupted by World

War II, efforts began afresh in the late 1940s. One of the first signs of success was the establishment of a nominally independent City Planning Commission in 1947. Although complete political control was not gained by the reform group until the 1951 election, the commission was instrumental in creating the final impetus to change.

The City Planning Commission was established as a result of the efforts of the "Young Turks," a group of wealthy and politically influential reformers (including Joseph Clark and Richardson Dilworth, both of whom would later be elected mayor, plus a planner, Edmund Bacon, an architect, Oskar Stonorov, and several other prominent members of the city's financial and civic elite). At least one account of that time reveals that this group argued that presenting an example of the physical changes to be made in the city would help convince the electorate of the need for political change. Accordingly, a large-scale model of both the city as it was then and the city as planned was made the centerpiece of an exhibit housed in the public meeting room of Gimbels, then the dominant department store in the city (Petshek 1973:15–25).

The success of the reform effort climaxed with the election of Clark as mayor and Dilworth as district attorney. The first priority of the new regime was the elimination of the old machine, the reorganization of local government, and the introduction of merit-based hiring and contract-bidding procedures under a new home rule charter granted by the state. Reconstruction and renewal of the city received nearly as much attention. They were jointly administered by the City Planning Commission and by an operational entity with which it worked closely, the Redevelopment Authority.

This examination of the early days of Center City revitalization has two reasons aside from simple nostalgia. First, as Jean Lowe (1967) so graphically pointed out, political reform and downtown renewal were mutually reinforcing in Philadelphia. When the reform movement ended, the role of planning, and the role of Philadelphia's elite, in the planning process changed dramatically. As will be shown in this chapter, the effects of the original plan were altered by changing political and economic factors. Nonetheless, despite the changes in political leadership, and despite changes in the economic base of the city and the region, an underlying theme has remained constant—the segregation of Center City from the other communities of the city, as well as a strategic argument that the center receive priority treatment.

The second reason to examine the origins of Center City development is to dispel a particular myth that surrounds this early "golden era" of planning in Philadelphia. In the memories of some of the planners, there remains a conviction that if only they had been able to reform the government, if only they had had the talent in the City Planning Commission that they had when Ed Bacon headed it, if they could only have reinspired the leadership of the city, then the original plans could have been completed. However, it is important to realize not only what *was* achieved, but what was *not*. In the mid-1970s, a conference was held that brought together some of the major actors of the early days of planning and renewal to reflect on the past. Two comments are worth noting. William Rafsky, who was director of the Redevelopment Authority and has remained involved in citywide urban renewal efforts since he left office, argued that the city never had the power to do much in the way of direct development and "only" packaged development options for the private sector (Rafsky 1975). The other comment of note was that of Edmund Bacon, who compared the early City Planning Commission efforts and its attitude toward the city as a whole to U.S. government propaganda in Vietnam. He had just seen the movie "Hearts and Minds," which is a chronicle of the contradictions in actions and words in Vietnam, and was struck by the similarities with how planning and development actually proceeded in Philadelphia. His message was simple—that in pursuit of the goal of winning the hearts and minds of Philadelphians over to their image of the city, planners and developers had overlooked the real needs of the city's neighborhoods (Bacon 1975).

Center City Development: A Study of Three Projects

Center City has presented several major problems to the City Planning Commission, which mainly concerned residence, retail office space, tourism, access to transportation, and their interrelationships. In order to give some idea of how Center City has developed, and "whose city" has been developed, I have focused on three projects. The first is the Society Hill/Independence Hall area, which has emerged as an interesting mix: a locus of gentrification and a tourist and corporate center. It is a product of the early, proactive planning commission approach, in which the city (as primary actor) tried to counter broad-based demographic and developmental trends by taking strategic action.

The second project, Market Street East, is predominantly a retail and transportation center (with some office development). The efforts, since 1984, to graft a convention center onto the plan for this area will also be considered here. Rather than countering basic trends, it was decided to alter the basic plan for this development to reflect new patterns of retail consumption (i.e., the preference for shopping malls), the increased reliance on a suburban work force in the redeveloped Center City, and a decreased role for comprehensive planning. Interestingly, the original image of the Center City revitalization was carried forward in this approach, as expressed in the city's 1947 and 1960 basic plans. In contrast, the government played a much larger role as initiator and primary actor in the Society Hill project. Direct control and significant guidelines for that project were dispensed with in favor of more indirect financing and tax options.

The most recent example of the Center City's revitalization, the Market Street West development effort, is the last to be examined; the new downtown office boom, and the reduced role of the city as an active "legitimator" of development, will also be considered. Almost exclusively a reaction to pressures for new office space for headquarters and business services, this project reduced the city's role virtually to that of a cheerleader. To some extent this reflects new fiscal realities; to a greater extent, it is the continuation of the role Rafsky and Bacon have described (i.e., the city as handmaiden to private development) as being evident in a new national and regional political and economic environment.

Indeed, it is significant that many people assumed the city would continue its rebound after World War II and regain its industrial and commercial strength. Even when the City Planning Commission performed a baseline study of the economy in 1951 (City of Philadelphia, City Planning Commission 1951a), data on the suburbanization of people and jobs were treated as a simple expansion of the economy over a wider space. Instead, this period proved to be the beginning of a difficult transition to a city of jobs and people lost. The new decentralized mixture of industrial, postindustrial, service-sector, and welfare economies undermined the traditional link between jobs and residences in many older neighborhoods.

For Philadelphia, the result has been to divide the city between winners and losers, between middle- and upper-class areas, and into low-income, white, black, and Hispanic neighborhoods. The political structure reflects this division; a black mayor, Wilson Goode, was elected in 1983 on the promise that he can both lunch in the corporate board rooms and talk on the street corners of the city. The City Council reflects the racial composition and differential economic interests of the city's neighborhoods amazingly well, but the result has been a declining degree of consensus about the city's developmental agenda.

As revenues have declined, and as the harsh realities of the scale of renewal needed for the city have been recognized, the entire concept of planning and revitalization has changed. Whereas "comprehensive" planning used to be done for the city as a whole, "strategic" planning now results in planning for economic development, with Center City being the main trigger. To a large extent, the rest of the city's neighborhoods will be forced to wait for the trickling down of benefits from this effort.

The change in planning strategies present in these three cases is not simply the result of the whims of political appointees to the planning commission, nor of the randomness of chance over a forty-year period, nor of disconnected fads and the foibles of planners. In large part, it reflects the attempts of a city government to reposition itself as its economic base and political power have shrunk.

Society Hill/Independence Hall. Located in the southeast quadrant of Center City, at the end of the 1940s this neighborhood was an amalgam of small industries and warehouses, and was a wholesale produce distribution center. The federal government had made some efforts to purchase the small hotels and shops immediately across Chestnut Street from Independence Hall. Much of the older historic district included both historic buildings and the commercial and small industrial buildings of the nineteenth century. These early efforts at historic preservation were spotty and had a negligible impact prior to the city's renewal efforts.

By the mid-1960s, it was clear that a remarkable physical transformation had occurred. Society Hill Towers, and a large number of town houses (some designed by I. M. Pei) had completely supplanted the wholesale food center and many of the warehouses. The area to the east of Washington Square was renamed Society Hill, after the meetinghouse of the Free Society of Traders that had stood at the crest of the hill on which the towers were located. Immediately to the west, Independence Hall had been substantially restored. There was now a park to the south and a three-block-long mall to the north, surrounded by federal offices (the Federal Reserve Bank, the Mint, and the federal courthouse and office complex), corporate headquarters (one bank, a television and radio station, and Rohm and Haas), two museums, and an office building (later converted to a combined mall and office building).

The areas between Society Hill and the newly created Independence Mall soon became a mix of high-priced housing (whose construction was strongly influenced by the historic preservation movement), an expanded historic district (including the Bank of the United States, the Customs House, restored buildings such as the Powel House, the site of Ben Franklin's house, and a new visitor's center), and, in the late 1970s, an upscale dining and night life center. In short, the utopian dreams of making a declining industrial slum neighborhood visually attractive and financially profitable were largely realized in this area. Indeed, the members of the City Planning Commission now speak of this area as worthy of "conservation," as it has acquired an aura of stability to accompany its success.

It is interesting to observe that the neighborhoods to the immediate south and north of Society Hill seem to have been affected by this revitalization movement. Queen Village, which borders Society Hill on the south and which had been a lower-class community of mixed ethnic heritage, was favored by young urban families seeking the amenities of Society Hill but lacking the necessary income. Eventually this group expanded, organized, and defeated a transportation plan that would have created an expressway cutting along the southern boundary of Center City. Queen Village now has an almost entirely different population and housing mix and is simply a cut below Society Hill in terms of rents and housing costs, with a higher-income, younger population.

Revitalization expanded to Old City, to the north of Society Hill, in the 1970s. An area composed largely of warehouses and wholesale outlets, Old City has begun to witness the conversion of lofts into apartments, and the fragments of historical sites have been made the subject of a general advertising campaign for the area. Both Queen Village and Old City have benefited from the increase in historic preservation tax credits in the 1970s and 1980s, which has helped attract private capital.

The Society Hill project was a primary consideration in the earliest discussions of the revitalization of Center City. Soon after the election of Joe Clark as mayor in 1951, a coalition of business and civic leaders sought to institutionalize the process of consultation and involvement that had been a part of the reform movement. This body, known as the Greater Philadelphia Movement, was a classic elitist body, in that much of the public debate of development and planning options took place within its membership, or in forums sponsored by it. The movement's primary focus was on its immediate environment—the downtown area. Early redevelopment efforts (roughly 1950–1956) had focused almost exclusively on slum clearance and housing renewal (Kleniewski 1981); however, city planners began to change their focus as soon as the scale of the city's housing problems and their attendant costs were recognized. By one estimate, more than one in four housing units in Philadelphia would need to be demolished, and 40 percent would need some form of treatment (Row 1960: 179).

After an exhaustive study of the Central Urban Renewal Area, published in 1956, the Redevelopment Authority head, William Rafsky, concluded that for reasons of expense, displacement effects on surrounding communities, increased housing problems in nonrenewal areas, and the reluctance of the private sector to invest in the renewal effort, the authority was developing an inventory of housing it could neither improve nor sell (Rafsky 1956:1). The authors of the CURA study, as it became known, recommended a diversified strategy of development but concentrated on the downtown area. By 1963, 45 percent of total city renewal funds was being expended on Center City, the bulk on Society Hill (Kleniewski 1986).

Although there is no clear set of data regarding the amount of local, federal, and private-sector dollars that went into the area's development, some of the major figures involved in the development have provided estimates. Bernard Meltzer, head of the City Planning Commission under Mayor Frank Rizzo (1971–1979), estimated in the late 1960s that each public dollar invested in Society Hill generated seven dollars in private investment, and that for every dollar from the city, forty-nine dollars was generated from state, federal, and private sources combined. Under Rizzo, he wanted to limit urban renewal elsewhere in the city, arguing that every dollar of improvements generated four to five dollars' worth of increased demands on the public infrastructure (Weiler 1974:150).

Such estimates of scale seem correct. By the 1970s, the renewal of Society Hill alone (not including the Independence Mall area) was said to have cost $49 million in public funds and over $250 million in private-sector funds (City of Philadelphia, City Planning Commission 1976). Given the impossibility of adjusting these figures to any single baseline value of constant dollars, it is not possible to obtain definitive values. Nonetheless, the signal success of Society Hill as a renewal project was a result of the use of public dollars as leverage. By contrast, the persistent problem of housing revitalization in the rest of the city, as pointed out in the CURA study, was that public-sector funds were the only funds available, and no private financing could be attracted to deal with the extensive dilapidation of the housing stock—by some estimates, more than one-third of the city's housing) (City of Philadelphia, City Planning Commission 1951b:1).

It would indeed be a significant addition to this discussion to be able to determine the actual costs incurred by the public sector and compare them with the changes in the city treasury, the city's amenities, or the general well-being. Unfortunately, like many cities, Philadelphia makes it difficult to ascertain the actual source of funds or the amount of public dollars that is spent for an area, or the amount of funds derived from it. Although it is possible to show that the Community Development Block Grant funds targeted for the Society Hill/Queen Village area during the 1970s were diverted to police, fire, and sanitation worker pension funds (the rationale being that these services were being provided to the neighborhoods), it is impossible, without access to city worker daily schedules, to apportion these subsidies to specific neighborhoods in a consistent and meaningful fashion. Changes have been made in city accounting and reporting practices since 1987, which may well change this situation in the future. At present, calculating a meaningful "return on investment" figure is impossible in such cases.

The city's role was not simply financial, however. Society Hill was not only a leveraging success, but the result of a successful public relations effort. Mayor Dilworth moved into one of the first units rehabilitated in the area, and was followed by a string of public officials and members of the local business and financial elite (Tate 1973). Lest the public think that this was an example of enlightened nobility, Mayor Dilworth was quite candid in giving the underlying reasons for his administration's development of Society Hill: It was a calculated effort to keep whites in the city and reverse the flow of the middle class and potential political leaders to the suburbs (Lowe 1967:351–352).

By any definition, the Society Hill/Independence Hall redevelopment effort has successfully achieved its goals. The area has been transformed from a mixture of slums, light industry, warehouses, and an open-air wholesale food market to the focus of postwar gentrification in Philadelphia. (For a graphic description of the area prior to renewal, see Tate 1973.) As a result of strong design restrictions maintained by the Redevelopment Authority, housing in the area has been consistently developed within a federalist mold. Today, the neighborhoods that hug the Delaware River between the original boundaries of Philadelphia, and to the south of them, are mixtures of lofts, apartments and houses, whose selling price ranges from $150,000 to $500,000. Efficiency apartments rent for $300 per month; two-bedroom units rent for $2,000 and up.

It is clear that this success was obtained by removing residents and housing them elsewhere. Although these people had been promised affordable housing in their former neighborhoods, this promise was largely ignored. By the time a lawsuit was settled in the early 1980s, the number of households of the area that had been promised housing of equivalent cost and returned to their neighborhoods totaled less than a dozen.

The impact of Society Hill's revitalization is long-term. Society Hill has demonstrated that a coordinated residential and office complex development project is possible and profitable, given enough time, a cooperative City Planning Commission and Redevelopment Authority, and sufficient private-sector dollars leveraged by direct investment and appropriate loan guarantees.

Market Street East. If Society Hill can be described as the City Planning Commission's major success story, Market Street East remains an enigmatic tale at best, largely because of the contrast of original plans with actual possibilities, and of "reform" vs. "mainstream" urban politics.

Originally, the land use plan of Center City called for the segregation of downtown Philadelphia from the rest of the city by two east-west expressways, running along the northern and southern borders of the city, respectively. When the design of Market Street East was made public in 1960 (City of Philadelphia, City Planning Commission 1960; 1963; 1976), it revealed that the concept of a segregated core was reinforced by plans to locate a combined transportation hub and megastructure office and retail complex along the north side of Market Street, between Seventh and Tenth Streets (see Banham 1976, for a good discussion of the megastructure design principle).

This megastructure was designed to be a four-block-long concourse, below street level but open to the sunlight, linking subway and commuter rail service. Rising above this concourse, at appropriate intervals, were four very substantial office towers. On the other side of the office towers would be a bus terminal and parking garage, which completely isolated the downtown retail area from direct access of the rest of the city.

Had Market Street East been Society Hill, there would have been a systematic bundling of the land, followed by a design competition in which several alternatives would be discussed, and then the full support of the formal and informal governments of the city, the elected and the corporate, would have been given to the project. No such development was forthcoming.

Neither expressway has been built. One has been scrapped altogether. (The South Street Expressway was removed after a titanic battle in which the city and the state joined in opposition to the residents, both new and old, of Queen Village, the neighborhood to the south of Society Hill. Construction of the Vine Street Expressway finally began in 1984, and is scheduled to be completed in 1992. As a result, much of the development strategy based on a transportation hub has been altered. One major part of the original plan has remained intact, however. A rail connection between the former Penn Central and Reading Railroad commuter lines was built in the late 1970s at a cost of $300–$400 million. The concourse is there, but in large part the megastructures have been replaced by a few relatively modest office towers.

Instead of megastructures, the bulk of the properties were to be transformed into an urban shopping mall of no more than three or four levels. The Gallery at Market East, as it was named, was expanded to include Gallery II, which lengthened the shopping area some three full blocks. There was one final change in the original plan. In the 1980s a plan was adopted to locate and build a new convention center and a new criminal justice center, cheek by jowl, to round out the development of Market Street East.

This departure from original design, from megastructure to strip development, was symptomatic of the breakdown of consensus within the political structure, the claims of the rest of the city's residential and commercial areas on development funding, the weakening of the reform elements within the elected government, and a discontinuation of the easy access to elected government officials by corporate leaders. In short, the developers of Market Street East had to contend with pressing competition for scarce development dollars, but lacked an effective power base.

This breakdown of broad-based support for a grand plan for Center City was accompanied by an increase in the demands of both black and working-class communities for shifts in the basic thrust of renewal. The demonstrations and riots in many black neighborhoods across the country during the 1960s produced immediate changes in urban budgetary priorities. High-profile physical changes in income and racially delimited communities such as Society Hill took second place to both the rhetoric and occasional reality of community and neighborhood planning.

At about the same time, in the early to mid-1960s, the focus of the Democratic party in Philadelphia shifted away from reform. The party was led by a union-progressive-black coalition, whose power was evidenced by the election of James Tate as mayor, after he had filled out the second term of Richardson Dilworth (who had resigned to run unsuccessfully for governor). In his unpublished autobiography, entitled "In Praise of Politicians," Tate vividly describes the tactics and methods by which he came to grips with the changing political realities of the city.

In contrast to the reform interests of Dilworth and Clark, Tate's key goals were the delivery of city services to the loyal party constituents—and the revitalization of Center City was not the most direct way to accomplish this (Tate 1973). Nonetheless, he supported this effort as long as it did not interfere with the broader agenda of service delivery.

This broader agenda necessarily caused a partial dissolution of the consensus regarding the reform movement and its original planning efforts. The dissolution is reflected by the declining fortunes and change in behavior of two pivotal elite bodies of the 1950s. The first was the Citizens' Council for City Planning, a group that paralleled and reinforced the major reform organization, the Greater Philadelphia Movement, and that began a long slide toward ineffectiveness and dissolution. The second body, the Greater Philadelphia Movement, had been a prestigious membership group of corporate, financial, and social elites. As the new composition of Philadelphia's postreform government became apparent, and the relative strengths of labor and nonbusiness interest groups increased, the movement changed its name to the Greater Philadelphia Partnership, indicating a change from a broad, consensual movement to a partnership of differing interests. Tate's discussion of his days in office reveals not a movement generating a new government, as had been the case under Clark and Dilworth, but substantial negotiations, an end to much of the "goodwill" between the public and private sectors, and indeed, a significant degree of rancor by Tate toward city and public-sector officials alike who did not realize the scope of a true citywide development effort.

The cohesive approach to a movement had collapsed and was replaced by a "partnership" of different interests, which often shifted from one policy to another. The implications of these developments for Market Street East are direct. The end of the reform era and the political liabilities of large-scale planning made a systematic, broad-based effort unlikely, at best.

What emerged was a diverse strategy in which, project by project, substantial pieces of the development were put in place, but with significant departures from the original plan. These components are, in order of their completion, Galleries I and II, the Center City Commuter Connection, the Lit Brothers conversion, and the Convention Center project (construction of which is to begin in 1989). The Gallery projects diverged markedly from the expected use of the space on Market Street but kept certain of the original design principles intact. It was the expectation of the City Planning Commission that the office center development in Philadelphia would be located along Market Street, between City Hall and the office complexes around Independence Hall and Mall. After many attempts to generate developers' interest in such an approach, a proposal was made by James Rouse, best known in the area for his successful development of two suburban malls that were slowly depleting the cash registers of the four remaining major department stores along Market Street (Gimbels, Strawbridge & Clothier, Lits, and Wanamaker's).

What Rouse proposed was to apply the principle of market agglomeration exemplified by suburban shopping malls to the retail strip along Market Street. If a four-level shopping mall were built and linked to the commuter rail lines of the city, he argued, the retail needs of both the Center City population and the working commuter population would be a ready market for this approach to retailing. After the first mall was successfully completed, he proposed linking a second mall to it, as well as building a two-office tower on one of the above-ground property sites. Construction of Gallery II was quickly agreed to by the Redevelopment Authority and the City Planning Commission.

Both Gallery projects embodied one major component of the early downtown plan—exposure of the public areas to the outside world through copious use of glass. Thus, the design principle advanced by Bacon from the very outset—that pedestrians not only should constitute free-flowing traffic but should feel connected to the city and to the outside world, even while they were walking in a subterranean concourse—was preserved.

Helping to drive the Gallery projects was the gradual realization of a long-held planning dream in Philadelphia—linking the old Pennsylvania and Reading commuter lines by means of an underground tunnel between Sixteenth and Eleventh Streets. Designed long ago, but not able to attract appropriate funding, the tunnel was becoming a reality in the early 1980s by virtue of a massive grant from the Urban Mass Transit Administration (UMTA). The linking of the two commuter systems resulted in creation of a regional rail network, thus facilitating the use of Center City by suburban commuters (and continuing the planning theme that Philadelphia needed to reattract the leadership potential that had escaped to the suburbs). It also guaranteed that an increased number of people would be exposed to the two Gallery shopping areas, as two rail stations service passengers along the connection.

These projects received substantial public-sector support, both direct and indirect. The commuter tunnel project was an almost entirely government project, with 80 percent of the cost paid for by the UMTA, and 20 percent funded by the local government. Small amounts were obtained from the cash boxes of the transit system to pay for overruns and special adjustments to the system. A total of approximately $400 million was expended on that aspect of the project alone.

Estimates of the expenditures on the Gallery projects are difficult to come by, as the amounts spent by the Redevelopment Authority to acquire the properties are not evident. What is clear is that Gallery I received about $25 million of the roughly $100 million in development expenditures from a variety of sources. One estimate from 1980 indicated that $245 million in urban renewal funds had been spent to assist in that development (*Philadelphia Evening Bulletin* 1980). A $5 million loan from the city to the developer, and $21.1 million in UDAG funds were required to complete the Gallery II project. Additionally, the city agreed to pay 55 percent of the maintenance costs at the Gallery and to become the tenant of last resort for at least one office tower. Although the Redevelopment Authority owns the land on which this development stands, the proceeds go substantially to the shop owners and the development company.

In recent years, the Galleries have contrasted too vividly with the small shopping area left between the City Hall and the Gallery area. Spiritualists, dojos, X-rated movie houses, sexual aids stores, tobacconists, pizza parlors, and small- to moderate-size clothing stores are interspersed with the one remaining department store not linked to the Galleries, the Reading Market (a Faneuil Hall–type of open market) and two new office towers, substantially inhabited by city offices.

In the aftermath of a coordinated approach to Market East, the city has pushed forward two additional plans for development: a justice complex and a convention center.

The justice complex is a straightforward public dollars, public use development. The convention center, however, fits the basic model of Galleries I and II: public-sector assembly of land and approval of plans; partial public funding, combined with an identified revenue base to pay off bonded debt; and private-sector control of running the center after construction. A blue-ribbon authority, appointed by the mayor and the governor and strongly dominated by private-sector interests, directs every aspect of the $500 million project, from assembly of the land (a responsibility of the Redevelopment Authority) to opening day.

Although this project has been at least as controversial among neighborhood organizations as the Galleries (which provoked demonstrations in the mall as well as in City Council chambers during their first months of operation), great pains were taken to assure the neighborhoods of the area that they would benefit from the project. Construction jobs and new jobs in the Convention Center were promised after its completion. A new ratable was also promised to ease pressures on an already shrinking tax base. One major dispute has focused on the rather dramatic claims of potential benefits made in the cost-benefit analysis that preceded approval of the project. But what is striking about the issue is the extent to which the city has been forced to change its legitimation of Center City development from "renewal for the sake of renewal" to "renewal as an investment with a payoff." This "payoff" as the bottom line for renewal should be understood as both a return to the city and a return to the private sector.

Indeed, the lesson of Market Street East's development has been the lesson of the conservative backlash of the 1970s and 1980s, albeit on a local level. Renewal that responds to generalized decay and that seeks a new city in its stead has been replaced by renewal that satisfies the basic investment criteria of risk, financing, and return. The final example of downtown renewal, a small area called Market Street West, provides a graphic illustration of both approaches.

Market Street West. Market Street West, the area abutting the main east-west artery from City Hall to the Schuylkill River, has a decidedly schizoid history. Originally, it was the site of one of the hallmark efforts of public renewal at its most extreme—Penn Center Plaza, the complete leveling of a major rail artery and its superstructure, and the development of a broad plaza of public space interrupted by office complexes. This was to serve as an anchor for further development of the corridor by the private sector. To some extent, that development has occurred. What marks this area as worthy of note, however, is the transformation in developmental decision-making that has become apparent since the mid-1950s.

The area to the west of City Hall, one of the pivotal elements in the original push for renewal, had been dominated by the railroad superstructure and the Broad Street terminal of the Pennsylvania Railroad, collectively termed the "Chinese Wall." The north side of Market Street was faced by a multistoried, four-block-long brick wall, supporting the rail lines terminating at Broad Street, immediately across from City Hall's northwest corner. Long regarded as an eyesore, the separate suburban station building erected in the 1930s had made the Broad Street Station superfluous as well. Even before its efforts in Society Hill, the city began the assembly and renewal of this land (specifically, the properties between Broad and Eighteenth Streets along the north side of Market Street).

What emerged was a complex plan for routing rail lines to the suburban station underground, rather than on or above the surface. The Broad Street station and the "Chinese Wall" were leveled, using public dollars, and plans for the new plaza-office complex and subterranean concourse were developed by the City Planning Commission. As with Market East, the underground concourse was a central design feature of the early plans.

The Uris Company, the major contractor for the project, quickly altered the basic design features. It eliminated the use of sunken gardens and skylights to open up the concourse level, as well as the vision of high-ceilinged open space at that level. This alteration provides an interesting insight to both the power and the limits of the development process in these early days of renewal.

As both Bacon (1975) and Tate (1973) recall, the refusal of Uris to adhere to the basic original plan for the Market West project led to an impasse, in the overcoming of which Mayor Clark took an active role. A meeting took place between the mayor and Uris in which the issues concerning the concourse level were explored. According to Clark, as quoted in Tate's memoirs, the result was an ultimatum that produced a compromise. Clark indicated that the project had to follow the plan or Uris could, in effect, get out of town. Holding the carrot of further development work and the threat of a lost contract, the city obtained some cooperation. The ceilings in the concourse were raised somewhat, though not to the levels specified. Some lower-level gardens (inaccessible by people in the concourse) and skylights were included, but not so that the concourse became an extension of the outside world.

In short, the city's only weapon in negotiations with Uris was the threat of forcing its total withdrawal—a Pyrrhic strategy. Withdrawal by Uris would have created a difficult atmosphere for alternative developers, and a much protracted delay in moving from vacant land to finished construction. The impact of any action by the City Planning Commission and the Redevelopment Authority was thus limited to the degree to which a mayor would be willing to "jawbone" the development community. The plans developed for the Penn Center project provided for no independent authority.

As the reform movement died, support for the overall plan for downtown Philadelphia became more fragmented, a process I have discussed somewhat in the context of Market Street East. A much more widely dispersed development was planned for the west side of City Hall. After the bulk of the Penn Center Plaza development was accomplished in 1963, four widely scattered buildings were constructed in the 1960s, and four more were erected in the 1970s (City of Philadelphia, City Planning Commission 1984a). In the late 1970s, a genuine office development boom began to impact upon Center City, concentrated in the Market West area. Six buildings were opened in four years, located mostly in a three-block area immediately to the west of the original Penn Center project, and on land that, in some cases, had been developed as ancillary to the plaza (for parking, in particular).

This office development boom, and the new form of renewal effort it represented, were exemplified by a proposal to develop the square block between Sixteenth and Seventeenth Streets, south of Market. Spearheaded by Willard Rouse (not to be confused with James Rouse of Market Street East), a proposal was made to build twin towers above a retail and hotel space. What made this proposal controversial was that Rouse proposed breaking the "Billy Penn's hat" rule in their construction. The Redevelopment Authority, with the agreement of the City Planning Commission, had an internal development rule that no building in Center City could rise higher than 491 feet, the distance from the street to the crown of William Penn's hat on the statue atop the City Hall tower. The first tower, completed in late 1987 (and already partially occupied), is proof that Rouse received the necessary permission to build. As expected, the skyline is now dominated by Liberty Place (styled after the Chrysler building); City Hall has been reduced to one of several large, but now far less significant, buildings in the downtown area.

There was, as might be anticipated, considerable opposition to the proposal to depart from tradition. Edmund Bacon came out of retirement to testify as to the legitimacy of the height rule. Many community groups argued that the Rouse tower simply deflected needed resources from the rest of the city. In the end, the debate was a classic disagreement over progress. Traditionalists ended up in the Bacon camp, arguing for a "livable" city, developed on a human scale on a low-rise model. Supporters of the Rouse proposal maintained that Philadelphia's success in renewing Center City had essentially undermined Philadelphia's own guidelines. The value, and hence the cost, of downtown land had driven up the cost of its redevelopment. Only a high-rise tower would succeed in deriving the rents sufficient to recoup the cost of development at a decent rate of return. Besides, the argument went, if Houston, Los Angeles, San Francisco, New York, and Chicago can all alter their skylines to remain competitive, why not stodgy old Philadelphia?

The criteria for deciding on this radical shift in the appearance of Center City are revealing, and, fittingly, mirror the change in the skyline. The City Planning Commission prepared an impact statement regarding the Rouse proposal and concluded that construction should proceed for the following reasons: (1) it would contribute to the overall competitive position of Philadelphia's office core; (2) it would help balance work being done on Market Street East, and help finish out the western developmental thrust; (3) retail areas would be increased by virtue of the mixed-use nature of the plan; and (4) the design and the plan were aesthetically appropriate for the city (City of Philadelphia, City Planning Commission 1984b). It is ironic that aesthetics, so much the hallmark of the earliest reform era plans, were now reduced to an afterthought.

What bears attention is that the City Planning Commission has placed itself firmly behind the development of Center City as an economic center that it expects will spur the rest of the city toward greater prosperity. The Rouse plan was presented exactly at the time that the commission was completing a five-year study of the physical, economic, social, and land-use characteristics of Center City (City of Philadelphia, City Planning Commission 1985a; 1985b; 1985c; 1986).

These studies, taken together, argue that (1) Center City is the basis of a postindustrial city economy; (2) facilitating the development of this economy is a key to the city's overall future economic development; (3) the gentrification of Center City neighborhoods does not impose an especially harsh burden on the surrounding neighborhoods; and (4) the jobs created downtown will benefit the entire city.

Conclusion

In this chapter I have examined three major areas of development that have been part of Philadelphia's much touted downtown revitalization;

however, I have not tried to examine the entirety of this renewal effort. The choice was deliberate; my aims were (1) to illustrate the shift from public-centered planning in the name of the greater good of the entire city, by agencies with relatively strong planning and redevelopment powers, to a planning and development process that has been diminished in both scope and scale; (2) to demonstrate the decline of the aesthetic planner and the increased use of the investment planning model; and (3) to indicate that the planning process itself has become a subject of political dispute rather than a mechanism of achieving political consensus.

There has been little systematic evidence concerning the issue of differential benefits derived from the renewal efforts of the city. Complicating even the desire to perform such research has been the recognition that funds for renewal come from multiple sources and that they are combined and then distributed among a number of different projects. Kleniewski (1981) has documented the shift in expenditures from neighborhoods to the Center City; such funds were devoted to "urban renewal." Adams (1988) has argued that the amount spent on neighborhood development, measured in capital investment dollars, has dramatically declined, while Center City investment levels have remained constant, and expenditures for citywide projects have increased. In an earlier study (Bartelt 1986), I examined the projected economic development payoffs ostensibly linked to downtown development and found them greatly exaggerated.

What is more striking than these findings, however, is the widening contrast between the neighborhoods of the city as a whole and the newer Center City. As elsewhere, the growth of a new office economy in Philadelphia has resulted in the erection of a gleaming new facade on the ruins of the commercial and industrial past. This new skyline has become symbolic of development in its entirety and invites the observer to equate downtown development and revitalization with the progress of the region. Simultaneously, however, the old industrial neighborhoods decline, the ghettoes empty out, and residents of the neighborhoods that are upgraded are displaced.

It is not surprising that residents of the city's neighborhoods feel disenfranchised. Their relative participation in development has clearly decreased: many of the development debates focused on what to do with Center City, not with the city as a whole; and the payments for development increasingly come from the pockets of users. This latter point carries an important political message to the planning and development community. As each project is considered, a significant issue will increasingly be its comparative ability to recover costs. As noted earlier, Bernard Melter asserted in the late 1960s that urban renewal projects like Society Hill were significant because they generated seven dollars in noncity funds for every one dollar spent. But he later concluded that urban renewal in general was a losing proposition, as it "forced the City to spend $4 to $5 in sewers and streets for every $1 in funds it spends on development" (Weiler 1974:150).

These conditions almost provide an imperative for high-density downtown development. Put differently, there currently exist no incentives that can guarantee neighborhood-oriented development. As tax revenues and provision of city services decline, even the slight power of the ballot diminishes. It is not surprising that the rhetoric of development battles thus becomes increasingly fierce while downtown development feeds on its own success.

In this chapter I have only scratched the surface of downtown development in Philadelphia. Since World War II, there has been a significant effort to revitalize Center City, as the downtown area is known. What has been indicated here is that the process has changed dramatically in that time. In the heyday of reform politics in Philadelphia, the planner was, if not king, at least the prince of the city. Creating an architectural model of a new city seemed only a small step away from the plan's realization. The relative ease with which the Society Hill project developed was followed by the more difficult and continuing effort to remake the face of Market Street East. All pretense of government control was finally abandoned in the Market West development; even the Redevelopment Authority, which had been able to demand adherence to architectural styles in the housing of the Society Hill community, could not enforce the Billy Penn hat limit.

It is, of course, still debatable whether the economic power represented by the Rouse development was integral to the earlier development of Penn Center. It is certainly arguable that the business community had a strong influence within the reform governments of Clark and Dilworth, and thus had no imperative to propose alternatives from outside the government. No one should be so naive as to expect that planning was independent of the corporate power evident in the reform movement. Nonetheless, clearly a greater degree of concern was expressed with a city in need of planning than with Center City development when the renewal effort was at its height.

What is striking about the entire period is the extent to which the city's role has changed from active partner to cheerleader and legitimator of Center City development. Early discussions of the Comprehensive City Plan (City of Philadelphia, City Planning Commission 1960) reveal a spatially and socially diverse approach to the needs of a broad range of the city's neighborhoods. Downtown development has dominated some of the more recent discussions of the Center City Plan: "The Central Business District of the nation's fourth largest metropolitan area, Center City provides a highly efficient environment for economic exchange. Center City is a true regional center, a center of enormous vitality, of power and prestige, of business acumen and financial resources. . . . The state of the Center City economy directly affects all residents of Philadelphia and the region, necessitating its maintenance and enhancement" (City of Philadelphia, City Planning Commission 1985b:1).

So we return to the original question: "Whose city is being revitalized?" Public dollars have meant private profits, the essential means of driving the development process, but they have also meant the creation of two cities—the Philadelphia of progressive revitalization, a combination of quaint and glitzy, and the forgotten city of row houses and empty factories. Many Philadelphians enter the 1990s fearing that the few decentralized development efforts that do exist will end and that Center City will continue to dominate the field of vision of the planning and development communities.

References

Abernethy, Lloyd M. 1982. "Progressivism: 1905–1919." In *Philadelphia: A 300-Year History*, ed. Russell Weigley. New York: Norton.

Adams, Carolyn T. 1988. *The Politics of Capital Investment*. Albany: State University of New York Press.

Bacon, Edmund. 1975. "What Was Attempted—The Planning Story." In "The Politics of Utopia: Towards America's Third Century," ed. Stanley Newman. Philadelphia: Temple University, Political Science Department (mimeo).

———. 1976. *Design of Cities*. New York: Penguin.

Banham, Reyner. 1976. *Megastructures*. New York: Harper and Row.

Bartelt, David W. 1986. "Linking Downtown Development to Housing and Job Training." Report to Philadelphia City Council, Hearings before the Housing Committee on Linked Development (photocopy).

Beauregard, Robert. 1982. "Urban Form and the Redevelopment of Central Business Districts." *Journal of Architectural and Planning Research* 3:183–198.

Borchert, John. 1978. "Major Control Points in American Geography." *Annals of the Association of American Geographers* 68:214–232.

City of Philadelphia. City Planning Commission. 1951a. "Economic Base Study of the Philadelphia Area." Philadelphia: City Planning Commission.

———. 1951b. "Philadelphia Housing Quality Survey." Philadelphia: City Planning Commission.

———. 1960. "The Comprehensive City Plan." Philadelphia: City Planning Commission.

————. 1963. "The Center City Plan." Philadelphia: City Planning Commission.

————. 1976. "Center City: The 1976 Plan." Philadelphia: City Planning Commission.

————. 1984a. "Center City Office Inventory" (technical report). Philadelphia: City Planning Commission.

————. 1984b. "Issues Raised by the Rouse Proposal" (staff analysis). Philadelphia: City Planning Commission.

————. 1985a. "Center City and Its People" (working paper). Philadelphia: City Planning Commission.

————. 1985b. "The Economy of Center City" (working paper). Philadelphia: City Planning Commission.

————. 1985c. "The Urban Form of Center City" (working paper). Philadelphia: City Planning Commission.

————. 1986. "The Future of Center City" (working paper). Philadelphia: City Planning Commission.

Clark, Joseph S., Jr., and Dennis Clark. 1982. "Rally and Relapse: 1946–1968." In *Philadelphia: A 300-Year History,* ed. Russell Weigley. New York: Norton.

Cybriwsky, Roman, and John Western. 1982. "Revitalizing Downtowns: By Whom and For Whom?" In *Geography and the Urban Environment,* ed. D. T. Herbert and R. J. Johnston. New York: Wiley.

Kleniewski, Nancy. 1981. "Neighborhood Decline and Downtown Renewal: The Politics of Redevelopment in Philadelphia, 1952–1962." Ph.D. dissertation, Temple University, Department of Sociology.

————. 1986. "Race and Urban Renewal: North Philadelphia vs. Society Hill." Paper presented at the annual meeting of the Association of Collegiate Schools of Planning. Milwaukee.

Levy, Paul. 1979. "Queen Village: Social Conflict at the Center's Edge." In *The Philadelphia Region,* ed. Roman Cybriwsky. Washington, D.C.: Association of American Geographers.

Lowe, Jean. 1967. *Cities in a Race with Time.* New York: Vintage.

Lukacs, John. 1981. *Philadelphia: Patricians and Philistines, 1900–1950.* New York: Farrar, Straus and Giroux.

Petshek, Kirk. 1973. *The Challenge of Urban Reform.* Philadelphia: Temple University Press.

Philadelphia Evening Bulletin. 1980. "Gallery II to Follow in Footsteps of Gallery I." (November):45.

Rafsky, William. 1956. "A New Approach to Urban Renewal for Philadelphia." Philadelphia: Office of the Development Coordinator (mimeo).

————. 1965. "New Housing Built through Urban Renewal." *Issues* (December). Philadelphia: Philadelphia Housing Association.

————. 1975. "What Was Attempted." In "The Politics of Utopia: Towards America's Third Century," ed. Stanley Newman. Philadelphia: Temple University, Department of Political Science (mimeo).

Row, Arthur. 1960. "The Physical Development Plan." *Journal of the American Institute of Planners* 26 (3):177–185.

Tate, James H. J. 1973. "In Praise of Politicians." Unpublished manuscript, Temple University Urban Archives.

Weiler, Conrad. 1974. *Philadelphia: Neighborhood, Authority, and the Urban Crisis*. New York: Praeger.

6. The Pittsburgh Model of Economic Development: Partnership, Responsiveness, and Indifference

G round was broken in October 1986 for the Pittsburgh Technology Center. Its forty-eight-acre site had just been cleared of a closed steel plant that had formed part of the "Pittsburgh Works," originally owned and operated by the Jones & Laughlin Steel Company. Symbolizing the city's traditional manufacturing base, Jones & Laughlin had been the city's single largest employer until the mid-1970s. By contrast, the Pittsburgh Technology Center, under the aegis of the Urban Redevelopment Authority (URA), would be facilitating the commercialization of research carried out by Carnegie-Mellon University and the University of Pittsburgh. The latter, in fact, was now Pittsburgh's largest employer. By 1988, steel production was peripheral to the city's economy; the universities were increasingly viewed as "engines of growth" and as being of central importance to the city's future economic base.

The replacement of a steel plant with a publicly sponsored technology center, although dramatic, raises the awkward question of who benefits from public policies aimed at economic development in a context of economic decline. The market forces typically unleashed during economic restructuring (which involves the contraction of the manufacturing sector and the redevelopment of city centers) disproportionately favor downtowns over neighborhoods, the well educated over the unskilled, and whites over minorities. Local government therefore must decide whether to accept and reinforce the outcomes favored by the market or whether to target substantial public expenditure at those who do not share proportionately in the benefits of that "rising tide" that economic development policies seek to encourage.

The dilemma is particularly difficult for local officials who are key actors in the public-private partnerships active in urban economic development. The goal of such partnerships is to facilitate market forces; and their activities thus favor downtown development and those with marketable skills. Can local government, on the one hand, actively participate in a public-private partnership that supports downtown and service-sector

103

development and, on the other, be responsive to neighborhood organizations, minorities, and manual workers, groups typically excluded from such a partnership?

Such a question is particularly appropriate in the case of Pittsburgh, for the city is a symbol in numerous ways. Pittsburgh, once synonymous with the might of the nation's steel, now symbolizes the cities of the rustbelt both because it has been hurt by the dramatic decline of manufacturing in its surrounding region and because it is diversifying its own economic base in response to such decline. Furthermore, its public-private partnership is perhaps both the oldest and most powerful in the United States. Because it was established long before the precipitous decline of the steel industry, it is possible to analyze the partnership's impact under conditions of both economic stability and economic decline. The longevity of Pittsburgh's partnership permits an analysis of who benefits over time and under varying conditions.

The experience of neighborhood organizations, minorities, and manual workers—three groups not included in Pittsburgh's public-private partnership—suggests both the opportunities and the constraints that are perhaps intrinsic to public-private partnerships. The experience of these groups indicates that the answer to the question just asked can be a qualified yes. A balancing act is possible, but only under a limited number of conditions.

Briefly, in this chapter I will argue that neighborhood groups in Pittsburgh have organized so effectively that they have been able, even under a system of at-large elections for the City Council, to extract substantial benefits from the city's economic development policies. City government is now responsive. By contrast, the black community, not organized as a strong political force, has faced indifference rather than responsiveness and has not received such benefits. However, a new system of district elections, by increasing the community's internal political cohesion, may improve the blacks' position. Finally, the local government has been more responsive to the *regional* than to the local demands of labor activists.

Since the late 1970s, therefore, the city government has been able to respond to neighborhood organizations and, to a lesser extent, to labor while very much remaining a member in good standing within the partnership.

Pittsburgh's Gradual Economic Transformation

The city of Pittsburgh has been undergoing a process of economic change for forty years, very gradually evolving into a service-oriented, postindustrial city. Although the Pittsburgh region has undergone a brutally rapid loss of manufacturing jobs, the city's earlier diversification insulated it somewhat from the impact of that loss.

While undergoing economic change, however, the city has lost population and become less important to its neighbors. Whereas in 1950, 45 percent of Allegheny County's population was within the legal boundaries of the city of Pittsburgh, by 1984 that figure had dropped to 29 percent. Similarly, the city constituted 18 percent of the metropolitan area's population in 1984, compared with 31 percent in 1950. Between 1970 and 1984, the city lost nearly one-quarter of its population (Giarratani and Houston 1986:25).

This loss of population was accompanied by a loss of jobs. Between 1940 and 1980, the city lost 52,500 jobs, a decrease of 24 percent. Its reliance on manufacturing jobs lessened. In 1950, 26 percent of the city's jobs were in manufacturing, and 12.8 percent of the labor force was employed in steel and metal manufacturing. By 1980, only 14.6 percent were in manufacturing and only 5.5 percent of the city's labor force was employed in steel and metal manufacturing (Jezierski 1987b:7–10). In the 1980s, the region has come to resemble the city. The former has lost so many manufacturing jobs that it is now more dependent on nonmanufacturing jobs than is the nation as a whole (Giarratani and Houston 1986). By 1985, manufacturing accounted for a slightly smaller percentage of total employment in the Pittsburgh metropolitan area than it did in the Columbus, Cleveland, or Cincinnati metropolitan areas (Federal Reserve Bank of Cleveland 1986:6–8).

Those jobs which have emerged have been concentrated in the areas of banking, health care, and education. Because these sectors export their services (Giarratani and Houston 1986:21), the city has been able to insulate itself to some extent from the troubles of its region. Nonetheless, the lag in the creation of new jobs, Pittsburgh's comparatively high unemployment rate in the recession year of 1982, and its population decline all indicate that the city of Pittsburgh is restructuring in a context of decline rather than of growth (U.S. Bureau of the Census, *County and City Data Book*, 1983).

In the aggregate, Pittsburgh, if compared with other declining cities, has coped well with economic change. The loss of manufacturing employment, coupled with steady population decline, has not led to fiscal crises; the city is certainly better off than its milltown suburbs, and its downtown has flourished since 1981. Louise Jezierski, in comparing Pittsburgh with Cleveland, concludes that "Pittsburgh is making a more successful transition to a service economy, and has been able to maintain a better educated, middle-class workforce than is Cleveland" (Jezierski 1987b:9).

The Politics of Redevelopment

Pittsburgh's city government has encouraged real estate redevelopment for forty years and is now encouraging the development of new advanced technology industries and a diversified economic base. Although its redevelopment efforts are internationally renowned, they have also aroused intense controversy and political conflict.

In particular, economic development policies involving the redevelopment of land have faced bitter opposition from neighborhood organizations. By contrast, economic development policies aimed at economic diversification have aroused relatively little opposition. They are not controversial, even though they affect the city's social structure as a result of their impact on the distribution of employment. Thus, intense political conflict in Pittsburgh is far more common over issues of territory than over issues related to the nature and social consequences of the city's future economic base. The process or urban renewal was conflictual, but the transformation of the city's occupational structure aroused little notice.

Neighborhood Organizations

The political discourse about economic development in Pittsburgh, when compared with similar discourse in many other cities, is more pragmatic and open to compromise and accommodation. That is so at least partly because the politics of economic development incorporate the political changes wrought by the previous politics of urban renewal. Two such changes are noteworthy. First, neighborhood organizations, as a result of the victories they achieved during the controversies over urban renewal, are significantly involved in economic development policymaking. Although the two largest black neighborhoods have not fared well, as we shall see, neighborhood activists by and large have been incorporated into the city's routine political life. Since such incorporation occurred relatively early in Pittsburgh, neighborhood representatives and various elites have not confronted each other long enough to develop unyielding and ideologically defined postures.

Second, the 1970s were marked by a relative absence of redevelopment and a weakening of the public-private partnership. Paradoxically, that absence dramatized both the costs and the benefits of redevelopment. Neighborhood organizations began to realize that development did have benefits as well as costs, whereas the private-sector members of the partnership were forced to acknowledge the mistakes and costs of the development carried out in the two previous decades. The 1970s were therefore sobering for both camps. By the late 1970s, when a new mayor simultaneously revitalized the partnership and redevelopment, the political dynamics of redevelopment had changed. Thus, although the politics of economic development has been shaped by the politics of urban renewal, the two are different.

Neighborhoods and the "Renaissance." The public-private partnership that oversaw Renaissance I, the first postwar period of redevelopment, ignored neighborhood concerns. The partnership was dominated by the mayor, David Lawrence, elected in 1945, and Richard King Mellon, the most important businessman in the city. Although it has changed, the partnership they created is still a significant actor in 1988.

Lawrence, the state chairman of the Democratic party, the boss of the Pittsburgh political organization or machine, mayor of Pittsburgh for four terms, and eventually governor of Pennsylvania, made redevelopment of the city's downtown his top priority. And Mellon's "decision to rebuild rather than abandon Pittsburgh" was the partnership's keystone (Lubove 1969:107). Organized labor was not asked and did not ask to participate in the partnership. Having failed to define its interests as being directly affected by the physical redevelopment of downtown, it left public policy decisions in Lawrence's hands.

The Allegheny Conference on Community Development, organized in 1943 as a result of Mellon's initiative, became the private sector's organizational actor in the partnership. The Allegheny Conference paid experts to draw detailed plans for redevelopment, which the public sector then reacted to, usually indicating its acceptance (Lubove 1969).

The public sector's own organizational arm was established by Lawrence in 1946. The Urban Redevelopment Authority has been and still is the key public-sector actor in the implementation of redevelopment policy; it is now charged with all public-sector activity in the areas of both housing and economic development. The mayor appoints all five members of the URA's governing board. Lawrence's legacy is still influential. The current chairman of the board had been Lawrence's executive secretary and was appointed by Lawrence as the URA's first executive director; Lawrence's grandson was appointed the URA's executive director in 1987.

Joseph Barr, Lawrence's handpicked successor as mayor, served from 1959 to 1969. Although his administration continued the physical redevelopment of the Lawrence years, it was much more sensitive to the social issues that marked the urban crisis of the 1960s (Coleman 1983). Nonetheless, neighborhood activists felt Barr gave professional planners who were insensitive to the needs of neighborhoods too much discretion (Coleman 1983) and that downtown redevelopment was given too high a priority. The Allegheny Conference did not respond to Pittsburgh's racial and social crisis until the appointment in 1968 of a new executive director who was concerned with social issues. (Robert Pease, as of 1989, continues as the conference's executive director.)

In fact, the routines of land redevelopment under Barr proceeded much as they had under Lawrence. Although the URA became more concerned with relocating displaced families, the emphasis on clearing neighborhoods largely remained. In response, however, neighborhoods organized to stop urban renewal projects or to change their focus from clearance to rehabilitation. Neighborhood groups learned the routines of organizing, protest, confrontation, and lawsuits. These groups began to have an effect; there are indications that, at the end of the Barr administration, the very planners and lawyers involved with redevelopment began to doubt their previously held assumptions about renewal.

In 1969, neighborhoods found an unexpected political champion. Peter Flaherty, a loyal member of the Democratic machine and Barr's heir apparent, broke with the machine and ran for mayor without the endorsement of the party. His campaign stressed his lack of ties to labor, business, and the party, and promised that neighborhood interests, rather than those of downtown, would be heeded (Stewman and Tarr 1982:89). He won easily.

The Flaherty administration emphasized fiscal soundness and an efficient city administration as well as neighborhood interests. He cut back city employment (by 27 percent over seven years), partly to save money and partly to end the flamboyant patronage practices that had reinforced the party organization's power (Stewman and Tarr 1982:91; Clark and Ferguson 1983:194). Flaherty did not view local government as an active, interventionist force either in social welfare matters or in downtown development. His policies and rhetoric were designed to minimize the cost of government and to increase its efficiency rather than to expand its role (Clark and Ferguson 1983:198–203). At a time when other cities were expanding social programs and increasing city expenditures, employment, and their dependency on the federal government, Flaherty did the opposite (Clark and Ferguson 1983:201).

Flaherty *was* concerned with neighborhoods rather than with the central business district, which had been the partnership's traditional focus. In fact, the legitimacy and institutionalized access that neighborhoods gained during his administration are Flaherty's most important legacy in the area of development. Rather than spending all federal moneys downtown, Flaherty allocated half to neighborhoods. He established a home improvement loan program and gave high priority to parks and recreation (Stewman and Tarr 1982:93). Flaherty diminished the power of the URA, which he viewed as antithetical to neighborhood interests, and reorganized the city planning department so as to institutionalize access by neighborhood groups. He *forced* the planning bureaucracy to act on neighborhood concerns. He clearly put neighborhoods in the center of the policymaking process.

The partnership was sickly when Flaherty left Pittsburgh in 1977 to join the Carter administration. Although his relations with the Allegheny Conference improved during his second term, Flaherty largely alienated it. He had not balanced his commitment to neighborhoods with a commitment to the partnership.

His successor, Richard Caliguiri, campaigned on the slogan "It's another Renaissance." He revitalized the partnership and encouraged major investments in the downtown area. However, Caliguiri's economic development policy, unlike Lawrence's, included neighborhoods as well as downtown. In fact, on November 15, 1987, Caliguiri admitted that he worked "a lot closer with . . . community organizations than I do with the business organizations" (Piechowiak and Perlmutter 1987:A12).

Caliguiri did indeed allocate a large portion of the federal funds received to neighborhoods: in the early 1980s, neighborhoods received 75 percent and downtown received 25 percent (Stewman and Tarr 1982:96). Almost 75 percent of the city's capital expenditures planned for 1986–1991 are allocated to neighborhoods. Housing and infrastructure development within neighborhoods have received priority. In 1985, Pittsburgh received $19 million in Community Development Block Grant funds, and most of those dollars have been allocated to housing and neighborhood economic development (Ahlbrandt 1986:127).

Urban Development Action Grants (UDAGs) have also been extremely important to the city's redevelopment efforts. Because tax abatements have been comparatively miserly, federal funds have allowed redevelopment to proceed without imposing a heavy burden on the city's taxpayers. In fact, Pittsburgh ranked fourth in the nation in the amount of UDAG funds received from April 1978 to June 1984. Such funds were given in the form of a relatively few large grants. Whereas Chicago received forty-one grants for a total of $77.6 million in that period, for example, Pittsburgh received eleven grants for $63.6 million in those years (Marks 1984:1514).

Large UDAGs were used to help finance the downtown portion of

Renaissance II; smaller ones were used in conjunction with other moneys for housing in neighborhoods. For example, the city used an $8 million UDAG, Community Development Block Grant funds, and proceeds from selling $23 million in municipal (mortgage) bonds to help stabilize six neighborhoods on the city's North Side (Ahlbrandt 1986:130).

The legitimacy of neighborhoods has led to city policies encouraging neighborhood economic development. The city, in conjunction with national and local foundations, has both encouraged and helped create community development corporations. Five such CDCs have become so visible and active that they are dominating the neighborhood agenda; economic development rather than provision of social services or advocacy is now viewed as the neighborhood issue deserving of highest priority.

This process has been helped by the switch in the focus of their neighborhood role by key community activists to a focus on economic development. One interviewee who has worked with various types of community-based organizations commented, "Talent is now channeled into development; we've lost the ability to be good organizers. We're all on the gravy train." The emphasis on economic development is so great that one key member of the establishment, viewed by neighborhood representatives as an advocate of downtown development, said he was "worried by the lack of advocacy" and the almost total absorption of neighborhood groups in economic development.

Whatever the costs and benefits to neighborhoods of an emphasis on economic development, it is clear that neighborhood organizations are very active in such redevelopment. It is also clear, however, that thus far the CDCs have tended to focus on real estate development (neighborhood housing and revitalization of commercial districts) rather than on identifying and assisting potential entrepreneurs. They tend to assume that real estate activity will stimulate economic activity and job creation. Partly because of their territorial focus, they have not become active in articulating how neighborhood programs should fit into citywide economic development efforts. Finally, CDCs face the problem that their economic development efforts, even if successful, may help increase the aggregate wealth of their neighborhoods (by increasing the level of economic activity) but will not necessarily help the poor, the unskilled, or manual workers.

The problems associated with the substance of their activities should not obscure the key role neighborhood groups play in making decisions that directly affect their respective neighborhoods. Clearly, organization is the key variable explaining both why neighborhood groups, excluded from the partnership in 1945, are now such legitimate actors in the politics of redevelopment and why they have received significant amounts of public money. Their participation in redevelopment policy has not alienated the private-sector members of the partnership from the mayor, however. Since the late 1970s, Pittsburgh's city government has been able to respond to neighborhood organizations while actively participating in a public-private partnership to which it is very much committed.

The Black Community

The black community in Pittsburgh constitutes 25 percent of the city's population and 22 percent of its electorate. Yet it has not been a participant in Pittsburgh's public-private partnership, nor has it achieved the kind of political access and legitimacy enjoyed by neighborhood organizations, nor has it received substantial benefits from economic development policy. It is treated more with indifference than with hostility. The reasons for the community's lack of success are complex, but they point out the interdependence between the incentives offered black community activists by the political system, on the one hand, and the internal political dynamics of the black community on the other.

The black community has not been completely excluded from the benefits of economic development. One predominantly black neighborhood has received substantial amounts of public money; moreover, small businessmen have received some assistance, and real estate redevelopment has improved housing in a number of black areas. Nonetheless, in the aggregate, conditions within the black community are so poor that the benefits of economic development policy have clearly not significantly helped that community. The statistics on black infant mortality and unemployment, for example, are noteworthy.

In 1982, black infant mortality rates in the city were the highest in the country (Health and Welfare Planning Association 1985:35). A report issued in December 1985 succinctly summarized the data concerning the relative level of Pittsburgh's black infant mortality rate:

> Pittsburgh has an extremely high infant mortality rate. . . . Three times between 1970 and 1982, the City had a higher rate than eleven other cities with populations of 500,000 or more. In the same period, Pittsburgh was one of the three worst cities eight times. The ratio of non-white to white infant mortality is startling, about 2.4 to 1. From a national perspective, the white infant mortality rate in the city is similar to that reported in other urban areas. Relative to urban areas of comparable size, black Pittsburgh babies die in excess numbers. (*Report of the Mayor's Consortium* 1985:4,6)

The mortality rate reflects other problems. In 1984, Pittsburgh ranked second on the list of the ten metropolitan areas with the highest rate of black unemployment. The Pittsburgh metropolitan area had 26.8 percent black unemployment compared with 7.6 percent white unemployment. The comparable figures for the Chicago metropolitan area were 21.4 percent and 6.2 percent; those for the Cleveland metropolitan area were 18.8 percent and 7.2 percent. First-ranked Detroit's metropolitan area had 28.1 percent black unemployment compared with 7.6 percent white unemployment (Hopey 1985:C1).

In 1986, black unemployment in the city of Pittsburgh was 19.7 percent (roughly equal to the 1985 figure), compared with 3.8 percent for whites. Whereas white males had a relatively low (4.3 percent) unemployment rate, the rate for black males was 24.3 percent. Rates for black females showed less divergence from those for white females—their respective unemployment rates were 3.1 percent and 15.1 percent (Commonwealth of Pennsylvania data). The figures for young black males are even more drastic than those for white youths. In 1983, 55 percent of black males aged 16–21 who were not in school were unemployed; the comparable rate for whites was 27 percent (Health and Welfare Planning Association 1985:34).

Finally, the labor force participation rate for blacks in the Pittsburgh metropolitan area is very low. In 1980, the national black participation rate was 59.2 percent (compared with 62.2 percent for whites); the black participation rate in Pittsburgh was 52.8 percent (compared with 57.2 percent for whites). The metropolitan areas of Atlanta (with 64.2 percent) and Cleveland (with 59 percent) had much higher black labor force participation rates than did the metropolitan area of Pittsburgh (Health and Welfare Planning Association 1985:18).

Clearly, the black community in the aggregate has not shared in the economic benefits flowing from Pittsburgh's redevelopment policies. In December 1985, after the *The Places Rated Almanac* had identified the Pittsburgh metropolitan area as the "most liveable" in the United States, a report to the mayor concluded that "what we have here is a tale of two cities: one ranked number one for quality of life and the other number two for rate of black unemployment" (*Report of the Mayor's Consortium* 1985:9).

The city government has not been completely inattentive to the black community. It requires a 10–15 percent "set-aside" for minority contracts for large projects receiving public moneys. Although monitoring has not been extremely careful, one major project receiving a $20 million UDAG was required to meet a 10 percent set-aside but reached the goal of 15 percent. The school board (with a black president) aggressively monitors its 15 percent set-aside requirements. Furthermore, most large projects are required to hire 50 percent of their nonsupervisory entry-level employees from those referred by the Employment and Training Division of the city's Department of Personnel and Civil Service; many of those referred are black. Business views this requirement as onerous; one economic development official stated that "we lose a lot of clients because of that requirement." The economic development division of the URA is encouraging entrepreneurial activity in the black community and is currently formulating an innovative program to create a venture capital fund that would help black firms participate in set-aside programs. Yet these requirements and efforts have not been sufficient to improve the relative status of Pittsburgh's black community.

The reasons are obviously complex. The decline of traditional manufacturing has hurt black workers more than white workers, for blacks are more heavily concentrated in manufacturing. Whatever the sociological explanations for the comparative severity of the problems faced by Pittsburgh's black community, its lack of political power reinforces the strength of social trends.

Black Politics. One of the ironies of black politics in Pittsburgh is that the very success of neighborhood organizations, territorially organized by definition, makes it more difficult for the black community as a whole to organize along racial lines. Racial and neighborhood politics can be compatible if the vast majority of black residents live in black neighborhoods that are both contiguous and internally cohesive. However, such is not Pittsburgh's political geography.

First, the black population is more dispersed in Pittsburgh than in many other cities, and black electoral power is therefore relatively difficult to organize. The five wards with black ward chairmen comprise only 54 percent of the city's black voters; another 34 percent are scattered among twenty-seven districts in the other wards (Fuller 1986:A6). Furthermore, although segregation occurs *within* neighborhood boundaries, neighborhood organizations, with a few glaring exceptions, tend to define their scope by territorial rather than by racial boundaries. Community development corporations, for example, reinforce neighborhood rather than racial identity.

Second, overwhelmingly black neighborhoods—those that consist primarily of public housing as well as those that do not—are not contiguous but are scattered throughout the city. The fact that Pittsburgh has no equivalent of Chicago's South Side has political consequences in that issues that could be defined in racial terms are much more likely to be defined territorially. Identification with neighborhood, even in overwhelmingly black neighborhoods, is more easily achieved than is identification with the larger, citywide black community.

The two largest black neighborhoods are eternally fragmented rather than cohesive. They are thus unable to "play the game" played by white neighborhoods; the access to city government won by neighborhoods is effective for any specific neighborhood only if that neighborhood is not torn by competing organizations. Thus, although neighborhoods in the aggregate benefit from their access to city government, the two largest black neighborhoods do not benefit as much as the aggregate figures would suggest.

In sum, Pittsburgh's black community is not a significant political force. The black vice chairman of the URA and dean of the School of Social Work at the University of Pittsburgh concluded that "presently, we're politically impotent. Blacks aren't in positions where they can help shape and make decisions. I don't believe the (white) political leadership is antiblack. I believe the political leadership just doesn't see us on the agenda" (quoted in Fuller 1986:A1). The city government, therefore, has not been forced to balance the commitment to the partnership with commitments to the black community.

Between 1953 and 1985, black council members were always chosen as candidates by the party organization; the council had either one or two black council members (out of a total of nine). In 1985, the party refused to endorse a black candidate and one was not elected. After the election of an all-white City Council, many argued that the question of black political power was primarily one of representation. In 1987, the endorsed black candidate won the election even though he was hospitalized throughout the campaign.

Because of the pressure of a lawsuit charging that the system of citywide elections discriminated against blacks, a referendum was held in 1987 to ascertain whether voters approved switching to a system of district elections. Voters did approve, and at the time of writing, various proposals for defining voting districts are being discussed.

The proposal to establish a system of district elections did not receive the unanimous support of the black political elite. The NAACP's executive board, for example, opposed the proposal until pressure from NAACP members forced it to reverse its position (Carter 1987:B1). The division over district elections is not surprising, for the numerous cleavages in Pittsburgh's black community run deep. A newspaper story reporting the results of a two-hour forum that brought together blacks holding influential positions began with the comment that "even casual observers of the black political scene in Pittsburgh have wondered whether representatives of its diverse interests could sit at the same table long enough to exchange concerns" (Byrd et al. 1986:A6).

The most obvious division is that of neighborhood. Black politicians have not always supported each other. The withholding of the Democratic party's endorsement in 1985 of the incumbent black councilman was preceded by lack of support from key black ward chairmen. A subsequent meeting between the incumbent, the black chairmen, and the NAACP president, called in order to construct a strategy to unify black primary voters behind the incumbent, broke up amid chair-throwing and vitriolic recriminations. The black chairmen decided they would rather have an all-white City Council than support the incumbent (Fuller 1986:A6).

Divisions are also deep within the two most heavily populated black neighborhoods. Such divisions help account for the fact that although neighborhoods in the aggregate have achieved many of their goals, black neighborhoods have not. Organizational rivalries have made it difficult for Community Development Corporations in both neighborhoods to mobilize support. Because various black "influentials" with a base in the neighborhood were able, in the words of one person, "to knock heads together" and override competing organizations, one of the two neighborhoods now does have a CDC that seems to be having some success. No one has yet been able to do that in the black neighborhood adjacent to downtown, however. Therefore, two CDCs, referred to as CDC (I) and CDC (II), exist in that neighborhood. Until the factions active in the neighborhood can be submerged, agreement on substantive proposals for economic development is unlikely.

Some proponents of district elections hope that factions within the black community will be less powerful if all competing leaders within a district must deal with a black council member elected from that district. In essence, the council member's control over the flow of government benefits will enable him to mediate between competing organizations and effect some kind of organizational coordination.

If district elections do indeed introduce a dynamic that leads to greater cohesion within at least those electoral districts with a substantial black electorate, the black community will then be in a better position than it is now to pressure city government to increase the benefits it is entitled to receive from economic development policy. The black electorate has recently participated much more actively in local elections, and district elections may indeed provide a way for neighborhood and racial issues to reinforce each other so that in the medium term the black community may become a more significant political force. Until now, however, the city government has felt relatively little pressure from the black community to balance its commitment to the public-private partnership with a commitment to improve the social conditions of the black community as a whole.

Organized Labor

Manufacturing workers, and the unions that represent them, are tied to the regional rather than to the city economy. The Pittsburgh city government is not very important to organized labor, both because the manufacturing sector is regional in scope and because by 1980, manufacturing accounted for less than 15 percent of total city employment. The public-private partnership is similarly not of direct relevance because even though some of its corporate members are important actors in the regional economy, its focus is citywide rather than regional.

The gradual nature of job loss in manufacturing in the city (the proportion of the labor force employed in manufacturing declined 6 percent in each of the two decades between 1960 and 1980) militated against activism over the issue of job loss. In fact, the loss of manufacturing jobs did not become a political issue until late 1982, when a coalition of unions, neighborhood groups, and churches formed the Save Nabisco Action Coalition and succeeded in keeping open a still profitable Nabisco bakery employing 650 workers. The coalition then lobbied for a plant closing notification bill, which was passed by the City Council; the mayor vetoed it and his decision was upheld in court. The corporate members of the partnership were strongly against the notification bill, and it is likely that had the mayor approved it, his relations with the partnership would have suffered. The threat that the coalition would force a confrontation between labor and the partnership never materialized. By 1985, the organization had ceased to be politically significant (Jezierski 1987a).

Sustained activism within the city was unlikely given the lack of regional activism. Two factors dampened regional mobilization against job loss even though 66,000 jobs related to the steel industry alone (88,000 manufacturing jobs in all) disappeared between 1979 and 1983. First, most steelworkers, accustomed to the cyclical nature of the industry, refused to believe that the downturn that began in 1979 represented secular decline. Second, the United Steelworkers Union played a problematic role. Intraunion politics had diminished the union's effectiveness. As one activist put it, "My local, one of the biggest in Western Pennsylvania, was a dissident local within the union. We thought McBride [the USW's president] and his men were a bunch of thugs." Ideas for retaining the manufacturing base in the Pittsburgh region were not accepted by the union's leadership, resulting in a stalemate. It was not "until McBride died, and Lynn Williams, to his credit, made a tentative peace with us that the leadership and various locals started working together."

Clergy and individual union members, rather than a labor union with resources, took the lead in protesting the decline of steel employment and the disinvestment perceived to be the root cause of such decline. However, the various protest organizations quickly split over the use of tactics. One group, The Denominational Ministry Strategy, chose dramatic confrontation; some of its members threw skunk water on corporate executives' children attending a church Christmas party (Paris 1984:1). Public reaction to the skunk water incident was so negative that all protest activity became suspect.

In this context, an Ohio-based organization, Tri-State Conference on Steel, began trying to persuade local officials in the region's steel towns to take economic development into their own hands. It suggested that municipalities join together to form a Steel Valley Authority, a special-purpose governmental unit that could exercise the right of eminent domain to reopen closed steel plants under local auspices, and issue tax-exempt bonds.

Organizers for Tri-State found that the furor over DMS impeded their efforts. They had to convince local officials that they were neither affiliated with the Denominational Ministry Strategy nor proposing confrontation and that the creation of such an authority was a feasible option. Persuasion literally took years, for many officials held the view that "economic development is not our responsibility."

In the city, an initially skeptical Mayor Richard Caligiuri (who died in 1988) gradually became convinced that a regional manufacturing base had to be maintained and that the public sector should be involved. He became a very strong supporter of the authority and lobbied suspicious local officials in various milltowns to support it. One organizer employed by Tri-State was so appreciative of the mayor's support that he concluded, "If all the steel plants in the region were in the city instead, we'd be in great shape."

In January 1986, the Steel Valley Authority was officially incorporated. Nine municipalities, including the city of Pittsburgh, are represented on its board. Its creation has been a triumph of organizing among extremely skeptical and wary local officials. Now the authority faces the problem of how to fund its proposed activities and is lobbying for state funds. Its future is still problematic.

Neither partnerships nor governments have addressed the problems raised by labor markets unrestricted by governmental boundaries. Labor activists have therefore striven for the creation of a *regional* governmental body that could focus its attention on some of the steel industry's problems. Labor in essence has had to design and create an institution that can relate the jurisdiction of government to the scope of labor markets. It has had to create a governmental unit so that it can eventually benefit from economic policy.

Mayor Caligiuri did not support city policies that would threaten his standing within the partnership, but he did actively support labor's regional demands. Such support was fairly costless for him because such demands do not run counter to the partnership's citywide thrust.

Conclusion

All forms of governance are limited with regard to what they can accomplish. The Pittsburgh experience may illustrate the limits—as well as the potential opportunities—intrinsic to governance by public-private partnership. Although the public sector in Pittsburgh is not as much a "junior partner" as it is in many other cities, the partnership did not address the investment decisions made by the private sector. Even a comparatively strong public sector working within the constraints of a public-private partnership could not protect Pittsburgh, and especially its surrounding region, from either economic restructuring or its attendant costs. Simply put, the partnership had not been designed to respond to the forces that shaped the rustbelt. That is the partnership's most serious limitation as a form of governance in times of industrial decline, restructuring, and diversification.

Nonetheless, the Pittsburgh experience also suggests the opportunities that the public sector can create and use while being active within a partnership. Pittsburgh's experience suggests that local officials can, under certain conditions, be responsive both to a public-private partnership and to groups that are not members of such a partnership. The patterns identified in this chapter are very much shaped by the longevity of the city's partnership arrangement. The city's balancing of neighborhood organizations and the partnership, for example, is only a decade old—but it is the culmination of the thirty years of experience that preceded that decade. Although the balancing act is not necessarily a permanent feature of Pittsburgh politics, its very existence tells us that various actors in the city were able to reach some kind of consensus. Their positions are not intrinsically irreconcilable.

Local government in Pittsburgh may be able to achieve a balance simply because the groups that have organized are territorially based (neighborhood organizations) or are concerned with economic trends largely outside the city (labor organizations). Whether the city can hold the partnership together while responding substantively to the demands of an organized black community is unclear. As long as urban renewal is not the issue, it may be easier to balance downturn and neighborhood interests, both of which are territorial, than it is to balance the demands for economic growth in the aggregate made by a partnership with demands aimed at improving the economic conditions of the black community.

The Pittsburgh experience provides a useful referent, but it is also a cautionary tale that should be heeded by those who wish to minimize the costs associated with economic development. Local government in Pittsburgh, even when actively participating in an urban partnership, can encourage economic development in neighborhoods. It can also be responsive to certain kinds of demands from spokesmen for manufacturing workers. Whether its economic development policy can provide the kinds of response, translated into substantive benefits, needed by the black community, however, is still very uncertain.

Note

I thank my colleagues at the University of Pittsburgh, who read an earlier draft, for their constructive criticisms and helpful suggestions. All matters of interpretation are mine alone. I also thank Anne Hileman for her research assistance.

References

Ahlbrandt, Roger S. 1986. "Public-Private Partnerships for Neighborhood Renewal." *Annals of the American Academy of Political and Social Science* (November):120–134.

Byrd, Jerry, Jean Bryant, and Alton Fuller. 1986. "Black Agenda Aired at Forum." *Pittsburgh Press* (October 28):A6.

Carter, Kevin L. 1987. "NAACP Members Vote for District Elections." *Pittsburgh Press* (March 11):B1.

Clark, Terry, and Lorna Crowley Ferguson. 1983. *City Money: Political Processes, Fiscal Strain, and Retrenchment.* New York: Columbia University Press.

Coleman, Morton. 1983. "Interest Intermediation and Local Urban Development." Ph.D. dissertation, University of Pittsburgh.

Commonwealth of Pennsylvania. Department of Labor and Industries. Office of Employment Security, Pittsburgh Office 1986. Unpublished unemployment data.

Federal Reserve Bank of Cleveland. 1986. *Annual Report*.

Fontana, Richard F. 1983. "SNAC becomes a Fighting Advocacy Group." *Pittsburgh Post-Gazette* (August 10):1.

Fuller, Alton. 1986. "Powerless Politics: Blacks Evaluate Strategies after Setbacks in City Government." *Pittsburgh Press* (October 27):A1.

Giarratani, Frank, and David B. Houston. 1986. "Economic Change in the Pittsburgh Region." Unpublished manuscript.

Health and Welfare Planning Association. 1985. *Toward Tomorrow: An Environmental Scan for the United Way of Allegheny County.*

Hopey, Don. 1985. "Out-of-Work Woes: Unemployment Curse Haunts Blacks." *Pittsburgh Press* (October 22):C1, C16.

Jezierski, Louise (1987a). "Neighborhoods and Public-Private Partnerships in Pittsburgh." Unpublished paper.

————. (1987b). "Political Limits to Development in Two Declining Cities: Cleveland and Pittsburgh." Paper presented at the annual conference of the Southwestern Political Science Association.

Lubove, Roy. 1969. *Twentieth-Century Pittsburgh: Government, Business, and Environmental Change.* New York: Wiley.

Marks, Marilyn. 1984. "The New Urban Agenda: The Focus Is on Helping Cities Help Themselves." *National Journal* (August 11), pp. 1513–1516.

Paris, Barry. 1984. "Church Diners 'Bombed' with Skunk Water." *Pittsburgh Post-Gazette* (December 17):1.

Piechowiak, Cynthia, and Ellen M. Perlmutter. 1987. "Region's Fast Change Challenges Old-Boy Network." *Pittsburgh Press* (November 15):1.

Report of the Mayor's Consortium to Improve Pregnancy Outcomes. 1985. (December).

Stewman, Shelby, and Joel A. Tarr. 1982. "Four Decades of Public-Private Partnerships in Pittsburgh." In *Public-Private Partnerships in American Cities: Seven Case Studies,* ed. R. Scott Fosler and Renee A. Berger. Lexington, Mass.: D. C. Heath.

U.S. Bureau of the Census. 1983. *County and City Data Book.*

Dennis Keating
Norman Krumholz
John Metzger

7. Cleveland: Post-Populist Public-Private Partnerships

Cleveland, Ohio, has been cited as an outstanding example of the use of public-private partnerships to promote urban revitalization in the 1980s. As a Midwestern rustbelt city with a declining population, continuing losses of manufacturing employment, and strong racial divisions, Cleveland has faced very serious economic and social problems since World War II. Recently, Cleveland has been hailed as a "comeback" city (*Time* 1980; Methvin 1983).

Under the leadership of conservative Mayor George Voinovich, who represents the reaction to a brief and turbulent period of urban populism under former Mayor Dennis Kucinich, the city has relied heavily upon the private sector (corporate and philanthropic) for leadership and financial support for urban redevelopment programs. Representatives of these interests have played a leading and, at times, decisive role in determining public policy. This has resulted in the initiation of major redevelopment projects, privately controlled and often publicly subsidized. The city's major focus has been on the redevelopment of its downtown, or central business district. This approach is similar to that of the city's urban renewal policies of the late 1950s and 1960s. Massive land clearance projects were aimed primarily at the private commercial redevelopment of downtown Cleveland. Both eras of public-private partnerships have assumed a benevolent operation of the trickle down theory of urban economic growth, which predicts that private downtown development creating jobs and increasing the tax base will at least indirectly benefit the rest of the city.

In this chapter we will argue that the emphasis on public-private partnerships during the administrations of President Ronald Reagan (1981–1988) and Cleveland Mayor George Voinovich (1979–1989) has resulted in an imbalanced development strategy for Cleveland. Downtown development has overshadowed the redevelopment of the city's neighborhoods. Although neighborhood-based development groups have received considerable assistance from the city and from private corporations and

121

foundations, this assistance has not been commensurate with that provided for major downtown development projects. The political influence of neighborhood nonprofit development groups is not nearly equal to that of their for-profit counterparts, which exert much more influence at City Hall.

The Decline of Cleveland's Economy, Downtown and in the Neighborhoods

Public-private partnerships are hardly an innovation in Cleveland. Like most U.S. cities, Cleveland embarked upon a major post–World War II urban renewal program, which was supported by the city's corporate leadership.

The vehicle they used to promote Cleveland's urban renewal program was the nonprofit development foundation. The first of these foundations, created in 1954, was the Cleveland Development Foundation, which helped the city's Urban Renewal Department prepare plans and programs for early Title I projects, including the St. Vincent's and Gladstone projects. In 1960, a second development foundation called the University Circle Development Foundation (later University Circle, Inc.) was established. Its purpose was to protect the medical, cultural, and educational institutions of the University Circle area, which were threatened by an enveloping black ghetto. Foundation consultants produced the University-Euclid renewal plan, which was then executed by the city.

Cleveland's urban renewal program was similar to that of most U.S. cities; it was run by a coalition of business and political leaders. The costs were not equally shared; they fell most heavily on the minority poor. Moreover, the city admittedly cut back on police, fire, and other services in designated urban renewal areas. In many projects, housing for poor blacks was demolished and replaced by institutional and commercial development. An estimated 1,780 poor and black families were displaced from the St. Vincent's project alone, and no replacement housing was constructed, nor was relocation assistance provided. Instead, a hospital and community college were built on the cleared land. The Kerner Commission cited such treatment as one reason for the racial riots that erupted in the Hough neighborhood in 1966 (*Report of the National Advisory Commission on Civil Disorders* 1968).

There are two differences that distinguished Cleveland's urban renewal efforts from those of most other cities, however. First, the city's program was controlled by the City Council, not by an autonomous urban renewal authority. This meant a slow process, for council members from

Cleveland's thirty-three wards negotiated or disputed the elements of various plans. The slow pace of redevelopment is exemplified by the Erieview urban renewal project, Cleveland's key downtown redevelopment project. Although this $45 million project is rated a success by most observers, many parcels that were cleared in the early 1960s still remained in 1987.

Second, Cleveland's program was wildly ambitious. It was assumed that if land were assembled in large parcels, titles cleared, and costs written down, a market would exist for an unlimited amount of land in the city. As a result, the city designated 6,060 acres of land (one-eighth of all the land in the entire city) for clearance. Unfortunately, urban renewal promoters were to be disappointed. The market proved unable to absorb even a fraction of that amount and, in 1967, the federal government suspended the city from further urban renewal assistance until it could better implement its program.

Cleveland found that urban renewal did not revive its downtown or stem the tide of suburbanization. Instead, the city experienced a steady loss of population and employment and an erosion of its tax base—what has been termed a "growth crisis" (Swanstrom 1985:Chap. 3).

The recent growth of downtown corporate and financial service employment and the creation of a new entertainment district in the formerly industrial Flats have not yet changed the overall economic picture in Cleveland. Like most other older, industrial cities in the Northeast and Midwest, Cleveland has experienced population loss, waves of manufacturing plant closings, rising unemployment and poverty, and the growing deterioration of an aging housing stock. Cleveland's population decreased by 177,081 during the 1970s, a drop of 24 percent. The city projects continued population decline through the year 2000, with the loss ranging from 42,000 to 101,000, depending upon various factors. Cleveland's traditional economic base of manufacturing industries has eroded significantly since World War II. Manufacturing employment in the city declined by 59 percent between 1947 and 1982. Service industry employment, nearly one-third of which is located downtown, has picked up some of the slack, although the new jobs created in this category have either been in highly skilled business and professional-technical services or in low-paying personal and support services (Bier 1987; Cambridge Systematics 1987; Fogarty 1987). Since 1980, Cleveland's poverty rate has increased by more than one-third; as of July 1986, it was 35 percent. More than 65 percent of the population of three black neighborhoods on the East Side is in poverty (Council for Economic Opportunities in Greater Cleveland 1987).

Growing poverty rates, combined with deteriorating housing conditions, have created a housing crisis in many Cleveland neighborhoods. An exterior conditions survey by the Cuyahoga County Regional Planning Commission in 1984–1985 identified 24,000 substandard one-to-four-unit structures in Cleveland, representing 19 percent of the total stock. The city's Department of Community Development estimates that nearly one-third of the housing stock is substandard if interior conditions are also considered. Much of the city's public housing is substandard and several thousand units are vacant despite long waiting lists. The estimated cost of repair is $140 million.

Much of the Cuyahoga Metropolitan Housing Authority housing is close to downtown and close to or within the boundaries of several public-private partnerships. These partnerships, which include the Mid-Town Corridor, the St. Vincent's Quadrangle, the Warehouse District, and the Ohio City Redevelopment Association, are often considered models. The city's successful application to be named an All-American City by the National League of Cities featured the work of the Mid-Town Corridor. But the partnerships do not include public housing tenants on their boards or committees and they tend to ignore the needs of tenants and the housing authority's physical facilities in their planning; so does the city. In a typical case, the city is making a $3.5 million capital improvement expenditure for sidewalks, street trees, lighting, and infrastructure in the Warehouse District in the hope of attracting a new, upscale population to live in mostly vacant downtown warehouse lofts. But the city has not addressed the substantial capital improvement needs of the 800 families now living in the authority's Lakeview Terrace, west of the Warehouse District. Similarly, the St. Vincent's Quadrangle and Mid-Town Corridor partnerships virtually ignore the 4,000 housing authority units located near their boundaries.

Cleveland's public-private partnerships have not adequately addressed such systematic problems as the decline of manufacturing, the increase in poverty, and racism, which cloud the prospects for future redevelopment.

Cleveland's Power Structure

To understand the basis for the creation and use of public-private partnerships in Cleveland, it is necessary to understand the city's power structure and its interest and role in redevelopment. The power structure of Cleveland's banks, utilities, and industrial corporations has been and is a tightly knit business establishment whose activities have long been chronicled by historians. From about 1870 to the turn of the century, Cleveland was one of the most powerful industrial cities in the world; Cleveland industrialists such as Mark Hanna and John D. Rockefeller were figures of international importance.

Close business and banking relationships are reinforced by a pattern of social relationships. Almost all Cleveland banks and corporations have memberships at the exclusive Union Club, almost all are members of the Cleveland Growth Association, and almost all are members of the same country clubs. Their officers lead civic committees and occupy chairs on the distribution committees of Cleveland's large foundations, whose grants and contributions to the city and to the city's nonprofit corporations help set the public agenda. Their leadership in large public projects can be decisive.

As Mayor Kucinich found out, the power structure can exercise decisive influence regarding solution of important problems such as the city's financial default. Any discussion of the power structure in Cleveland would be incomplete without mention of the new players in the game and their agenda. The older banking and industrial elite generally favors conservative growth politics in which the city government is expected to play a passive role, merely providing basic services and keeping taxes low. Since the 1950s, however, a new group of service-sector business elites has emerged and has shaped public policies in favor of their substantial investments in the city's downtown. This group, made up of developers, property owners, and businessmen, favors liberal growth politics in which the city government is expected to play an active role in facilitating and providing subsidies (such as Urban Development Action Grants, or UDAGs) to further downtown development. Urban renewal, convention center and hotel development, entertainment attractions, modernization of infrastructure, and higher taxes to support better service are all part of this growth coalition's agenda. The group now dominates the development program of the city of Cleveland and the Cleveland Growth Association.

Another significant change has been the change of corporate leadership resulting from the takeover of Cleveland corporations by non-Cleveland and multinational groups (e.g., the 1987 takeover of Standard Oil of Ohio by British Petroleum and the 1988 announced sale of Higbee's, one of two major downtown department stores, to a national chain and developer Eddie DeBartolo).

The Cleveland Growth Association is Cleveland's renamed Chamber of Commerce. It functions as a civic booster (especially for the downtown); a promoter of development, tourism, and business subsidies; and a powerful representative of local business interests. In 1987 it had a budget of $4.2 million and a staff of eighty. The association has been an enthusiastic supporter of the public-private partnership concept. One of the most important recent examples of the association's role in such partnerships is its underwriting of much of the cost of the Voinovich administration's Civic Vision plan.

Cleveland Tomorrow, founded in 1982, is composed of the chief executive officers of forty-eight of Cleveland's major corporations. It has played a leading role in decision-making with regard to major policy issues affecting the city. It too has underwritten part of the Civic Vision planning process. In 1987, Cleveland Tomorrow was chosen to administer the Cleveland Neighborhood Partnership program, a new initiative to support neighborhood development. The program provided $1.1 million from four foundations and the city over two years to support six community development corporations (CDCs) chosen in a competition for funding. In January 1988, Cleveland Tomorrow announced proposals for redevelopment of both the downtown and the neighborhoods, to be promoted through nonprofit development corporations.

Cleveland's two major community foundations play a critical role in civic decision-making. In 1986, the Cleveland Foundation had assets of $427 million and distributed $22 million in grants. Its Distribution Committee is composed of leading corporate and civic leaders, headed by corporate attorney Richard Pogue. The foundation has been an active participant in virtually all major development decisions in Cleveland. It has provided substantial financial support for such projects as Playhouse Square and lakefront development and has also underwritten the Civic Vision plan. The Cleveland Foundation has provided generous support for Cleveland's neighborhood organizations. Since 1981, it has provided $2.2 million to individual CDCs. It has also supported the Center for Neighborhood Development at Cleveland State University, an organization that provides technical assistance, training, and research support for CDCs. Since its creation in 1979, the Cleveland Foundation has provided $435,000 to the center. The foundation has provided substantial support to the Cleveland Housing Network and the Cleveland Neighborhood Development Corporation. The former is a coalition of nine CDCs involved in housing; the latter is a citywide coalition of CDCs involved in commercial development. In 1987, the Cleveland Foundation announced that it was allocating $5 million for neighborhood development during the next several years.

The Gund Foundation has joined the Cleveland Foundation in most of these ventures. The Gund Foundation in 1986 had assets of $56 million and made grants totaling $8 million.

The third major source of funding for CDCs has been the Standard Oil Company of Ohio. In 1986 its Social Investment Fund contributed $270,000 to Cleveland CDCs, $250,000 to the Enterprise Foundation for support of CDCs, and additional funding to national organizations involved in neighborhood development.

The philanthropic contributions of these three funders has been supplemented by those of two national funders: the Local Initiatives Support Corporation and the Enterprise Foundation.

In 1987, Cleveland Tomorrow, the private funders, and representatives of neighborhood organizations joined forces to develop a comprehensive community development strategy. The purpose of this group was to coordinate funding for neighborhood development in Cleveland. A major question will be the degree to which neighborhood groups should have a role in the decision-making process, including the allocation of equity capital and the choice of which CDCs are to receive operating support.

A Downtown-Corporate Redevelopment Strategy

Cleveland's revitalization strategy has not been detailed in any written plan or program, although a new general land use plan called the "Civic Vision" was developed in the second half of the 1980s. Like the plans of many other central cities, Cleveland's general plan was very outdated. The city's previous general land use plan had been formulated in 1949. It reflected the expectation that Cleveland would continue to grow, even though Cleveland's postwar population decline was well under way. However, in 1974 the City Planning Commission did adopt a social policy plan that addressed the city's economic and social inequities (Krumholz 1975; 1982).

In November 1984, Mayor Voinovich announced that the city would develop the Civic Vision plan (*Planning* 1988). Prominence would be given to the downtown plan, to be financed by the Greater Cleveland Growth Association, Cleveland Tomorrow, the office building association, and the foundations. There was no delay in decisions concerning the award of UDAG grants and major development projects while the new general plan was being developed (although after the fanfare of the mayor's announcement in a City Club speech, development of the plan proceeded slowly). According to the City Planning Commission, "local business and civic leaders on the Downtown Plan Steering Committee will guide the planning process." In addition to the downtown plan, the Civic Vision plan was to include a citywide plan to provide a comprehensive and coordinated approach to land use, zoning, expenditure of the city's capital budget, and the use of Community Development Block Grant funds. The chairman of the Citywide Plan Steering Committee was the director of the Cleveland Housing Network. Three of the seventeen community representatives represented CDCs.

Although support has been given to neighborhood development groups, the city's main emphasis has been to encourage private development, primarily in the downtown area, and to provide all available subsidies—local, state and federal. Private developers have largely determined land use decisions.

Specific project development efforts now being made make clear the outlines of Cleveland's primary strategy—the redevelopment or maintenance of five areas: (1) downtown, (2) the riverfront and Flats, (3) a commercial-institutional corridor on the East Side, (4) a university-cultural center, and (5) housing and neighborhoods. With the exception of (5), virtually all the focus is on areas to the east of the Cuyahoga River.

Downtown is said to be the financial, administrative, and entertainment center of metropolitan Cleveland. The largest share of the city's resources and administrative energies is targeted at that area. New development plans for downtown include office, commercial, and entertainment facilities emphasizing a rehabilitated Playhouse Square, the largest theater restoration project in the United States. Planned facilities also include a commercial-recreational project on the lakefront modeled after Baltimore's Inner Harbor and possible redevelopment of the city-owned stadium and lakefront airport; a new domed stadium; a new Rock 'n Roll Hall of Fame; and Tower City, an expanded office-hotel-retailing center located above and integrated with the area's rapid transit system. New hotels are to be built in the vicinity of the newly refurbished Convention Center to allow Cleveland to aggressively compete for national convention business. New high-rise housing is to have high priority downtown in order to provide a somewhat permanent population, as well as a market for restaurants and entertainment facilities.

The Flats area along the Cuyahoga River is to be developed as a restaurant-bar-entertainment complex that will take advantage of its proximity to the waterfront. It is to draw its market from downtown and the entire region. The city hopes to develop upper-income housing in the Flats if possible, supplemented by selected redevelopment of commercial and recreational activities compatible with riverfront uses.

The Euclid Corridor, or Dual-Hub Corridor, runs from Public Square in the heart of downtown through Playhouse Square to University Circle, the metropolitan area's center of cultural, university, and medical services. City planning efforts here include the acquisition, clearance, and preparation of sites for entirely new industrial or commercial investment. The Dual-Hub Corridor may be the location of a proposed $700 million rail transit system that will tie downtown to University Circle.

University Circle, the eastern end of the corridor, is the home of the city's art and history museums, Case Western Reserve University, the Cleveland Orchestra, and several large medical complexes including the Cleveland Clinic, the city's largest employer. Plans for this area include the addition of new market rate housing and the expansion of these institutions.

Planning objectives for Cleveland's housing and neighborhoods include housing rehabilitation, new construction where possible, and promotion of neighborhood revitalization throughout the city. The activities of the city's many neighborhood-based, nonprofit housing development corporations are to be assisted by CDBG funds, state funds, and contributions from local and national foundations. Local corporations are also beginning to get involved in neighborhood-based development by providing financial and staff support for some of these neighborhood corporations.

Overall, in Cleveland, as in most large U.S. cities, the driving force shaping the city's investment policies and development plans is a downtown-corporate strategy. The city is to be transformed primarily into a corporate headquarters center, with banking, legal and professional support services. Although Cleveland is known throughout the world for its heavy industry and manufacture of durable goods, no emphasis is being placed on reindustrialization. Instead, the efforts are being directed toward developing commercial office buildings, hotels, and recreational and retail activities centered in the downtown area. The most active participant in developing this blueprint is a coalition of downtown developers, bankers, corporate executives, the political establishment, the media, and the private foundations.

Financing Public-Private Partnerships: Urban Development Action Grants and Tax Abatements

The key financial mechanism for implementing public-private partnerships in Cleveland during this era has been the Urban Development Action Grant (UDAG) program. Mayor George Voinovich's status as a leading Republican big-city mayor and his aggressive lobbying efforts have enabled Cleveland to enjoy a windfall of UDAG moneys since the election of Ronald Reagan in 1980. Cleveland's share of the UDAG program far exceeds that of other Ohio cities; in 1985 the city was ranked

Table 7.1. Distribution of UDAG Projects in Cleveland, 1981–1988

Location	Project Type				
	Commercial/ office	Industrial	Housing	Health/ institutional	Total
Downtown[a]	16	0	0	1	17
University Circle	2	0	1	1	4
Neighborhoods	6	0	3	3	12
Other areas[b]	0	6	0	1	7
Total	24	6	4	6	40

SOURCE: City of Cleveland, Department of Economic Development.
[a] Includes central business district, Playhouse Square, Warehouse District, and the Flats.
[b] Includes industrial and institutional areas outside of downtown, University Circle, and the city's residential neighborhoods.

fourth nationally in grant dollars obtained—behind New York, Detroit, and Baltimore. Between 1981 and 1988, Cleveland was awarded forty UDAGs totaling $103,308,548. According to city data, this has made possible "the leveraging of $672.9 million in private investment and allowed Cleveland to retain 3,973 jobs and to create a projected 7,875 jobs, of which only 1,096 have been created to date (City of Cleveland 1988).

Tables 7.1 and 7.2 show the distribution of UDAG projects and dollars in Cleveland since 1981 by geographic location and project type. The most common UDAG in Cleveland has been that for downtown commer-

Table 7.2. Distribution of UDAG Dollars in Cleveland, 1981–1988

Location	Project Type				
	Commercial/ office	Industrial	Housing	Health/ institutional	Total
Downtown[a]	$72,221,495	$ 0	$ 0	$ 351,750	$ 72,573,245
University Circle	1,350,000	0	5,500,000	1,200,000	8,050,000
Neighborhoods	10,047,493	0	4,606,000	2,276,810	16,930,303
Other areas[b]	0	4,300,000	0	1,455,000	5,755,000
Total	$83,618,988	$4,300,000	$10,106,000	$5,283,560	$103,308,548

SOURCE: City of Cleveland, Department of Economic Development.
[a] Includes central business district, Playhouse Square, Warehouse District, and the Flats.
[b] Includes industrial and institutional areas outside of downtown, University Circle, and the city's residential neighborhoods.

cial-office projects. The sixteen UDAGs in this category have accounted for 70 percent of the program's dollars in Cleveland since 1981. In contrast, only four UDAGs have been awarded for housing projects.

The largest and best-known recipient of UDAG money in Cleveland has been the Tower City Center project. First announced in 1974, it includes renovation of the Terminal Tower building (the largest downtown structure and the historical centerpiece of Cleveland's Public Square), and redevelopment of the adjoining real estate for construction of a multi-use retail, office, and hotel complex at an announced cost of $279 million. Since 1980, Tower City has been awarded five UDAGs totaling $31.5 million for bridge, street, and public transit repairs; retail development; and conversion of the old central post office facility to commercial and office space. The project has also received $54 million in additional subsidies from the Federal Urban Mass Transit Administration, the Ohio Department of Transportation, and the Greater Cleveland Regional Transit Authority. Tower City has benefited from state-subsidized improvement of the adjacent Public Square at a cost of $12 million.

The redevelopment of Tower City Center did not begin until 1988. Expected to be the anchor for the rebuilding of Cleveland's downtown retail market, Tower City now faces competition from the newly completed Galleria, a large, modern retail facility built by the Jacobs brothers with the benefit of $3.5 million UDAG on the old Erieview urban renewal site near the lakefront. Whether the heavily subsidized Tower City, whose management hoped to begin leasing new retail space during 1989, can compete and coexist with the Galleria and other proposed new downtown commercial developments still remains uncertain fourteen years after the project was originally announced. The two Jacobs brothers announced the development of an office tower and hotel adjacent to Public Square and the mall, a project estimated to cost $250 million. They received a $10 million UDAG to assist in restoration of the historic Society Bank building, which is part of the project. Each Jacobs brother (collectively they bought the Cleveland Indians' baseball franchise in 1986) is worth approximately $345 million (*Forbes* 1987). A son is developing several projects in the Flats, including the powerhouse restoration project, which received a $4 million UDAG in 1988. The Tower City grant and the recent Galleria UDAG indicate that subsidizing upscale retail development that attracts upper-income suburban consumers to Cleveland's downtown continues to be a linchpin of the city's public-private partnership development strategy.

The Voinovich administration has been less aggressive in initiating public-private partnerships that use UDAGs for low- and moderate-income housing projects sponsored by CDCs. Only two UDAGs, both used for the Lexington Village housing project, have been obtained for this purpose. Lexington Village was developed in 1985–1987 on twelve acres of land in Hough (a low-income black neighborhood that had been devastated by riots in the late 1960s) by the Famicos Foundation, a local nonprofit housing rehabilitation organization, and McCormack, Baron & Associates, a private developer. Phase I, a $13.7 million project financed with a $2.6 million UDAG and an additional $3.5 million of city subsidies as well as $3 million of foundation money, resulted in construction of 183 low- and moderate-income townhouse apartments, all of which have been leased. Phase II is a $7.1 million project with a $1.4 million UDAG that will add 94 housing units to the existing development in 1989. Tower City's $86 million in direct subsidies dwarfs the $10 million committed to Lexington Village.

The city has used UDAG repayments to capitalize a small-business revolving loan fund, which as of August 1987 had awarded eight loans totaling $626,000 and committed an additional $1.1 million for thirteen more loans. This fund has also been used to help small businesses relocate away from the announced site of the proposed domed stadium. Unlike other cities, however, Cleveland has not used UDAG repayments to fund housing rehabilitation programs operated by CDCs (City of Cleveland 1988).

Tax abatements for selected residential development projects were revived by the Voinovich administration in 1986. Tax abatements had been abandoned as a development incentive policy during the late 1970s, after public outcry over the tax breaks granted to several downtown development projects helped to elect Dennis Kucinich as mayor on an antiabatement platform (Swanstrom 1985:Chap. 6). Initially, the revival of tax abatements occasioned little controversy.

Currently, residential projects must be located in a community reinvestment area designated by the city in order to qualify for a tax abatement. These areas are created on a project-by-project basis, and usually include only the land parcels that encompass the specific project. Abatements are granted on all new real property taxes generated by the project for seven years. As of June 1987, the city had approved eight abatements projected to cost $4 million in new property tax revenues over the next seven years. The two largest abatements have been granted for the Mayfield–Euclid Triangle apartment complex in University Circle and new residential development in the historic Warehouse District bordering downtown, both market rate projects. The city has also begun to use the abatement tool to support low- and moderate-income housing sponsored by nonprofit developers. It has granted abatements for Lexington Village, for new housing built in the impoverished Central neighborhood, and most recently for the renovation of existing housing units in the Olympia Theatre building in the Broadway neighborhood.

The Voinovich administration has also designated six enterprise zones (located in virtually all of Cleveland's industrial areas) in which industrial tax abatements can be granted. New business investment within these zones is eligible for a tax break, which abates all tangible personal property taxes for ten years. Tangible personal property includes machinery, equipment, leasehold improvements, and inventory.

In 1986 the LTV Steel Corporation received the first abatement granted under this program, for a $37 million investment in its hot and cold strip mill. The city's abatement applies to $19 million of this investment because half of the mill is located in adjoining Cuyahoga Heights. The value of this abatement is estimated at $3.6 million over ten years.

In March 1988 the Jacobs brothers and Forest City Enterprises both asked for twenty-year tax abatements worth an estimated $120 million, in addition to $20 million in UDAGs, to subsidize the building of two downtown luxury hotels and an office building. The Voinovich administration supported their requests and thus provoked a public debate over the necessity for this subsidy, the absence of conditions limiting the abatements, and the substantial loss of revenue to Cleveland's beleaguered public schools. The Voinovich administration, under pressure, agreed to some limited restrictions but rejected any linkage between these tax abatements and requests that the developers invest in neighborhood projects. In May 1988 the City Council overwhelmingly approved such abatements. After protracted negotiations, the opponents agreed not to contest them in a proposed referendum.

Although it has provided financial incentives like UDAGs and tax abatements, the city has largely left development planning to the private sector. Individual and corporate developers such as Forest City Enterprises and the Jacobs brothers and civic groups such as the Playhouse Square Foundation, the Domed Stadium Committee, and the North Coast Development Corporation have taken the lead in downtown development planning. In 1988 Cleveland Tomorrow proposed the creation of a citywide development corporation to promote large-scale development projects.

Community Development Corporations: Cleveland's Junior Partners

The CDCs play a secondary role in the city's development strategy. Unlike their private-sector counterparts, they are heavily dependent upon subsidies, for both their operation and their projects. Because of the

Table 7.3. CDBG Allocation and Nonprofit Housing Groups in Cleveland, 1981–1988

CDBG	Year	Total CDBG allocation	Number of non-profit housing groups funded	Amount of nonprofit housing funding	Nonprofit housing as % of CDBG
VII	1981–1982	$37,626,000	5	$1,711,000	4.5
VIII	1982–1983	33,116,084	12	2,013,000	6.1
IX	1983–1984	31,403,000	12	1,800,000	5.7
X	1984–1985	29,139,000	11	1,225,000	4.2
XI	1985–1986	28,816,000	15	1,250,000	4.3
XII	1986–1987	24,471,000	14	914,500	3.7
XIII	1987–1988	$24,569,000	18	$1,005,500	4.1

SOURCE: City of Cleveland, Department of Economic Development.

continual cutbacks in the federal Community Development Block Grant (CDBG) program, the level of city support for CDCs is a critical issue.

Table 7.3 reveals the decline of Cleveland's total CDBG allocation since 1981 and the shrinking proportion of funding for nonprofit housing. The city's CDBG allocation decreased 35 percent between year VII (1981–1982) and year XIII (1987–1988) of the program. Although the number of nonprofit housing groups funded by a CDBG grew from five to eighteen in that period, their portion of the total CDBG dollar pie shrank by $1 million in these years. In 1987, the city used CDBG money to create a new program, the Neighborhood Development Impact Grant, which in two funding rounds has targeted $1.3 million for real estate development and commercial improvement projects sponsored by nonprofit CDCs. It also has supported numerous CDCs involved in commercial development.

When neighborhood interests were concerned, the private philanthropic foundations took the lead in providing financial assistance. Cleveland Tomorrow, a corporate coalition, also began to express interest in neighborhood redevelopment. In 1987 it supervised a fund to support the Cleveland Neighborhood Partnership program, which provided aid to six neighborhood groups. Foundation financial support contributed to the survival and expansion of the network of CDCs in Cleveland and the growth of citywide umbrella organizations like the Cleveland Housing Network. In 1979 the foundations financed creation of the Center for Neighborhood Development at Cleveland State University. The city, of course, also contributed key financial support in the form of CDBG allocations to the CDCs and their projects. Allied and individual CDCs sought the support of both. Additional investment support came from the AmeriTrust Development Bank created in 1986.

The CDCs developed their own priorities and projects. The funders determined the direction of neighborhood development to the extent that they made their funding priorities known (e.g., housing rehabilitation and weatherization). The funders were not asked to fund large-scale neighborhood projects. The exception was Lexington Village in Hough. However, it pales in comparison with the investment being made in the development downtown and around the Cleveland Clinic and University Circle. For the most part CDCs were involved only in small development projects; therefore, most CDCs remained small in terms of their budget, staff, and project development.

With fewer subsidies available to attract private developers to inner-city rehabilitation and with the city's public housing agency beset by problems, CDCs have emerged as important actors in low- and moderate-income housing and commercial development. Nonprofit CDCs have influenced the housing situation in several ways. First, nonprofit developers have weatherized and rehabilitated hundreds of housing units for low- and moderate-income persons. As of July 1987, the Cleveland Housing Network and its member groups had rehabilitated 366 units of low-income housing under a lease-purchase program in which vacant homes are acquired and rehabilitated at low cost and subsequently leased, with an option to purchase, to low-income families. Three CDCs in Cleveland are producing an average of 25 renovated homes per year in the conventional market. In addition, four CDCs have renovated 165 units of multifamily rental housing in seven buildings scattered across the city.

Second, nonprofit CDCs have generated additional public and private housing investment. The Cleveland Housing Network has invested $3.5 million of government money and $2.8 million of bank and foundation funds in its housing rehabilitation projects. The CDCs have used CDBG funds in rehabilitation programs that leverage seven to ten dollars in private funds for every CDBG dollar.

Third, nonprofit developers have influenced the creation of innovative public policies for solution of specific housing problems. In response to a growing arson rate, three housing advocacy groups formed the Cleveland Anti-Arson Coalition in 1981. The coalition worked with city officials and Cleveland State University to develop an Arson Early Warning System that has contributed to lower arson rates in the neighborhoods. The Union-Miles Development Corporation worked with the Center for Neighborhood Development to develop new state receivership enabling legislation that was passed in 1984 as a remedy to the problem of vacant abandoned property.

Finally, nonprofit CDCs have worked with banks, foundations, and state and local government to leverage resources and create new public and private institutions that support low- and moderate-income housing development. For example, the New York–based Local Initiatives Support Corporation has matched the contributions of Cleveland corporations and foundations to create a $3.1 million neighborhood development loan and grant fund, of which $2.4 million has been invested in more than forty Cleveland community development projects since 1981. The Enterprise Foundation, likewise, has created a $2.1 million loan and grant fund and has given $250,000 in technical assistance for CDCs providing low- and moderate-income housing. The CDCs have worked closely with the newly created AmeriTrust Development Bank to finance housing and commercial development projects. The CDCs have also worked with the Ohio Department of Development and the Ohio Housing Finance Agency to create state-funded programs that support low- and moderate-income community development.

The Politics of Revitalization

Economic and racial divisions have pervaded Cleveland's postwar politics. Carl Stokes, the first black mayor of a major U.S. city, was elected in 1967 in the wake of the 1966 Hough race riot. When a conservative Republican mayor succeeded Stokes, community activism had not yet peaked. During the 1970s there was a surge of neighborhood organizing in Cleveland, aided by the Commission on Catholic Community Action and focusing on such issues as redlining, disinvestment, and tax abatements. This movement in turn provided the basis for the 1977 victory of upstart Dennis Kucinich, campaigning on a populist platform (Swanstrom 1985; Clavel 1986). It was the turbulence associated with Kucinich's brief reign as mayor, his adamant opposition to tax abatements for corporate developers, and his support for the municipal power company that eventually united corporate and business opposition and led to his defeat in 1979 (he had narrowly survived a 1978 recall election) and the election of conservative Republican Mayor Voinovich.

Cleveland's power structure, unlike that of some other major U.S. cities, has not always presented a united front on development issues. In recent years, there has been considerable disagreement over whether a proposed new domed stadium should be sited on the lakefront, where other competing development has been proposed, or elsewhere in the downtown area. A proposal to hold a dome-financing referendum was defeated in 1984 and the future of a new stadium remains controversial, even though acquisition and clearance of a site are already under way. A similar rift has occurred over whether the city's lakefront airport should be replaced by housing and commercial development. The mayor and City Council, civic and business interests, and the *Plain Dealer*, the city's only major newspaper, have long bemoaned the lack of downtown hotel space sufficient to attract convention and tourist business. But they have been unable to attract developers. In fact, when a powerful Democratic leader and hotel owner did not receive city support for a tunnel to connect the renovated, city-owned convention center with one of his downtown hotels, he threatened to withdraw altogether from the city's convention bureau and to sell his hotels as sites for future office development. Thus, in some circumstances where there have been competing economic interests and conflicting views among the local civic elite and developers, it has proved difficult to develop a consensus and put together a public-private partnership that can efficiently accomplish downtown development goals.

By the early 1980s, there was relatively little community organizing in Cleveland. Only a few community organizations were left that had a mass membership base. Consequently, the CDCs, many of which had been created by parent community advocacy organizations, had emerged as the major vehicle representing neighborhood interests in Cleveland's redevelopment process. Funding was not available for community organizing and organizers. The Commission on Catholic Community Action, which had played so critical a role in galvanizing Cleveland's neighborhoods in the 1970s, no longer acted as a catalyst for community organizing. The CDCs did not involve themselves in partisan politics, as evidenced by the refusal of most CDCs to back Dennis Kucinich against those campaigning for his recall in 1978, despite his administration's support for neighborhood development. Dependent upon the largesse of the city in awarding CDBGs, as well as on the private foundations and, to a lesser extent, corporate investment (e.g., through the Local Initiatives Support Corporation, the Enterprise Foundation, and Cleveland Tomorrow), CDCs could not easily afford to antagonize their funders by taking contrary positions on controversial public issues (e.g., the awarding of development subsidies like tax abatements and UDAGs). Cleveland's neighborhood groups, unlike those in cities such as Boston, Chicago, and San Francisco, did not become involved in citywide coalitions that were backing progressive reform mayoral candidates such as Ray Flynn, Harold Washington, and George Moscone who were elected on pro-neighborhood platforms (Hartman 1984; Squires et al. 1987). Although a few members of the City Council were associated with neighborhood groups, they did not attempt to rally a neighborhood constituency based on citywide issues. Thus, for example, demands for downtown-neighborhood linkage policies to bene-fit poor neighborhoods that were ultimately successful in these three cit-ies did not emerge in Cleveland when there were signs of a revival of major downtown commercial development (Keating 1986). When the Voinovich administration revived tax abatements as a policy, at least for residential construction and rehabilitation, there was virtually no opposi-tion from neighborhood groups to the subsidizing of market rate and lux-ury housing. Rather, they understandably sought tax abatements for their housing projects as well. The opposition to tax abatement for downtown commercial development in 1988 did not involve CDCs.

The CDCs' lack of clout is reflected in the pattern of the awarding of UDAGs. Under Republican Mayor Voinovich Cleveland did very well. Most UDAG recipients were commercial and industrial and were located in the central business district. The only major neighborhood UDAG was the Lexington Village project. Unlike many other cities, Cleveland made no special provision for seeking and supporting UDAG awards to neigh-borhood groups. The UDAG payback funds did not automatically go into neighborhood investment or housing trust funds. Instead, the city re-served the right to determine the future use of these funds, and they were used mostly for small business. Although some neighborhood groups sought UDAG payback funds, their use has not yet become a major public issue.

What neighborhood-based CDCs have gained during the Voinovich administration is credibility; they have earned respect for their accom-plishments locally and nationally. Voinovich's Community Development Department has continued CDBG allocations to support CDCs despite the massive federal cutback in CDBG funding. The Civic Vision planning process has included neighborhoods, and the mayor did select neighbor-hood representatives to chair and sit on the Steering Committee. This could be viewed as an effort to gain credibility for this process in the neighborhoods; however, it does reflect the fact that Cleveland's neigh-borhoods cannot easily be ignored.

Conclusion

All of this support for neighborhoods from the public and private (cor-porate and philanthropic) sectors suggests that public-private partner-ships in Cleveland have been a resounding success. However, this is not the case. First, despite these well-intentioned efforts over an eight-year period (1980–1988), the many problems facing Cleveland's poor neigh-borhoods have not been alleviated by public-private partnerships. Poverty, unemployment, crime, substandard housing, racial tension, and physical blight persist in all too many of the city's neighborhoods. As Tim Hagan, liberal Democratic president of the Cuyahoga County Commissioners, stated, "The focus of our attention should not be on what we are doing for the Jacobs brothers or DeBartolo but on how we respond to the poor, sick, wounded and the people in our community who have no voice." This is in part simply a reflection of the reduction of federal urban aid by the Reagan administration, the inability of a state government with limited resources to make up for this loss of federal aid, and the unwillingness of Cleveland's more affluent suburban neighbors to share their tax base with an impoverished city.

Second, although these factors have been important constraints, it is also true that only a fraction of available public and private resources has been directed to neighborhood development. Much more investment, both public and private, has gone into downtown development than has gone into neighborhood reinvestment.

Third, and perhaps most important, this allocation choice reflects the lack of political power of the CDCs. They have received what has been deemed possible by Cleveland's power structure. No one suggests that this is adequate to deal with neighborhood problems, but it does reflect the primary emphasis on downtown development. Cleveland is a typical example of the creation of public-private partnerships whose main focus is downtown development—an indication of the continued dominance of the trickle down theory of economic development. Although Cleveland's revitalization does not approach that of many other cities, there is little evidence to suggest that trickle down will have any more effect in Cleveland's poor neighborhoods than in those of other cities. A much more progressive public interventionist policy to promote redistribution programs at the municipal level would be required to more equitably extend the benefits of central business district growth to Cleveland's poor and working-class neighborhoods. Redistributionist policies could include such policies as:

conditioning UDAGs and similar subsidies on the creation of jobs for poorer city residents

encouraging more neighborhood-based UDAG projects and using UDAG paybacks from major downtown projects to support neighborhood development

increasing the use of declining CDBG funds to support CDCs

implementing a city-linked deposit policy (adopted in 1988) to generate more lender investment in neighborhood projects requiring concessions from private developers benefiting from public subsidies like tax abatements downtown to support neighborhood development

This redistribution can only happen under a different leadership representing neighborhood and minority interests—one that is better able to implement programs to deal with the issues raised under Kucinich that his brief administration could not effectively translate into viable policies. Kucinich's inability to heal racial divisions and his antagonizing of his neighborhood constituency have set back the development of a progressive neighborhood-based political movement in Cleveland, however.

If CDCs are to make a more noticeable impact on urban revitalization, all levels of government and the private sector will have to commit much greater resources than they have in the past. Cleveland's limited commitment to CDCs does not differ from the commitment made by other cities. In addition to a more equitable policy at the local level, there must be greatly increased federal support for neighborhood-based housing and economic development programs if urban problems are to be seriously addressed.

References

Bier, Thomas. 1987. "Population and Housing Projections." Report prepared for the Cleveland City Planning Commission, Civic Vision Program.

Cambridge Systematics, Inc. 1987. "City of Cleveland Retail Market Study." Report prepared for the Cleveland City Planning Commission, Civic Vision Program.

City of Cleveland. Department of Economic Development. 1988. Unpublished data.

Clavel, Pierre. 1986. *The Progressive City*. New Brunswick, N.J.: Rutgers University Press.

Council for Economic Opportunities in Greater Cleveland. 1987. *Poverty Indicators and Trends, 1980–1987: Cuyahoga County, Ohio*.

Fogarty, Michael. 1987. "Cleveland: Economic Analysis and Projections." Report prepared for the Cleveland City Planning Commission, Civic Vision Program.

Forbes. 1987. "The 400 Richest People in America" (October 26).

Hartman, Chester. 1984. *The Transformation of San Francisco*. Totowa, N.J.: Rowman and Allanheld.

Keating, W. Dennis. 1986. "Linking Downtown Development to Broader Community Goals: An Analysis of Linkage Policies in Three Cities." *Journal of the American Planning Association* 52:133–141.

Krumholz, Norman. 1982. "A Retrospective View of Equity Planning: Cleveland, 1969–1979." *Journal of the American Planning Association* 48:163–183.

Krumholz, Norman, Janice Cogger, and John Linner. 1975. "The Cleveland Policy Planning Report." *Journal of the American Institute of Planners* (September):298–319.

Methvin, Eugene H. 1983. "Cleveland Comes Back." *Reader's Digest* (March).

Planning. 1988. "Cleveland Takes on . . . Everything" (May).

Report of the National Advisory Commission on Civil Disorders (Kerner Commission). 1968.

Squires, Gregory D., Larry Bennett, Kathleen McCourt, and Philip Nyden. 1987. *Chicago: Race, Class, and the Response to Urban Decline*. Philadelphia: Temple University Press.

Swanstrom, Todd. 1985. *The Crisis of Growth Politics*. Philadelphia: Temple University Press.

Time. 1980. "Fatter City: Cleveland Makes a Comeback" (December 29).

8. Detroit: The Centrifugal City

Detroit is the city that illustrates most clearly the negative effects of dependence on one basic industry. It has suffered severe economic decline, yet because one industry basically dominates the economy, suggesting a monolithic power base, and because the labor force is well organized, one might possibly expect public-private partnerships to have arisen to save the city. Such expectations are unfounded; modest public-private partnership efforts have been made and have met with some success, especially those directed at specific institutional and downtown projects. But these efforts have not solved the problems of this rustbelt city, since whatever benefits accrued from them simply have not counterbalanced the simultaneous exit of capital and people.

Birthplace of the assembly line and the mass production of automobiles, Detroit has gradually lost its high position in the hierarchy of U.S. urban economies. Like a number of other Northern cities, it has not been able to successfully rebound from the trauma of industrial decline. Reliance upon the manufacture of automobiles was once a source of strength but has become a distinctive liability.

Possibly only one other U.S. city, Pittsburgh, relies to such an extent upon one manufactured product for its economic viability (Hill 1983). Although policy analysts such as Dan Luria and Jack Russell have suggested schemes for ending Detroit's dependence on automobile manufacturing, the city remains very much bound to the production of cars (Luria and Russell 1984; Hill 1984a; Anton 1983). The metropolitan region relies on automobile production as well, and suffers when the industry fluctuates and declines. But in general the region fares better than the city, which has steadily lost much of its manufacturing sector to the surrounding suburbs. Economic dispersal has combined with the continual decentralization of the white population and the middle class to create a severely fragmented metropolis.

In many U.S. cities, growth coalitions of economic elites have affected the economic usefulness of central cities by essentially managing their redevelopment for the benefit of local business interests. Sometimes educational or other service institutions have shaped redevelopment efforts in a similar fashion (Mollenkopf 1983). Often, those industries or businesses of primacy in the local economy controlled these public-private partnerships. In Detroit, which is dominated by a single industry, one might expect industrial leaders to have strongly influenced redevelopment activities. Coalitions, institutions, and automobile magnates have influenced renewal efforts in the city of Detroit, often to their own benefit. On the whole, however, it is the economic, racial, and class fragmentation of the metropolis that has had the greatest effect on the city. The pivotal determinants of the contours of Detroit's postwar redevelopment policy have been (1) its decentralizing economy, largely caused by the flight of the manufacturing sector, but by decline in other sectors as well; and (2) high levels of white flight, and related fragmentation of population by income and race. Since the early 1970s, the city has responded to these centrifugal trends with a redevelopment strategy heavily oriented to economic development of the central business district, riverfront, and industrial sectors. These efforts have had moderate success in achieving their limited aims, yet they have not resolved the fundamental dilemmas of the centrifugal city.

A Decentralizing City

Since World War II, two processes, the geographic decentralization of Detroit's economy and of its population, have occurred simultaneously as separate but mutually supportive phenomena.

Although the decentralization of Detroit's economy began before World War II, the central city still dominated the region's supply of industrial employment in the late 1940s (Conot 1986). The city's share of manufacturing employment in the metropolitan area rose from 57.7 percent in 1939 to 60.3 percent in 1948. After that year, however, the proportion declined steadily, falling to 40.6 percent by 1963, and 25.0 percent in 1982 (Darden et al. 1987:22).

The initial reason that manufacturers left the city was lack of space and the growing popularity of one-story plants. As early as 1945, planning publications noted that the city had an insufficient amount of land suitable for either expansion of existing facilities or assemblage of large parcels for new industrial development (City of Detroit, City Plan Commission 1944). In 1958 an industrial-sector planning report, based in part on an exhaustive survey of industries, warned that "many industries today find themselves in old, outmoded, multi-story plants. Some of these industries have moved out of the city and, in the process, have abandoned millions of square feet of factory space" (City of Detroit, City Plan Commission 1958:1).

Because of its heavy dependence on an automobile-based economy, the city was especially vulnerable to national economic downturns. In time, the problem ceased to be simply the flight of manufacturing plants; as the automobile industry began to change, its reliance upon Michigan workers decreased. By 1980, the automobile manufacturers had established a process of global production and were building components in South America, Asia, and Western Europe. Aging city plants, with their fatal combination of high wages and outmoded facilities, became more and more dispensable in this new world of international production, silicon chips, and industrial robots. Contraction or closure of plant operations became routine (Hill 1984b). As automobile plants left, so did their parts suppliers and other support businesses.

People were leaving as well. In the early postwar years, the extent of the flight was not yet apparent, and city politicians still spoke of the need to cope with excessive growth (City of Detroit, City Plan Commission 1946). In 1953, central city population peaked at 1.8 million. However, the number of city residents had fallen to 1.67 million by 1960, and to just over 1.2 million by 1980.

The racial differentiation of the population movement was striking. In 1960, 75.3 percent of central city residents were white. Twenty years later, only 34.4 percent of the central city population was white. The recorded total number of city blacks had risen from 482,000 in 1960 to 759,000 in 1980. During the same years, the city's white population fell from 1,138,000 to 414,000. This startling figure—a decrease of 724,000 whites over a twenty-year period—is a reflection of not only the tendency of whites to leave the city, but also the tendency of blacks *not* to leave the city. Racial separation is such a persistent characteristic of the region that segregation between municipalities has actually increased over the years. In 1950 the index of dissimilarity between Detroit metropolitan municipalities was 26.6, meaning that just over one-fourth of the people in a metropolis would have had to move between municipalities in order for even racial distribution to exist. By 1960 that index had increased to 44.4. In 1980, the index stood at 75.3; three-fourths of area residents would have had to move between municipalities to approximate an even distribution (Darden et al. 1987:78). Little wonder that in 1970, Detroit's rate of black suburbanization was among the lowest of all the cities that Thomas Clark studied—Atlanta, Chicago, New York, Washington, D.C., and seven other metropolitan areas (Clark 1979:47).

Blacks were moving into Detroit's suburbs, although they tended to become segregated in a few municipalities. But low-income blacks were not part of the trend toward decentralization. In 1983, the disparity between central city income and metropolitan area income was greater in

Detroit than in any other of the thirty-three largest U.S. metropolitan areas (Darden et al. 1987:99). The presence of an oversupply of poor citizens is one reason that the city of Detroit continues to have a higher rate of fiscal distress than other U.S. cities, even in times of relative economic prosperity (Peterson 1986:28).

White and middle-class flight strongly affected the viability of the city of Detroit. Population loss combined with economic dispersal to confound many city attempts at redevelopment.

Postwar Redevelopment

During all the years of deleterious economic and population decentralization, the city government was trying to redevelop the inner city so that it would be attractive to regional firms and residents. In order to promote redevelopment, it worked with a number of prominent business and special-interest groups. Before the 1967 riots, these groups did not form a unified, identifiable growth coalition; instead, various growth promoters worked to facilitate specific projects.

Several years before the federal government enacted Title I of the Housing Act of 1949, Detroit had started its own urban renewal program. Eugene Greenhut, a developer backed by East Coast financial interests, approached the city in 1945 with a proposal. In exchange for land assembled by the city and tax breaks, Greenhut promised to transform a slum into new low- and moderate-income housing (Emery 1945). Nothing came of this particular scheme, but the committee formed to examine the proposal, influenced by the testimony of local real estate and business interests, suggested that the city set up a program to assemble land for developers. This led Mayor Edward Jeffries to announce the Detroit Plan in 1946, under which the city would clear blighted land at the rate of one hundred acres a year.

The federal government's 1949 urban renewal program gave the city the money to carry out what it had already planned. The first two renewal sites were Gratiot, a 129-acre portion of a black neighborhood near Hastings Street, and a 77-acre project in a white ethnic neighborhood popularly known as Corktown. As in most cities, the process of removing existing families and completing renewal projects took much longer than originally expected. One complicating factor was that the Gratiot site's black families had very little alternative housing available to them because of blatant racial discrimination in public and private housing. The city dealt with this difficulty as did many other cities across the nation—by simply forcing existing residents out with little relocation assistance.

Another difficulty was the initial unwillingness of local builders to buy cleared land in the middle of a black residential neighborhood (Mowitz and Wright 1962).

The projects dragged on slowly, so a coalition of sorts formed to speed their progress. As has been typical in postwar Detroit, the coalition included local labor leaders such as the president of the United Auto Workers (UAW), Walter Reuther. It was Reuther who responded to a *Detroit News* article with a telegram to the mayor and the Common Council asking them to set up a citizens' committee to oversee redevelopment. In the telegram Reuther pledged $10,000 from the UAW to help fund the effort. Mayor Albert Cobo, a conservative who actively distrusted the "Communist" UAW, yielded to pressure and set up a committee in 1954, but he made sure it included adequate corporate representation (Conot 1986: 444). Local bankers, merchants, and unions contributed $50,000 to supplement the UAW's contribution to the new Citizens Redevelopment Committee. The committee became the Citizens Redevelopment Corporation in 1955 and was supported in part by funds from the big three automobile firms—Ford, Chrysler, and General Motors—and other local business interests. The group focused on the Gratiot project, and the major apartment tower in the renamed Lafayette Park project opened in late 1958.

The driving forces behind several of the city's other redevelopment efforts were the institutions, most notably the medical organizations associated with the Medical Center and the institutions affiliated with the Cultural Center and Wayne State University. The Medical Center offers a representative example of the institutional development projects.

The Detroit Medical Center project began in 1954 when four hospital directors, representing Grace, Harper, Woman's, and Childrens' Hospitals, met with the Detroit City Plan Commission to discuss expansion needs and the problems of blight surrounding their facilities. The four hospitals formed a "citizens' committee" that included the dean of the College of Medicine at Wayne State University and the directors of the four hospitals. They hired a consultant, whose expenses were partially funded by the city, to put together a 1956 plan for a "fully self-contained urban complex" of medical facilities, housing, and retail services. The city declared the Medical Center an urban renewal project, but much of the money for land purchase and for the eventual construction of new hospital facilities came from local foundations; wealthy individuals such as Mrs. Edsel Ford, daughter-in-law of Henry Ford, who gave $750,000; and, later, the U.S. Department of Health, Education, and Welfare. The chairman of the Medical Center Fund was Joseph L. Hudson, Jr., of the family that owned the region's largest department store chain, Hudson's.

The Detroit Medical Center was the first renewal project to generate well-organized citizen protest. The Gratiot residents had not waged a resistance battle, although the Detroit Urban League protested the shoddy treatment of relocatees. Corktown residents opposed the destruction of their neighborhood, but their techniques were rudimentary and ineffective. In the case of the Medical Center, however, three groups—the Urban League, the National Association for the Advancement of Colored People, and the Fellowship of Urban Renewal Churches, an alliance of blacks whose churches were slated for demolition—mounted a moderately effective campaign of protest. Specifically, they opposed the wholesale clearance of black residents for the benefit of hospitals with well-known policies of discrimination against black health professionals and patients. In the end the project proceeded, but the protest groups forced several of the hospitals to implement less discriminatory policies, and several member churches of the Fellowship of Urban Renewal Churches gained permission to rebuild within the new Medical Center. Years later a few of the black churches sponsored nonprofit housing in the project area—the only Medical Center housing affordable by former residents of the site (J. Thomas 1985).

Throughout the postwar period, urban renewal projects in Detroit have faced the same problems of delay and red tape that slowed projects in other cities. After a number of what must have seemed tortuously slow years, most of the projects, including Gratiot/Lafayette, the Medical Center, the Cultural Center, Corktown, and University City (near Wayne State University), managed to achieve visible accomplishments. But the projects generated an escalating number of neighborhood protest movements, more vociferous than the Medical Center protests, and fueled by increasing indignation over the number of neighborhoods the city was clearing. The protests culminated in the passage of a 1972 state law requiring organized citizens' councils to help guide redevelopment projects (J. Thomas 1985). It was at about that time, as well, that rehabilitation became established as the policy approach preferable to wholesale clearance. But the pain caused by the old redevelopment battles was not easy to alleviate.

Economic flight, administrative delays, and neighborhood protests influenced redevelopment. Also important, however, was the simultaneous, convulsive population flight. Citizens who moved into newly built housing in the Gratiot/Lafayette project were racially, and eventually economically, diverse. By the time other projects were completed, however, the effects of depopulation had already taken their toll. The Cultural Center and University City projects, for example, facilitated the construction of several new cultural and university buildings, but the number of residents in the surrounding neighborhoods dropped drastically. In certain neighborhood redevelopment projects, such as Jefferson Chalmers, the city could not rehabilitate fast enough to keep up with the high level of abandonment aggravated by wholesale white flight. Redeveloping some areas was very much like repairing holes in a bathtub whose plug had already been pulled.

The Role of the Private Sector

In spite of the participation of Detroit's economic elite in institutional projects such as the Medical Center, its role was not nearly as strong as that of similar groups in other cities. Attention focused upon specific projects such as the Medical Center, the Gratiot/Lafayette site, the Cultural Center, and the downtown area. No overall growth and development organization of any significance existed until after the riot of 1967. Linda Ewen, in her 1978 empirical study of interlocking kinship and organizational ties among the wealthy of Detroit, analyzed major civic and business organizations in the city. Directors of major Detroit firms held leadership positions in several of these groups. But Ewen offers no empirical evidence that these elites strongly influenced pre-riot redevelopment. With the exception of the fairly innocuous Central Business District Association, not one of the business or civic organizations that she analyzed focused on the redevelopment of Detroit, until the creation, after 1967, of New Detroit, Detroit Renaissance, and the Economic Development Corporation of Greater Detroit (Ewen 1978).[1]

Detroit also differed from many other cities, such as San Francisco, in that it did not have a strong municipal development agency. Instead development powers were shared by the Detroit City Plan Commission, the Housing Commission, and other agencies, which constituted a confusing hodgepodge that the city did not reorganize until the early 1970s (J. Thomas 1988).

The balancing effect of organized labor in the city partially explains the absence of stronger redevelopment leadership by the economic elite, particularly the automobile magnates. In Detroit, this has led to what Jones and Bachelor call "either a very structured form of pluralism or a fairly open system of elite rule, depending on one's perspective" (Jones and Bachelor 1986:46). In addition, economic interests had been rapidly leaving the city throughout the postwar period, and in many cases automobile firms were the first to go. On the whole, the automobile industrialists had never been particularly tied to the city, even though many of their plants were located there. Henry Ford, founder of the Ford Motor Company, established Ford World Headquarters and the massive River Rouge complex in suburban Dearborn. Chrysler was headquartered in Highland Park, a suburban enclave surrounded by Detroit. The headquarters of General Motors, a large and decentralized company, were located in the city, but the company was not an active city booster.[2]

The riot of 1967 had the effect of a cold bath for the corporate elite, who evidently began to realize the imperatives of the times. Several authors, notably Ewen and Hill, have written about business leaders' reaction to the 1967 crisis and subsequent creation of organizations such as New Detroit, Detroit Renaissance, and the Economic Development Corporation of Greater Detroit. Henry Ford II, grandson of the company's founder, was particularly active in these efforts. The most visible legacy of this period is the shining Renaissance Center, a privately developed complex that Henry Ford II financed in part by coercing local corporate firms that were dependent on the Ford Motor Company to contribute funds. Although the Renaissance Center could hardly be called a public-private venture, since it was built privately, it did suggest a fledgling commitment to the central city, or at least to the central business district. Also dating from this period is New Detroit, Inc., dedicated to funding social and economic programs for the benefit of city residents (Ewen 1978; Hill 1983).

Even as they contributed to these organizations, however, the controllers of the city's economic base continued, and escalated, their flight from the city. In the five years before the riot, the central city gained 8,500 manufacturing jobs. In the five years after 1967, the city lost 28,700 manufacturing jobs; in the next five years, it lost 21,700; in the following five years (1977 to 1982), it lost an additional 47,600 (Darden 1987).

The Economic Imperative

The reality confronting contemporary Detroit is the necessity of pushing for redevelopment of a city center in the context of continued capital and population dispersement to the periphery. Because of scarce resources and the negative effects of private-sector decisions, the city cannot afford redevelopment projects of sufficient size to counteract the wide-ranging effects of decline. In general, the city has responded to this situation by funding both housing and economic development activities, but focusing on economic development. It has emphasized two major economic development areas: central business district/riverfront development, in order to create a center at least comparable to the capital investment nodes of the region; and industrial renewal, in order to halt the flight of manufacturing jobs. Residential neighborhood redevelopment has received much lower priority.

The Central Business District and the Riverfront

Detroit's leaders, like the leaders of many cities, view the status of downtown as indicative of the status of the city's image. Coleman Young's administration, in particular, has made the central business district a high priority.

Detroit has been involved in central business district development for some years, dating back to efforts in the late 1940s and early 1950s to establish a downtown civic center. As the city sponsored residential renewal projects, it also promoted central business district renewal projects, planned for both institutional and retail use (City of Detroit, City Plan Commission 1962). But redevelopment efforts could not counterbalance private market trends. Even after construction of the shining, symbolic Renaissance Center, an independent 1980 survey of the downtowns of thirty-eight cities ranked Detroit's downtown in the bottom one-third in terms of economic growth and retail strength. Detroit was one of only six cities with no new downtown office space under construction, and 35 percent of available first- and second-floor retail space was vacant. According to the survey, central business district sales in Detroit were one-half their 1967 level (*Detroit Free Press* 1983). During the 1970s and 1980s, the Renaissance Center sustained chronic, sustained financial losses.

By the late 1980s, the city was experiencing some success with its downtown and riverfront projects. These projects include the once-troubled Detroit People Mover, a monorail that encircles downtown with a three-mile loop; Millender Center, a new retail-hotel-apartment-parking complex across the street from the Renaissance Center; Greektown's newly developed retail mall, Trapper's Alley; the expansion of Cobo Hall; Harbortown, a retail and residential complex on the city's east riverfront; and older city projects such as the Joe Louis Arena and Riverfront West Apartments.

Industrial Redevelopment

The central business district/riverfront is only one focus of the city's contemporary economic development policy. Another is the crucial industrial sector. Industrial renewal projects are not new; as early as 1945 the City Plan Commission, encouraged by local labor leaders who advocated that the city establish an industrial development authority, seriously considered selecting industrial redevelopment sites (City of Detroit, City Plan Commission 1945). One of the first urban renewal projects, Corktown (officially known as the West Side Industrial Project), was planned for light industrial reuse. Another early urban renewal project, Milwaukee Junction, prepared seventeen acres for industrial redevelopment. In the early 1960s, the city planned to develop yet another industrial project, Research Park, which was to cover sixty acres (J. Thomas 1987).

On the whole, however, the city's pre-1974 redevelopment efforts had little industrial emphasis. In some cases, such as the Research Park project, protest from surrounding neighborhoods succeeded in convincing the Common Council to revise the planned project and develop housing on the property. In the early 1960s, a number of residents organized to change the master plan's industrial designation of their neighborhoods back to residential. Additional reasons for the paucity of city industrial projects were the reluctance of the federal government to allow industrial urban renewal projects, in spite of the nonresidential "set-aside," and the lack of sufficient economic development tools (J. Thomas 1987).

The situation changed in 1974, when the city's new charter strengthened the economic development structure. By then federal agencies concerned with programs for economic development, such as the Small Business Administration and the Economic Development Administration, had grown in size and influence. Cities could also use programs funded under the Housing and Community Development Act—including Community Development Block Grants, Urban Development Action Grants, and Section 312 loans—for economic development activity (So et al. 1979). In Detroit, a prodevelopment black mayor, Coleman Young, took office in 1974, and one of his first actions was to organize a 1975 report to the federal government that requested $2.5 billion in economic development assistance, including $526 million for industrial development. Simultaneously, the city supported passage of state enabling legislation for development corporations and established several such agencies in Detroit, with the Detroit Economic Growth Corporation as the umbrella organization. The Young administration worked closely with President Jimmy Carter's administration to refine economic development programs.[3]

Such tools came very late in the process of economic decentralization, however. Of particular concern by the mid-1970s was the continuing exodus of automobile plants and the anticipated demise of the Chrysler Corporation. One city report claimed that 23,951 Detroit residents would lose jobs if Chrysler carried out its contraction plans, and the city announced in 1979 that it was considering building a new plant for Chrysler. In 1980 Chrysler did close its large Dodge Main plant, thus idling thousands of workers. But within a year General Motors challenged the city to assemble a site large enough for the company to build a modern automobile plant.

Poletown, the project that developed as a result of that challenge, heralded a new era in Detroit's redevelopment history. A mammoth and ambitious undertaking, the Central Industrial Park Project, as it was officially known, required a concentrated investment that, it was hoped, would provide thousands of jobs in one stroke. The site of just over 400 acres that the city selected included more than 1,000 residential, commercial, and industrial structures, and provided homes for over 3,400 people (Blonston 1986). All land would have to be cleared within months. The project represented in microcosm a contemporary dilemma: the city had to choose, quickly, between the plant and the local neighborhood. It chose the plant.

In reality, of course, the dilemma was much more complex. Some neighborhood activists who opposed the Poletown project claimed that the city could have reduced the amount of neighborhood clearance required. Others championed Poletown as beneficial for the city's neighborhoods, since it would allow the retention of perhaps as many as 6,000 industrial jobs. Improved relocation policies meant that many residents welcomed the chance to sell their homes and move elsewhere. In the final analysis, the true value of the project may have been its dramatization of the cost of reversing what would surely have been General Motors's alternative decision, to build the plant somewhere else besides the city of Detroit. That cost was at least $200 million in federal, state, and local economic development assistance (Jones and Bachelor 1986). One city councilman, Mel Ravitz, has estimated that the true governmental costs are far higher, since the total cost in tax abatements and land acquisition alone reached $200 million, or $44,000 for every job at the new plant when it ran at full capacity, which turned out to be about 4,500 hourly jobs (Ravitz 1987; Blonston 1986).

At least one disinterested analyst has calculated that the benefits to the city will not outweigh the costs (Fasenfest 1986). Although General Motors had always warned that the Poletown plant would replace, rather than supplement, existing older city assembly plants such as Fleetwood and Clark Street, it was still a shock in the fall of 1987 when the company closed down assembly operations at those two older plants for a loss of 6,000 jobs. In the year before this announcement, General Motors had been operating the Poletown plant with only one shift of about 3,000 workers, and it laid those workers off temporarily during model changeover in November 1987.

In spite of this experience, the city intends to repeat the Poletown strategy at least once, for expansion of Chrysler's Jefferson Avenue plant. Again the city is offering a package of financial incentives, including city, federal, and state funds.

The Poletown experience has been particularly sobering. A city so dependent upon one industry sorely needed a clearly successful automobile-related project to help it retain its manufacturing base. What better private entity could one forge a link with than the largest domestic car company, General Motors, historically headquartered in Detroit? The disappointing cut in expected employment, and the subsequent closure of other General Motors plants, only left open the question of where the industrial component of private enterprise, the supposed partner, was leading Detroit. The experience also emphasized the reality of the reduction in scale of the previously leviathan automobile industry.

Neighborhood Redevelopment

Poletown and other industrial, central business district, and riverfront "partnership" ventures all required government funds. Some of the money used, such as Urban Development Action Grants, could only be used for these or similar projects. Other funds, such as Community Development Block Grants, could be used for neighborhood projects. In general, the opportunity cost of the success of the economic development projects, that is, the alternative that did not receive the funds, was neighborhood redevelopment.

An examination of Community Development Block Grant allocations is particularly important, since it is the federal program designed to serve housing and community development needs. A 1979 city report claimed that, in fiscal years 1975–1976 to 1979–1980, the block grant program allocated 78 percent of its funds to neighborhoods and 22 percent to economic development. A simple mapping of major expenditures that can be identified by geographical area (approximately 45 percent of funds), however, reveals a different story for the years 1975 to 1982. Block grant money that went to the central business district and to what the city defines as the riverfront—including downtown and those parts of the city that border the riverfront—totaled 40.1 percent of the traceable allocations for those years, or $62 million. If one adds expenditures for the Woodward Corridor, which includes housing and institutional projects in the Medical Center, Wayne State University, and the General Motors–sponsored New Center area, the total of the geographically identifiable funds going to the Woodward Corridor, downtown, and the riverfront is 51.8 percent, or $80 million.[4]

This pattern of industrial, institutional, and downtown-riverfront targeting has caused conflict between the mayor and the Common Council, as well as dissatisfaction among many neighborhood activists. The council wishes to channel more money to residential neighborhoods (Ravitz 1987). The mayor, in contrast, holds fast to his centralization policy. His staff argues that the city is too large for unfocused investment, that the city supports neighborhoods but must target resources where they can make a visible difference—an argument not entirely without merit.

Neighborhood activists' protests against the city's expenditure priorities have been sporadic. The Poletown case generated a large, well-organized protest movement that, under different circumstances, could have succeeded in stopping or modifying the project. Their protest movement did not succeed because the industrial crisis was so terrifying that it influenced all parties involved, even some Michigan Supreme Court justices, according to the dissenting opinion of Justice James Ryan, who described "how easily government, in all of its branches, caught up in the frenzy of perceived economic crisis, can disregard the rights of the few in allegiance to the always disastrous philosophy that the end justifies the means."[5] For several years, community organizations such as the Michigan Avenue Community Organization vocally protested the city's expenditure priorities. But as time passed, the protest abated, in part because of the seemingly irreversible popularity of Coleman Young as mayor, and in part because of modest city funding of some neighborhood organizations under programs such as the Neighborhood Opportunity Fund (Ravitz 1987).

Economic growth has steadily continued in most suburban areas, unhampered by public concerns over priorities. Exceptions exist, such as the downriver communities south of the city, which have their own special problems of industrial decline. Areas of particularly heavy growth are Macomb and Oakland Counties, which lie just to the north of Detroit, and Dearborn, southwest of the city of Detroit. What has happened, therefore, is not merely decentralization of economic prosperity and growth, but decentralization and simultaneous concentration of prosperity in certain specific nodes (Darden et al. 1987).

Detroit's Future Needs

In summary, Detroit stands at the threshold of the 1990s as a city that has tried to buttress its core in a context of widespread, if nodal, regional decentralization. The steady flight of capital investment and of the white middle class has severely hampered attempts to *keep* businesses and people, much less attract them. Yet, at the same time, in some sense the city's redevelopment projects have succeeded in what they set out to do. The older urban renewal projects managed to create institutional enclaves for hospitals, cultural institutions, and a university; beautify the civic center portion of the downtown; and create a varied and well-designed residential complex at Gratiot/Lafayette. More recent projects induced an automobile company to build a modern facility in the inner city; they also included erection of a number of new central city buildings downtown, and beautification of the riverfront.

For all that effort, the city and its people remain distressed, because of persistently negative private market and population trends. These trends cannot be reversed merely by changing central city governmental policies. The efforts that the private-sector entities put into various redevelopment projects, it would seem, could have been more profitably expended on checking their own relentless decentralizing tendencies.

Since city policymakers will continue to attempt to redevelop the city, however, an obvious and immediate need is improved integration of economic development and housing policies. Other, more long-term, substantial needs are to make decisions necessary to cope with a postmanufacturing economy, and to improve the economic and political unity of the region as a whole.

The problem with centralized investment, as implemented by the city, is that steady deterioration of neighborhoods and municipal services, including the school system (which is under the jurisdiction of the Board of Education, not the city government), has made residence in the city increasingly less attractive. Several downtown projects provide upper-income housing, but existing middle-income neighborhoods have received less attention. Low-income neighborhoods have gradually disappeared; residential abandonment has continued to the point that several neighborhoods now include only a fraction of their original housing units. It would do little good to have a stellar city center and riverfront if no one lived in the rest of the city. Therefore, at some point, greater attention will have to be given to retaining existing residents.

Integration of economic and housing development, one of several possible approaches to resolving this dilemma, is a policy option that the Young administration considered in the mid-1980s. When he announced the new Jefferson Avenue Chrysler plant expansion in 1986, Coleman Young revealed his ideas for a new East Side project that encompasses not only plant development but also housing. Although he was careful to call these ideas a "dream," with no immediate plans for implementation, their announcement was a progressive sign (*Detroit News* 1986). A project that tied housing and retail development with industrial redevelopment would be more holistic than Poletown had been. But financing would prove difficult, especially if the housing were to be affordable. In a linked project, one might expect the industrial firm, in this case Chrysler, to contribute to the costs. Although this makes sense theoretically, a practical drawback is that most automobile firms are still disinvesting from Detroit, and Chrysler is making limited investment only when its funds are supplemented by government money.

Although adjustments to the city's internal redevelopment strategy are important to consider, it is even more important to address other, long-term problems of economic decline and regional fragmentation. As it becomes less feasible to rely upon the manufacturing sector, it will be more important to provide employment alternatives for people who once could depend on factories for jobs. Automobile plant closings make the future of blue-collar workers bleak. A 1984 task force charged with assessing the economic future of the state of Michigan described the situation succinctly in its report: "To be competitive in a changing national and international marketplace, Michigan must shift its economic base toward those products and processes that are less vulnerable to low-wage competition because of their dependence on human skills" ("The Path to Prosperity" 1984:52). It recommended a strategy of targeting state resources to support technologically advanced manufacturing, but frankly admitted that although such a strategy could ensure economic survival, it could also mean a reduced need for unskilled workers. Because this report formed the basis of the state's new economic development policies, acknowledgment of such a flaw was particularly unsettling.

Under the circumstances, a top priority should be to design a strategy for those who do not fit into the new technological parameters. For example, a stronger education and training system is a well-known need, mentioned often by consultants hired to analyze strategic planning for the city (Williams 1987). Yet the quality of Detroit's school system has declined precipitously over the years, and significant numbers of young people are not being prepared to participate in a new economy. In fact, significant distractions, such as the increased possession of handguns and murders among teenagers, hamper their educational and maturation process and drive even more families away. Employment and educational programs should be linked more strongly with economic development. Those programs which work, such as that of Focus Hope, Inc., a Detroit civil rights organization with an established training and economic development component, deserve stronger support. More creative community economic development programs, which build upon programs of existing neighborhood organizations, are also an important option (Mier 1984; R. Thomas 1987). The distinct advantage of such programs is that those most in need can participate in the process of defining and implementing social and economic revitalization.

Linked development policies may be of less applicability to the city of Detroit than to more "marketable" cities; nevertheless more linkage between city and suburban projects should also be explored. As an example, the city could negotiate, with the state's help, an agreement between the central city and the suburbs that would require developers of a certain size and under certain conditions to invest in both city and suburbs. This would elaborate upon the current agreement, mandated by state law, that a firm seeking tax abatement from Michigan municipalities receive the consent of any Michigan municipality from which it is disinvesting. Another, related approach would be to implement a rational policy for regional infrastructure investment.

Such steps would have to be taken in the context of resolution of a broader problem: the need to increase regional unity. Previous attempts to implement regional governance have not worked, because of the opposition of protective city politicians and the opposition of the exclusive suburbs. But cooperation has become increasingly important. Racial and income segregation have cut off the city from its neighbors. It is hard to envision any real and lasting success for the redevelopment of the central city if it remains isolated from the rest of the region.

Achieving greater regional cooperation is not a hopeless aim. The route to such cooperation, however, will probably not be the old one of single-level metropolitan governance. Cooperation will have to come in a way that does not weaken what blacks see as their hard-earned political autonomy within the central city (Darden et al. 1987). It will require greater mixing of incomes and races within the metropolis–for example, in suburban housing. It will require serious statewide attention to the problems of social and economic distress that have unfairly shackled the city of Detroit. And it will require, in the final analysis, a true societal commitment to a strategy of urban and regional development that includes all citizens—rich and poor, skilled and unskilled, black and white.

Notes

1. See her pp. 203–204, which include charts listing the organizations and the percentage of leadership positions held by corporate directors.
2. Ford's grandson Henry Ford II, who took over the firm in 1945, took a more active interest in the city of Detroit, especially after the 1967 riot. In addition, the Ford Foundation supported facilities and institutions such as Ford

Hospital and the Detroit Symphony Orchestra. In the 1970s, the General Motors Company began to actively redevelop the New Center area, in which its corporate headquarters were located. For a history of the relationship between the auto companies and the city, see Conot (1986).

3. For specifics of 1975 dollar requests, see City of Detroit (1975), 21A. For an overview of new policies, see City of Detroit (1978), 210–213.
4. Calculated from City of Detroit (1982), 4–32. Includes only those funds geographically identifiable as having been in a particular sector or subcommunity. Does not include CDBG administration, planning, public and social services or neighborhood opportunity funds. For maps, see Darden et al. (1987). Much of the rest of this chapter draws on Chapter 5 of that book.
5. *Poletown Council* v. *Detroit* (1981):646.

References

Anton, Thomas J. 1983. *Federal Aid to Detroit*. Washington, D.C.: Brookings Institution.

Babson, Steven. 1986. *Working Detroit: The Making of a Union Town*. Detroit: Wayne State University Press.

Blonston, Gary. 1986. "The Plant: A Second Chance for Detroit." *Detroit Free Press Magazine* (September 8):6–15, 29.

City of Detroit. City Plan Commission. 1944. "Planning Detroit, 1944." Detroit: City Plan Commission.

———. 1945. "Planning." *Detroit City Plan Commission Newsletter* (May).

———. 1946. Minutes of the Commission meeting. Burton Historical Collection, Detroit Public Library, Detroit Mayors. Box 2. File: City Plan Commission (November 21).

———. 1958. "Industrial Renewal Program: Progress Report." Detroit: City Plan Commission.

———. 1962. *Renewal and Revenue: An Evaluation of the Urban Renewal Program in Detroit*.

———. 1975. "Moving Detroit Forward: A Plan for Urban Economic Revitalization" (April).

———. 1978. "Overall Economic Development Program," 2d draft (August).

———. 1982. "Community Development Entitlement Grant Program: Program and Project Descriptions" (January).

Clark, Thomas. 1979. *Blacks in Suburbs: A National Perspective*. New Brunswick, N.J.: Rutgers University, Center for Urban Policy Research.

Conot, Robert. 1986. *American Odyssey*. Detroit: Wayne State University Press.

Darden, Joseph, Richard Child Hill, June Thomas, and Richard Thomas. 1987. *Detroit: Race and Uneven Development*. Philadelphia: Temple University Press.

Detroit Free Press. 1983 (May 11).

Detroit News. 1986 (January 19).

Emery, George. 1945. Letter to Mayor Edward Jeffries. Burton Historical Collection, Detroit Public Library, Detroit Mayors. Box 2. File: City Plan Commission.

Ewen, Linda. 1978. *Corporate Power and Urban Crisis in Detroit*. Princeton, N.J.: Princeton University Press.

Fasenfest, David. 1986. "Community Politics and Urban Redevelopment: Poletown, Detroit, and General Motors." *Urban Affairs Quarterly* 22 (September):101–123.

Hill, Richard Child. 1983. "Crisis in the Motor City." In Susan S. Fainstein, Norman I. Fainstein, Richard C. Hill, Dennis Judd, and Michael P. Smith, *Restructuring the City: The Political Economy of Urban Redevelopment*. New York: Longman.

———. 1984a. "Economic Crisis and Political Response in the City." In *Sunbelt/Snowbelt: Urban Development and Regional Restructuring*, ed. Larry Sawers and William K. Tabb. New York: Oxford University Press.

———. 1984b. "Transnational Capitalism and Urban Crisis: The Case of the Auto Industry and Detroit." *Cities in Recession*, ed. Ivan Szelenyi. Beverly Hills: Sage.

Jones, Bryan, and Lynn Bachelor. 1986. *The Sustaining Hand: Community Leadership and Corporate Power*. Lawrence: University Press of Kansas.

Luria, Dan, and Jack Russell. 1984. "Motor City Changeover." *Sunbelt/Snowbelt: Urban Development and Regional Restructuring*, ed. Larry Sawers and William K. Tabb. New York: Oxford University Press.

Mier, Robert. 1984. "Job Generation as a Road to Recovery." *Rebuilding America's Cities: Roads to Recovery*, ed. Paul R. Porter and David C. Sweet. New Brunswick, N.J.: Rutgers University, Center for Urban Policy Research.

Mollenkopf, John H. 1983. *The Contested City*. Princeton, N.J.: Princeton University Press.

Mowitz, Robert J., and Deil S. Wright. 1962. *Profile of a Metropolis: A Case Book*. Detroit: Wayne State University Press.

"The Path to Prosperity: Findings and Recommendations of the Task Force for a Long-Term Economic Strategy for Michigan." 1984. n.p.

Peterson, George E. 1986. "Urban Policy and the Cyclical Behavior of Cities." *Reagan and the Cities*, ed. George E. Peterson and Carol W. Lewis. Washington, D.C.: Urban Institute.

Poletown Council v. *Detroit*. 1981. 410 Mich. 616 (March).

Ravitz, Mel. 1987. Personal interview (March 11).

So, Frank, Israel Stollman, Frank Beal, and David Arnold. 1979. *The Practice of Local Government Planning*. Washington, D.C.: International City Management Association.

Thomas, June. 1985. "Neighborhood Response to Redevelopment in Detroit." *Community Development Journal* 20 (April):89–98.

———. 1987. "Planning and Industrial Decline in Detroit." Paper presented to a meeting of the Association of Collegiate Schools of Planning, Los Angeles (November).

————. 1988. "Racial Crisis and the Fall of the Detroit City Plan Commission." *Journal of the American Planning Association* 54 (Spring):150–161.

Thomas, Richard W. 1987. "The State of Black Detroit: Building from Strength. The Black Self-Help Tradition in Detroit." Detroit: Detroit Urban League.

Williams, Kristine. 1987. "Planning Detroit's Future." *Planning and Zoning News* (September).

Larry Bennett

9. Postwar Redevelopment in Chicago: The Declining Politics of Party and the Rise of Neighborhood Politics

In many respects, the post–World War II economic evolution of Chicago, as well as the city government's responses to population loss and the decline of older industries, parallel the experience of other U.S. cities. In contrast, the Cook County Democratic party's domination of Chicago politics during this period was unique. Mayor Richard J. Daley, who governed the city from 1955 until his death in 1976, presided over what has been called the last of the big city political machines. Yet ultimately, the objectives and effects of Chicago's post–World War II redevelopment strategy worked at cross-purposes to the perpetuation of the Democratic machine. The principal objective of this chapter is to trace the connection among orthodox redevelopment strategies, political realignment, and the emergence of neighborhood-based redevelopment strategies in Chicago.

From the mid-1950s until the mid-1970s, Mayor Daley was the pivotal figure shaping local planning, redevelopment, and economic development policy. The Kennedy and Johnson administrations, cognizant of the Cook County Democratic party's role in delivering the presidential election vote, rewarded Chicago with substantial urban renewal funding. When the city's business leaders and developers sought cooperation from municipal government, their first stop was the fifth floor of City Hall, where Mayor Daley's office was located. If Mayor Daley could be convinced to throw his support behind a particular project, the city's redevelopment and housing officials could be expected to execute the necessary municipal action in an expeditious fashion (Rakove 1975:76–89; Squires et al. 1987:158–163).

Beginning during Daley's term and continuing into the 1980s, the face of Chicago was reshaped by municipally sponsored redevelopment and partnerships linking city government with universities, hospitals, developers, and major corporations. As a result of these initiatives, the downtown Loop area has been substantially rebuilt, and "back office" business operations, retail districts, and residential areas now ring the old downtown. On the North Side of the city along the shore of Lake Michigan, gentrification has proceeded in a band of neighborhoods including Old Town, Lincoln Park, and Lakeview.

Chicago has not been completely rebuilt, however. The neighborhoods south and west of the Loop include thousands of decayed, abandoned, and wrecked housing units. The unemployment and poverty rates of their residents far exceed the national averages. In addition, public services and infrastructure are clearly inadequate. The fiscal neglect of neighborhoods located from the Loop and the lakefront has been documented by the research of political scientist James Greer, who observed that "public and private investment are disproportionately distributed in the very best neighborhoods" (Greer 1983:181).[1]

Nor has private investment and municipally sponsored redevelopment shored up the local economy's traditional centerpiece, heavy industry. In sections of the city such as South Chicago, where several steel mills have closed in recent years, plant closings and job losses have resonated throughout the neighborhoods (Bensman and Lynch 1987). Local retailers have lost business, home maintenance has been deferred, and families have left to seek better fortune in other communities.

The interaction of redevelopment policy, its social and spatial consequences, and economic transformation has had important political consequences. Urban renewal–spawned neighborhood disruption in central Chicago spilled over to the outlying parts of the city as dislocated residents sought new places to live. Neighborhood preservation became a principal theme of neighborhood activists and some ward-level political party organizations. However, because the city government was a principal agent of neighborhood change, local Democratic organizations could not easily manage this issue, and neighborhoods frequently mobilized in opposition to the municipal planning and redevelopment agenda.

With the death of Mayor Daley in 1976, the municipal government's ability to build support for and execute redevelopment policy declined precipitously. Since the late 1960s, neighborhood mobilization had spread across the city, and even toward the end of Daley's term the city government had to either anticipate and coopt neighborhood opposition to city plans or accept some neighborhood-based participation in planning and redevelopment efforts.

In a sense, the 1983 election of Harold Washington, Chicago's first black mayor, was the culmination of these trends. His predecessors, Michael Bilandic and Jane Byrne, had struggled unsuccessfully to achieve Daley's renown as a city builder. Byrne, through her efforts to promote redevelopment, managed to antagonize many neighborhood groups. Washington entered office pledging to reorient the city government's redevelopment policy. During Washington's four and one-half years as mayor, planning, housing, and economic development officials often worked closely with neighborhood organizations, and in general sought to forge policies attentive to neighborhood concerns.

The following section is a review of general trends in the postwar economy of Chicago. We then turn to the development coalition built by Mayor Daley and analyze the relationship between redevelopment and the decline of ward-level Democratic party organizations by examining two neighborhood redevelopment initiatives: the University of Illinois–Chicago campus and the Sandburg Village project. Finally, we look at new directions in planning, downtown redevelopment, and neighborhood development since 1983.

Chicago's Post–World War II Economy

From the mid-nineteenth century until the Great Depression Chicago grew at an enormous pace, in large part because of its emergence as the manufacturing center of the Midwestern United States and the hub of the intercontinental rail system. In the years immediately following World War II, the city's economic well-being remained bound to its status as a manufacturing and transportation center. Among its leading industries were steel, heavy machinery, consumer appliances, and food production (Cutler 1982:159–199). Although the railroad industry declined across the country in the years following World War II, Chicago compensated to some degree by constructing O'Hare Airport, which became a leading airline junction.

Although the heart of Chicago's postwar economy remained industrial, economic activity there was more diversified than in many older industrial cities. For example, Chicago and its suburbs trailed only New York as a location of Fortune 500 corporate headquarters (Cohen 1981:302). Financial institutions, insurance companies, and real estate firms also employed thousands of workers. With the construction of a huge exhibition hall, McCormick Place, in the 1960s, Chicago became the country's leading location for conventions and trade shows (Cutler 1982:171).

However, by the late 1950s the decentralization of the Chicago metropolitan region was beginning to undercut the central city's economy. As a result of construction of the metropolitan expressway system, residential development on the metropolitan periphery advanced and soon, major businesses were also relocating. In 1961 International Harvester shut down its huge assembly plant on Chicago's West Side. Newer facilities in the Chicago suburbs were available to make up for the production capacity lost with the closing of one of the city's largest industrial units.

National economic restructuring also affected Chicago businesses. By the 1960s the meat-packing industry had decentralized its production facilities, thereby vastly reducing the expense of transporting livestock. Chicago, whose concentration of meat-packing firms was a vestige of the more centralized production structure, experienced a major decline in this industry. Indeed, in 1971 the storied Union Stockyards closed down permanently.

As measured by the decennial Census, the city of Chicago's population peaked in 1950 at 3,621,000. In the next thirty-five years the city lost 20 percent of that figure. Paralleling this population decline were declines in jobs, number of businesses, and income. To take the most dramatic instance of job loss, between 1947 and 1982 manufacturing employment in Chicago declined from 668,000 to 277,000 (Squires et al. 1987:26). Similarly, in a little more than a decade, 1970 to 1981, the number of the city's manufacturing firms declined from 8,087 to 6,127 (Longworth 1981). Ultimately, the disappearance of businesses and jobs affected the material well-being of Chicago's residents. After the 1960s, the city's unemployment rate, especially of minority residents, persistently exceeded the national average. From 1969 to 1979, real income of families in Chicago *declined* by slightly more than 10 percent (Squires et al. 1987:41).

By the late 1970s the principal exception to this pattern of business shutdowns, job loss, and income decline was a surge of investment in downtown Chicago real estate. Between 1979 and 1984, there was more than $4.5 billion in new construction and rehabilitation in Chicago's Loop and immediately adjoining neighborhoods (Ludgin and Masotti 1985). Construction of headquarters and speculative office development were substantial. For the first time in decades, new hotel construction and major renovation of existing hotels resumed. On the south and west sides of the Loop, two new residential communities, Dearborn Park and Presidential Towers, took shape. Also, to the north, west, and south of the old downtown, the rehabilitation of factories and warehouses produced more residences and office and commercial space. Yet the tangible economic consequences of this real estate prosperity have remained illusive. Less than one-quarter of the city's work force is employed in the Loop and its environs; in spite of the huge investment in the late 1970s and early 1980s, the downtown job increase was a modest 8 percent (about 18,000 jobs) between 1972 and 1982 (Squires et al. 1987:35). Furthermore, there are no signs that laid-off industrial workers claimed more than a handful of these new jobs.

In part, Chicago's downtown boom was indicative of a larger investment pattern that produced similar building booms in other cities. However, although the quantity of recent real estate investment in Chicago is striking, the character of that investment is essentially consistent with the city's long-term, post–World War II pattern of development. The latter was forged by the development coalition organized by Richard J. Daley. In order to understand how Chicago came to be restructured in the fashion described thus far in this chapter, it is necessary to examine that development coalition.

Richard Daley's Growth Coalition

At the time of Richard Daley's election as mayor in the spring of 1955, the fortunes of the Cook County Democratic party were at a low ebb. In 1946, Mayor Edward Kelly, who, along with party chairman Patrick Nash, had presided over the Democratic party's institutionalization as the dominant force in city government, was prevented by party insiders from seeking reelection. In the 1940s several scandals had damaged the Kelly administration, and eventually, Kelly lost the support of a substantial number of the party's ward committeemen (Biles 1984:133–151). The Democrats then nominated and elected as mayor for two terms Martin Kennelly, a businessman who had not been active in the party. Mayor Kennelly hazarded some ventures in reforming the city administration, yet he made little effort to oversee the City Council. The latter fell under the control of a handful of regular Democratic aldermen, and interfactional squabbling became commonplace (Meyerson and Banfield 1964: 61–88; O'Connor 1976:83–92).

Richard Daley had held the post of eleventh ward Democratic ward committeeman since the 1940s, and beginning in the 1930s he had occupied a series of elective and appointive local and state government positions. He took over as party chairman two years in advance of the 1955 mayoral election and at the end of 1954 received the party's endorsement as its mayoral candidate. Daley defeated Kennelly, his principal opponents, in a three-way Democratic primary. In a closely contested general election, Daley won the mayoralty over Robert Merriam, a lifelong Democrat and opponent of the machine who was nominated by the Republican party (O'Connor 1976:106–125).

Thus, when Daley assumed the mayoralty, the Democratic party had weathered a decade of internal fighting and declining repute among local voters. Furthermore, Chicago's business and civic leaders had begun to perceive a city in decline; and like similar elites in other cities, they had taken some steps toward addressing what were, in their minds, the city's pressing problems. Historian Arnold Hirsch has recounted the efforts of business leaders like Milton C. Mumford and Holman C. Pettibone, and of a private civic group, the Metropolitan Housing and Planning Council, to initiate urban redevelopment in the city. In the years preceding Daley's election as mayor, their great victory was the clearance of a large Near South Side area for the expansion of Michael Reese Hospital and the Illinois Institute of Technology and the development of two large-scale, middle-income housing projects, Lake Meadows and Prairie Shore (Hirsch 1983:100–134).

Despite the scope of the Near South Side redevelopment efforts, much remained to be done if the city were to be substantially reshaped. Under Richard J. Daley, the pace of redevelopment increased markedly. In 1957, the municipal government established a Department of City Planning, which was separate from the longstanding and semiautonomous Chicago Plan Commission, and the new agency promptly produced a *Development Plan for the Central Area of Chicago* in 1958 (City of Chicago, Department of City Planning 1958). In the early years of the Daley administration there were substantial increases in the city planning staff and in agency funding, as well as the initiation and execution of a far more extensive urban renewal program (Squires et al. 1987:201 n. 21).

Daley's term in office coincided with massive public works investments. His administration oversaw the construction of the city's expressway network and the expansion of its system of rail mass transit. McCormick Place was built along Lake Michigan just to the southeast of the Loop. To the northwest of the city Daley accomplished the annexation of a large parcel of suburban territory, on which O'Hare Airport was developed.

Daley's planning, redevelopment, and public works initiatives were consistent with the expectations of Chicago's business leaders. His biographers notes that he devoted considerable energy to cultivating personal relations with important business figures. Just as important, the substance of Daley era redevelopment was consistent with the preferences of important business groups such as the Chicago Central Area Committee. Planning documents such as the 1958 central area *Development Plan* portray a future downtown area devoted to business management and finance, retailing, and residence—a vision quite in keeping with the emerging consensus of the committee (Bennett et al. 1988). Chicago's business leaders were also impressed by the highly professional planning and redevelopment officials hired by Daley. They included Housing and Redevelopment Coordinator James Downs and City Planning Director Ira Bach.

Daley's development alliance should be viewed as part of a larger strategy by which the mayor sought to expand his political coalition and overcome the obvious weaknesses of the mid-1950s Democratic machine. Business leaders, given personal access to the mayor, favored with appointments to various municipal boards and commissions, and impressed by a forward-looking redevelopment program, at the very least lost any inclination to attempt to unseat the mayor. Moreover, Mayor Daley developed a low tax–good service philosophy of government that appealed to small business and middle-class residents who were less concerned about city planning and downtown redevelopment.

For Daley, the extension of his political coalition had several advantages. The perceived efficiency of his administration reduced criticism of the Democratic machine, and this permitted the ward-level organizations to go about their work of recruiting activists and mobilizing voters without interference. Mayor Daley centralized the patronage process, which in effect reduced the power of ward committeemen. However, he increased the size of city government, and through the late 1960s his city had a very healthy economy. Thus, ward-level job opportunities were numerous, and over time most ward organizations in the city developed a firm loyalty to Daley. Finally, the strong economy, big public works policy, and favorable treatment of municipal workers meant that Daley could count on the active support of Chicago's organized labor. In the end, Richard Daley reinvigorated the Democratic machine in Chicago through the promotion of important public policy initiatives, thus substantially widening the net of his political coalition. Redevelopment was, if not the linchpin, at least a main spoke in this restructured political coalition.

Two Cases of Daley-Era Urban Redevelopment

Three features of urban redevelopment during the Daley administration account for the neighborhood backlash that was evident by the late 1960s. First, the principal aim of city planning in general and of particular redevelopment projects was downtown protection. Like the downtown business community, the city administration took the position that maintenance of the Loop as an attractive place for business, cultural facilities, and residences was an overriding objective of local public policy. Second, particular projects were initiated by parties outside the city government. The Dailey administration's approach to restructuring the city was procedural, not substantive. Although documents such as the 1958 central area *Development Plan* outline a vision of the future Chicago, impetus for the execution of particular projects came from actors apart from the city administration. Third, Daley administration planners and redevelopment officials did not, as a rule, extend themselves to consult with the neighborhoods affected by the redevelopment projects. This is not surprising, as particular projects tended to be justified in reference to the larger objective of downtown protection, and their nongovernment sponsors were their true initiators. In effect, redevelopment planning was carried out for communities and not with communities.

Two of the most ambitious urban redevelopment projects during the Daley administration were the Harrison Street–Halsted Street site on the Near West Side, which became the University of Illinois at Chicago (UIC) campus, and a middle-income residential project on the Near North Side, Sandburg Village.[2] By examining the execution of these redevelopment projects, we can observe how they conform to the overall pattern of redevelopment in Chicago. Furthermore, we can observe how redevelopment tended to undercut the legitimacy of local party politicians and spur nonparty neighborhood mobilization.

Although the specific rationales used to justify clearance of the Harrison-Halsted area for the new UIC campus and the North Avenue–LaSalle Street site for Sandburg Village were rather circuitous, each project ultimately played a role in preserving the downtown Loop area. For the most of its history the Harrison-Halsted area, just to the southwest of the Loop, was a port of entry for Italian immigrants. By World War II, its physical appearance was quite unseemly, and there was the prospect of substantial black replacement of the older Italian population (Nelli 1970:25–40; Rosen 1980:94–100). On the North Side, the North Avenue–LaSalle Street redevelopment area straddled the decrepit Old Town neighborhood to the west and the very affluent Gold Coast to the east. After World War II, the Gold Coast was the city's only remaining upper-income, central area neighborhood. Thus, it was easy for the city to agree with groups such as the Greater North Michigan Avenue Association that a "wall" should be built between the Gold Coast and the slums encroaching on the west (DeClue 1978).

The UIC campus and Sandburg Village were both initiated by actors separate from city government. In the Near West Side neighborhood that presently houses UIC, an indigenous redevelopment effort had been under way since the 1940s, but in 1960 Mayor Daley unilaterally turned over the designated urban renewal site to the University of Illinois, which for several years had sought a location for a permanent campus in Chicago (Rosen 1980:61–87). The Sandburg Village project grew out of pressure by a well-known developer, Arthur Rubloff, and the Greater North Michigan Avenue Association, which was allied with him. Their frequently stated intention was to insulate the Gold Coast from the rundown neighborhood to its west (Gapp 1961).

As might be anticipated, given the impetus for these two projects, there was limited neighborhood participation in their planning and execution. In the case of the UIC–Near West Side redevelopment area, Mayor Daley committed the site to the University of Illinois *before* notifying the area's chief neighborhood organization, Hull House. By the time neighborhood opposition to the city's decision mobilized, the available forums for debating the proposal were outside the community: City Council, the state legislature, the Illinois Housing Board, and the courts. In none of these places could opponents offer alternative proposals or debate the substantive merits of the UIC-city proposal. In any event, each of these forums upheld the decision to turn over the site to the university (Rosen 1980:112–121).

Sandburg Village was a clearance project carried out under the provisions of the 1947 Illinois Blighted Areas Redevelopment Act, which did not require advance neighborhood hearings. Incumbent project-area businesses were assured that they could relocate to a commercial complex to be developed on the Sandburg Village site, but in fact, new space was never made available (Gapp 1964; Moore 1966).

Interestingly ward-level politicians in both areas were also bypassed in project planning. This was in spite of the fact that two prominent machine aldermen, John D'Arco of the first ward (UIC site) and Paddy Bauler of the forty-third ward (Sandburg Village), represented local residents. Redevelopment in each of these wards threatened to dislocate numerous constituents, and failure to protect these constituents would mean that the ward organizations could anticipate losing some part of their reputation for clout in City Hall. The degree of disillusionment that might follow this turn of events is suggested by this comment from George Rosen, historian of the UIC planning process, regarding alderman John D'Arco's first-ward constituents: "the Italian, Greek, and Spanish-speaking residents of the area didn't believe it could happen. They knew the fabled power of the Italian political leaders of the area and felt those leaders, who were close to the Democratic city leaders, would never agree to such a proposal which would change already committed plans for the area from residential renewal to institutional use" (Rosen 1980:86). In fact, both D'Arco and Bauler were unhappy with the redevelopment projects in their wards, but Mayor Daley overruled their objections (Bach 1983; DeClue 1978; Rosen 1980:87).

There was neighborhood opposition to both the UIC and Sandburg Village projects, but in neither instance were opponents able to block or substantially amend project plans. As we have already noted, the very vocal opposition to the UIC plan mobilized only after the city had committed the Near West Side site to the University of Illinois. The momentum of the project was such that, at this stage, its opponents engaged in a futile exercise of protesting before forums, such as the City Council, whose endorsement of the plan was foreordained.

The planning of Sandburg Village managed to avoid widespread neighborhood opposition. The city did not hold hearings in the neighborhood, and site acquisition and demolition were carried out very expeditiously. Opposition to the redevelopment plan did occur at the point when displaced businesses recognized that no provision would be made for their on-site relocation. However, by this time the old neighborhood had been demolished and its residents dispersed, and the arguments offered by the displaced businesses focused on the guarantees they thought they had received. Thus, they had no constituents to mobilize and no platform that transcended their particular concerns.

In each of these cases redevelopment generated substantial resentment toward the Daley administration, and furthermore, demonstrated the first and forty-third ward organizations' inability to defend community interests. By the late 1960s, neighborhood mobilization was occurring all over Chicago. Some of this mobilization was a response to new redevelopment and highway construction proposals, such as the longstanding movement to block a proposed "crosstown" expressway that would run along Chicago's western border (Pavlos 1975; Pick 1978). In other cases, neighborhood groups formed to cope with problems such as block-busting by real estate firms, street crime, and poor city services, that were not the direct result of urban redevelopment initiatives. Yet both types of mobilization bypassed the traditional channel of neighborhood activism, the Democratic ward organizations. The atrophy of the ward organizations was signaled by the declining voter turnouts, even when Mayor Daley sought reelection (Bennett 1987a:14). It has been documented by observations of ward-level politics such as Thomas Guterbock's case study of a North Side regular Democratic ward organization (Guterbock 1980).

Neighborhood backlash against urban redevelopment is not the sole factor explaining the collapse of the Democratic machine by the early 1980s, but it is one important element in the constellation of factors that worked to undercut that machine. Furthermore, when Harold Washington successfully sought the mayoralty in 1983, advocating a platform that included staunch opposition to the Democratic machine, neighborhood groups played an important role in putting him in office and defining the programmatic agenda of his administration (Kleppner 1985:143–147).

Emerging Trends in Neighborhood and Economic Development

Neighborhood activism is a longstanding component of politics in Chicago. Thus, in considering the program of the Washington administration in relation to new approaches to planning, redevelopment, and economic development, it is essential to note that even before 1983, neighborhood-based organizations were working on a variety of innovative programs. For instance, in the 1970s West Side community groups formed the nucleus of the Metropolitan Area Housing Alliance, which played a major role in the national anti-redlining movement.

In 1984, the Chicago Reinvestment Alliance, which includes three dozen neighborhood and housing groups, as well as the National Training and Information Center, a veteran of the anti-redlining mobilization, joined three major Chicago banks to initiate the Neighborhood Lending Program. The reinvestment alliance, using as leverage provisions of the federal Community Reinvestment Act that allow local groups to review and challenge the practices of lending institutions, convinced the three Chicago banks (the First National Bank, the Harris Trust, and the Northern Trust) to commit funds to neighborhood residential and commercial projects. Two of the reinvestment alliance's member organizations, the Chicago Rehab Network and the Chicago Association of Neighborhood Development Organizations, link the three lender banks with neighborhood housing development corporations, landlords, and businesses. Although implementation of the program began slowly, by late 1987 reinvestment alliance members were pleased with its progress. Under the terms of the agreement, the three banks will ultimately invest nearly $200 million in neighborhood projects (Swift and Pogge 1984; DeMuth 1985; Metzger and Weiss 1988).

Another notable partnership united the Center for Neighborhood Technology, Peoples Gas (a local utility), and the Chicago Energy Savers Fund, established by the Washington administration. The city government and Peoples Gas provided $15 million for loans to landlords making weatherization investments in their property. The Center for Neighborhood Technology oversees the program (Moberg 1987:7). Although establishment of the Energy Savers Fund is partially attributable to the initiative of the Washington administration, the center predates the administration and well before 1983 had identified neighborhood energy conservation as a major objective.

Nonetheless, Harold Washington campaigned for the mayoralty as a critic of orthodox redevelopment strategies; and far more than mayors Bilandic or Byrne, he sought to set a new economic development agenda. Within weeks of assuming office, Washington appointed a series of task forces to examine critical issues such as the city's declining steel industry (Mier et al. 1986). By the spring of 1984 the Washington administration had released a detailed economic development agenda that emphasized balanced economic growth benefiting the downtown as well as outlying neighborhoods, job creation as the principal criterion for allocating public subsidies, and neighborhood participation in defining economic development policy (City of Chicago 1984). By its estimate, between the 1984–1985 and 1986–1987 fiscal years, the Washington administration doubled the number of neighborhood-based groups receiving support in the form of Community Development Block Grants (City of Chicago, Mayor's Office of Inquiry and Information 1985; 1987). For the first time, under the Washington administration the city debated linked development measures to channel back to the neighborhoods some of the benefits accruing from downtown investment.

In many respects, the specific programmatic initiatives of the Washington administration matched its vision of an alternative economic development agenda. The Department of Housing and the Department of Economic Development introduced and enlarged a series of programs aimed at neighborhood problems: loans and grants for single-family homeowners and the owners of multifamily structures, emergency loans to prevent housing abandonment, loans for small businesses, and technical assistance for neighborhood-based firms (Moberg 1987).

The administration also sought to reshape the impacts of past administrations' planning and economic development initiatives. From the Bilandic and Byrne administrations Harold Washington inherited a controversial downtown redevelopment plan, the North Loop project (Bennett 1986). The city carried on with that project, but by imposing affirmative action standards on developers sought to ensure some degree of job creation for disadvantaged local residents (McCarron 1985). Similarly, the Washington administration renegotiated the financing of another controversial Byrne venture, the Presidential Towers residential complex to the west of the Loop, winning from the developers approximately $15 million for a trust fund to finance affordable housing (Clark 1987).

In other instances, the Washington administration was less able to re-orient economic development policy. For example, both of the city's major league baseball franchises, the Cubs and the White Sox, as well as the city's 1986 Super Bowl champion Bears, were dissatisfied with their stadiums. The Bears and White Sox complained that Soldier Field and White Sox Park, respectively, were antiquated. The owners of the Cubs wished to install lights in Wrigley Field, the last major league ballpark in which only day games were played. In each case the sports organizations held out for substantial assistance from the city, in the form of either fiscal help or negotiation with affected neighborhood residents and organizations. By the middle of 1987 the city and the Bears had agreed on a site for a new football stadium, but some leaders in the selected West Side neighborhood were highly skeptical of the city's promise to find relocation housing for about one thousand incumbent residents (Barry 1987). In late 1987 Mayor Washington made a compromise proposal to the Cubs and Wrigleyville neighborhood activists. The mayor's plan called for the installation of lights at Wrigley Field, but it also limited the number of evening games that the Cubs could schedule. Opponents of lights in Wrigley Field nevertheless accused the mayor of betrayal (McCarron 1987).

The Washington administration also sought to steer a middle course in the linked development debate. In 1984, a neighborhood group called the Save Our Neighborhoods/Save Our City Coalition (SON/SOC) induced Mayor Washington to establish a committee to study linked development and make recommendations that could guide the drafting of a linked development ordinance. The coalition also offered a linked development proposal, whose centerpiece was a five dollar per square foot levy on downtown construction in excess of 100,000 square feet. These funds would then be distributed to neighborhoods around the city.

The mayor's committee included neighborhood activists, representatives of the development and banking communities, and municipal administrators. The business representatives strenuously opposed the SON/SOC plan; and although the committee ultimately made a series of recommendations that included elements of the SON/SOC proposal, Mayor Washington did not take action on the committee report. Instead, the administration's planning and economic development agencies began to negotiate development contracts that required various kinds of commitments from developers, such as public infrastructure investments and technical assistance to neighborhood groups. The administration called this practice linked development, but the SON/SOC leadership objected to this "voluntary linkage" (Bennett 1987b).

The linked development and stadium controversies illustrate a major constraint on the Washington administration and its economic development agenda. In dealing with the development issues or particular projects that mobilize the major actors in Chicago's economy—the city's half dozen largest banks, its headquartered corporations, major developers, its major league sports franchises—it is difficult for the municipal administration not to acquiesce to at least some of the demands of capital. These dominant economic actors can threaten to take their investments elsewhere, and to some degree any administration must heed this threat. The political fallout from major corporate pullouts, or from the relocation of a major league sports franchise, is also a hazard that an administration must consider. It would be an exaggeration to claim that the Washington administration sold out to the city's major corporate actors, but the administration did make deals. Often, these deals entailed substantial fiscal commitments by the city, and the money thus committed was not available for other kinds of economic development or the provision of basic city services.

Some neighborhood activists in Chicago also contended that the Washington administration was a wellspring of numerous good, effective neighborhood-oriented programs, but they did not perceive the outlines of an overarching city policy for economic development. Members of the city administration would disagree, but even Mayor Washington's staunchest supporters acknowledged that the fruits of many of the administration's programs would be long in appearing. Moreover, by Washington's second term in office, major components of the city's service delivery system, such as the public schools, which in the long run must be considered an essential ingredient for overall economic recovery, had hardly been addressed.

On November 25, 1987, after attending the groundbreaking ceremony for a low-income housing project on Chicago's South Side, Mayor Harold Washington suffered a fatal heart attack. Washington's unexpected death will complicate the process of judging the success of his administration's planning, redevelopment, and economic development program. During Washington's first term, City Council opposition hampered his efforts. Throughout his four and one-half years as mayor, changes in the national economy, federal government fiscal cutbacks, and a nervous local business community were additional hurdles the mayor and his administration had to face. Ultimately, the consequences of many of the Washington administration's initiatives will depend on the stewardship of his successors as mayor. What is not in doubt, however, is that future municipal administrations must continue to address the neighborhood needs and heed the mobilized neighborhood residents whose role in the Washington administration gave it much of its distinctive character.

Notes

1. Despite its commitment to redirect resources to neighborhoods located away from the Loop and the lakefront, the administration of Mayor Harold Washington, at least in the case of public works expenditures, had difficulty implementing this pledge. Greer (1986:37) comments that there was "little difference between recent administrations in terms of this area of public resource allocation." Greer's most recent figures (personal communication) indicate that the city of Chicago capital budget for 1985 to 1991 allocates 51 percent of the spending to three of the city's seventy-seven community areas: O'Hare Airport, the Loop, and the Near North Side. Only about 3 percent of the city's residents live in these areas, but the airport is a major economic institution undergoing expansion, the Loop is the city's locus of corporate and commercial investment, and the Near North Side is the city's primary area of gentrification.
2. This discussion of the Near West Side urban renewal project draws on Rosen (1980).

References

Bach, Ira. 1983. Interview with Chicago's director of development (December 21 and 23).

Barry, Patrick. 1987. "Deal-Making Begins as West Side Stadium Gets Nod." *The Neighborhood Works* (July):9–11.

Bennett, Larry. 1986. "Beyond Urban Renewal: Chicago's North Loop Redevelopment Project." *Urban Affairs Quarterly* 22:242–260.

———. 1987a. "In the Wake of Richard J. Daley: Chicago's Declining Politics of Party and Shifting Politics of Development." Paper presented at the annual meeting of the American Political Science Association, Chicago (September).

———. 1987b. "The Dilemmas of Building a Progressive Urban Coalition: The Linked Development Debate in Chicago." *Journal of Urban Affairs* 9:263–276.

Bennett, Larry, Kathleen McCourt, Philip Nyden, and Gregory D. Squires. 1988. "Chicago's North Loop Redevelopment Project: A Growth Machine on Hold." In *Business Elite and Urban Development*, ed. Scott Cummings. Albany: State University of New York Press.

Bensman, David, and Roberta Lynch. 1987. *Rusted Dreams: Hard Times in a Steel Community*. New York: McGraw-Hill.

Biles, Roger. 1984. *Big City Boss in Depression and War: Mayor Edward J. Kelly of Chicago*. DeKalb: Northern Illinois University Press.

City of Chicago. 1984. *Chicago Development Plan, 1984*.

————. Department of City Planning. 1958. *Development Plan for the Central Area of Chicago*.

City of Chicago. Mayor's Office of Inquiry and Information. 1985. *Neighborhood Bulletin* (Winter).

————. 1987. *Neighborhood Bulletin* (Summer).

Clark, Thom. 1987. "Luxury Towers Seed Housing Trust Fund." *The Neighborhood Works* (March):3.

Cohen, R. B. 1981. "The New International Division of Labor, Multinational Corporations, and Urban Hierarchy." In *Urbanization and Urban Planning in Capitalist Society*, ed. Michael Dear and Allen J. Scott, pp. 287–315. New York: Methuen.

Cutler, Irving. 1982. *Chicago: Metropolis of the Mid-Continent*. Dubuque, Iowa: Kendall/Hunt.

DeClue, Denise. 1978. "The Siege of Sandburg Village." *The Reader* (January 20).

DeMuth, Jerry. 1985. "Downtown Bank Lending Programs Finally Get Rolling," *The Neighborhood Works* (March):9–11.

Gapp, Paul. 1961. "Land Group, Chief Clash." *Chicago Daily News* (March 21).

————. 1964. "Anti-Shopping Center Plan Stuns Carl Sandburg Area." *Chicago Daily News* (April 23).

Greer, James L. 1983. "The Politics of Decline and Growth: Planning, Economic Transformation, and the Structuring of Urban Futures in American Cities." Ph.D. dissertation, University of Chicago.

————. 1986. *Capital Investment in Chicago: Fragmented Process, Unequal Outcomes*. Chicago: University of Chicago, Center for Urban Research and Policy Studies.

Guterbock, Thomas M. 1980. *Machine Politics in Transition: Party and Community in Chicago*. Chicago: University of Chicago Press.

Hirsch, Arnold R. 1983. *Making the Second Ghetto: Race and Housing in Chicago, 1940–1960*. New York: Cambridge University Press.

Kleppner, Paul. 1985. *Chicago Divided: The Making of a Black Mayor*. DeKalb: Northern Illinois University Press.

Longworth, R.C. 1981. "How Much Time Do We Have? . . . No Time." *Chicago Tribune* (May 10).

Ludgin, Mary K., and Louis H. Masotti. 1985. *Downtown Development: Chicago, 1979–1984*. Evanston, Ill.: Center for Urban Affairs and Policy Research, Northwestern University.

McCarron, John. 1985. "City Sets 30 Percent Minority Goal for N. Loop," *Chicago Tribune* (October 27).

————. 1987. "Mayor Says to Turn on Cubs Lights." *Chicago Tribune* (November 14).

Metzger, John T., and Marc A. Weiss. 1988. *The Role of Private Lending in Neighborhood Development: The Chicago Experience*. Evanston, Ill.: Center for Urban Affairs and Policy Research, Northwestern University.

Meyerson, Martin, and Edward C. Banfield. 1964. *Politics, Planning, and the Public Interest: The Case of Public Housing in Chicago*. New York: Free Press.

Mier, Robert, Kari J. Moe, and Irene Sherr. 1986. "Strategic Planning and the Pursuit of Reform, Economic Development, and Equity." *Journal of the American Planning Association* 52:299–309.

Moberg, David. 1987. "The Next Four Years: Neighborhood Agendas." *The Neighborhood Works* (May):1–8.

Moore, Ruth. 1966. "Propose Razing Buildings by Sandburg Village." *Chicago Sun-Times* (April 22).

Nelli, Humbert S. 1970. *The Italians in Chicago, 1880–1930*. New York: Oxford University Press.

O'Connor, Len. 1976. *Clout: Mayor Daley and His City*. New York: Avon.

Pavlos, Elliot Arthur. 1975. "Chicago's Crosstown Expressway: A Case Study in Urban Expressways." In *The Manipulated City*, ed. Stephen Gale and Eric G. Moore, pp. 255–261. Chicago: Maaroufa Press.

Pick, Grant. 1978. "The New Improved Crosstown." *The Reader*, (January 13).

Rakove, Milton. 1975. *Don't Make No Waves—Don't Back No Losers: An Insider's Analysis of the Daley Machine*. Bloomington: Indiana University Press.

Rosen, George. 1980. *Decision-Making Chicago-Style: The Making of a University of Illinois Campus*. Urbana: University of Illinois Press.

Squires, Gregory D., Larry Bennett, Kathleen McCourt, and Philip Nyden. 1987. *Chicago: Race, Class, and the Response to Urban Decline*. Philadelphia: Temple University Press.

Swift, Larry D., and Jean Pogge. 1984. "Neighborhood Reinvestment Partnership: Community Groups Lead the Way for First Chicago Corporation." Chicago: Woodstock Institute (May).

10. Congenial Milwaukee: A Segregated City

Milwaukee presents a clear example of the nature and working of public-private partnerships in an industrial city because of its unchanging political scene. The city had only two mayors between 1948 and 1988, and a single group of business leaders, the Greater Milwaukee Committee, was the leading voice of the private sector throughout that period. This stability blocked the entry of new political forces and ensured consistent policy implementation.

For forty years, the goal of the Greater Milwaukee Committee and its political allies has been to keep the city from falling behind other industrial cities across the country by initiating downtown projects to facilitate transportation, shopping, and entertainment. During this time, the public sector has played a tag-along role, mainly funneling federal dollars into private development.

The partnership ignored the changes taking place in manufacturing during this period: An industrial boom brought prosperity and an influx of workers, many black; then a manufacturing decline undercut corporate profits. The worsening economic conditions affected many people—especially blacks and older white factory workers. At the end of the 1980s, encouraged by the success of new downtown development and by a partial revival in the manufacturing sector, Milwaukee, like many other industrial cities, is looking to economic diversification as a way of overcoming the loss in manufacturing employment, while also continuing its half-hearted and stumbling response to the urban problems resulting from the long manufacturing decline.

The Three Milwaukees

Milwaukee is often regarded by outsiders as a backwater place, a conservative, provincial city that lags far behind the advance guard of more modern U.S. cities. Milwaukeeans have been the butt of many jokes; for example, the nerds on the television shows "Laverne and Shirley" and "Happy Days," both of which were set in the city.

Closer analysis reveals a city with an attractive downtown, prosperous suburbs, and a congenial atmosphere combining both cosmopolitan and traditional values. When judged by some important measures of quality of

178

life—unemployment and crime rates; the level of public services; educational, cultural, and entertainment facilities—Milwaukee scores well. The ethnic heritages of its residents are many and strong. Germans constitute a large group; the Hmong from Laos are the most recent arrivals.

Milwaukee has a complex political history, which has often displayed a maverick trend. Elsewhere in Wisconsin this has been evident in the progressive movement and the efforts of Joe McCarthy. In Milwaukee there is a rich tradition of both left-wing and right-wing politics. But although the left and progressive traditions have had great moments in Milwaukee's history, the 1980s have been dominated, in this city as elsewhere, by the right.

The left wing has supplied Milwaukee with three socialist mayors in this century, whose terms spanned thirty-eight years; they have served as recently as 1948–1960. There have also been a socialist congressman whom the House of Representatives at first refused to seat; communists who built the industrial unions in the 1930s and 1940s; and radical priests who challenged segregation and war in the 1960s and 1970s.

But Milwaukee's politics in the late 1980s is more red-neck than radical. Milwaukee's black community, 25.3 percent of the city's population in 1985, is probably excluded from power more totally in Milwaukee than in any other large city in the United States. In no other metropolitan area does as high a proportion of the black population live in the central city. (98 percent of Milwaukee's blacks lived there throughout the 1980s.) No other major metropolitan area has as high a rate of black unemployment; 25.9 percent in 1986, compared with 5.1 percent for nonblacks (McNeely and Kinlow 1987:27,42; *Milwaukee Journal*, December 27, 1987). Not until 1988 was there a black department head in city government. People say that the Sixteenth Street bridge is the longest in the world, for it connects Poland, on the South Side of the city, with Africa, on the North Side.

These are the three ways of looking at Milwaukee—as a slow, conservative city; a well-run, congenial metropolis; and a seriously segregated community notwithstanding a strong radical tradition. All are accurate.

The guiding force behind Milwaukee's development has been the alliance between the business community and local government. This public-private partnership dates back to the first months after World War II, when a small group of businessmen organized what was the forerunner of today's Greater Milwaukee Committee. Since then, city government has generally played a passive role in the partnership, letting the GMC set the agenda and mostly channeling tax dollars into projects for housing, highways, and downtown buildings.

Conservative Democrats have controlled city government throughout the twenty-eight years (1960–1988) served by Mayor Henry Maier,
thought to be the longest mayoral reign ever in a large U.S. city. The
city's bond rating remains high (AA + in 1987, according to Standard &
Poor's), blizzards and garbage are handled efficiently, and there is not
much public corruption. The metropolitan area has developed without
the booms and busts experienced by faster growing areas; the downtown
is attractive, though it lacks bustle and excitement.

But the 1980s produced a crisis: business leaders were shaken up by
the recession of 1980–1983; the growing black population did not share
in the recovery from that recession; and parts of the once prosperous
South Side suffered from the loss of the city's manufacturing employment. These events elicited a varied response from the governing partnership. On one side were those, including some influential business
leaders, who wanted to extend the partnership to include certain neighborhood groups, albeit on terms dictated by the establishment. On the
other side were those, including more conservative elements in city government, who were trying to continue to isolate the neighborhood groups
and minority communities. The election of John Norquist as mayor upon
Maier's retirement in 1988, brought forces into city government that at
least nominally recognized the need to work with rather than to isolate
these forces.

Why were some business leaders more willing than the city's political
establishment to recognize the problems of the neighborhoods? Perhaps
because they were taught a lesson by the recession of the early 1980s.
Those whose businesses survived learned, from the Japanese and others,
to think things through from a new perspective. But the voters of Milwaukee did not teach Mayor Maier a similar lesson.

In this chapter I will examine the history of Milwaukee since World
War II, and particularly the crisis of the 1980s. My focus will be on the
public-private partnership and the economic issues that have been most
important in the city's development, especially downtown development
and housing.

A Brief History of Milwaukee

According to 1987 estimates, Milwaukee is the nation's eighteenth
largest city, with a population of 605,090. The four-county metropolitan
area (Milwaukee, Ozaukee, Washington, and Waukesha Counties), with
1.4 million people, is the twenty-fourth largest consolidated metropolitan
area. The city's population is declining; the metropolitan area's population is relatively stable.

The city is on the shore of Lake Michigan, ninety miles from Chicago. Originally a fur-trading center, it has been in the shadow of the windy city ever since the 1850s, when Chicago's population surpassed Milwaukee's. Even during Milwaukee's most dramatic moments, such as the 1886 Bay View massacre prompted by strikes for the eight-hour day, Milwaukee took a back seat to Chicago, in that case to the Haymarket protests occurring the same week.

In the 1860s Milwaukee was the largest wheat market in the world. A leather industry developed from the fur trade; a brewing industry developed from the grain industry. It became an industrial city that supplied machines for grain and saw mills, and later motors, and then turbines and electrical switches. At the turn of the century it was a boom town with a vigorous economy and high-technology machinery. Milwaukee was the Silicon Valley of its day, the home of basement inventors. The typewriter was perfected in a downtown machine shop, then sold to an Eastern company named Remington & Sons. Business names included Pabst and Schlitz and Blatz, Evinrude, Harley and Davidson, Briggs & Stratton.

The city matured economically in the first half of the century, becoming a world leader in the production of heavy machinery. During World War II, Milwaukee's machine shops did most of the metalwork required for the intricate and massive atom bomb project. By one estimate, the employees of seventy-seven local companies, led by Allis-Chalmers, worked on the Manhattan Project (Lankevich 1977:71). But today's world uses big machines less. Milwaukee's machinery manufacturers have been overtaken by the new technologies. The economy has been diverse enough to avoid a crash, however. For example, important service industries have developed in Milwaukee: residential mortgage insurance, pioneered by the Mortgage Guaranty Insurance Corporation; and temporary employment led by Manpower Incorporated.

Overall, the metropolitan economy has recovered from the recession of the 1980s, but there are fewer manufacturing and more service jobs, and there is a new emphasis on reviving the entrepreneurial spirit of the turn of the century, as well as an increased number of what a city report calls the "new poor" and the "old poor":

> The "new" poor used to be Milwaukee's traditional household, employed in blue-collar jobs. With the loss of 25,000 manufacturing jobs since 1975, many of these blue-collar households have lost significant earning power and economic security and have median household incomes of less than $15,000 and median per capita incomes of $5,000. The "new" poor appear to be located on the near south side and the neighborhoods adjacent to the poorest on the north side (City of Milwaukee, Department of City Development 1987:19)

The old poor are mainly black. In 1980, before the emergence of the new poor, 59.7 percent of Milwaukee families below the poverty level were black; of children below the poverty level, 70.5 percent were black (McNeely and Kinlow 1987:72).

Milwaukee's Emergence as a Major City, 1945–1962

World War II was beneficial for Milwaukee's economy. In 1939 the city ranked eleventh in the U.S. in the value added to raw materials in its factories, and by 1947 Milwaukee was eighth—the fastest rise of any U.S. city during that decade (Research Clearinghouse of Milwaukee 1950:60).

The city was in a strong financial position. In 1932 the city government adopted a pay-as-you-go policy: no general obligation bonds. By 1943, a debt-amortization fund exceeded the amount of money still owed, and Milwaukee was debt-free. But the private sector had been as unwilling as the public sector to spend, and Milwaukee in 1945 looked very much as it had in 1929, except that it was more crowded and shabbier.

The suburbs were growing, which concerned city leaders (who called them an "iron ring"), though the city population was also growing. Their response to suburbanization was annexation and an unsuccessful fight to avoid being forced to provide water service to suburban industry. From 1945 to 1962, the area of the city proper increased 116 percent, to its present 96 square miles.

There was a postwar housing shortage for veterans and for blacks who had come to Milwaukee during the war. Blacks were 3 percent of the city's population at war's end, but they were a major contributor to population growth. From 1940 to 1950, the city's population grew from 587,472 to 637,392; 25.9 percent of the increase was a result of growth in the black population, from 8,821 (1.5 percent of the city population) to 21,772 (3.4 percent).

Progress on housing was slow. In 1946 the leader of a citizens' group complained about "the 'general hopelessness' of the attitude of the city housing authority" (*Milwaukee Journal*, December 5, 1946). That attitude did not change quickly. Despite a 1948 city referendum authorizing $2.5 million in slum clearance bonds, city plans were not advanced enough to allow the bonds to have been sold by the time the authorizing action for them expired in 1951.

Six small housing projects, totaling only 2,849 units, had been built by the early 1950s. These projects, along with private real estate development, led officials to declare in 1953 that the housing shortage had eased. But as Mayor Frank Zeidler put it, "The lack of enough bare shelter has disappeared, but there is a tremendous amount of substandard housing in which people should not be living" (*Milwaukee Journal*, July 1, 1953).

In the 1950s, efforts turned to modernizing downtown. The main movers were members of the Greater Milwaukee Committee, which had been organized in the first months after the war. ("A bank president, an attorney, a theatre executive, two retailers and several industrialists" gathered in a downtown bank, according to GMC's 1955 annual report.) Their focus was on improvements that could be achieved during the 1948 Wisconsin centennial; the group was thus called the 1948 Corporation. It became the Greater Milwaukee Committee in 1948, having outlived its original function.

As described in the 1958 GMC annual report, the group's founders shared

> alarm over what they considered the degeneration of Greater Milwaukee. The city had not had a major improvement in fifteen years. It was obvious to the group that traffic congestion was strangling the community, that off-street parking was desperately needed, that cultural facilities were sadly lacking, that the core of the community was in effect disintegrating. Even more disturbing to these leaders was the apathy of the community. The feeling seemed to prevail that nothing could be done. No inspiration or guidance emanated from the public bodies which normally would provide such leadership.

The 1948 Corporation stepped in to provide guidance. Its first step was to support a yes vote in a 1947 city referendum on whether the city should abandon its no-debt policy. Voters agreed, 54,036 to 40,909. The following year, bonds were authorized for expressways, blight removal, veterans' housing, parking, and a sports arena. Zeidler was elected mayor (prevailing over Henry Reuss in the general election), though he had opposed the new debt policy.

Zeidler was the last socialist to win public office in Milwaukee. In the thirty-eight years they ran city hall, the socialists never succeeded winning municipal ownership of utilities, but they did leave a legacy of clean government and sound finances—so-called sewer socialism. Business leaders were wary of Zeidler, especially because of his support for public housing. They were quite satisfied to have city government play a subordinate role to the business community.

The late 1940s also saw the purging of communists and their supporters from Milwaukee's labor community, the most dramatic being the expulsion of Harold Cristoffel from United Auto Workers Local 248 at Allis-Chalmers, after a long strike in 1946–1947. The purges effectively eliminated any possibility of strong labor opposition to the new GMC-led group that would set the course for Milwaukee's development.

The GMC, drawing on the influence of the private sector and using the platform provided by city newspapers, facilitated a slow increase in civic improvements in the 1950s. The efforts were rewarded in 1953 by the relocation of the Boston Braves baseball team to Milwaukee's new county-financed stadium, the first transfer of a major league franchise in modern baseball. The 1955 GMC annual report said that "[the committee's] members and supporters can look back upon a decade of civic progress unparalleled in this community's history." Construction of two museums, a civic center, a zoo, a war memorial, a library addition, downtown parking facilities, expressways, and an airport had begun, and a slum clearance program was under way.

The report also revealed how much economic power the GMC wielded. The group's 150 members, it said, owned or managed businesses representing one-fourth of the city's total assessed value of business property, or $198.9 million of $804.7 million. Yet there had been little downtown investment by the private sector. The GMC projects had thus far used taxpayer money. But the new downtown was only half complete.

"Yes, the citizen of Greater Milwaukee sees the rise of a new skyline," wrote GMC President George Kasten in the 1959 report. "But he also sees other skylines and rightfully asks, 'Are we ahead, abreast or behind?' " Kasten's answer: "The Milwaukeean who travels realizes that his city is not keeping pace with San Francisco, Baltimore, Detroit, Pittsburgh and dozens of other centers."

There were even signs of decline. By 1954, the downtown was no longer the area leader in retail sales (*Milwaukee Journal*, July 15, 1956). The real per capita property tax base leveled off in 1952 and began falling in 1957 (Booth n.d.:6). The civic monuments were not bringing people downtown. "Downtown in trouble for lack of decision and action" was the headline of a *Milwaukee Journal* editorial on January 13, 1959. The obstacles to development during the period included: not enough parking space; slow progress on construction of expressways; wrangling among private developers; a state requirement for jury approval of property condemnation; and complicated ownership of many downtown buildings, which had been subdivided for multiple descendants.

There were also racial problems that became political issues. The situation exploded during the 1956 mayoral election, when Zeidler ran for a third term and was tagged a "nigger-lover." Rumors spread that he had used city money to put up billboards across the South inviting blacks to Milwaukee. The issue reached such proportions that members of the Milwaukee Federated Trades Council wrote labor organizations in ten

Southern states, asking if they knew of such billboards. None did. *Time* magazine ran an article on "The shame of Milwaukee" (April 2, 1956), debunking the rumors. Zeidler won reelection with 55.6 percent of the vote, substantially less than the 72.5 percent he received in 1952.

In 1959, the St. Lawrence Seaway was opened, thus fulfilling the city's long-held dream of being an ocean port. The celebration of the opening was classic Milwaukee kitsch. A U.S. Navy flotilla visited the city, and 1,500 marines staged a mock invasion of a Lake Michigan beach. A quarter-million people welcomed the amphibious assault, which was capped off with a simulated nuclear bombing of Milwaukee by a navy plane.

There were more serious battles to come, however. For the first time since the 1920s, the private sector wanted to invest downtown. The Marine National Exchange Bank proposed in 1958 construction of a twenty-eight-story building but insisted on an assessment freeze, under an unused 1943 law that allowed a freeze at the assessed value of the old building. The mayor and Common Council would accept a freeze extending into the 1970s, but the proposal was challenged in 1959 by the Marine Bank's across-the-street neighbor, the First Wisconsin National Bank. The "battle of the banks" brought the enmities existing among the ruling business elite into the open for the first time. "Hot statements continued to fly and the public looked on in amazement" (Wells 1970:249). The Marine Bank won a compromise; a GMC spinoff had helped bring the parties together. The fight had proved to be something of a catharsis, and at last the private sector began investing its own money downtown.

With the retirement of Mayor Zeidler in 1960 and the election of Henry Maier, who had defeated Henry Reuss, rule of City Hall passed to someone who was not perceived as antagonistic to the interests of the business community. Maier consolidated control over the city's development functions by combining three departments into the new Department of City Development. In 1961, a state referendum resulted in abolition of jury trials in land condemnation proceedings, thus, paving the way for an increase in federally funded urban renewal programs. Raved the *Milwaukee Journal* in a 1962 editorial: "The downtown area is stirring out of what has been a long slumber. Though agonizingly slow, the progress of the last five years gives evidence that the renaissance predicted by optimists may not be far off" (March 25, 1962).

Protest, 1962–1968

A renaissance was coming, but it was not the kind the *Milwaukee Journal*'s optimists had predicted. In Milwaukee, as elsewhere, the 1960s saw a renaissance of political protest. The voices of dissent there were still being ignored early in the decade, though, since there was so much good news. For example, when construction of a twenty-one-story addition to the Pfister Hotel, the city's finest, began in 1964, the *Journal* writers editorialized: "The spectacular transformation of Downtown . . . is rushing forward by the hour these days. It is a breath-taking prospect when you envision it all together" (May 14, 1964). Milwaukeeans felt safe; their city had the nation's lowest crime rate in its population category (Lankevich 1977:77).

By 1965, city leaders were talking about creating a "little Rockefeller center" downtown on the Milwaukee River. The metaphor then changed, and there was talk of recreating Copenhagen's Tivoli Gardens, a riverfront showcase of food, music, fountains, and gardens. The county board of supervisors appropriated $1,000 so that its chairman could join businessmen making a trip to Denmark to study the original Tivoli (*Milwaukee Sentinel*, March 9, 1965).

Former Mayor Zeidler sniped at the new mood, saying that "the city needs a more sophisticated type of planning that includes economic and social planning, as well as physical planning." He charged city officials with bottling up blacks in a ghetto. City leaders wanted none of Zeidler's remarks. In an editorial the *Milwaukee Sentinel* commented that: "Zeidler's repeated accusations against Maier, all in general terms and without specific details, are becoming a little tiresome. . . . It would be refreshing—it might even be helpful—if Zeidler were to tell us, in full detail, just what he did during his twelve years in office, to meet those developing problems. We do not recall that he did very much" (*Milwaukee Sentinel* 1963).

In these years, the white population was declining, after showing an 8.8 percent increase during the 1950s (to 668,351). Between 1960 and 1970, it decreased 11.8 percent (to 589,783), almost to its 1940 level. In 1960, the city was 8.4 percent black; in 1970, blacks constituted 14.7 percent.

The movement of industry to the South was becoming noticeable. In 1962, a front-page story in the *Milwaukee Journal* reported that the Hytrol Conveyor Company would close its fifty- employee factory and move to Jonesboro, Arkansas. Wages there for an assembler were $1.60 per hour, compared with $2.20 in Milwaukee, the company's president said. Arkansas offered "cheaper labor, lower taxes, better production facilities and a new plant financed through a Jonesboro bond issue" (August 22, 1962).

Since manufacturing was concentrated in the city rather than the suburbs, the exodus of factories was felt most strongly there. During the 1950s, median family income in the city remained constant relative to that in the suburbs; about 96 percent of the suburban level. But during the 1960s, the proportion fell to 91 percent, reflecting the loss of high-paying manufacturing jobs (Booth n.d.:2). The city government took notice, and in 1962 created industrial land banks on vacant city land, which it offered at favorable rates. Sales of land were slow, and even twenty-five years later there were only 3,000 jobs in the land banks (*Milwaukee Sentinel*, January 21, 1987). The city's decline was brought home in 1966, even to those who paid no attention to economic trends. The Braves, whose arrival in 1953 had symbolized the beginning of the city's growth period, left the city for Atlanta.

With the increase in federal money for urban renewal and no need for jury decisions in land condemnation proceedings, there was an increase in city-sponsored housing programs. Of the 266 acres of land cleared during the 1960s and early 1970s, 56 percent was used for residential development, 30 percent for business development, and 14 percent for expansion on the campus of Marquette University, just west of downtown. Downtown projects included the development of office space and construction of high-rise, higher-rent apartments (Booth n.d.:45).

Many blacks were complaining that city development policies were doing nothing for them. The bulk of low- and moderate-income urban renewal housing was in already black areas (Booth n.d.:45), and attempts to pass open-housing legislation were defeated 18−1 in the Common Council, the only support coming from the sole black member, Vel Phillips. In 1963, the executive director of the Milwaukee Urban League, Wesley Scott, complained that there was "not a single Negro renting outside the core area, unless he is renting from a Negro." Black attorney David Beckwith told a suburban meeting of Democrats that "each day he searches the newspapers looking for some sign that Mayor Maier has found that the Negro problems 'won't just go away' " (*Milwaukee Sentinel*, October 11, 1963).

A group of black leaders issued a public statement attacking Maier: "It is disappointing that the mayor of our city, by his words and actions, has beclouded the hopes and aspirations of Milwaukee Negroes." The statement referred to housing policies, employment opportunities, and "the meager involvement and participation of Negroes in the operations of city government" (Lankevich 1977:130−131). In 1964 and 1965, there were brief boycotts of the Milwaukee schools by groups protesting school segregation.

White flight, or as the city planners called it, "push," began (City of

Milwaukee, Department of City Development 1987:11). Migration to the suburbs before the mid-1960s had been a result of families choosing to move to a nicer house. But the phenomenon of push, or white flight, was the move away from a neighborhood, not just from a house. It was the result of people feeling "they are in the path of change and that their property values will drop" (City of Milwaukee, Department of City Development 1987:11). This was expressed politically in 1964, when George Wallace won 25 percent of the vote in Wisconsin's Democratic presidential primary—his first show of strength outside the South. Wallace won 31 percent of the vote in Milwaukee's South Side congressional district and 46 percent in a new district in the northern and western suburbs. "If ever have to leave Alabama I'd want to live on the south side of Milwaukee," Wallace said (*Milwaukee Journal*, April 8, 1964).

In June 1967, blacks and their white supporters began public actions against the resistance to open-housing legislation. One target of picketing was the home of Common Council President Martin E. Schreiber. The next month, tensions finally exploded in a two-day riot-insurrection. Three people died; more than 100 were injured (including dozens of policemen) and more than 1,700 were arrested. Maier imposed a strict ten-day curfew.

The violence and the tough response by Maier and his police chief, Harold Breier, did not deter open-housing supporters. Less than a month later they began marches that continued for more than 200 consecutive days. In August, about 200 people, led by a white priest, James Groppi, and by the Commandos of the National Association for the Advancement of Colored People Youth Council, marched across the Sixteenth Street bridge to Kosciuszko Park on the South Side. They were met by a crowd of hostile whites estimated by police to number 13,000. Following this incident, 22 people were reported injured and 45 were arrested. According to a newspaper account, "Along the route, both to and from the park, the demonstrators were targets of eggs, bottles, rocks, firecrackers and beer cans. Police were also hit by the missiles. The march began shortly before 7 p.m. and ended about 9:30 p.m. with the demonstrators on a dead run for safety and police guarding them. Hundreds of whites ran alongside" (*Milwaukee Sentinel*, 1967).

On the occasion of the 100th consecutive day of marching, the *New York Times* reported that "the marchers [had] received the support of business, religious, civic and labor leaders. But they [had] failed to win the votes they need most—a majority of aldermen on the Milwaukee Common Council" (December 3, 1967). Nor had they received the support of Maier, who insisted that segregated housing was a metropolitan issue and that white flight would intensify if the city took open-housing action without passage of similar legislation in the suburbs. In April 1968, Maier won reelection for a third term with 86 percent of the vote, having defeated a liberal open-housing supporter. But Martin Luther King's assassination helped spur enactment of legislation nationwide, and by the end of the month, after sixteen suburbs had passed laws, Maier had swung his support in favor of city action. It was taken soon thereafter.

The immediate task facing business and political leaders was to repair the city's image. Maier saw the situation as an opportunity to launch a program he had first proposed in 1961—a massive summer lakefront festival of music and other entertainment. The nine-day Summerfest drew an estimated 1.2 million people for events ranging from performances of the Royal Philharmonic Orchestra of London to "the world's largest polka party" (Wells 1970:263). The period of intense social activism would soon be over.

The Downtown Area vs. the Neighborhoods, 1968–1980

Some of the activism of the pre-Summerfest days continued; neighborhood organizations sprang up west and north of downtown and lobbied in reaction to the destruction of housing for expressways. But it was soon clear that these organizations would have little strength. In 1969, for example, when elections were held to choose representatives to Neighborhood Resident Council boards, the governing body for determining allocation of Model Cities funds, only 6 percent of the eligible voters participated, and Maier-backed candidates defeated those of the largely black Organization of Organizations (Lankevich 1977:80).

Milwaukee's attractiveness as a community dominated attention at the end of the 1960s. The Performing Arts Center opened downtown on the Milwaukee River. The city continued to win such honors as "Beautiful City USA" and a first place in a national "Clean Up, Paint Up, Fix Up" competition. Crime and traffic accident rates were down, and in 1970 major league baseball returned with the transfer of the Seattle franchise to Milwaukee.

Investment downtown continued at a slow but steady pace. The 601-foot-high First Wisconsin Center, still the tallest building in Wisconsin, was completed in 1973. Other private downtown developments completed in the 1970s include the Mortgage Guaranty Insurance Corporation Plaza office complex, Juneau Village high-rise apartments, an addition to the Northwestern Mutual Life Insurance headquarters building, and a new office building for Blue Cross and Blue Shield United of

Wisconsin. The Blue Cross building indicated a moderation in the pace of downtown building, since the project as completed in 1977 was substantially scaled down from the original plans. Another public project, a new convention center, was completed in 1974.

During this period there was a change in the structure of the public-private partnership. In 1973 the GMC, which had always operated through private relationships rather than formal arrangement, created a for-profit subsidiary, the Milwaukee Redevelopment Corporation, in order to channel the increasing federal and city dollars into private development projects. The city also became a funding channel and provided technical expertise through its Department of City Development. One of the things that had paved the way for this new relationship was the GMC's pattern of working behind the scenes rather than as the object of public acclaim.

Rudolph Schoenecker, then GMC's executive director, explained how he had helped establish lines of influence for GMC members.

> City officials viewed the executives with tremendous distrust, [Schoenecker] said. Schoenecker set out to change the executives' image by arranging civic progress dinners. The seating was crucial, he recalled, allowing executives to meet and get to know public officials. Once there was trust, the executives could call City Hall, the County Board or state officials when they needed help on a project, he said. "On that basis we got more things done," Schoenecker said. "And when anything good happened, the credit always went to the elected official. They were the ones on the line every few years to get re-elected." (Bauer 1987)

The GMC also enjoyed the support of the Journal Company, the city's largest media corporation and publisher of both the *Milwaukee Journal* and the *Milwaukee Sentinel*. Journal chairman Irwin Maier (no relation to the mayor) was a devoted member of the GMC, and his media outlets backed the group's efforts. Maier was considered one of the two leading figures on the GMC, the other being the chairman of the Northwestern Mutual Life Insurance Company, Edmund Fitzgerald—later, Francis Ferguson.

Ferguson was the architect of the plan for GMC's spinoff of the Milwaukee Redevelopment Corporation, whose funding came from a number of blue chip Milwaukee companies. Mayor Maier endorsed it and the new corporation was announced in a joint GMC-mayoral statement at City Hall. It was not an immediate success, though, since its major project of the 1970s, a plan to redevelop the old Blatz downtown brewery and convert it to shops and housing, did not get off the ground. In the 1980s, however, the Milwaukee Redevelopment Corporation completed a number of downtown projects.

Meanwhile, housing problems in the black community intensified. Census figures for 1970 showed Milwaukee to be one of the most segregated metropolitan areas in the United States, with only 3.5 percent of the nonwhite population living outside the central city. (Most of these individuals were not black.) Furthermore, the nonwhite population living in the city was one of the most rapidly growing of such populations in all U.S. metropolitan areas, increasing 38.8 percent during the 1970s, to 145,832. The non-Hispanic white population dropped 23.1 percent, to 453,576. The Hispanic population increased 67.5 percent to 26,111. In 1980 Milwaukee was 22.9 percent black (up from 14.7 percent in 1970) and 4.1 percent Hispanic (Beverstock and Stuckert 1972:24; McNeely and Kinlow 1987:12).

The housing situation worsened with initiation of the urban renewal and expressway projects. Between 1960 and 1974, 11,066 housing units were demolished for these purposes, but only 7,689 new public housing or rent-subsidy units were built. Another 12,908 units were destroyed for other city projects, mostly as part of federally funded code enforcement programs. The total demolition amounted to 9.7 percent of all housing units in 1970 (Beckley 1978:150).

Those who were displaced crowded even more intensely into black neighborhoods. "Relocation did not have any net desegregating effect since it merely contributed to increasing concentrations in other parts of the ethnic area and to the lateral expansion of that area. . . . Besides the fact that federal assistance has torn down more housing that it has helped build, it appears that this assistance has also contributed to crowding, neighborhood disruption and relocation" (Beckley 1978:151).

Growing community opposition focused on expressway construction, now considered less critical since the major routes through the downtown and out to the suburbs were completed. Maier flip-flopped on the issue of construction, sometimes arguing that completion of the planned eighty-two-mile network had to be postponed until funding for replacement housing was increased and sometimes arguing, as a result of pressure from union and real estate groups, that the work should carry on (Booth n.d.:45–46).

Eventually, work was halted on a loop that was supposed to circle the downtown area. One resulting embarrassment was an elevated highway whose connecting link was not completed for a decade, during which the road came to a dead end in mid-air. That fiasco was memorialized in a John Belushi film, *The Blues Brothers*, in which the heroes try to escape down what turns into a dead-end expressway.

A worse expressway mess was the 1967 demolition of houses along a one-and-a-half-mile strip extending through the black community, for an expressway that was never built. Twenty years later, only 10 percent of the vacant land had been developed. A nineteen-acre site north of downtown also remained vacant in 1987, twenty years after the demolition of houses. In 1978, the Department of City Development took notice of the housing situation and adopted a new "Preservation Policy," which "explicitly [gave] priority to the existing housing stock over new construction" (City of Milwaukee, Department of City Development 1987:11).

Meanwhile, conservatism was tightening its hold on public opinion. In 1976 a federal judge ordered the Milwaukee school system to develop plans to desegregate the schools, but disputes over how to achieve change continued through the rest of the decade and into the 1980s. Just one month after the ruling, an American Nazi party candidate received 4,790 votes in the mayoral primary. Maier easily won reelection to his fifth term and in 1980 won a sixth term.

Recession and Restructuring in the 1980s

For Milwaukee, the 1980s have been a time of sweeping economic change in the form of a downturn that was felt first in the business community. In 1982, corporate losses ran as high as $207 million at Allis-Chalmers, $77 million at Harnischfeger, and $17 million at A. O. Smith. Then, as layoffs increased and wages braked, the impact spread through the neighborhoods. As the business community began responding to the blows it had suffered, the change began to have a visible effect on the political establishment. Business became even more influential in setting the political agenda, especially in state government.

The economic crisis was a surprise, since the last years of the 1970s had been relatively prosperous. Politicians and business leaders frequently cited a 1977 *Wall Street Journal* story that referred to Wisconsin as the "star of the Snowbelt." Indeed, the number of manufacturing jobs in the city of Milwaukee held steady during the last years of the decade, peaking at 100,526 in 1978.

When the recession hit, it hit hard. In 1980–1982, the number of manufacturing jobs in the city plummeted by 22.1 percent. At first service-sector jobs merely held steady, but in 1981 they exceeded for the first time the decreasing number of jobs in manufacturing (City of Milwaukee, Department of City Development 1987:50). Wisconsin was hit less hard than Michigan or Illinois, but compared with most of the rest of the nation, it suffered more because of its concentration in metal-bending manufacturing. The average annual wage of a Wisconsin worker fell from about 94 percent of the U.S. average in 1980, a stable level that had been maintained since the late 1960s, to a low of 89.8 percent of that average in the first quarter of 1983 (*Milwaukee Journal,* February 16, 1986).

The turnaround began in 1983. On a frigid January morning more than 10,000 people waited outdoors at Milwaukee's State Fair Park to apply for 175 jobs at the A. O. Smith Corporation. The resumption of hiring by one of the city's largest employers was at once a symbol of both the recession and the beginnings of recovery. Overall employment in the metropolitan area had peaked in 1979 at approximately 680,000. By 1983 it had plunged to 640,000. It then increased, hitting the 700,000 mark late in 1987. By the end of 1988, unemployment in the city had fallen to 4.1 percent, the result of both growth in the service sector and a rebounding manufacturing economy that benefited especially from a surge in exports because of the fallen value of the dollar.

The recovery of the late 1980s was strong enough to support a rebirth of downtown development, centered around a 250,000-square-foot enclosed shopping mall, the Grand Avenue, completed in 1982. Built by the Maryland-based Rouse Corporation, the mall was intended to be (and has since its completion been regarded as) the piece of downtown development that gave momentum to other efforts, and thus changed downtown Milwaukee from a stagnating environment to one that was rejuvenating.

There was a debate in the late 1970s, however, about the wisdom of investing so much money in a downtown project at a time when many neighborhoods were in disrepair. Some black aldermen, in fact, threatened for a while to block the Common Council's approval of an application for federal Urban Development Action Grant (UDAG) funds for the mall project unless the city abandoned plans for a freeway to be built through the black neighborhoods and simultaneously applied for grants to rebuild the blocks already demolished for the proposed highway.

Their protest failed; the argument that downtown development would also help the neighborhood carried the day. In two editorials, the *Milwaukee Journal* chastised the black leaders, commenting that "inner city aldermen, especially, should remember that their constituents have much to gain from the downtown mall-hotel proposal: jobs, improved shopping opportunities and an enhanced city tax base" (December 28, 1977). "Inner city residents should not find the downtown proposal threatening. In fact, the inner city—perhaps more than other areas— stands to gain from downtown revival" (December 24, 1977).

The UDAG was approved by the federal government, thus providing $12.6 million for the project. The city contributed $20 million, raised by floating municipal bonds with the mall used as a tax-incremental financing district. Rouse put in between $15 million and $20 million, and local corporations—forty-seven in all, including most of the city's best-known old-line manufacturing and financial firms—invested almost $20 million, using the Milwaukee Redevelopment Corporation as their intermediary to own the project and lease it back to Rouse.

What made the Grand Avenue happen were strenuous efforts to achieve a public-private partnership. Francis Ferguson, the unofficial leader of the GMC, described to a reporter the final deal with Mayor Maier that enabled the Grand Avenue project to proceed:

> The mayor, said Ferguson, "was willing to bend a few rules to make them fit the circumstances. And by that, I'm not suggesting anything wrong. For example, the thing that finally made the Grand Avenue work was the concept that the mall area—where people are actually walking—is a city sidewalk. And that's the first place and the first time in the U.S. that we know of that it's ever been done." Declaring the inside of the mall a public area allowed the city to use tax incremental financing to remodel and extend the central arcade. (Bauer 1984)

As William Drew, commissioner of city development, said later, "The Grand Avenue changed the way everyone looked at how things could be done here. As important as anything I can point to is how the Grand Avenue proved that government and the private sector could put something together" (*Milwaukee Journal*, April 30, 1987).

The Grand Avenue has been an acknowledged emotional success, for even its original critics have come to agree that it has added brightness to the downtown area and contributed to the building spurt that has continued throughout the 1980s. It is unclear to what degree it has been a financial success, since the mall operators have never been willing to reveal financial results. City figures show that in the first five years after the mall opened, tax proceeds from the downtown area including the Grand Avenue were $18.6 million, or about $2.7 million more than projected when the tax-incremental financing district was created (*Milwaukee Journal*, April 30, 1987).

In arguing against the neighborhood-based critics, the *Milwaukee Journal* had asserted that: "revitalization of neighborhoods—including their shopping strips—should not get lost in the downtown shuffle. . . . It is ridiculous to suggest that Milwaukee shouldn't press for downtown renewal. And since it isn't a question of one or the other, but of how best to do both, residents should press city officials to act on neighborhood redevelopment, too" (December 24, 1977).

But the private sector's willingness to push for and invest in the city was exhausted in its Grand Avenue effort, as well as in several subsequent downtown projects that took the Grand Avenue as their model. Though the project was billed as an investment, many corporations looked on their Redevelopment Corporation involvement as more charity than profit-seeking. And although they were willing to part with some money in order to do their part to bring Milwaukee's downtown into the 1980s, they had no interest in giving money to develop the neighborhoods. Nor did there exist at this time an idea that would begin to emerge among a few business leaders toward the end of the 1980s—that it might make good business sense to keep the neighborhoods from deteriorating. And the city administration was not inclined to press for neighborhood development. Its willingness to act was limited by the agenda set by the private side of the ruling partnership.

The Grand Avenue became the project that brought together $70 million in partnership funds to help make Milwaukee's downtown a congenial place. It also provided rhetorical ammunition for arguments that the city had avoided deterioration and was advancing, though all the while it was ignoring the increasing plight of the neighborhoods.

Attention remained focused on the downtown area throughout the 1980s. Projects included five high-rise office buildings, a number of additions to and renovations of existing corporate headquarters buildings, a new sports arena, several high-rise luxury apartment complexes, and an expanded downtown skywalk.

There was even a burst of optimism about housing when the Department of City Development concluded in 1982 that "rapid movement out of the inner city had stopped; housing maintenance had improved dramatically; troubled neighborhoods had improved; and fewer of the city's neighborhoods needed ongoing special programs" (City of Milwaukee, Department of City Development 1987:12). But the department's optimism was short-lived. "By 1985 neighborhood conditions were changing," it reported (City of Milwaukee, Department of City Development 1987: 12). Some of the changes detected in its 1985 survey were: vacancy rates in the central city climbed from 10.8 percent in 1980 to 13.7 percent in 1985; there was a growing shortage of low-rent housing, with 64,300 low-income households but only 52,100 low-cost units; the proportion of households spending more than half their income on rent doubled, from 15 percent in 1980 to 32 percent in 1985 (City of Milwaukee, Department of City Development 1987:12;15;16). Other studies confirmed that redlining continued to be a problem in minority neighborhoods (Squires and Velez 1987).

By the mid-1980s, the Department of City Development was reporting that South Side neighborhoods were in distress for the first time; they exhibited "many of the housing problems that were present in 1978 in the inner city on the North Side" (City of Milwaukee, Department of City Development 1987:5). This situation was due in part to the layoffs of middle-aged white factory workers. The worst problems were still concentrated in the black population, however. The disparity between black and white unemployment, 25.9 percent versus 5.1 percent in 1986, was worse than in other metropolitan areas (McNeely and Kinlow 1987:72). A survey in *American Demographics* magazine revealed that in terms of blacks' economic well-being, Milwaukee ranked forty-fifth of the forty-eight largest metropolitan areas in the United States (O'Hare 1986).

One reason things were so bad was that the business community's first response to the downturn was, in accordance with the standard practices dictated by the business cycle, to lay people off and to be tougher in bargaining with the unions. Some unions took a stand against concessions, but lost. In 1983, for example, in two of the most significant labor actions, unions lost strikes against Briggs & Stratton, in suburban Milwaukee, and against Kohler, about forty miles north. Both unions were forced to accept two-tiered wage scales. Overall in Wisconsin, the average manufacturing wage had been climbing relative to the national average throughout the 1970s, reaching a peak in 1983, when it was 11.3 percent higher. That difference began to decrease in 1983, and by 1986 it had fallen to 8 percent, roughly the same level as in 1971 (*Milwaukee Journal*, February 16, 1986).

But once managers had succeeded in shrinking their work forces and reducing the share of revenues going to labor, many of them began to discover that the secret of competitive excellence was to adjust the variables that had little relation to labor costs. One of the most important ingredients of the success of the Japanese was their integrated approach to design, manufacturing, inventory, and quality control. So Milwaukee's manufacturers began learning how to run their businesses differently. At Harley-Davidson, for example, managers were aware that the invasion of Japanese heavyweight motorcycles had ended the company's 99 percent market domination of the 1970s; its share was only 12 percent in 1982. By using a combination of tactics, including application of Japanese-derived techniques, reduction of the work force, and successful lobbying of the federal government to obtain three years of tariff protection, they reversed the trend. Harley's market share rose to 38 percent in 1987, and the company was the leader again (*Milwaukee Journal*, December 6, 1987).

Business leaders also rediscovered the importance of both small business risk-taking and entrepreneurs. There was considerable concern over the fact that both Milwaukee and Wisconsin lagged behind other areas in new business formation. Some business figures began complaining publicly that the Milwaukee business community was too conservative and complacent, afraid of risk (*Milwaukee Journal*, April 6, 1986). What these critics wanted was a return to something more like the entrepreneurial spirit prevalent in Milwaukee at the turn of the century.

Seeking to realize their aim of improving the business climate, politically minded business leaders found common cause with a number of conservative and moderate Democrats. Together, they implemented a series of new state programs and obtained cuts in the state personal income tax. They also created a number of new public-private partnerships designed to boost economic development, including: Competitive Wisconsin, to frame policy suggestions; Forward Wisconsin, to market the state to out-of-state companies looking for new factory or headquarters sites; the Strategic Development Commission, to propose a framework for long-term economic growth; the Wisconsin Community Development Finance Authority, to fund community-based business ventures; and a revitalized state Department of Development, to provide technical assistance for business. In 1986, dissatisfied with Democratic Governor Tony Earl's commitment to their agenda, this coalition helped elect Republican Tommy Thompson, whose platform had emphasized more support for economic development.

In Milwaukee, one of the indications of the increased political influence of the business establishment was the growing importance of William Drew, head of the city's Department of City Development, which worked at the technical level with the Milwaukee Redevelopment Corporation, the GMC spinoff, on a number of downtown projects. The city government jealously guarded its authority over economic development in Milwaukee, and metropolitan-area coordinated economic planning remained as difficult as ever to achieve. The idea was floated—as it had been from time to time for decades—but went nowhere. It was a good idea, many argued, but it could not overcome the strong opposition of Drew, among others, who did not want to share their power (Norman 1986).

There were occasional bursts of protest from the black community in the early 1980s that signaled the potential for a political challenge to city government. In 1981, for example, the death while in police custody of a young black man, Ernie Lacy, led to street marches by more than 10,000 people, the largest demonstrations since the open-housing protests of the 1960s. There were also other, much less dramatic events, such as controversy about the absence of blacks in high-ranking positions in city government and the police department, and a continuing struggle over how to deal with the still-segregated school system, which was being waged with lawsuits and judicial orders. But none of these things prompted much change at City Hall. When the Department of City Development released a major reassessment of its housing policies in 1987, it did not directly address the black issue but only referred to it obliquely—there were four occurrences of the world "minority" in the forty-nine-page report (City of Milwaukee, Department of City Development 1987).

With political leaders often demonstrating a see-no-evil-hear-no-evil tendency, it is not surprising that the business side of the partnership was quicker to perceive the seriousness of the problems of the neighborhoods. In the middle of the decade, the GMC entered, cautiously to be sure, into a relationship with a group of neighborhood organizations from the depressed area west of downtown.

These community-based organizations had made changes that made them more congenial in their relations with the business community. Among other things, they had tried to adopt a business point of view, either by managing housing cooperatives or by working with small businesses such as a tavern, laundromat, grocery store, and business incubator. There was thus a natural meeting ground for the GMC and some other business groups and neighborhood organizations such as the Cooperation West Side Association, the Westside Housing Cooperative, the Westside Conservation Corporation, and the Northwest Side Community Development Corporation. Also, settlements were negotiated between the city's major banks and coalitions of community organizations that used the federal Community Reinvestment Act as leverage to win commitments for increased banking activity in their neighborhoods. The Department of City Development itself participated in a business incubator in a black neighborhood, the Milwaukee Enterprise Center.

All these projects, however, were small, slow to develop, and clearly inadequate to do more than make a dent in the overall solution of neighborhood problems. What can be said for them is that they were attempts to bring community groups into the partnership that had previously been closed to them. The business community was willing to work with them on their own business terms. Community groups, such as Jobs With Peace, that did not follow the business-venture model for their new projects were not accepted into the partnership.

What Next?

One way to answer the question of where do things stand? is to summarize the situation faced by some of the major players in the late 1980s.

The GMC, and the business community in general, are generally prospering, certainly relative to their situation in the first half of the decade. The manufacturing firms that remain have for the most part reorganized and are once again competitive on a world scale. Service firms have continued to grow; and though new-business formation continues to lag behind national rates, the perception is that the climate for entrepreneurs is much improved. Many of these changes are criticized for being too little too late, however. The true measure of their success, from a business point of view, will not come until the 1990s when some of the new strategies have had a chance to exert their effect. The GMC's work with neighborhood organizations is proceeding very slowly, with little indication of concrete results beyond the education of a few community leaders in the methods of investment finance. Some business leaders have also become deeply involved in discussions about integration and quality of education in the city schools.

The neighborhood organizations are slowly becoming more sophisticated in their approach to business and are learning about planning, investment, and management. They have no great success stories to tell, have made no major impact on city policy, and have not increased their power base by substantially increasing their grass-roots involvement. They have done some work focusing on voter registration, with an eye to increasing their power in elections in the 1990s.

The black community continues to focus on survival issues—education, drugs, teenage pregnancy—but is limited by scattered and paltry resources. Housing is a continuing problem; more people (virtually all of them black) died in house fires in 1987 than in any year since 1967. There has been little growth in that community's political power except for the appointment of some blacks to leading positions, for the first time, in both city and county government.

The conservative South Side remains politically strong, as does the tradition of fiscally conservative city government. Both major candidates in the 1988 election to replace retiring Mayor Maier based their campaigns on appeals to conservative homeowners and the business community. The focus of winner John Norquist has been more on holding down property taxes for homeowners than on establishing new programs.

Business development is in its second growth cycle since World War II. The first cycle included the increase in improvements in the 1950s and private downtown building projects in the 1960s, the city's glory years. That progress was interrupted by the black activism of the mid-1960s, the slower business growth of the 1970s, and the recession of the early 1980s. How long will the current upturn last? The answer depends largely on national and international economic events, since Milwaukee's economy is still too fragile to endure another serious recession. It also depends on the extent of changes in business attitudes and practices and the success of efforts to stimulate new business formation.

Will there be a revival of political activism? Or rather, when will the revival occur? The ground is fertile because of the economic distress of the 1980s, the departure of much of the old guard in both the political and business establishments, and the integration of a few activists into the new administrations in city and county government. But the remnants of Milwaukee's leftist and progressive movements did not win much during the 1960s, and are not in a strong position to mount another serious challenge to business and to politics as usual. How fast will the conditions in many neighborhoods deteriorate? How quickly will community leaders gain sophistication and build the power base necessary to become a political force? Will these leaders join the business-government partnership, or will they challenge its guiding principles? All these questions remain to be answered in the 1990s.

At the beginning of this chapter, it was noted that Milwaukee provides a clear example of the role of public-private partnerships, because of the long stability of its ruling structures. That continues to be the case as the city enters the 1990s, even though there has been a large turnover in local political and business leaders in the late 1980s. Despite a more diversified economic base and a new generation of leaders, the goal of public and private leaders remains the same: to bring in enough investment in major facilities to keep the downtown competitive with comparable-sized cities across the nation in the hope that a general economic revival, rather than sharply focused and well-funded programs, will be adequate to solve the problems of urban decay.

References

Bauer, Fran. 1984. "Francis Ferguson a Driving Force." *Milwaukee Journal* (September 28).
———. 1987. "Executives' Attention Turned to Social Ills." *Milwaukee Journal* (September 20).
Beckley, Robert M. 1978. "The Effects of Federal Programs on Housing and the Quality of Life: The Milwaukee Case." In *Milwaukee's Economy*, ed. John P. Blair and Ronald S. Edari. Chicago: Federal Reserve Bank of Chicago.
Beverstock, Frances, and Robert P. Stuckert. 1972. *The Metropolitan Milwaukee Fact Book: 1970*. Milwaukee: Milwaukee Urban Observatory.
Booth, Douglas E. n.d. "City Government Finances in an Era of Economic Decline." In "The City Life Cycle and City Government Finances: Milwaukee, 1852–1977." Unpublished report.

City of Milwaukee. Department of City Development. 1987. *Toward Preservation Partnerships*. Greater Milwaukee Committee. Annual Reports. 1955, 1958, 1959.

Lankevich, George J. 1977. *Milwaukee: A Chronological and Documentary History*. Dobbs Ferry, N.Y.: Oceana.

McNeely, R. L., and Melvin Kinlow. 1987. *Milwaukee Today: A Racial Gap Study*. *Milwaukee:* Milwaukee Urban League.

Milwaukee Journal. 1962. "There's Movement and Optimism" (March 25).

————. 1964. "Word's Spectacular for Developments Downtown" (May 14).

————. 1977a. "Downtown vs. Neighborhood Shops" (December 24).

————. 1977b. "Get Cracking on Downtown Project" December 28).

Milwaukee Sentinel. 1963. "Frank Talk" (October 8).

———— . 1967. "Marchers Pass Mob of 13,000" (August 25).

New York Times. 1967. "100th March Set for Milwaukee" (December 3).

Norman, Jack. 1986. "Yet Another Economic Council." *Milwaukee Journal* (August 17).

O'Hare, William. 1986. "The Best Metros for Blacks." *American Demographics* (July):26–33.

Research Clearinghouse of Milwaukee. 1950. *Milwaukee Today and Yesterday*. Milwaukee: Research Clearinghouse.

Squires, Gregory D., and William Velez. 1987. "Insurance Redlining and the Transformation of an Urban Metropolis." *Urban Affairs Quarterly* 23:63–83.

Time. 1956. "The Shame of Milwaukee" (April 2):23.

Wall Street Journal. 1977. "Star of the Snowbelt" (September 16):27.

Wells, Robert W. 1970. *This Is Milwaukee*. Milwaukee: Renaissance Books.

Scott Cummings
C. Theodore Koebel
J. Allen Whitt

11. Redevelopment in Downtown Louisville: Public Investments, Private Profits, and Shared Risks

L ocal business elites and growth coalitions exercise considerable influence over the direction and content of downtown redevelopment policy (Logan and Molotch 1987; Whitt 1982). Nonetheless, it is does not always follow that partnerships between public and private interests necessarily contradict the public good. Profit-sharing agreements, increased tax and parking revenues, and related remuneration arrangements mean that public partners need not be excluded from the benefits provided by successful urban development programs. In some cities, as a result of enlightened linkage policies (Swanstrom 1987), the activities of nonprofit development corporations and neighborhood organizing (Daykin 1987), and progressive city administration (Clavel 1986), public-private partnerships have been formed along more equitable and financially lucrative lines.

In this chapter we describe the urban redevelopment experiences of Louisville, Kentucky. Special attention is given to the financial arrangements underwriting a major revitalization plan begun in 1980 that is currently transforming part of the city's downtown. A partnership between public and private interests directs Louisville's redevelopment program. Local business elites are deeply involved in the effort, and most observers concede that private interests have disproportionately influenced the content, form, and direction of Louisville's revitalization agenda (Whitt 1987). The plan has drawn little or no opposition from community groups and is proceeding with a remarkable degree of civic cohesiveness and support. What is not clear, however, is the extent to which the city itself will benefit financially from the comprehensive redevelopment plan. The case study shows that certain aspects of the redevelopment program are highly favorable to the city's financial interests. Other components of the revitalization scheme, however, may transfer significant risks to city government and have the potential to seriously compromise the city's ability to realize a social return on its investment of public dollars.

Our case study is presented in four parts. First, we identify those forces that frequently lead to the utilization of public dollars primarily for the purpose of underwriting private gain in the urban redevelopment process. Second, we describe the Louisville redevelopment program, paying special attention to the financial arrangements driving the plan. Third, we examine and analyze the financial data, attempting to ascertain the potential benefits to be derived by the city. Our purpose is to evaluate the unequal nature of Louisville's public-private partnership through the analysis of several financial variables: (1) risk exposure, (2) profit-sharing opportunities, (3) sales and property tax revenues, and (4) other revenue-generating possibilities. Fourth, we conclude our case study with a discussion of the political tradeoffs required to promote more equitable partnerships between the public and private sectors. We also identify those issues about which city officials need to be more aggressive when negotiating the terms of partnerships with private developers, financiers, and speculators.

Working Partnerships: A Critical Appraisal

Local governments are often confronted with organized pressure from local business elites to subsidize the development costs of firms making capital investments within their boundaries. Feagin (1987) contends that

> local governments are pressured by business elites to provide parking facilities, tax abatements, public services, zoning permissions, and administrative assistance in finding federal grants and loans. Hidden government subsidies for the builders of downtown developments include zoning changes to permit development, tax abatements sharply reducing taxes, cheap land provided by clearance programs, and utilities. All across the country government officials have played a role in downtown office development, providing money for services such as new roads and sewers, giving away public land by closing streets and by urban renewal projects, and constructing business-oriented projects such as convention centers and parking garages. (209)

Feagin argues that although local government is often in "partnership" with private entrepreneurs, its role is confined to providing the essentials to guarantee profitmaking and creating a friendly business environment.

Bluestone and Harrison (1982) argue that private investment decisions often contradict the public good and reveal serious conflicts of interest between "capital" and "community." In pursuit of higher profits and lower investments in the cost of labor, many corporations have abandoned cities altogether and relocated in rural regions or even in other parts of the world. Plant closings and shutdowns virtually destroy the employment base of a city, weaken its ability to provide services, and undermine the structure of neighborhood life and culture.

The mobility of capital and the willingness of firms to encourage the highest municipal bidders unleash destructive competition among cities to attract runaway U.S. businesses and international investment dollars. Irrational and unrestrained competition has lead some municipal jurisdictions to seriously compromise their revenue base with lucrative tax abatement incentives, or to make rash commitments to finance infrastructure improvements or to initiate land use changes through high-risk public indebtedness or fiscally questionable bonding programs (Bluestone and Harrison 1982). In addition, those growth centers that have been successful in attracting industry appear to be developing the same kinds of urban problems experienced by cities that corporations abandoned only a few years earlier (Feagin 1987).

When private investors are drawn to profit opportunities in the central cities, revitalization and redevelopment plans typically reflect the need to change the user of land from one class of users to another. In part, gentrification can be understood as a systematic attempt to reverse upper- and middle-class migration to the suburbs. The loss of middle- and upper-income consumers to suburban developers and merchants doing business in large shopping malls represents a tremendous drop in profits and revenues for businesses with fixed locations and investments in the central city. To compete with their suburban counterparts, downtown business elites often lobby for significant state investments in infrastructure improvements, loan guarantee and tax reduction packages, exemptions from established zoning and building code ordinances, and land use policies that ensure the removal of the urban working class and the poor from areas targeted for renewal. Louisville's downtown redevelopment program reveals the potential contradictions between private gain and the public good and illustrates the public policies that are necessary to attract investment capital to the central city (Cummings 1987).

The Local Business Elite and Municipal Government: Downtown Redevelopment in Louisville

Like many other cities, Louisville has seen a deterioration of its downtown area that has its origins in national economic events that have transformed the city's base of industrial employment, and in the rapid suburbanization of its population. Since the mid-1970s, Louisville has suffered a serious decline in industrial employment. Foreign competition, plant closings, runaway industry, and robotization have forced numerous workers to join the ranks of the unemployed or driven them into the low-wage, service sector of the economy. Between 1950 and 1980, manufacturing jobs in the nonagricultural sector decreased from 40 percent to 24.8 percent of the city's total employment base. Between 1960 and 1980, the city lost nearly 100,000 residents, a population movement similar to that found in other "smoke-stack," industrial cities (Yater 1987). Many of those residents relocated in the surrounding suburbs or left the region altogether. By the mid-1970s, the population of Jefferson County (in which Louisville is located) exceeded the number of residents remaining within the city limits.

In the face of deindustrialization and radical demographic transformations, the city's downtown deteriorated during the 1960s and 1970s. Only one major downtown office complex was completed between 1953 and 1968. For almost two decades, development activities in the central business district remained at a virtual standstill. During the 1960s and 1970s, numerous offices, hotels, department stores, restaurants, and commercial establishments closed their doors, many abandoning the downtown altogether. The Urban Land Institute reports that between 1963 and 1982, the number of retail establishments in the central business district declined from 811 to 387 (Yater 1987). The city actively participated in various urban renewal projects during the 1960s and was the beneficiary of numerous federal grants through the Community Development Block Grant program, the Model Cities program, and related federal urban programs during the Johnson, Nixon, and Carter years. It was not until the late 1970s and early 1980s, however, that attention was systematically given to downtown revitalization through public-private partnerships.

The Broadway Renaissance

The corner of Fourth and Broadway in downtown Lousiville is the southern anchor of the central business district. In 1920 this section of Broadway included stately mansions that were soon to be replaced as a result of commercial expansion. The burgeoning downtown economy brought major redevelopment projects and transformed the central business district into the commercial heart of a growing metropolis. The transformation was nowhere more apparent than at Fourth and Broadway.

In 1923 J. Graham Brown, a local millionaire, started a redevelopment effort that established Fourth and Broadway as Louisville's "magic corner"—the place to see and be seen; the hub of entertainment and excitement. Within five years, Brown had built the $4 million, fifteen-story

Brown Hotel on the northeast corner, the adjacent ten-story Brown Medical Office Building and the Brown Theatre; the four-story Martin Brown Office Building (expanded to twenty-three stories in 1955) on the northwest corner; and the Louisville Union Bus Depot and the Brown Garage on the southwest corner. Additional development by others produced the seventeen-story Heyburn (office) Building on the southeast corner, and a host of theaters: the Mary Anderson, the Majestic, the Kentucky, the Rialto, and Lowe's State Theatre.

The magic corner symbolized the centrality of the cities of this era and became part of local folklore about the Depression, the '37 flood, World War II, the Kentucky Derby, first dates, proms, and romance in general. But suburbanization took its toll, gradually at first and then with stunning acceleration. The Brown Hotel closed in 1971 and was purchased by the Jefferson County Board of Education for administrative offices and classrooms. By the end of the decade the school board had decided to sell the property and to consolidate its administrative offices elsewhere. The theatres converted to adult entertainment. Some ran what seemed to be an endless stream of Bruce Lee movies; others closed. The bus depot was torn down and the Brown Garage was allowed to become delapidated. The Heyburn Building was auctioned to its mortgagor and was in serious need of upgrading.

During the 1970s the magic corner became the forgotten corner, as redevelopment efforts focused on the northern half of downtown: the development of a riverfront plaza, an arts center, and a hotel near the river; the construction of two office towers, financed by the city's larger commercial banks; construction of a court building and convention center by the state; and plans for an enclosed retail "galleria." The surviving major occupant of the corner was the Capital Holding Corporation, one of the fastest growing and most successful insurance holding companies in the United States. The Commonwealth Building, opposite the Brown Hotel, was its headquarters. Unwilling to stay in a depressed area, Capital Holding's chief executive officer, Thomas C. Simons, faced the choice of moving or leading an effort to redevelop the Broadway area. In 1978 the Louisville Central Area, whose members are primarily the major corporate residents of downtown, formed a task force to study the redevelopment potential of the Broadway area. Under the leadership of Simons, the Broadway Project was created in 1979; representatives of the major businesses and property owners in the area and the local government thus formed one of the city's first urban development partnerships.

Preliminary development concepts were prepared for the Broadway Project and the Louisville Central Area within the year by Zuchelli,

Hunter & Associates, a Maryland development consulting firm. The proposed three-stage development plan focused on three square blocks constituing approximately thirty-five acres north of Broadway between Second and Fifth Streets. Phase I would include renovation of the Brown Center (hotel and office complex), 325 units of residential development north of the Brown Center, 100,000 square feet of new office space, street-level commercial space, a 1,125-space parking garage, and open space. Phases II and III would add 1,175 residential units, 295,000 square feet of office space, 110,000 square feet of commercial space, and additional open space. The total project was estimated to cost $154.8 million in roughly equal amounts per phase.

Initially, the path to redevelopment was uncertain. There was some hope that the University of Louisville would buy the Brown Hotel and the Brown Medical Office Building from the school board for use as a downtown campus. But such an expansion was not planned by the university. By 1980 the school board was actively seeking a buyer. An attempt by the Broadway Project to buy the hotel and office building for $4 million failed when the city refused to borrow $1 million against future Community Development Block Grant receipts to help finance the purchase on the grounds that such a move was too risky. In 1981 the school board leased the building to a developer interested in life-care housing for the elderly. Later that year the Broadway Project Corporation assumed the lease. It increased its efforts to have an urban renewal plan formulated and to secure financing for purchase of the Brown Center, as well as other properties included in Phase I.

As plans for Phase I were refined, the development was scaled down to better reflect available resources and the market realities of Louisville. Phase I of the Broadway Project (renamed the Broadway Renaissance) was completed in 1985 and included renovation of the Brown Hotel and the Brown Medical Office Building, construction of a 475-space garage, and development of Theatre Square (40,000 square feet of new commercial space, open space, and restoration of the Kentucky Theatre and the facade and lobby of another theatre).

Phase II of the Broadway Project is currently under construction and features a strikingly designed residential complex of 550 units of townhouse, low-rise, and mid-rise apartments and condominiums, with a 346-space, ground-level garage. These residential buildings will include 26,000 square feet of additional retail space. The centerpiece of Phase II is two rows (arranged in a crescent shape) of three-story apartments that face each other from opposite sides of Third Street. J. Bruce Graham, of the Chicago office of Skidmore, Owings & Merrill, designed the project.

Table 11.1. Broadway Project, Phase 1: Investment, risk, and return

Investment type	Amount	Source	Risk	Return
Grant (property acquisitions and clearance)	$5 million	City (federal CDBG moneys)	100% up-front subsidy.	No direct return. City owns open space. Possible indirect return through increase from developed properties.
Direct loan	$5 million	City (federal UDAG moneys)	Potential loss if project defaults. Subordinate lien position.	Tax revenue 10% interest after 5 years; 50% of net cash flow; 50% net proceeds.
Parking garage bonds	$3 million	City (parking authority)	Operating deficits ($76,000 in 1986). offset by in-lieu-of tax payments.	100% of net cash flow from garage.
School bonds	$5 million	City (outstanding bonds from earlier renovation)	Secured by title to the hotel.	None; however, outstanding bonds being paid by partnership.
Direct loan	$1.5 million	State (Industrial Finance Authority)	Potential loss if project defaults. Subordinate lien position.	11.25% interest.
Economic development bonds	$7.6 million	State	Portion of debt service comes from general fund if net cash flow is insufficient.	11.25% interest; however, a portion of interest and principal is deferable and accruing.
Private mortgage	$12.2 million	Private bank	Secured by loan guarantees from members of the Broadway-Brown Partnership.	12.6% interest.
Equity	$6.1 million	Broadway-Brown Partnership (private)	Liable for operating deficits, which are only partially convertable to equity. Equity at risk if sold for less than debt on property.	15% return on equity if net cash flow is positive; 50% of net proceeds.

The target market consists of middle- and upper-income professionals and administrators who work downtown. All phases of the redevelopment scheme were financed by significant state grants, investments, and public bonding programs.

Financing Redevelopment: Shared Risks and Liabilities

Private investment is an act of balancing risks and rewards. From the developers' perspective, rates of return are maximized by using OPM, "other people's money." Risks are minimized by targeting markets where there is some history of success. Traditionally in the United States, the public sector enters the development game with the intention of underwriting risks and increasing private rates of return by minimizing development costs. The private sector frequently sees the risks involved in center city redevelopment as substantial, as evidenced by tracts of idle urban renewal land where free is even too high a cost. In Louisville, however, we found that local officials enter the development arena seeking to maximize the city's own returns as well as to underwrite the costs of private initiative.

The private sector led the redevelopment effort. Five downtown corporations, along with the two general contractors for the project (Cranston of Pittsburgh and Sturgeon-Thorton-Marrett of Louisville), formed a private redevelopment corporation, the Broadway-Brown Partnership. In perhaps an unprecedented move, a local pension fund representing the firemen's and construction unions joined the partnership.

The partnership has a significant equity position and total liability for operating deficits (except for those of the garage). The partnership's equity, originally $4.6 million and now $6.1 million, represents approximately 17 percent of the value of the properties. In addition, the corporations involved in the partnership (except for the two co-managing partners) secured a $12.2 million private mortgage with letters of credit (see Table 11.1).

Whereas the members of the partnership invested or pledged their own money, the city effectively leveraged federal and state funds to provide the public financing of Phase I. Although state and federal dollars are still drawn from the public treasury, the enterpreneurial mode of Lousiville's city officials appears to be consistent with the OPM principle driving private investments. The city tried to minimize its exposure to risk by packaging noncity money. Federal dollars committed to the project totaled $10 million, half of which was allocated for property acquisition and clearance. The other half was loaned to the project by the city for twenty-five years (callable after twenty years) at 10 percent interest starting after the first five years. In addition, the city is to receive, as additional interest, 50 percent of net cash flow less a 15 percent return on equity to the partnership and 50 percent of net proceeds upon sale of the property (80 percent if partnership interests are sold that exceed the partnership's equity). Thus, the city loaned the project its federal UDAG money, will receive a reasonable rate of return after the first five years, and stands to share equally with the partnership in profits or capital gains.

At the same time, the city's liabilities are very limited. It has no liability for negative cash flow, except with regard to the parking garage, which it owns through its parking authority. The garage was financed with $3 million from a parking authority consolidated bond. To secure a portion of the overall parking authority bonded indebtedness, the city pledged payments in lieu of ad valorem taxes from the partnership. These payments ($96,700 for 1986, increasing to $126,700 in 1988 and thereafter) were calculated on the basis of estimates of the tax liability if the property was assessed. Since the city has title to the Brown Complex property until the school board bonds are repaid, the property is tax exempt anyway. (Taxes are levied on the retail property, which had a tax liability of approximately $13,400 in 1986). Additionally, the city is guaranteed a minimum of $60,000 per year from the partnership for rental of parking spaces. Financial statements from the parking authority reveal that the garage had a debt service coverage ratio of 1.12 for fiscal year 1987, in effect generating $30,680 in net income. However, without the obligated payment in lieu of taxes from the partnership, the garage would have been unable to cover 30 percent of the debt service for a $76,000 loss.

In contrast to the city, the state has issued the partnership a direct loan of $1.5 million from the Kentucky Industrial Finance Authority and has issued $7.6 million in economic development bonds for the project. Payback on $3.8 million of the latter is based on cash flow, and is deferrable.

Liability for operating deficits is the responsibility of the private-sector partners. To date the project has not been a success, at least as measured by positive cash flow. The hotel, which is the project's main source of income, has yet to reach a profitable level of occupancy. By industry standards, an occupancy rate of 60 percent is necessary to return a profit; the Brown Hotel remains 10 to 15 percentage points below this threshold. Only 75 percent of the office space and 69 percent of the retail space in the Brown Medical Office Building is occupied after three years of operation. (The overall downtown occupancy rate for office space in Louisville is 85 percent.) The retail space in Theatre Square has been even less profitable, with only a 50 percent occupancy rate. Retail trade has been marginal, at best. Whether this situation will improve after completion of

Phase II is uncertain, but the hope is that the additional demand from residents will have a significant impact. What is certain is that the hotel and the retail space must generate more revenue in order for the project to have a positive cash flow.

Original projections of a positive cash flow by 1987 have proved incorrect. The partners' equity position has increased to $6.1 million and is likely to increase further as cash infusions into the property continue. Debt service on the deferrable state loan has not been paid and the interest has accrued. Further losses by the partnership seem probable, since the market for the retail space and for hotel space continues to be weak. Because debt service on the city's UDAG loan starts in 1990, an even larger cash flow will be required to meet operating expenses.

The financing package for Phase II of the Broadway Project is dramatically different from that for Phase I. The city was declared ineligibile for a UDAG and the state reduced its share of the financing package to less than 10 percent of the total after having financed nearly one-fourth of Phase I. The developer was unwilling to put cash into the property and failed to obtain private financing. Clearly, if there was to be a Phase II, it would require a more active involvement of the city in financing. Just as the need for the city's backing was becoming essential, the city received a substantial payment from its subsidiary water company as a result of bond refinancing.

The chief negotiator for the city, a private attorney specializing in land development, was instrumental in redesigning the financing for Phase II. The city offered to be the principal source of financing for the development, to include $17 million in industrial revenue bonds (issued by Manufacturers Hanover Trust), a $1.9 million direct loan, and $2.6 million in equity. The state provided $2 million in economic redevelopment bonds and the county provided a $1 million direct loan. A local foundation (set up by J. Graham Brown, the original developer and owner of the Brown Complex) provided a $1 million grant to the development for open space. A local bank provided a $2.1 million loan for the construction of condominiums, and a consortium of downtown businesses active in the project guaranteed the loan through purchase commitments.

The city did not provide the property to the developer for a nominal sum as it had in Phase I. Instead, the city charged the developer the full cost of acquisition and clearance. This charge was indicative of the city's willingness to become more actively involved in the project as an investor rather than as a gift giver or a passive mortgagor. The city's stance was articulated by its chief negotiator: the city would be willing to provide needed cash, but only if the potential for long-term return was equivalent

Table 11.2. Broadway Project, Phase II: Investment, risk, and return

Investment type	Amount	Source	Risk	Return
Revenue bonds	$17.0 million	City (through Manufacturers Hanover Trust)	Secured by first mortgage. City has no liability.	Floating interest rate. No return to city.
Direct loan	$1.9 million	City (local funds)	Potential loss if project defaults. Subordinate lien position.	5% interest deferable and accruing based on cash flow net of city's 10% preferential return.
Direct loan	$1.0 million	County (local funds)	Potential loss if project defaults. Subordinate lien position.	5% interest deferable and accruing based on cash flow net of city's 10%.
Economic development bond	$2.0 million	State	Potential loss if project defaults. Subordinate lien position.	5% interest deferable and accruing based on cash flow net of city's 10%.
Equity (limited partner)	$2.6 million	City (local funds)	Equity at risk if sold for less than debt on property; liability for operating deficits.	10% preferential; 90% of net cash flow up to $2.6 million, then 62.5%; 80% of tax losses; possible capital gain if limited partnership interest on property sold. Will receive 62.5% of net proceeds after return of $2.6 million equity investment.
Operating losses (general partner)	Operations not started	Caldwell American Investments, Inc.	100% if net cash flow is insufficient to service debt and pay operating expense, however, some working capital in project budget.	Not applicable. Management fee is 5% of gross operating revenue. Will receive 37.5% of net proceeds (net of city's $2.6 million equity investment).

to the risks taken. Thus, in Phase II of the redevelopment project the city became even more aggressively entrepreneurial.

The city's approach was to become a limited partner through a subsidiary corporation, with the developer serving as the general partner. The city's negotiator insisted that the city receive the typical benefits of a limited partner and engaged an independent attorney experienced in limited partnerships to verify that the city's interests as a limited partner were being protected. As a limited partner, the city has no liability for operating deficits. It is to receive a 10 percent "preferential" return on its equity position out of gross revenues and 90 percent of net cash flow up to $2.6 million, after which it will receive 62.5 percent of net cash flow. Eighty percent of tax losses are distributed to the city's corporation, for which the city has not attempted to get a federal tax exemption. Originally, the city planned to syndicate its interest in the property and had estimated a sales price of $6 million prior to tax reform. Although these plans have been delayed by tax reform, a future syndication is possible.

The city will receive 100 percent of the proceeds from any syndication or sale of its partnership interest. Upon sale of the property, the city will receive 62.5 percent of net proceeds, with its $2.6 million equity position paid out of gross proceeds.

The general partner, Caldwell American Investments, has a minor equity position in the property. Caldwell American will receive 5 percent of gross operating revenue as a management fee; an incentive fee if net operating income exceeds projections; a 10 percent return on $0.4 million in equity; 10 percent of net cash flow (increasing to 37.5 percent after the city is paid $2.6 million from net cash flow); and 37.5 percent of net proceeds after the city's $2.6 million in equity is returned from gross proceeds. Caldwell American is fully responsible for operating deficits.

Given the operating deficits in Phase I (Phase II adds 26,000 square feet of retail space in what is an already soft market), it is reasonable to question how the city was able to obtain such favorable agreements on net cash flow and net proceeds. Given the operating deficits in Phase I, the agreements on net cash flow and net proceeds in Phase II are clearly favorable to the city. In Phase I, the developer was a consortium of local companies apparently motivated by civic interest and not solely by investment criteria. (The fiduciary rationality of pension fund investment in such a situation is clearly questionable.) In Phase II, the city is the primary equity investor and provides the bulk of the financing through industrial revenue bonds (for which it has no significant financial liability) and a direct loan. The private-sector partners in both phases are liable for operating deficits, but there are significant (but not unusual) development and management fees, and there is the possibility, however remote, of income from positive cash flow and net proceeds upon sale.

The city's primary rationale for involvement is, of course, to serve not as an investor but as a promoter. The hope is that redevelopment will increase tax revenues not only from the developed properties but from adjacent areas. There is some evidence that the hoped-for ripple effects are occurring. Capital Holding invested $2 million in renovation of its corporate headquarters opposite the Brown Hotel and now plans to build a new $66 million headquarters building in the area. The nearby Heyburn Building was purchased and renovated and is being successfully operated by a local developer with the help of $6 million from industrial revenue bonds issued by the city. Property assessments in the three blocks within the project area (most of which has not been redeveloped) declined steadily from 1962 to 1981 with a cumulative decline of 78 percent in real dollars, but have since increased substantially: 80 percent in nominal dollars and 47 percent in real dollars. The city's annual property tax revenues from this area have increased 82 percent (in nominal dollars) since 1980 after having declined 40 percent during the previous twenty years. The city's interests as a promoter of development notwithstanding, the principal advocate of the Broadway Project has been the consortium of downtown businesses led by Capital Holding (Schimpeler-Corradino Associates 1982; Broadway-Brown Partnership 1987).

The city of Louisville's investment interests in these developments has been protected through: (1) use of federal and state moneys; (2) protection against operating deficits; (3) agreements governing distribution of net income and net proceeds; and (4) preferential treatment of interest on equity. A failed project—as evidenced by continuing operating deficits or failure to meet required debt payments—would be harmful to all partners, public and private. Obviously, the private partners will not be willing to sustain operating losses indefinitely, and some reordering of liabilities between the public and private partners will probably be requested if gross income does not increase significantly. Negotiations for such a reordering have already begun. The five downtown corporations involved in the partnership have requested that the partnership's equity investments be returned from net proceeds from sale of the property prior to repayment of the loans made by the city and state. The city and state have tentatively agreed, thus substantially increasing their risk exposure (Shafer 1987).

Conclusion

Although the equality of public-private partnerships has no exact yardstick, the city of Louisville appears to have aggressively pursued financial rewards roughly in proportion to some calculus of costs and fiscal risks. Certain elements of Louisville's partnership are not as unequal as those found in other cities. Public officials in the city have attempted to make strategic use of their ability to negotiate in behalf of the public interest. We are not claiming that Louisville's partnership is equalitarian, but we do think this case study reveals important lessons about the nature of public-private partnerships.

Overall, we think that the public sector can never really become a coequal partner in urban redevelopment programs unless it stands to profit in the same manner as a joint investor or limited business partner. However, most local officials do not negotiate urban redevelopment deals in the same manner as their private sector "partners." In fact, it does not appear that the public sector is really a "partner" in the business and financial sense of the term. There are numerous factors that undermine the business relationship between public and private partners.

When private investors make choices, it is always in the face of incomplete market information, uncertainties about future profits, and concern over external constraints that cannot be controlled by the actions of their business partners. Important contingencies may be overlooked in the initial planning process, projections may be inaccurate, one or more of the partners may change their minds, changes may occur in the national or local economy, and so on. There are no guarantees that a specific redevelopment project will benefit each of the participants or the city as a whole. Most important, private investors make decisions on the basis of projected revenues. Local officials are not driven by the same financial calculus, a fact that makes them an unusual business partner.

To the extent that effective planning has been done, however, private investors will take steps to assemble as much relevant information as possible and try to reduce fiscal uncertainties to manageable levels. Important sources of inequality between private and public partners are asymmetries of *information*, *risk*, *capital*, and *power*. If private-sector partners are significantly unequal in their abilities to secure relevant information and financing, or to reduce uncertainties, the outcome may be redevelopment agreements that are substantially more beneficial or less risky for some of the investors. Likewise—whatever the uncertainties—if one of the partners has more power (from whatever source) in the relationship, that partner may be able to force the other into a relatively disadvantageous position or extract more of the benefits and profits generated.

To simplify, let us assume that each of the private-sector partners acts independently and calculates its stake in the proposed redevelopment plan. Much of the assessment is, of course, based on reliable information,

Figure 11.1. Calculation of Potential Risks and Benefits by Each Partner

Potential risks

		High	Low
Potential Benefits	High	Speculation	Sure thing
	Low	Bad deal	Matter of indifference

and bottom line reasoning, but much is also based on incomplete data, guesses, and subjective calculations tempered by civic pride and local boosterism. Figure 11.1 shows the possibilities. Each partner will opt for the *sure thing*, if that is possible to achieve. If not, the next best option is *speculation*. No one wants the *bad deal*; and if risk and benefits are both low *(matter of indifference)*, private partners are unlikely to make substantial investments. Miscalculations and blunders may result from unrealistic calculations brought about by unpredictable events, lack of information, or faulty projections of costs and benefits. In addition, it is possible that one of the partners may be forced into an undesirable position (square) if there are significant differences in the bargaining power of the partners. Thus, problems of information and power may result in disadvantages for one or both of the partners. If private-sector partners are forced into an undesirable position (square), however, they can leave the negotiation table, thus terminating the "deal."

Public-sector partners do not have the political or financial flexibility to allow them to walk away from the negotiation table. If market forces have driven the downtown into deterioration, local officials do not have access to the money or the power to finance urban redevelopment by themselves. In order to generate the capital and political commitment to a major urban development program, the public sector must forge some type of relationship with private developers, investors, and speculators. Figure 11.2 depicts hypothetical relationships between private and public partners when they attempt to form development agreements.

Many public-private partnerships can be accurately placed in the *exploitation* category. Proponents of partnership strategies argue that both parties should benefit, but not necessarily in direct relationship to the amount of money invested in the project. Conservative businessmen of-

Figure 11.2. Types of Business Relationships between Public and Private Partners

Public Benefits

		High	Low
	High	Equal partnership	Exploitation of the public partner
Private benefits	Low	Public enterprise	Depressed urban economy

ten see the possibility of bureaucratic inefficiency when the state enters the development arena, and typically stand in opposition to the idea that local government is a bona fide, profitsharing business partner. All analysts would consider a depressed urban economy the result of unsuccessful policies. In this situation, there is assistance from neither public nor private investors. Many private businesses have abandoned the downtown, and local government faces a high demand for welfare and social services with little money to pay for either. A number of hypothetical possibilities may produce partnerships that are both unequal and undesirable. From the vantage point of the public-sector partner, there are numerous forces at work making exploitation and a depressed urban economy likely policy outcomes.

There are at least two factors that produce major inequalities between public and private partners. The first is what Friedland and Palmer (1984) call the "capacity to exit." One way to have more influence and power in a negotiated arrangement is to possess more options for action. If one or more of the private-sector partners is able to move physically away from the area—and is thus able to avoid or withdraw from local negotiations or agreements—that partner has more options. This greater freedom of action may be translatable into greater power in negotiations. A central problem facing governments is that they are physically immobile, whereas most private-sector partners (developers, firms, financial institutions) are, at least in principle, able either to shift capital (to other investments outside the area) or to move their base of operations. Capital is mobile, but communities and governments are not (Bluestone and Harrison 1982).

Second, there may be unequal information available to the partners, for two reasons. First, intrafirm information is better than that of outsiders, including government agencies. Political scientists Bryan Jones and Lynn Bachelor (1984) analyze the problems related to what they term the "corporate surplus." They specifically examine the efforts of city governments to attract production plants to the local area; however, similar considerations undoubtedly affect efforts to formulate redevelopment schemes. City governments often provide incentives for private developers to undertake projects. "The corporation knows just what is necessary for a city government to provide in order to attract the facility, while city officials are not privy to that information" (Jones and Bachelor 1984:247). Given the economic and political pressures for urban growth and development, city officials want the new facility, and astute private developers want all the concessions they can get.

The game of urban development (Feagin 1983) can be compared with a high-stakes poker game in which it is in the interest of the private partners not to reveal the minimum levels of public subsidies required to induce their participation in the project. Through skillful negotiations, they might be able to gain extra concessions. This pattern is apparently the norm since as a result of "the asymmetry of information characterizing the negotiations, officials are inclined to grant concessions up to the statutory limit" (Jones and Bachelor 1984:247). In other words, public officials may become preoccupied with the question, How much can the city *afford* (politically and economically) to give? rather than with asking, Will this turn out to be of real benefit to the city in the long-run?

The "corporate surplus" is thus "the extraction of concessions by a corporation beyond what would be strictly necessary to attract the facility" (Jones and Bachelor 1984:247). To the extent that such asymmetries of information and differences in the ability to move capital exist, public partners may be excessively concession-prone, tipping the balance toward exclusively private benefits. This may be exacerbated by the fact that elected officials frequently desire to be associated with dramatic, highly visible projects whose ultimate fate and resulting benefits may not be obvious for many years, if at all, to voters.

Another reason for unequal information pertains to the special roles played by financial institutions in business affairs generally and redevelopment plans in particular. City and state governments do, of course, have considerable ability to collect relevant information about the local economy and thus to assess likely future economic developments. However, as the idea of the corporate surplus implies, there may be important gaps in this information. Not only do individual development firms have a much better idea of what their own internal incentives are, but privately held information may be more complete in at least one other important way. Michael Useem (1984) has demonstrated that corporate directors serving on the boards of several firms simultaneously are in a strategic position to gain information about a broad range of business conditions affecting different firms, and to play valuable intrabusiness-community roles because of this enhanced "business scan."

In Louisville (Whitt and Mizruchi 1986), as elsewhere (Mintz and Schwartz 1985), financial institutions are typically at the center of networks formed by shared directorships. Since banks and insurance companies occupy such positions in the local economy, and since banks in particular are involved in information exchanges based on lenders' need to know and have relationships of trust with their local corporate clients, it is reasonable to suppose that banks are likely to possess a great deal of pertinent information concerning local business conditions, financial and growth-related plans of clients, and possible bases of joint interest in urban redevelopment plans. This may well be an information resource that cannot be matched by local government. Banks and other financial institutions and their executives are central players in local redevelopment schemes. These organizations are often the sources of construction loans, and multiple corporate directors (frequently bankers) are likely to be disproportionately represented in civic and policymaking organizations, including those involved in planning urban redevelopment (see, for example, Useem 1980).

Although cities are constrained in their negotiations with developers, the Louisville example demonstrates that they are not powerless. Several lessons can be learned from our case study, which can place a city in a better position to protect its own interests and to establish a more balanced relationship with private-sector partners. We recommend that when negotiating the terms of a public-private partnership, city officials pay close attention to the following principles.

1. *Determine what financial roles the city is capable and willing to play.* The financial roles cities can play range from gift-giver to equity partner. Gift-givers can hope to attract development where it might not otherwise occur, but the city is constrained to negotiate regarding the physical characteristics of the development, not its own position in the development package. Being limited to a "front-end" role clearly has its disadvantages and is likely to place a city in a strategically disadvantageous position. On the other hand, equity partners can bargain concerning distribution of fees, net cash flow, preferential returns, and net proceeds. This is the fullest range of bargaining that can occur.

2. *Play with other people's money.* Use federal or state money to the extent possible. The city's strategy for using federal and state funds in a project should depend on the direction of repaid funds. If payments return to the other levels of government, the city should try to use these funds as gifts. If

payments return to the city, it should bargain for guaranteed returns with the highest security possible.

3. *Tie returns to the risks taken.* A clear assessment of the risk of the venture is needed by the public as well as the private partner. Better knowledge of the risks involved for both sides can help the city bargain for a greater or lesser rate of return. The more firmly the city guarantees the private partner's return, the less the rate of return should be for that partner. The "sure thing" warrants a rate of return approximating that of annuities.

4. *Look at all sources of returns, or "watch the money."* The more money the city provides and the greater its risks, the more the city should tap all types of proceeds: interest payments, fees, net cash flow, and net proceeds upon sale.

5. *Get qualified help.* If the city's staff has limited development experience, contract with lawyers and accountants who are knowledgeable about joint property ventures and syndications.

6. *Limit exposure to cash infusions.* Operating deficits should be borne by the private-sector partner, but any development scheme should start with sufficient working capital to enable the property manager to offset slow market acceptance of the project.

Louisville's urban redevelopment program represents a case in which the public sector extracted a share of the potential benefits in return for the amount of dollars it brought to the negotiation table. Although the potential benefits were obviously not in direct proportion to those that might have been claimed by a private partner who invested a similar amount of money in the project, it does seem apparent that the Louisville case does not fit the exploitation category in Figure 11.2. We submit that the Louisville case is more consistent with the public enterprise and equal partnership categories, although the city is clearly not a full financial partner. Considering the amount of public dollars invested in the renovation effort, the city did manage to position itself as a more active business partner in comparison with officials in other municipalities.

When conservative public officials argue that government ought to be run "like a business," we doubt that they have public enterprise in mind. At the same time, our evidence and argument suggest that local officials ought to enter public-private partnerships with a tough entrepreneurial attitude, and negotiate a fair share of rewards in return for the public dollars invested in private redevelopment projects. To do less raises critical questions about the collective good and the ability of local government to pursue the public interest.

References

Bluestone, Barry, and Bennett Harrison. 1982. *The Deindustrialization of America*. New York: Basic Books.

Broadway-Brown Partnership. 1987. Unpublished data.

Clavel, Pierre. 1986. *The Progressive City*. New Brunswick, N.J.: Rutgers University Press.

Cummings, Scott. 1987. *Business Elites and Urban Development*. Albany: State University of New York Press.

Daykin, David. 1987. "The Limits of Neighborhood Power: Progressive Politics and Local Control in Santa Monica." In *Business Elites and Urban Development,* ed. Scott Cummings, pp. 357–387. Albany: State University of New York Press.

Feagin, Joe. 1983. *The Urban Real Estate Game*. Englewood Cliffs, N.J.: Prentice-Hall.

———. 1987. "Tallying the Costs of Urban Growth under Capitalism: The Case of Houston. In *Business Elites and Urban Development*, ed. Scott Cummings, pp. 205–234. Albany: State University of New York Press.

Friedland, Roger, and Donald Palmer. 1984. "Park Place and Main Street: Business and the Urban Power Structure." *Annual Review of Sociology* 10: 393–416.

Jones, Bryan, and Lynn Bachelor. 1984. "Local Policy Discretion and the Corporate Surplus." In *Urban Economic Development*, ed. Richard Bingham and John Blair, pp. 245–267. Beverly Hills: Sage.

Logan, John, and Harvey Molotch. 1987. *Urban Fortunes*. Berkeley: University of California Press.

Mintz, Beth, and Michael Schwartz. 1985. *The Power Structure of American Business*. Chicago: University of Chicago Press.

Schimpeler-Corradino Associates. 1982. *Broadway Project Area Urban Renewal Plan*. Louisville: Schimpeler-Corradino Associates.

Shafer, Sheldon. 1987. "Companies May Spend Millions of Dollars More on Broadway Project." *Courier-Journal* (November 9):B1.

Swanstrom, Todd B. 1987. "Urban Populism, Uneven Development, and the Space for Reform." In *Business Elites and Urban Development*, ed. Scott Cummings, pp. 121–152. Albany: State University of New York Press.

Useem, Michael. 1980. "Corporations and the Corporate Elite." *Annual Review of Sociology* 6:41–77.

———. 1984. *The Inner Circle*. New York: Oxford University Press.

Whitt, J. Allen. 1982. *Urban Elites and Mass Transportation*. Princeton, N.J.: Princeton University Press.

———. 1987. "The Role of the Performing Arts in Urban Competition and Growth." In *Business Elites and Urban Development*, ed. Scott Cummings, pp. 49–69. Albany: State University of New York Press.

Whitt, J. Allen, and Mark Mizruchi. 1986. "The Local Inner Circle." *Journal of Political and Military Sociology* 14 (Spring):115–125.

Yater, George H. 1987. "Louisville." In *Cities Reborn*, ed. Rachelle L. Lauh, pp. 55–104. Washington, D.C.: Urban Land Institute.

Robert K. Whelan

12. New Orleans:
Public-Private Partnerships
and Uneven Development

Students of public policy innovation in the United States have often found that the South lagged behind other parts of the country. For many reasons—cultural, economic, political, and social—New Orleans was left behind other Southern cities in terms of urban development. Since 1970, New Orleans leaders have recognized the same kinds of problems in their city that were evident in other southern and rustbelt cities: white flight to the suburbs, overdependence on one sector of the economy (in the case of New Orleans, energy), and the economic difficulties faced by a black underclass.

As a result, New Orleans has developed some of the same kinds of partnerships that have been formed in other cities. Although New Orleans came late to urban renewal (for example, until 1986, there was no dominant association of key downtown business actors, of the kind found in many cities), we will see that public-private partnerships were responsible for major downtown redevelopment efforts in the 1970s. At the neighborhood level, New Orleans now has an active Neighborhood Housing Services program. Public-private partnerships have had a positive effect on city government services. An accountant from the private sector was made the chief administrative officer in the Barthelemy administration, and a major public-private partnership has made recommendations on governmental efficiency.

All this was achieved in a context of uneven economic development. While the central business district was being developed during the oil boom of the 1970s, the city continued to have a high rate of unemployment. Blacks had an especially high rate of unemployment, even during the best years of the boom. The housing stock is old, and 10 percent of the city's population lives in public housing. As Smith and Keller (1986) point out, "the city's lack of investment in public education has produced a largely unskilled black underclass" (p. 131). The high level of poverty is related to other serious problems, such as a high rate of violent street crime.

The city's demography is extremely important for our purposes. Other observers have accurately pointed out that New Orleans resembles the declining industrial cities of the Northeast and the Midwest in a number of respects (Mumphrey and Moomau 1984:91). In the decade 1970–1980, the city's population decreased from 593,471 to 557,616, a decline of 6.1 percent. A mid-decade Census Bureau report estimated the city's population at 559,101, a slight increase over 1980. In the same time span, the New Orleans Standard Metropolitan Statistical Area (SMSA) grew by 13.5 percent, from 1,045,809 in 1970 to 1,187,073 in 1980. The racial makeup of the city also changed in that decade, from 45 percent black and 54 percent white in 1970, to 55 percent black and 43 percent white in 1980.

The city's geography is also extremely important for urban development. New Orleans is surrounded by water, with Lake Pontchartrain to the north and east of the city, and the Mississippi River dividing the city. New Orleans has 363.5 square miles, but only about 200 square miles are land. The remaining square mileage is marsh and swampland in the eastern part of the city. Much of the built-up space is contained in an area from the lakefront to the river (north-south) and from the Bullard Road area in eastern New Orleans to the Jefferson Parish line (east-west). In brief, there has been high-density utilization of the developed land. Developable land is at a premium.

I begin with a discussion of the changing structure of the local economy. This is followed by an examination of postwar redevelopment strategies and the effects of development activities. In New Orleans, as in many other cities, dominant redevelopment strategies have been challenged. I discuss these challenges. Finally, I make some projections concerning future development.

The Changing Structure of the Local Economy

Since the 1960s, New Orleans' local economy has had a tripartite base: the port, oil and related industries, and tourism. Given the city's location near the mouth of the Mississippi River, the port has been central to its growth. Port-related activities were vital to the health of the economy as New Orleans grew to be the third largest city in the country according to the 1840 Census, and retained its status as the largest Southern city until the 1950 Census. More recently, the port has faced problems of competition from other cities, and of decreases in tonnage passing through. The port provided 11 percent of the city's jobs in 1979. A steamship company executive, W. James Amoss (1985), notes that the number of workers who loaded and unloaded ships in the port dropped from 5,103 in 1970 to 2,088 in 1984. At the same time, the number of hours worked decreased from 7.51 million in 1970 to 2.96 million in 1984. Since most of this dock labor force is black, the effects on the black community are especially severe, as blacks have lost relatively high-paying unionized jobs on the docks. Since 1986 the Dock Board, the state agency that runs the port, has been headed by Ron Brinson, a dynamic young executive. Under his leadership the volume of cargo and the number of jobs have risen. However, the Dock Board faces difficult problems in constructing the kinds of riverfront facilities it needs to match those of its competitors, because of Louisiana's fiscal problems (Katz 1987). We discuss the state's fiscal problems more fully later in the chapter.

The oil industry became an important part of the New Orleans economy after World War II, with the discovery and drilling of oil in the Gulf of Mexico off the Louisiana coast. As the oil industry developed, an industrial corridor emerged, extending from Baton Rouge to the Gulf of Mexico along the Mississippi River. Petrochemical industries are the most important component of this area. The Chamber of Commerce estimates that one-quarter of the jobs in the seven-parish metropolitan region relate to oil. The expansion of the New Orleans central business district was largely a result of the rental of office space by oil firms. (One such major facility is the million-square-foot office building at One Shell Square, the tallest in New Orleans.) These corporations provided over 9,000 jobs in the central business district (about 15 percent of the district's employment) in 1980 (Ryan 1985), mostly in their regional or exploration headquarters.

As economist Timothy P. Ryan (1985) has pointed out, the New Orleans economy became overdependent on the oil and gas industry in the 1970s. Ryan's research shows that oil and gas provide jobs not only in the mining sector, but also in other sectors of the economy, such as construction, manufacturing, services, and transportation. Ryan suggests that a more accurate description of the local economy in the 1970s and 1980s would be "the big one" (oil and gas) and "the little two" (tourism and the port).

The drop in the price of petroleum and related products depressed the New Orleans local economy in the 1980s, while much of the rest of the United States enjoyed economic prosperity. The city had a double-digit unemployment rate for more than three years. Collapse of oil-and gas-related industries led to a population out-migration; well-educated young professionals were the most likely to leave the area. The housing market was weak. This decline in oil-related unemployment ended in 1987, as things finally bottomed out. A rise in the price of oil to $20 a barrel started some exploration and gave the state's economy some stability. The unemployment rate for the New Orleans area dropped into single digits in 1987, even though the area still had a high (9.1 percent) unemployment figure in July 1987. However, the office vacancy rate in the central business district was 27 percent in the second quarter of 1987, far above the national average of 16.3 percent (Stuart 1987).

The move toward economic recovery is attributed to an increase in tourism-related jobs. According to the U.S. Travel Survey, tourism provided 45,000 jobs in the New Orleans metropolitan in 1986. In the late 1980s, tourism displaced petroleum as the mainstay of the local economy. Indexes such as airport deplanements and hotel-motel taxes showed large increases (Katz 1987).

Tourism accounted for 27.3 percent of the city's jobs in 1979. The number of hotels, conventions, and tourists has increased substantially since the 1960s. Most tourism-related jobs are in service industries and are largely low-paying positions, with high turnover rates. There is little career mobility, with few chances for advancement. The opening of the Louisiana Superdome in 1975 had a catalytic effect on tourism (as it did on rental of downtown office space). The number of hotel rooms increased from 10,000 in 1970 to 20,000 in 1980 and had increased to 25,000 in 1985, in part as a result of the 1984 World's Fair. Tourist business increased only marginally, and hotel occupancy rates dropped from 1980 to 1985, although they increased again in 1987 (Marcus 1985; Perales 1986). The number of convention delegates increased from 58,000 in 1960 to 580,000 in 1980. With the opening of the new convention center in 1985, the number of convention delegates increased to more than one million per year.

Manufacturing has historically played only a small role in the New Orleans economy and used to be of much greater importance than it is at present. In the third quarter of 1981, there were almost 53,000 manufacturing jobs in the New Orleans area. In the first quarter of 1984, there were 39,000 jobs. The loss of 14,000 relatively high-paying manufacturing jobs in less than three years was devastating for the local economy (Ryan 1985).

An important consideration is that the three major segments of the local economy (the port, the oil industry, and tourism) are controlled by outside interests and are highly subject to swings in the national and international economy. In many instances, the New Orleans area has been a loser that has been unable to control its own destiny. Port-related activities are affected by changes in the worldwide price of energy. Since the energy crisis of 1973–1974, the oil industry has been influenced by the behavior of the OPEC (Organization of Petroleum Exporting Countries) nations and other international actors. It should also be noted that the major oil companies are not based in New Orleans. When the price of oil fell, many workers lost their jobs; many others were transferred to company headquarters in Houston or other cities. The hotel industry is dominated by major national chains, such as Hilton, Sheraton, Marriott, and Hyatt —a situation that has many ramifications. A national chain often feels no particular obligation to a community when a closure is considered. The same may be true in regard to labor policy. Hyatt, for example, has refused to sign a union contract at its New Orleans hotel, thus helping to keep down local wages (Perl 1986). The national chains have done little to create career opportunities that might contribute to a solution of some of the economic problems afflicting the city. Moreover, the lack of local capital has historically been cited as a major reason for the city's relatively slow development. The Superdome and other 1970s redevelopment projects were financed by banks in other cities (notably Atlanta and Dallas).

National and international forces shape developments in the New Orleans area in many ways. Changes in the price of oil are the most obvious. A drop in the price of oil can create havoc in the many economic sectors dependent upon the petroleum industry. Changes in technology can also be important. For example, the port of New Orleans lost business in the 1970s because other cities were quicker to adapt to the new technology of containerization, and because many international companies in port-related industries turned to "mini-bridging." (In brief, it became cheaper for a Japanese company to bring goods to a West Coast port and then ship them by rail than to bring the goods through the Panama Canal, and, ultimately, through the port of New Orleans.) The tourism industry is subject to the overall health of the national economy. Moreover, when air fares are low, New Orleans booms with tourists. Tourism is cyclical, however, and there are frequent downturns, as in the summers of 1983 and 1985. National trade legislation is another example of an external force shaping the local economy. When Congress considered protectionist trade legislation in 1987, many in New Orleans were fearful concerning its effects. Port director Ron Brinson observed that "anything that restricts imports is bad for the port, period" (Powers 1987).

In summarizing the present state of the local economy, it is fair to say that New Orleans is relying more than ever on tourism as a base of its economy. The port has dynamic leadership but needs financial help for capital projects from a financially strapped state government. The port, and the oil industry, are still hostage of the OPEC nations, which set the price of oil. That the local economy is subject to national and international forces was especially evident in fall of 1987, when the city and Martin-

Marietta lost to Boeing and to Huntsville, Alabama, in the bidding for a lucrative contract to build the NASA space station. Optimism was high because of the anticipated infusion of jobs, capital, and spending into the local economy. It is not clear why NASA chose Huntsville over New Orleans. What is clear is the city's continued pattern of losses in these competitions.

Postwar Redevelopment Strategies

The New Orleans power structure resembles that of other Southern cities. In addition to major actors in port-related businesses and in the tourism and petroleum industries, the city's power structure includes representatives of banks, utilities, major law firms, department stores, hotels, the media, and other major proponents of downtown development. In many ways, New Orleans is an interesting city because of what has *not* happened in the area of urban redevelopment. The immediate postwar era saw a promising start. Under the direction of Mayor de-Lesseps Morrison, urban development included a new City Hall and judicial complex, and a new union railroad station. A World Trade Center was built, and trade with Latin America was thriving (Haas 1974). The Louisiana state legislature did not pass state enabling legislation for urban renewal until 1968. Thus, New Orleans was not involved in the nation's major postwar redevelopment effort until twenty years after the program began. Business leadership did not immediately come forward, as it did in other cities; not until the 1970s and 1980s did it play a major role in the city's revitalization program. In contrast to Atlanta, which integrated public schools peaceably in the early 1960s, New Orleans faced bitter opposition in that period. The failure of the city's initial efforts has thus rightfully been called the "failure of an elite" (Crain 1969).

Executive leadership was crucial to the city's redevelopment efforts in the postwar period. The efforts made by Morrison in the late 1940s and early 1950s were not followed up in any systematic way until the administrations of Moon Landrieu and of Ernest "Dutch" Morial, the first black to be elected mayor, in the 1970s.

One way in which New Orleans differs from other U.S. cities is that countervailing forces have sometimes emerged as a check on the dominant downtown business interests. Chief among these forces is the relatively strong preservationist movement. Its strength was most evident in its defeat of the proposed Riverfront Expressway in 1969. The Riverfront Expressway was to have been a six-lane, 108-foot wide, 40-foot-high elevated highway along the Vieux Carré (French Quarter) riverfront.

Originally suggested by New York planner Robert Moses in the 1940s, the expressway would have dwarfed the area's historic buildings. The plan had the support of a group of downtown financial and business interests organized into an umbrella coalition known as the Central Area Committee of the Chamber of Commerce, and of numerous politicians. Against the plan were historical preservationists, affected neighborhood groups, and other civic elites. This controversy between the preservationists and the pro-growth coalition drew national attention. The preservationists prevailed when the secretary of the Department of Transportation bowed to national pressure and stopped all federal aid to the project (Baumbach and Borah 1981). Historian Arnold Hirsch sees this as an instance of "productive non-action." He notes that "the attraction of a French Quarter unspoiled by Moses' elevated highway was critical to the 1970's revival of the CBD" (Hirsch 1983:118).

White working-class and middle-class homeowners have also been a force in opposition to major downtown interests. On numerous occasions, the white homeowner's vote has been decisive in defeating major tax incentives supported by the downtown growth coalition. Typical have been votes against raises for policemen and firemen, and the defeat of a bond issue to help the school board in the 1986 election. These initiatives were supported, by and large, by downtown business interests.

Since the 1960s, the city of New Orleans has pursued an economic development strategy that emphasizes revitalization of the central business district and promotion of tourism. In the mid-1960s, plans were formulated to construct the Superdome, a megastructure that would serve as a downtown convention center and sports arena and would announce to the world that New Orleans was no longer a parochial and insular city. The Superdome was the key to a tourist-based strategy for the future development of downtown New Orleans. When the project was first proposed, it had widespread political and community support; voters gave their overwhelming approval for Superdome bonds, to be included in a 1966 state constitutional amendment. Support began to wane because the project was beset by large cost overruns (proposed cost, $35 million; actual cost, $163 million) and rising deficits, which the state agreed to cover through a lease-financing arrangement.

The fact that a six-lane thoroughfare was available (the entire length of Poydras Street) was a major consideration in deciding on the location of the Superdome. The publicly financed widening of Poydras Street had been initiated under former Mayor Victor Schiro in the 1960s. Construction of the domed stadium paved the way for much private-sector development, starting with construction of large chain hotels in the early

1970s, and continuing with erection of large office buildings, stimulated by the heavy demand of major oil companies for office space for themselves, as well as space for smaller firms offering ancillary services.

The Superdome opened in 1975. A number of assessments of its impact were made when the dome celebrated its tenth anniversary. City officials say that the Superdome has been an economic catalyst in that it has aided in generating more than $2.5 billion in construction and renovation, opened the Poydras Street corridor from Claiborne Avenue to the river, and rejuvenated what was a deteriorating central business district. On the negative side, the dome never achieved its goal of becoming a multipurpose facility. It has provided space for many conventions and trade shows, but it is not ideal for that purpose (as evidenced by the construction of the Exhibition Hall, or New Orleans Convention Center). It is too large for most concerts. It is ideal as a professional sports facility. Since the city does not have a major league baseball team, the Superdome is used only ten days a year for pro sports (by the New Orleans Saints football team). A study by the University of New Orleans Division of Business and Economic Research, commissioned by the Louisiana Stadium and Exposition District, stated that "no urban renewal project in the history of New Orleans is likely to have beneficially impacted a surrounding area as has the development of the Louisiana Superdome." According to the report, for every dollar Louisiana has put into the Superdome's construction, operating facilities, maintenance, and improvements, it has received $96.40 in return. In short, the study concludes that the Superdome has been a very good investment for the city and the state (Ragas et al. 1987). A different analysis might place higher value on the state subsidy to the dome from the start, the increased subsidies to the Saints football team after it threatened to move in 1985, and the slim chance of the city's ever having a major league baseball team.

Although I am not particularly an admirer of domed stadiums (as a sport fan or as a student of public policy), the Superdome's contribution to New Orleans should be abundantly clear. The 1988 Republican party national convention was held in New Orleans and brought in thousands of journalists, delegates, and others who spent millions of dollars during their stay. Moreover, the favorable national image projected during the convention will bring in other conventions and tourists in the future. Without a facility like the Superdome, New Orleans could not ever host a political convention, a Superbowl (pro football championship), or a "Final Four" National Collegiate Athletic Association basketball tournament. Just before the Republican convention, the New Orleans Centre (an upscale shopping mall, anchored by major national stores such as Lord and

Taylor, and Macy's) opened, adjacent to the Superdome. This development would not be located in New Orleans, were it not for the proximity of the conventions and sporting events held at the Superdome. The Superdome has not solved the intractable problems of unemployment, but the unemployment situation would be worse without the tourism and service-related jobs provided by, and other jobs stimulated by, the Superdome.

In the 1970s, the city became the recipient of large amounts of federal economic development money. Two major projects undertaken by the city with Economic Development Administration and other federal moneys were Armstrong Park and the Piazza d'Italia. Armstrong Park is a thirty-one-acre park and entertainment complex at the periphery of the French Quarter that is built around the Municipal Auditorium. The Piazza d'Italia is a downtown city block consisting of plaza, fountain, and historic buildings to be restored for hotel and commercial uses. These were the earliest economic development efforts by the city government; neither has achieved its potential because the city found them both costly to operate and difficult to lease under city ownership. Both projects still have a great deal of potential; their development was spurred (particularly in the case of the Piazza d'Italia) by the 1984 World's Fair (Mumphrey and Moomau 1984).

New Orleans has been extremely active in the Urban Development Action Grant (UDAG) program. The city's largest grant has been for the Exhibition Hall/Sheraton Hotel project. The city received $14 million, which represented 16 percent of the cost of a new convention facility not including land. The Exhibition Hall served as the Louisiana Pavilion for the 1984 World's Fair (Young 1984).

The most controversial project financed by a UDAG is Canal Place, a downtown mixed-use development that straddles the boundary of the historic French Quarter. Canal Place has pitted preservationists, who fear that the scale and height of the project will detract from the coherence of the historic district, against developers and city officials, who see the project as helping to provide the jobs and taxes that the city needs to sustain itself (Brooks and Weeter 1982).

It is important to note that development along the riverfront and in areas close to the river was given impetus by the 1984 World's Fair. The opening of the Rouse Company's Riverwalk, another project using UDAG funds, in 1986 gave the city another major tourist attraction. Luxury condominiums are also being constructed.

The Morial and Barthelemy administrations attempted development of the 9,000-acre Almonaster-Michoud industrial district in eastern New Orleans. As a key part of Mayor Morial's economic development program, the city committed itself to providing infrastructure improvements and developing the area as a planned industrial park (Marak 1982). Much of the city's industrial base was already located in this area, including heavy and light industry and deep-water port users, processing industries, high-technology plants, and trucking terminals. In October 1983, SFE Technologies Inc., a manufacturer of computer parts, opened a plant in a new-enterprise zone in the Almonaster-Michoud corridor.

The Almonaster-Michoud industrial district is located along the curves of the Mississippi River gulf outlet. The area lacks both proper drainage and sanitary sewer systems and an adequate road network. There is already substantial industrial development in the corridor, including the NASA Michoud assembly facility, Folger Coffee, Georgia Pacific, the TANO Corporation (a producer of navigation and energy control equipment), Siemens-Allis Electronics, Litton Industries, and SFE Technologies.

In 1987 Sidney Barthelemy became the second black to be elected mayor of New Orleans. Barthelemy's coalition was unusual for a black candidate. In a runoff election against another black candidate, State Senator William Jefferson, Barthelemy's support had come from a *minority* of black voters and the overwhelming *majority* of the city's white voters. Barthelemy provides a stylistic contrast with Morial. Morial, who had been active in the civil rights movement, was often confrontational and combative in his relations with the white community. Barthelemy, whose background was the seminary, social work, and city and state government, preaches consensus and is often conciliatory in his relations with opponents of his administration.

In regard to economic development, Barthelemy had taken a somewhat different approach than Morial. Tourism has revived, and Barthelemy has made tourism his major emphasis. The keynote of his tourism strategy is the construction of a $40 million aquarium and park on a 10-acre site along the riverfront, stretching from the Bienville Street Wharf to the Moonwalk (in front of Jackson Square). In 1986, voters approved $25 million in bonds for the project. The Friends of the Zoo, a private, nonprofit organization that has played a key role in the renovation of the city's zoo, will raise the remaining $15 million. Aquarium supporters believe that it will bring tourist families to New Orleans and will stimulate development of the riverfront in the Decatur Street and French Market area. Another major venture is the attempt to have the Tivoli people from Copenhagen, Denmark, operate a Tivoli-style amusement park on the underutilized Armstrong Park site. Still another major Barthelemy effort was to encourage the Louisiana state legislature to provide financing for expansion of the New Orleans Convention Center during the 1987 legislative session. In addition, the Greater New Orleans Marketing Committee is conducting the first advertising campaign to promote New Orleans. The initial campaign focused on marketing in the Birmingham and Dallas metropolitan areas; $480,000 was raised for the campaign by a combination of public and private groups—evidence of the existence of a public-private partnership in economic development.

As noted earlier, the port as a base of the economy revived somewhat in 1986–1987. Part of the revival was in the economic and marketing areas. Also significant for future economic development was the port's cooperation with the city government. In 1988, the city and the Dock Board concluded a successful land swap, in which the city took over the Rivergate (the original convention center) from the Dock Board, and the Dock Board took dock land from the city.

Several other economic development efforts of the Barthelemy administration should be mentioned. In the summer of 1987, the city was able to attract the Pic-N-Save corporation, a discount chain, to the Almonaster-Michoud industrial district, where it will open a regional distribution center. The administration was also involved in a major effort to try to obtain a $2 billion contract for the Martin-Marietta Corporation, to build part of the proposed NASA space station at its New Orleans Michoud facility. Although the effort failed, many felt that the city government demonstrated cohesion and coordination that were not previously evident. The city is also investigating the possibility of building a second airport. Moisant Airport, which opened in the immediate postwar period, is a cramped, inadequate facility. Although the city is well served by the major airlines, it is argued that a second airport would enable New Orleans to become an airline hub and thus attract significant economic development. Finally, Mayor Barthelemy led a large New Orleans delegation to France in October of 1987 in search of companies interested in the opportunity to invest or build in the New Orleans area.

In summarizing postwar redevelopment strategies, we should note that the political actors in New Orleans are somewhat different from those in other cities. First, until the mid-1980s, downtown business leaders were not as dynamic or as forward-looking as their counterparts in other cities, such as Atlanta. Second, New Orleans has a strong preservationist movement that has prevented the destruction of the French Quarter and has succeeded in preserving many buildings of historical and architectural interest. Third, New Orleans has an influential white homeowner group that is opposed to taxes and to almost any action by the public sector. Its members have defeated many bond issues. Although they are a minority of the total electorate, in combination with a minority of black voters they chose the "more acceptable" black candidate, Sidney Barthelemy, to win the last mayoralty election.

The overall aim of redevelopment policies can be summarized as development of the central business district in 1970s, with preservation of the French Quarter and tourism. In the 1980s, the city has turned to tourism as the major base of its strategy, with the aquarium project on the riverfront as the keystone. But the city is not neglecting other areas, such as the development of its port and industrial facilities.

The Many Effects of Development Activities

In this section, I examine the spatial, demographic, and economic effects of redevelopment initiatives in New Orleans.

Several points should be made in discussing the spatial effects of downtown development activities. First, the major emphasis of economic development activities in New Orleans has been downtown revitalization. The skyscraper development along Poydras Street (the "Fifth Avenue" of New Orleans), and revival of the central business district, the French Quarter, and the tourism industry, are testimony to the success of such activities. Relatively few redevelopment efforts have centered on the city's neighborhoods. Those that have (such as the Neighborhood Housing Services rehabilitation effort in the Milan area) have been narrow in scope, particularly in comparison with such major downtown initiatives as the Superdome, Riverwalk, and aquarium. The relative neglect of neighborhoods has been a mixed blessing. Neighborhoods that have interesting historical structures are better off left alone, protected by the preservationists. The deterioration of other neighborhoods, however, has exacerbated such problems as unemployment and the high crime rate.

Second, the city has never emphasized displacement as part of its strategy, although there have been three main instances of displacement in the city's history: (1) displacement for the Civic Center and railroad station in the 1950s; (2) displacement along Claiborne Avenue, when the interstate highway was completed in the 1960s; (3) displacement in the Treme neighborhood for the Armstrong Park project in the 1970s.

In each case, low-income blacks were displaced to complete a public project. Overall, however, the numbers of people displaced and the amount of displacement in New Orleans are relatively small compared with other cities. The combination of a "machine politics" tradition and a strong preservationist movement has led to an emphasis on rehabilitation and renovation in the city's redevelopment efforts.

Third, many observers of New Orleans urban affairs are concerned about enroachment into the Vieux Carré (French Quarter). The eighteenth-century settlement of the city began in the French Quarter. The Quarter was largely a residential area until the 1950s. Although the Quarter's historic structures have been preserved (as a result of the efforts of the Vieux Carré Commission, created in the 1930s), many of those structures are now being used for commercial purposes, some of which seem unnecessary to long-time residents, who note the proliferation of T-shirt shops. Moreover, the construction of the Jackson Brewery additions, and other high-use development along the river, represent threats to the architectural integrity of the French Quarter in the eyes of many preservationists. In developing the riverfront, the city could destroy the area that gives New Orleans its "Old World" character and makes the city a favorite destination for North American and European tourists.

Finally, the city has a mixed record with regard to the location of its public housing. About one resident in ten (or about 50,000 people) resides in public housing. The city's oldest public housing (such as the Magnolia projects) was placed in close proximity to downtown, to transit lines, and to viable residential neighborhoods. Postwar public housing, such as the massive Florida and Desire projects, and the Fischer projects across the river in Algiers, were placed in isolated areas far from the city's economic mainstream. It is these later projects that provide the worst evidence of the social pathologies that we associate with public housing.

Many indicators of economic conditions do appear, on the surface, to be consistent with a declining central city. For example, both the mean and the median income for New Orleans remain well below the levels for the SMSA in comparable periods.

The percentage of families below the poverty level, however, showed little change between 1970 and 1980, increasing from 21.6 percent to 21.8 percent in that ten-year period (U.S. Bureau of the Census 1970; 1980). With the downturn in the oil industry, and the slowness to recover from the national recession of the early 1980s, the New Orleans area jobless rate reached an all-time high of 11.6 percent in early 1985 and has remained in the neighborhood of 10 percent since that time (U.S. Department of Labor 1985–1988).

New Orleans continues to have a two-tiered economy and society, with a depressed level of per capita income (compared with other cities), which suggests relative economic distress in the New Orleans SMSA. This unequal development of New Orleans has been important both economically and socially. One segment of the population is largely white and consists of affluent, well-educated people who hold professional positions in the community. Those who constitute the other segment, which is largely black but includes a sizable white component, struggle with the problems of unemployment and marginal employment.

The educational system has traditionally been the vehicle for upward mobility and opportunity in the United States. However, the New Orleans public schools (like those in the rest of the nation, and other Western industrial nations) are in a state of crisis. School facilities are deteriorating and teacher quality is low. Poor performance by students at all levels of the educational system has obvious implications for the local economy. The number of unskilled, poorly educated people in New Orleans has meant that the city has been unable to attract many high-technology industries (McQuaid 1987).

The demography of New Orleans creates fundamental problems in the delivery of city services. The large low-income population needs government services, but the city is financially unable to provide many of these services, for two reasons. First, the city is limited by the state of Louisiana's property tax legislation, which exempts from property taxes the first $75,000 of assessed valuation for owner-occupied homes. This creates a regressive tax situation, in which the city relies on sales taxes (generated in part by tourism) as opposed to property taxes, which are more responsive to the local economic climate. Second, the city is limited by the multiplicity of local governments in the metropolitan area. Much of the middle-income population, which provides local governments with much of their revenue base, lives in the outlying suburban parishes. Areas in the SMSA that are beyond city limits are outside the range and power of the New Orleans city government.

Overall, the city's redevelopment policies have served to reinforce the major demographic trends. Except for developers' construction of a few luxury condominiums along the riverfront and in the warehouse district, no attempt has been made to lure the middle class into the city. Redevelopment policies, by and large, have not addressed the needs of the large poverty-level population in regard to jobs, housing, and education.

It is reasonable to conclude that the major redevelopment efforts have brought jobs and business growth to the New Orleans area. Certainly, the Superdome must be mentioned as a major catalyst. The dome's impact —the increase in land values, tourism (as a result of events held at the stadium), new construction, and taxes generated—has been estimated at $2.68 billion in its first decade (Ragas et al. 1987). Having the dome has enabled New Orleans to host such major events as the Super Bowl, the Final Four of the NCAA basketball tournament, and the 1988 Republican National Convention. These events have generated hundreds of millions of dollars for the local economy.

Such projects as Riverwalk, the Jackson Brewery, and other hotel and retail development downtown can clearly be said to have generated jobs and business growth in the central business district. The questions, of course, are: What sorts of jobs are generated? Do we want an economy that is driven by tourism?

Challenges to Dominant Redevelopment Strategies: Projections for the Future

In New Orleans, the major challenge to dominant redevelopment strategies has come from the preservationist movement. Largely white and upper income, the preservationists have the money and skills to effectively challenge downtown interests. But one wonders if their influence is on the wane, as the city deals with the problems of economic development. In 1969, the preservationists prevented construction of the proposed Vieux Carré Riverfront Expressway. In 1986, opponents of the aquarium bond initiative obtained only one-third of the vote of an electorate that has historically been opposed to government expenditures. Subsequent challenges to the aquarium (legal, environmental) were widely heralded in the media as being "the third battle of New Orleans." These challenges all seemed to fizzle, as the aquarium project moved forward in 1987.

Perhaps the environmental movement has the potential to challenge redevelopment strategies. The mere mention of a proposed second airport in eastern New Orleans generated a strong response from numerous environmental groups. Given the city's fragile ecology, it may be that environmentalists will pose the most significant challenges to future redevelopment efforts.

In making projections concerning the city's future development, it should be remembered that different types of leaders will be making the decisions. Perhaps this is best exemplified by the Business Council (or Committee of Fifty), created in 1986. The first association of downtown development interests, it was the idea of Jim Bob Moffett, a Texan who heads Freeport McMoran, an energy company. The Business Council, like similar groups in other cities, includes developers and the heads of petroleum-related industries, port-related companies, banks, utility companies, department stores, hotels, and restaurants. Although the organization has not been as successful as some of its counterparts in bringing black and white business leaders together, it does include at least one major black businessman (the operator of a radio station) and the presidents of two black universities. It is too soon to assess the impact of this group, but the city's economic development policies may change because of its existence. Moffett himself has been a force for change. For example, he has emphasized the need for fiscal and tax reform and sales taxes, which could have profound implications for the city's economy. A group called the Young Leadership Council, formed after the 1986 mayor's race, also has significant potential. This group includes two hundred young professionals between the ages of twenty-one and forty-two. Forty percent of its members are women; 20 percent are black. Most of the members are in such fields as law, banking, investments, stocks and bonds, advertising and public relations, insurance, tourism, real estate, and the maritime industry. Thus far the efforts of the Young Leadership Council have focused on education; many members also served as volunteers at the 1987 NCAA Final Four Basketball Tournament and the 1988 Republican National Convention. It seems clear that there will be a new group of civic leaders who will be more involved with problems of economic development.

The 1987 revision of the 1975 growth management plan suggests other directions for future downtown development. The plan includes new pocket parks, better sidewalks, more effective traffic controls, the continuing construction of offices and housing downtown, new parking garages, and improved landscaping. It emphasizes the preservation of Canal Street as the city's traditional retail center and makes provision for office development between Canal and Poydras Streets, residential development in the old warehouse district, upscale development along the riverfront (especially hotels and convention facilities), and the easing of traffic problems in the central business district, by promotion of mass transit and coordination of parking plans.

"Public-private partnerships" has been an abused and overworked term in the 1980s. Nonetheless, it seems clear that in New Orleans, as in many other Southern and rustbelt cities, many ventures have been undertaken by such partnerships. Some are successful, some are not; some present a mixed picture. None have really addressed the problem of uneven economic development.

When we speak of "public-private partnership," we must ask who are the partners. Like many U.S. cities, New Orleans must deal with governmental fragmentation. In addition to the city government and the Dock Board, many other agencies play important roles in economic development, such as the City Planning Commission, and the Levee Board. Such proliferation of government agencies makes it difficult for the city to pursue coherent economic development policies because agencies are more interested in guarding their own turf than in creating jobs. The private sector is similarly fragmented. There have been many instances in New Orleans of private-sector division on an issue. Major developers may conflict on the potential use of a site. Outside interests, such as railroads, are most interested in obtaining the best possible price for their choice property. Before the creation of the Business Council, New Orleans lacked a downtown organization that spoke with one voice. (The Chamber of Commerce represents several other parishes in the region, in addition to the city.) Such fragmentation makes it difficult to deal with the seemingly intractable problems of uneven economic development.

References

Ahlbrandt, Roger S., Jr., and Clyde Weaver. 1987. "Public-Private Institutions and Advanced Technology Development in Southwestern Pennsylvania." *Journal of the American Planning Association* 53:449–458.

Amoss, W. James. 1985. "The Troubled Port: What It Needs to Do to Survive." *New Orleans Times-Picayune/States-Item* (May 25):A11.

Baumbach, Richard, and William Borah. 1981. *The Second Battle of New Orleans: A History of the Vieux Carré Riverfront Controversy*. University: University of Alabama Press.

Brooks, Jane S., and Deborah Weeter. 1984. "The Jackson Brewery." *Urban Land* 43:20–25.

Committee for Economic Development. 1982. *Public-Private Partnership: An Opportunity for Urban Communities*. New York: Committee for Economic Development.

Crain, Robert L. 1969. *The Politics of School Desegregation: Comparative Case Studies of Community Structure and Policy Making*. Garden City, N.Y.: Anchor Press.

Doig, Jameson W., and Erwin C. Hargrove, eds. 1987. *Leadership and Innovation: A Biographical Perspective on Entrepreneurs in Government*. Baltimore: Johns Hopkins University Press.

Haas, Edward F. 1974. *Delesseps S. Morrison and the Image of Reform: New Orleans Politics, 1946–1961*. Baton Rouge: Louisiana State University Press.

Hirsch, Arnold R. 1983. "New Orleans: Sunbelt in the Swamp." In *Sunbelt Cities: Politics and Growth Since World War II*, ed. Richard M. Bernard and Bradley M. Rice, pp. 100–137. Austin: University of Texas Press.

Katz, Allen. 1986. "A Gift of Tourists." *New Orleans Times-Picayune* (December 14):B3.

———. 1987. "Facing Reality." *New Orleans Times-Picayune* (October 25):33.

McQuaid, John. 1987. "Grim: New Orleans Blacks among Nation's Poorest." *New Orleans Times-Picayune* (April 10):A1.

Marak, Robert. 1982. "The Biggest Industrial Park of All." *Planning* 5:10–12.

Marcus, Frances F. 1985. "New Orleans Hotel Business Depressed Since Fair." *New Orleans Times-Picayune* (June 25):10.

Mumphrey, Anthony J., Jr., and Pamela H. Moomau. 1984. "New Orleans: An Island in the Sunbelt." *Public Administration Quarterly* 8:91–111.

Perales, Nan. 1986. "Tourism Officials Won Conventions at Working Party." *New Orleans Times-Picayune* (July 29):A1.

Perl, Peter. 1986. "Organized Labor Fights the Battle of the Brunches." *Washington Post* (February 27):A3.

Powers, Nan. 1987. "Concern Growing over Trade Bill's Effect in Louisiana." *New Orleans Times-Picayune* (September 13):G1.

Ragas, Wade R.; Ivan J. Miestchovich, Jr.; Eddystone C. Nebel III; and Timothy P. Ryan. 1987. "Louisiana Superdome: Public Costs and Benefits, 1975–1984." *Economic Development Quarterly* 1:226–239.

Ryan, Timothy P. 1985. "The New Orleans Economy: What Makes It Tick?" *Louisiana Business Survey* 16:3–12.

Smith, Michael P., and Marlene Keller. 1986. "Managed Growth and the Politics of Uneven Development in New Orleans." In Susan S. Fainstein, Norman I. Fainstein, Richard Child Hill, Dennis Judd, and Michael Peter Smith, *Restructuring the City*. Rev. ed. New York: Longman.

Stone, Clarence N. 1986. "Partnership New South Style: Central Atlanta Progress." In *Public-Private Partnerships: Improving Urban Life*, ed. Perry David. New York: Academy of Political Science.

———. 1987. "Race and Regime in Atlanta." Paper presented to the Southeastern Conference on Public Administration, New Orleans (October 7–9).

Stuart, Lettice. 1987. "CBD Vacancy Rate Remains High." *New Orleans Times-Picayune* (August 29).

U.S. Bureau of the Census. 1970. *1970 Census of Population*, Table 901.

———. 1980. "Social and Economic Characteristics." *1980 Census of Population*, Table 125.

U.S. Department of Labor. Bureau of Labor Statistics. 1985–1988. *Employment and Earnings* (monthly report).

Weiss, Marc A., and John Metzger. 1987. "Technology Development, Neighborhood Planning, and Negotiated Partnerships: The Case of Pittsburgh's Oakland Neighborhood." *Journal of the American Planning Association* 53: 469–478.

Young, Alma H. 1984. "Urban Development Action Grants: The New Orleans Experience." *Public Administration Quarterly* 8:112–129.

Joe R. Feagin
John I. Gilderbloom
Nestor Rodriguez

13. Private-Public Partnerships: The Houston Experience

With the demise of large-scale urban renewal programs, public-private partnerships are increasingly viewed as the key to urban revitalization, particularly in the areas of housing and economic development. As a result of the accelerated investment of capital on a global scale, numerous growth coalitions have been forged between business interests and public officials at the municipal level to promote new investment in cities. In the mid-1980s there were perhaps 15,000 governmental units with specific economic development programs (National League of Cities 1987).

These new public-private partnerships have been cited as examples of the growing power and significance of the local and national governments with regard to urban development in the United States. Some recent social science analyses of the federal government's role in the development of U.S. cities have included the generalization that state actors act independently of local business elites and business interests in pursuing local urban development (Mollenkopf 1983; Gurr and King 1987). Mollenkopf (1983:9) concluded from his study of U.S. cities that a business dominance theory of urban development decision-making must be discarded for the alternative view that "public actors, not private actors, generally possessed the critical initiative, and the results of their actions shaped private interests just as much as private interests shaped public action." Mollenkopf's theory emphasizes the points that political entrepreneurs pressing for economic development are autonomous actors using state power and that "governmental action follows its own logic rather than that of private interests." Gurr and King (1987:9–11), in generalizing about U.S. cities, have argued that state actors are "relatively autonomous" of local or national capitalists. State actors constitute a "new class" of bureaucrats whose interests lie in preserving their agencies and enhancing the state structure; they "pursue interests distinct in degree" from those of business elites. Although much of their analysis of local actors focuses on their dependence on state actors and national programs, Gurr and King suggest that at the local level, the concentration of state power means that local actors have distinctive interests separate from local economic actors and their interests.

From the perspective of this "independent state" theory, the new public-private partnerships in the cities signal the growing importance and independence of state actors and state agencies in urban development. Houston, the nation's fourth largest city and the city often called the "capital of the sunbelt," provides an interesting case study for examining some of the issues raised by these independent state theories, especially as regards city development and the authority of governmental officials vis-à-vis the local business leadership.

Boom and Bust in Houston: Old and New Partnerships

The Sunbelt Boomtown

Metropolitan Houston experienced an uninterrupted economic boom from World War II to the early 1960s. The export of oil tools and oil-related services and agricultural shipping intimately connected Houston with various cities in importing countries around the world. For nearly a century, metropolitan Houston's economic development has been based on the import of domestic and overseas capital and labor and the export of oil-related products, agricultural goods, and capital. Houston's economic history is distinctive not only in the dominance of the extraction and resource industries but also in the role played by public-private partnerships.

From the 1930s to the early 1980s, Houston's business leadership made no significant use of certain conventional public-private partnerships to implement public housing programs or programs aimed at redeveloping downtown areas, such as the urban renewal programs of the 1950s and 1960s. Moreover, the city's business elite was one of the last to develop the newer public-private partnerships that have assumed the guise of economic development and industrial recruitment agencies. The reason for this seems clear. In the twentieth century the city's growth coalition has been dominated by the city's business elite. And this elite has not wished to be encumbered by federal restrictions and requirements, such as those associated with urban renewal programs. Drawn mostly from the business community, the governmental actors in Houston have been under little pressure, until the mid-1980s, to use traditional urban housing and economic development programs for their real estate developers, downtown community, or moderate-income citizenry. The "free market" has been regarded as more than sufficient to produce untarnished prosperity for all Houstonians.

By the late 1970s, Houston had become a widely cited model of the positive consequences of a free enterprise approach to urban development. Conservative think tanks such as the Adam Smith Institute in Great Britain have cited Houston as a prototypical example of the prosperity that results from an unrestrained free market approach to both housing and economic development (Jones 1982:23–25). In the United States conservatives, including those in the government and in prominent think tanks, have proclaimed Houston as a free market model for the provision of economic development and affordable housing (see Siegan 1972).

Houston's First Major Economic Crisis

Interestingly, during the 1930s Houston was discussed in the mass media as the "city the Depression missed." Although somewhat exaggerated, this image was largely accurate because in the 1930s the oil-based economy was doing relatively well. Ironically, it was the gradual integration of the Houston economy into the global oil market that finally brought Houston its first major recession in the twentieth century—the near depression of the 1980s. The high price of a barrel of oil plummeted as nations fought recession and as they conserved and changed to new forms of energy; the dropping prices hurt the Houston economy at the same time that agricultural exports were also falling. A crucial part of the problem was the high value of the dollar, which priced Houston's exports so high as to cost the southwestern corporations major markets around the globe. In the early 1980s the long era of boomtown growth ended. Growth and development were replaced by high unemployment rates, thousands of bankruptcies, and some worker out-migration. By the mid-1980s it was clear that the city was no longer immune to business cycles (Feagin 1988). Unless there was a significant restructuring of the metropolitan market economy, serious long-term stagnation, or worse, was probable. Cities and regions with mature extraction industries can survive economically only by diversification or by replacing the declining base with a new economic base. In 1984 Houston's unforeseen economic crisis stimulated formation of the first visible public-private partnership aimed at economic development and diversification in the city's history.

We will now examine in more detail the recent history of Houston in regard to two major areas in which public-private partnerships have been of consequence in many other U.S. cities: housing and economic development. Our basic findings are that (1) public-private partnerships, as generally defined, are of relatively recent origin in Houston, and (2) it is the private partners that have dominated, and the most vulnerable segments of the population that have suffered, in attempts to deal with the city's housing and economic development problems.

Public-Private Partnerships? The Case of Housing

A Free Market Model?

Real estate experts in the United States often cite Houston as the only U.S. city without an affordable housing crisis. In the 1980s, the Reagan administration proclaimed Houston as a model for the production of affordable housing. The key ingredient for affordable housing, according to the President's Commission on Housing (1982), is the free market: no zoning, little planning, lax environmental regulations, and no rent control. Because these conditions exist in Houston, it has served as a model to the rest of the nation for the provision of affordable housing, according to the authors of a book on housing policy, *Resolving the Housing Crisis*, edited by the conservative Bruce Johnson. A top Reagan official (Johnson 1982:14) declared that this book is a valuable complement to the efforts of President Reagan to privatize housing programs. Praise for Johnson's book has been given by, among others, prominent housing analyst George Sternlieb, director of the Rutgers University Center for Urban Policy Research. Drawing on Siegan (1972), Johnson (1982:14) asserts in this book that only the free market is capable of producing affordable housing:

> Houston's lack of land use controls is actually a more efficient system in protecting neighborhoods than the scandal-ridden, bribery-prone zoning boards found elsewhere. The private market is capable of allocating a scarce commodity such as land if given the chance. . . . The Houston experience demonstrates that new construction is the natural market response to increasing demand. . . . The market works in Houston because Houston has no zoning and, thus, cannot use zoning ordinances to restrict supply and exclude "undesirable" developments and people.

The extraordinary claim that Houston has no housing affordability crisis is without any empirical support in the 1980s, as it has been in prior decades. Even with a 20 percent rental housing vacancy rate, no zoning, and little planning, Houston has a major housing crisis: at least 10,000–15,000 homeless persons, 18,000 persons waiting to get into public housing, half a million low- and moderate-income persons making unaffordable housing payments, a quarter of the low-income persons living in overcrowded houses, and a zero percent vacancy rate for housing accessible to Houston's large disabled population.

Despite this emergency, landlords have an almost free rein in the city; there have been few countervailing public or nonprofit entrepreneurs. Thousands of rental units are demolished by mortgage holders or owners each year for tax and other reasons or are simply abandoned. In addition, Houston has the most inequitable landlord-tenant laws of any major U.S. city. Landlords deny tenants just-cause eviction rights, the standard lease stipulates that the first $50 of any repair is charged to the tenant, and landlords restrict the rental of middle-income apartments by minorities by charging a $50 application fee and by recording hair and eye color on applications. Numerous apartment complexes in the inner city are virtually all-white. Landlords play an important role in perpetuating Houston's residential segregation, a point underscored by presidential candidate Jesse Jackson in a 1988 visit to the area (Gilderbloom 1985; Massey and Heimer 1987; Bullard 1987).

Housing Quality and Affordability

Despite the relatively large number of new rental units built in Houston since the late 1970s, problems remain for the poor and the disabled. A recent study found that 15 percent of the low- and moderate-income families live in substandard housing; one out of ten Houston renters lives in overcrowded housing, and close to one out of three Hispanic renters lives under these conditions. Amenities supportive of housing access are also missing. Houston remains an invisible jail for the disabled and elderly. Over 70 percent of the disabled and elderly do not have sidewalks with curb cuts in their neighborhoods to afford them access to buses. Houston is, perhaps, the least accessible city of any major city in the country (Gilderbloom et al., 1987).

Houston's free market in housing has not guaranteed cheap rents. The 1983 Annual Housing Survey indicated that median rents in Houston were higher than in cities on the West and East coasts. Houston's median rent was $77 higher than that in other Southern cities and $72 more than that in Northeastern cities. The federal government has determined that a tenant is paying an excessive amount whenever rent is more than 25 percent of income. By this standard, more than half of Houston's renters—most low- and moderate-income families—are paying excessive rent (Gilderbloom 1985:149).

Public housing. In the face of the chronic housing crisis, the developers and builders in Houston's private sector have been unwilling or unable to supply sufficient housing for moderate-income Houstonians. And public-private partnerships have made only the most feeble attempt to remedy the deficiencies of the "free" housing market by providing housing for Houston's less privileged communities. The city's business and governmental leaders have never targeted the housing problems for major public action. Since the New Deal programs of the 1930s, the business elite has opposed construction of most public housing and other low-income housing programs. As a result, only a modest number of public housing units were constructed during the 1930s and 1940s; few have been constructed since them. Houston now has approximately 3,000 public housing units, down from 4,000 just a few years ago. This contrasts sharply with New York's 207,000 units, Chicago's 47,000 units, Los Angeles's 26,000 units, and Philadelphia's 23,000 units. In Texas, Houston ranks third behind the smaller cities of Dallas and San Antonio in terms of public housing units.

The situation is the same in regard to other federally subsidized housing. Of those Houstonians who qualify under federal government guidelines for Section 8 aid, only 6 percent of low-and moderate-income families have received help, and only 9 percent of the disabled and 5 percent of the elderly who qualify have been given assistance. The percentage of persons receiving Section 8 assistance in Houston is well below the percentages in other cities. The President's Commission on Housing (1982: 13–15) estimates that nationally, 27 percent of all persons who qualify for Section 8 assistance receive it (Gilderbloom et al. 1987; Huttman 1987: 12). Houstonians have not gotten their fair share of Section 8 certificates. Historically, Houston's business leadership has not worked for public-private partnerships in this housing area and has not been aggressive in pursuing its claim for a "fair share" of the federal housing assistance pie.

Including the Section 8 rental housing vouchers program, in 1987 the Houston Housing Authority was involved in the subsidization of only 11,754 housing units—far fewer units than such cities as Philadelphia, Baltimore, Fort Worth, and Atlanta. In 1987 there were more than 13,000 people on the Houston Housing Authority's limited waiting lists for *all* types of publicly subsidized housing. Many other cities have used public-sector money to help remedy deficiencies in the private housing market. But Houston has not. In addition, the local government has provided little or no support for such programs as house sharing, congregate services, equity conversion, cooperative housing, and urban homesteading. There has been a fear among private investors that public intervention would harm the profitability of the private market. This intentionally created shortage of publicly subsidized low-income housing has produced a *chronic* housing crisis for Houstonians with modest incomes.

A private-public partnership to reduce the amount of low-income housing. In Houston public-private partnerships have sometimes taken a perverse form, as exemplified by the public-private partnership to get rid of Houston's largest public housing project. Despite the chronic housing crisis and the relatively few available public housing units in Houston, city officials have been working for several years to demolish the largest public housing project, Allen Parkway Village (APV). Mostly minority in its tenant composition, APV is a two-story, low-rise project consisting of 1,000 units on 37 acres. Although city officials, responsive to local developers, argue that APV is obsolete and cannot be rehabilitated, professional planners and social scientists disagree (Cuff 1985; Bullard 1987). They point out that APV could be rehabilitated at one-half the cost of building new public housing. The village was recently added to the National Register of Historic Places because of its architectural significance. Opponents of demolition point out that the real reason for demolishing APV is its prime downtown location; it is located within a few hundred yards of gleaming glass skyscrapers built by leading development corporations. Developers see Allen Parkway Village as an ideal site for construction of upper- and middle-income condominiums (Griffiths 1985). According to Tom Armstrong, formerly in charge of the Southeast regional office of the Department of Housing and Urban Development (HUD), "That was without doubt the most valuable piece of property in that metroplex . . . developers were applying significant pressures on Washington and area (HUD) offices to acquire properties that were located in highly appreciated situations" (Flournoy 1985:435). The unique aspect of this situation is not the outside business pressure, which has occurred in many cities, but the close partnership of public housing officials working with developers and with the Chamber of Commerce to materially reduce the amount of low-income housing.

The demolition of APV is the cornerstone of the city's ambitious plans to redevelop the entire Fourth Ward area surrounding the village. The Fourth Ward is Houston's oldest black neighborhood and dates back to the time of slavery. The overall development plan is to demolish 2,500 homes in the neighborhood and sell the tract of ninety acres to a developer to construct new office towers, condominiums, and shops (Flournoy 1985:435). The estimated value of the land could be in excess of $250 million. Kenneth Schnitzer, chairman of Century Development Corporation nad the nation's tenth largest developer, has been a prime mover to get the city to redevelop the Fourth Ward (Flournoy 1985:437). In early 1988, federal officials were on the verge of approving the city's application to demolish the village.

The Reagan administration adopts Houston Model: Reduced federal support for housing programs. The Reagan administration modeled its strategy for housing on the free enterprise approach that Houston exemplifies in conservative analysis. The administration made drastic cutbacks in all low-income housing programs and relied, as did the Houston leadership, on the private market to provide affordable housing. New public-private partnerships in the development of moderate-income housing made as much sense to Reagan conservatives as snow in Phoenix. When President Ronald Reagan assumed office in 1981, the amount of money being spent by the federal government for defense was already much greater than low-income housing expenditures, but by 1987 the amounts for defense had increased and the amounts for housing programs had been cut sharply. Money targeted for Section 8 had been cut by 82 percent; the Section 202 program (elderly and handicapped) had been abolished and Section 235 (homeownership program) had been eliminated.

Nonprofit cooperative housing and the public sector. Government officials in numerous countries, such as Canada, Sweden, France, and Italy, and in many U.S. cities have enacted and funded major programs to construct or facilitate construction of cooperative housing. Cities like San Francisco, Los Angeles, Boston, Chicago, and New York have hundreds of private community-based nonprofit corporations. These public-private partnerships have targeted the housing needs of many in the central cities and have led in some instances to a dramatic decrease in the percentage of income many tenants pay for housing. Neighborhood-based nonprofit development corporations have also helped to revitalize low-income neighborhoods.

Houston's moderate-income housing needs could be met in part by a public-private partnership, such as government-assisted cooperatives. Cooperatives with resale restrictions are attractive candidates for multi-family community-based housing, since they provide many of the guarantees associated with ownership. Cooperatives are operated by a non profit corporation that holds a single mortgage on the property and is controlled by elected directors. Each new owner purchases a share for a minimal downpayment; monthly payments include a share of the mortgage, plus maintenance. Whereas nonprofit organizations in Boston and New York can rehabilitate abandoned housing for $70,000 a unit, cooperative organizations in Houston can develop as many as fifteen units at that cost.

Despite the tremendous potential of these public-private partnership programs, Houston's public and private leadership has resisted the concept of cooperative housing. For example, during the 1980s the Enterprise Foundation attempted to organize a Neighborhood Development

Foundation to assist nonprofit organizations in setting up housing cooperatives in Houston. The Neighborhood Development Foundation has been successfully organized in twenty-seven cities across the nation and has served as a catalyst for more progressive and humane housing redevelopment. The Enterprise Foundation pledged $100,000 to the Houston city government for organization of a Neighborhood Development Foundation, but was unable to get *any* matching funds from the city. Nor was there any support from local private foundations or local corporations. In 1987 the Enterprise Foundation discontinued its efforts to set up this type of public-private partnership in Houston. The failure of the Enterprise Foundation was a major defeat for community efforts to create affordable housing for moderate-income persons. Houston has benefited from its share of philanthropy on the part of its wealthy families, but much of that money has gone into hospitals and medical facilities, not to support low-income housing efforts or other programs for the poor.

The possibility of new public-private partnerships. Although the future of housing construction for Houston's low- and moderate-income persons looks bleak, three positive signs emerged in 1987–1988. Private Sector Initiatives, an organization that provides services for nonprofit organizations to assist them in creating housing development proposals, presented during the fall of 1987 a series of seminars on organizing nonprofit cooperatives in Houston. It also established an $850,000 community investment fund for development by neighborhood-based groups. Another promising activity is a result of the efforts of Coop Houston, established by Jim Robinson, a charismatic lawyer and former college professor who has raised more than a million dollars to rehabilitate abandoned apartment units and convert them into cooperatives. Focusing on the housing needs of the city's poor black neighborhoods, Robinson has educated the city's leadership concerning the critical need for cooperatives. If Robinson meets his goals, he will have produced almost three times as much moderate-income housing as the city government has in the last fifty years.

One modest example of a recent *public*-private partnership active in the area of housing is the Houston Housing and Transportation Advisory Committee. Organized in the mid-1980s by progressive city council member Eleanor Tinsley originally to develop accessible housing for the disabled, the committee, composed of government and community leaders, has become a powerful influence. It prepared a detailed report and set up a conference on urban housing and transportation policy for the disabled and disadvantaged. Its recommendations to increase the amount of affordable and accessible housing aroused the interest of some government officials in a real public-private partnership in the area of housing, especially for the disabled. HUD was pressured to consider doubling its allocation of housing vouchers for Houston to make up for past inequities and to give serious attention to providing a demonstration grant to provide one hundred units of disabled housing units. At the local level, the Department of Planning and Development pledged half a million dollars from its Community Development Block Grant funds for cooperative housing developments by local nonprofit organizations. METRO (the region's public transportation agency) gave preliminary approval to develop an "accessibility corridor" that would allow the disabled to ride on a regularly scheduled bus route. The new infrastructure development would be funded by Community Development Block Grant funds, METRO physical improvement funds, and HUD demonstration grant moneys. Although the focus was on the disabled, it was clear that some of Houston's community, business, and political leaders were willing to consider new public-private partnerships in the area of housing problems.

Unfortunately, this interest in new partnerships was not shared by most members of the powerful business elite, the local growth coalition. Even though the aforementioned committee developed the respect and support of some of the more sympathetic government and community leaders, the business elite—with a few notable exceptions—was unwilling to support its recommendations. Initially, the Apartment Owners Association had supported formation of the committee to provide "help" to house the disabled. However, when the committee expanded its agenda to include housing problems of the poor generally, the apartment association refused to participate in its activities. A representative of the Apartment Owners Association claimed that the organization was not interested in tenants with Section 8 certificates and in modifying rental housing for the disabled. Moreover, when Houston's Center for Public Policy sponsored a conference on designing and financing housing services for low-income persons, fewer than ten landlords were among the two hundred participants at the conference. The Apartment Owners Association refused to announce the conference in its monthly newsletter sent to thousands of landlords. The future of public-private partnerships in the area of housing is severely limited by this antagonistic attitude of the city's real estate elite. Thus far in Houston's history, the private sector has rarely participated in any public-private venture generated by the public sector in regard to housing.

A Private-Public Partnership:
The Houston Economic Development Council

Reliance on State Aid

Virtually all public-private partnerships in Houston's history have been generated from and dominated by the city's powerful business elite. Virtually all such arrangements have in effect been *private*-public partnerships. Houston has not, of course, been strictly a free market city, its image in the conservative literature notwithstanding. The close relationship between the local and federal governments and the business elite is one of the less well known factors contributing to Houston's prosperity. For example, governmental aid for infrastructure projects, such as federal money for highways, substantial military-industrial aid for the local petrochemical industry during World War II, and the millions of dollars needed to build the Johnson Space Center, has been aggressively sought by a series of powerful Houston business elites. Members of these elite business groups have, as a matter of fact, long controlled and frequently staffed top positions in city government. Although Houston is frequently advertised as *the* free enterprise city, its business leadership has regularly taken major governmental assistance for projects that facilitate private profitmaking.

A Belated Partnership for Economic Development

As hard as it may be for analysts familiar with public-private partnerships in other major cities to believe, Houston's leadership waited until the 1980s to seriously consider a public-private partnership specifically designed to recruit corporations willing to locate in the city and to stimulate economic development and diversification. Only slowly did the implications of the economic bust that the city experienced in the 1980s penetrate the thinking of the business leadership organized through the Chamber of Commerce. They realized that in the future, the city's economy would be battered by the negative swings in the capitalist business cycle that had been avoided in the past. given the extraordinary weakness of local government planning departments, the chamber has traditionally been the effective local planning agency that has developed business-oriented solutions for city problems too serious for the ruling elite to ignore. Thus the economic recession of the 1980s generated a growing apprehension in Houston about the need for greater economic diversity.

Consequently, the chamber created investigative committees to assess economic development. In 1984 the chamber's leadership belatedly established the Houston Economic Development Council (HEDC). Headed by a local developer, the HEDC had as vice chairmen the top executives of the two local newspapers and the four largest banks, an oil executive, a business leader who was the head of a city booster group, and one union official. It is noteworthy that Houston's mayor and the chief county executive were appointed by private-sector officials, leaders of the Chamber of Commerce, to serve on what was ostensibly a public-private partnership. In reality, this was a *private*-public partnership (Feagin 1988:167–168).

Partial state funding. Where did HEDC funding come from? The HEDC obtained $6.3 million for the first two years from the local business community. A second two-year budget totaled $7.2 million. The HEDC was created by the business community, but local governments have played a considerable role in financing the organization since 1986. In that year Mayor Kathy Whitmire tried to stop this governmental subsidy because of the new taxes required, but she was defeated. Not recognizing the irony, business leaders called it the "first true economic wedding of the public and private sectors" in the city's history. This was not true, since the city's business leaders have often utilized state aid for their business needs. But what they were thinking was that this was the first aboveboard, public-private partnership for general economic development and reorientation of economic direction in the city's history (O'Grady 1987:1F).

Because of this new character of the public-private partnership there has been some conflict over the makeup of the bureaucratic structure and over the relationship of the HEDC to the chamber. Some have argued that the HEDC should be an entirely separate organization; others have argued that it should remain a committee of the chamber. This dispute was finally resolved in 1987 when the HEDC became officially separate from the chamber, although it continued to utilize chamber resources. There have also been squabbles between the public partner and the private partner. For example, during the summer of 1986, City Council members became irritated that the HEDC had not signed a contract with the city government to fund a portion of the public-private partnership. One problem was that HEDC leaders were afraid that such a money linkage to local government would bring too much surveillance of the sometimes secret HEDC and chamber operations and expenditures (Gravois 1986:1A). By 1988 the relationship of the HEDC with the local governmental authorities, including the city government, the county government, and the Port of Houston authority, appeared to have stabilized. The HEDC, now with a staff of thirty employees, secures one-third of its total funding from these governmental sources; the remainder of the funding comes from private sources, including the chamber.

Goals for the development of a free enterprise city. There has been some shifting of goals in this unique public-private partnership. Initially, HEDC established nine categories of sought-after economic development: (1) biomedical reserach, (2) research laboratories, (3) medical and computer equipment, (4) communications equipment, (5) chemicals, (6) materials-processing research, (7) computers and office machines, (8) engineering and architectural services, and (9) distribution services. When these target categories were proclaimed, they were criticized by some local and state analysts. For example, the lead priority of biomedical research seemed naive because Houston's medical center had not yet spun off a major medical-technical firm (Clark 1985:9–11; Feagin 1988:168).

Moreover, the Center for Enterprising of Southern Methodist University prepared a commissioned report that counseled Houston's business leaders to reject the national obsession with biotechnology and computers and to examine instead traditional manufacturing areas that had potential but that had been overlooked at the quest for diversification ideas, especially the processing of paper, agricultural and food products, printing, and pharmaceuticals. Looming above diversification was the problem of the inability of Houston's educational institutions to financially support a high-technology economic base. Gradually, business leaders acknowledged that metropolitan areas with high-technology industries industries tended to bankroll first-rate educational institutions and research laboratories. So the HEDC suggested that its parent, the chamber, create a task force to work to improve research and training in local universities and to press for greater federal funds for the medical center and NASA facilities. The HEDC's 1986 revised agenda targeted energy, biotechnology, space enterprises, international business, and tourism as areas of emphasis for economic development (Crown 1986:1; Houston Economic Development Council 1986:4). Moreover, by 1987 the HEDC had a new chief executive—Lee Hogan, a local engineer and entrepreneur. Hogan adopted an even more pragmatic approach to economic development, focusing on recruitment of new corporations and on diversification efforts, specifically emphasizing aerospace, petrochemicals, and medical technology as the principal areas.

Although some efforts have been made to nurture small businesses, the HEDC has for the most part functioned as a public relations and booster organization for Houston. Much money and effort has been expended on marketing efforts. Business leaders have repeatedly attacked the national media for depicting Houston negatively. The HEDC has conducted a number of national advertising campaigns to improve the city's image and to attract enterprise to the area. Officials of the HEDC sponsored a European trade mission, made an attempt to secure the proposed General Motors automated Saturn automobile facility, and worked very hard to obtain a major Navy home port for the Houston-Galveston area. Military-industrial corporations have been the target of recruitment efforts. In October 1986 the HEDC took some credit for inducing the military-industrial firm Grumman to relocate to the NASA area in south Houston. The incentive package that attracted Grumman included $20 million in tax abatements from the city government. Although as of early 1988, Grumman had not moved to the site because of shifts in the national space program, its relocation was still expected. In 1987 the HEDC proudly proclaimed its role in getting twenty-two companies to locate to or expand in the city, adding 3,000 new jobs. Officials of the HEDC were also pleased that two of Australia's largest firms and several large Japanese firms had decided to locate in the greater metropolitan area, in part the consequence of the falling dollar (Feagin 1988:170–171). By the late 1980s, Houston's business leaders announced with some satisfaction that they were learning to play the "economic development game" (Brubaker, 1986:1).

The Failure of El Mercado del Sol

A Real Public-Private Project

Aside from this *private*-public partnership of the HEDC and the city government, few examples of the new public-private partnerships so prevalent in many cities can be found in metropolitan Houston. One of these rare examples is the El Mercado del Sol shopping center, which opened in 1985. The idea for the center emerged from discussions among white and Hispanic business leaders and certain city officials, especially the city's chief planning officer. In 1983 city government officials contributed $500,000 of a Community Development Block Grant for a $13 million public-private partnership project that promised to help minority business leaders revitalize an old Mexican-American section adjacent to the city's downtown by developing a Mexican-style marketplace called El Mercado del Sol. It was hoped that the project would emulate the success of and follow the precedent set by San Francisco's Cannery and other Mexican-style marketplaces that were attracting tourists in San Antonio and Santa Barbara. The government officials pledged $2.5 million in additional Community Development Block Grant (CDBG) funds to improve the infrastructure of the parks and roads, but this pledge has not, as of

1988, been implemented. The project was aimed at converting an abandoned mattress factory located on the edge of a Mexican-American barrio (neighborhood) two miles from downtown into a retail shopping center of 400,000 square feet. This shopping mall would provide space for eighty stores and restaurants with Mexican cultural themes (Downing 1988:1D; Downing and Friedman 1988:1A).

The barrio where the El Mercado project was situated had originally been settled by Mexican immigrant workers who had been imported in the 1910s by the city's major railroad company, Southern Pacific, for railroad construction. This settlement of a few hundred laborers living in old, abandoned boxcars was now one of the country's largest Hispanic neighborhoods. In the late 1980s its residents constitute a diverse population of Mexican Americans, as well as Mexican, Salvadorean, Guatemalan, Honduran and other Latin American immigrants. But the barrio's economic development did not keep pace with its population growth. Its largely working-class population worked elsewhere in the city, and the relatively low earnings of the Hispanic workers did not provide the consumer power to support mall development. Consequently, the barrio did not have a retail shopping center.

If the El Mercado project were successful, it would be one of the nation's largest Hispanic commercial centers. This project was implemented by a public-private partnership whose two goals were neighborhood physical improvement and Hispanic business growth. El Mercado was the first serious attempt by the local government to improve conditions in a rundown area where a large proportion of Houston's 300,000 Hispanics reside. Moreover, it was the first major attempt by the local government to display the contributions made to Houston by Mexican-Americans. Given the barrio's blight, the El Mercado project was seen by some city administrators, especially Efraim Garcia, the city planning director, as crucial for local business revitalization because it would provide assistance to the Hispanic community, with benefits trickling down to the poorest residents. But the dream of economic and neighborhood improvement turned into a nightmare in 1987 when the El Mercado owner, Encore Development Corporation, filed for bankruptcy; the financing bank went into receivership and the Federal Savings and Loan Insurance Corporation foreclosed on the shopping center. After a brief delay it was sold to new owners, Mercado Partners II; the city of Houston injected $5 million in federal CDBG money into the center in 1987 to prevent total financial collapse (Downing and Friedman 1988:1A).

There are a number of reasons why the El Mercado public-private enterprise never reached its goals of being profitable and neighborhood-enriching. The project was affected by poor timing; it opened in the middle of Houston's dramatic economic decline, which caused a drop in disposable income and retail sales. On the center's opening day, fewer than five stores were open; the large crowd had few places to shop. Some critics of the city government involvement argue that El Mercado's premature opening with so few shops open was politically timed by the mayor, Kathy Whitmire, to draw Hispanic votes to her campaign and to upstage her opponent's announcement of candidacy in an upcoming election. Other critics point to the lack of planning intended to lessen the negative image of the marketplace's barrio setting. The street that leads to El Mercado from the downtown area, an important source of shoppers, winds through blocks of dilapidated warehouses, bars, and run-down hotels were vagrants and prostitutes congregate. There is no exit ramp at a nearby freeway that could bring large numbers of shoppers from more affluent areas of the city, nor is there an effective public transportation system to bring customers from the downtown area. Given the problem of accessibility, critics suggest that El Mercado should have been located downtown in one of many historic brick buildings alongside the historic Buffalo Bayou. For some of the owners of the fewer than twenty stores remaining in El Mercado, the chief problem is the lack of advertisement by the mall's owners. A few store owners have sued the new owners of El Mercado and the city's planning director for mismanagement of the project (Byars 1988, Sec. 1, p. 18; Urban 1988, Sec. 1, p. 3).

There were also underlying problems. Houston's city government leaders lack the tradition, experience, and skill needed by public-private partnerships to pursue general (and minority) economic development. This is a direct consequence of the enduring free enterprise philosophy that economic development be accomplished by unhindered, private driven capitalism. The second underlying problem is that the Hispanic and black communities have been viewed by the city's white growth coalition as labor reservoirs and low-priority areas for development. For over a hundred years, these communities have received little attention or assistance from the business elite and have thus remained foreign areas to the white leaders and affluent residents of the city. For example, business and government leaders have never felt the need to build effective street systems leading into the East Side barrios. In a sense, the problems of El Mercado are more than a problem of attempting the experiment of a rare public-private partnership in this free enterprise city. More fundamentally the problem is the pernicious racial and ethnic discrimination, the persistent racial neglect and exclusion long characterizing the city.

Conclusion

Houston is the premier example of the free enterprise city where the business of government is business. For that reason, there have been few truly "public-private" partnerships. Whereas other cities have seen a variety of public-private partnerships, many generated from the public sector, it is rare for a Houston public official or governmental agency to take the lead in suggesting or developing a public-private partnership of any kind. Most often, partnerships are initiated by the private sector in the form of public-private partnerships where the public sector is little more than the funding handmaiden of private business interests. Moreover, business interests have opposed partnerships for such government activities as public housing, cooperative housing, rental aid programs, new infrastructure for moderate-income neighborhoods, many types of general public services, and social welfare programs.

Our data on the private origination of certain state action (e.g., by the HEDC), and on private suppression of state action (e.g., by the real estate elite) raise serous questions about some generalizations in the theories of the state and cities cited earlier. The nation's cities are not all of one piece. They vary greatly across a continuum, from cities where relatively independent political entrepreneurs and political machines have had an effect on local economic development and on other important urban decisions, to major cities such as Houston where there are rarely politicians or significant political decisions that are not highly dependent upon the powerful business elite. We find little evidence in Houston of the independent political entrepreneurs or independent state bases of power discussed by Mollenkopf (1983:3–39; see also Skocpol and Amenta 1986).

Nor do our data on partnerships corroborate the arguments of Gurr and King (1987:14) that local and national governmental "officials tend to hold and pursue interests distinct in degree from those of groups [e.g., business] outside the state" and that "the vast majority of officials share some central, common interests in the perpetuation of the state's institutions and authority." The commitment of some city government officials, including those in Houston, to the expansion and independence of the government is not different in degree from that of the local business elite. And that commitment to the independence of governmental institutions ranges from nonexistent to very weak, because these local government officials are drawn from, are dependent upon, and soon return to the day-to-day actions of, the business elite (if they depart from business enterprise and investments while in office).

In the twentieth century, all mayors and most council members in Houston have thus far been drawn from the city's business circles. Moreover, the actions of Houston's business elite on matters of housing and economic development reveal no state actors working to enhance and expand the state institutions *against* the interests of the local business elite. Moreover, the dominance of that elite with regard to Houston's economy and politics has created a tragic situation for those who constitute the bottom half of Houston's population, because they, and their allies, cannot rely upon Houston's *private* market sector to provide full employment at decent wages or affordable housing for Houston's moderate-income communities.

Paul Goodman (1984) wrote that a person "has only one life and if during it he has no great environment, no community, he has been irreparably robbed of a human right." From a progressive citizen's viewpoint, cities might be judged great not by the number of monumental buildings, corporate headquarters, or rich people within their borders, but by their ability to provide a decent place for all to work and live. According to these terms, public-private partnerships should be measured by the kinds of job, housing, educational, and life satisfaction opportunities they offer to all citizens. Up to this point Houston's public-private partnerships have failed to meet these standards.

References

Brubaker, Laurel. 1986. "How Houston Really Landed Grumman." *Houston Business Journal* (October 13):1

Bullard, Robert. 1987. "Invisible Houston: The Black Experience in Boom and Bust." College Station: Texas A & M Press.

Byars, Carlos. 1988. "Tenant of Mercado Del Sol to Appeal Eviction Ruling." *Houston Chronicle* (January 26), section 1, p. 18.

Clark, Rosanne. 1985. "Development Council Maps Economic Strategy." *Houston* (February):9–13.

Crown, Judith. 1986. "HEDC Sets Goals for Growth by Year 2000." *Houston Chronicle* (April 2):1.

Cuff, Dana. 1985. "Allen Parkway Village and Houston's Low-Cost Housing." In *Public Housing Needs and Conditions in Houston*. Hearings before Subcommittee on Housing and Community Development, Committee on Banking, Finance, and Urban Affairs, House of Representatives, 99th Cong., 1st sess. (October 14). Washington, D.C.: Government Printing Office.

Downing, Margaret. 1988. "El Mercado Could Work, Analysts Say." *Houston Post* (February 14):1D.

Downing, Margaret, and Steven Friedman. 1988. "Warning Unheeded by City Planners?" *Houston Post* (February 14):1A.

Feagin, Joe R. 1988. *The Free Enterprise City: Houston in Political-Economic Perspective*. New Brunswick, N.J.: Rutgers University Press.

Flournoy, Craig. 1985. "Allen Parkway Village." In *Public Housing Needs and Conditions in Houston*. Hearings before Subcommittee on Housing and Community Development, Committee on Banking, Finance, and Urban Affairs, House of Representatives, 99th Cong., 1st sess. (October 14). Washington, D.C.: Government Printing Office.

Gilderbloom, John. 1985. "Houston's Rental Housing Conditions: A Longitudinal and Comparative Analysis." *Public Housing Needs and Conditions in Houston*. Hearings before Subcommittee on Housing and Community Development, Committee on Banking, Finance, and Urban Affairs, House of Representatives, 99th Cong., 1st sess. (September 18). Washington, D.C.: Government Printing Office.

Gilderbloom, John, and Richard Appelbaum. 1988. *Rethinking Rental Housing*. Philadelphia: Temple University Press.

Gilderbloom, John, Mark Rosentraub, and Robert Bullard. 1987. *Designing, Locating, and Financing Housing and Transportation Services for Low-Income, Elderly, and Disabled Persons*." Houston: University of Houston, Center for Public Policy.

Goodman, Paul. 1984. "Growing Up Absurd." In Gar Alperovitz and Jeff Faux, *Rebuilding America*, p. viii. New York: Pantheon.

Gravois, John. 1986. "HEDC Weighs Strings Attached to Tax Dollars." *Houston Post* (April 14):1A.

Griffiths, Bruce V. 1985. "Statement of Bruce V. Griffiths, Staff Counsel of American Civil Liberties Union." *Public Housing Needs and Conditions in Houston*. Hearings before Subcommittee on Housing and Community Development, Committee on Banking, Finance, and Urban Affairs, House of Representatives, 99th Cong., 1st sess. (October 14). Washington, D.C.: Government Printing Office.

Gurr, Ted Robert, and Desmond S. King. 1987. *The State and the City*. Chicago: University of Chicago Press.

Houston Economic Development Council. 1986. "Strategic Priorities Agenda." Unpublished paper.

Huttman, Elizabeth. 1987. "Homelessness as a Housing Problem in an Inner City in the U.S." Paper presented at American Sociological Association meetings, August.

Johnson, Bruce M., ed. 1982. *Resolving the Housing Crisis*. Cambridge, Mass.: Ballinger,

Jones, Robert. 1982. *Town and Country Chaos*. London: Adam Smith Institute.

Massey, Douglas, and Karen Heimer. 1987. "Residential Segregation." *American Sociological Review* 52: (December) 802–825.

Mollenkopf, John. 1983. *The Contested City*. Princeton, N.J.: Princeton University Press.

National League of Cities. 1987. *The Visible Hand: Major Issues in City Economic Policy*. Washington, D.C.: National League of Cities.

O'Grady, Eileen, 1987. "HEDC Surpasses Goal, Raises $7.2 Million." *Houston Post* (February 28):1F.

President's Commission on Housing. 1982. *Report of the President's Commission on Housing*. Washington, D.C.: Government Printing Office.

Siegan, Bernard. 1972. *Land Use without Zoning*. Lexington, Mass.: D.C. Heath.

Skocpol, Theda, and Edwin Amenta. 1986. "States and Social Policies." *Annual Review of Sociology* 12:131–157.

Thomas, Kate. 1988. "Hotel Needs More Debate." *Houston Post* (February 18):1C.

Urban, Jerry. 1988. "El Mercado Squabble Is on Hold Pending Appeal of Eviction Orders." *Houston Chronicle* (January 28), section 1, p. 3.

Michael Peter Smith
Gregory A. Guagnano
Cath Posehn

14. The Political Economy of Growth in Sacramento: Whose City?

Power is not only what you have but what the enemy thinks you have.

Saul Alinsky

The concept of public-private partnership is depicted by its proponents as a process in which private entrepreneurs work hand in hand with government officials to develop better cities within a capitalist economy (Catanese 1984). This limited view reduces public policymaking to a situation where local government is restricted to supplying infrastructure and incentives to improve the profitability of private enterprise as an indirect means of creating local employment and sustaining the local tax base. A more complete view of public-private partnership requires a consideration of the complex interplay between citizens and political institutions. The critical question is: How do citizens gain access to local decisionmaking processes originally created to represent their interests? Gittell (1980) notes that access is achieved through formal government structure or through extragovernmental organizations and groups that may influence governmental policy. Analysis of these forms of collective citizen action is crucial to understanding the complex nature of the state-society interplay since it is "only as a part of organized action that most segments of the population can exercise any form of power" (Gittell 1980:20).

Our goal in this study is to explore the dynamics of the struggle over the meaning and value of urban space as expressed in a major land use decision in the city of Sacramento, California. Whereas the authors of other studies in this book have extensively discussed "public-private partnership" as the manifestation of the relationship between corporate influence and the policies of city government, our intent is to focus greater attention on the way in which this "partnership" is mediated by a second state-society interaction, namely, the relationship between the local state and community groups attempting to increase the use value resulting from development policy. (On the concept of the local state as the interplay of local government and social forces, see Cockburn 1979; Gottdiener 1987.) The Sacramento case offers a unique vantage point for understanding the dynamics of public-private partnerships for three reasons. First, unlike many declining cities whose public officials have been forced by financial circumstances to enter into alliances with the growth coalition, Sacramento is experiencing a strong economy. Accordingly, the initial contours of linked development have been proposed by the major private developers rather than by city government officials. Second, because Sacramento is a sprawling postindustrial city with abundant undeveloped land, the usual components of linked development plans (e.g., moderate-income housing funds, employment funds to compensate for job displacement) have not been key features of linked development in that city. Third, the growing awareness of the environmental costs of economic growth throughout California has encouraged the formation in Sacramento of numerous community organizations favoring slow growth. These groups are typically composed of well-educated, middle-class professionals who know how to use the legal and political system to achieve their goals.

In this case study, we will define and locate the mechanisms utilized by developers, local government officials, and environmental activists to shape and mediate the outcomes of a specific large-scale land use decision and describe how the conflict over contradictory uses of urban space was managed. This focus on the local dynamics of development is not meant to deny the importance of the macro-level political and economic forces that help shape a locality but to assess the local interactions that occur within these structural constraints.

The objective of this study is to investigate the social construction of *place* as it results from the interactions of groups and institutions pursuing opposing goals. Economists typically make the abstract assumption that people act as individuals to produce aggregate efficiency; however, Logan and Molotch (1987) point out that a more sociologically and historically grounded assumption is that "people tend, in their market behavior as everywhere else, toward coalition and organization. It is the efficiency of results that is open and problematic" (see also Smith 1988a, Chap. 1).

In our expanded view of the development process, we delineate how various segments of the community contest the *use* and the *exchange* value of any land use decision. In an insightful recent work, Logan and Molotch (1987:2) suggest that the most traditional representation of the use–exchange value distinction is one between "residents, who use place to satisfy essential needs of life, and entrepreneurs, who strive for financial gain by intensifying the use to which their property may be put. The pursuit of exchange values in the city does not necessarily result in the maximization of use values for others. Indeed, the simultaneous push for both goals is inherently contradictory and a continuing source of tension [and] conflict." Conflict between use and exchange value is not always the result of entrepreneurs pursuing exchange value and citizen groups trying to protect use values. Citizen groups occasionally coalesce to resist a specific policy (e.g., low-income housing, parking ordinances, services for the homeless) that they perceive as impacting on property values and the eventual resale of their houses.

Some groups in Sacramento think the city has an image problem. It has been described as a "cowtown" for well over a decade. The pro-growth coalition has used this perception to promote the ideology that Sacramento can quickly be transformed from "cowtown" to "world class city," complete with a twenty-four-hour downtown, cultural amenities, and a skyline to match. Opponents of rapid growth fear that this will produce dangerous environmental hazards including declining air and water quality, traffic congestion, improper waste management, exurban sprawl, and vanishing open space, as well as ill-defined urban boundaries and unclear and conflicting regional policy directions due to governmental overlap.

Sacramento Assemblyman Phillip Isenberg has said, "The problem with slogans like 'world class city' is that they wind up meaning so many different things to so many different people, and folks wind up arguing past one another like ships passing in the night. The premise is wacky, the logic is irrelevant, and only the passion is meaningful" (Trainor 1987:61). Isenberg's comment points to a pivotal component of this process that is often overlooked in the analysis of urban development: interpretive meanings. These meanings, rooted in the use–exchange value dialectic, shape the way that opposing forces work out their conflicts and hence socially construct the locality.

The Changing Economic Base of Sacramento

Located at the confluence of two major waterways, the Sacramento and American rivers, Sacramento has some of the richest agricultural soil in the United States, which supports a wide variety of cash crops including rice, tomatoes, fruits, nuts, and grains. Greater Sacramento encompasses four counties with a combined area of 5,141 square miles and a population of 1.3 million (Sacramento Chamber of Commerce 1987). Once a relative backwater relying primarily on government employment and agriculturally related manufacturing, Sacramento is currently one of the fastest growing and most economically diversified metropolitan areas in California. Since the late 1960s the area has experienced very rapid economic and population growth, mainly in its suburban areas. This growth has been fueled by lower land, labor, and housing costs relative to those of California's booming coastal urban areas. Metropolitan area employment growth has been the greatest in the nongovernment service sector, followed by retail trade, financial, insurance, and real estate, high-technology manufacturing, and construction. Government employment in Sacramento, although it still accounts for 29 percent of the regional labor market, has shown a 20 percent decrease between 1977 and 1987 (*Sacramento Bee*, March 6, 1988:D1). Job growth forecasts predict strong growth for the service industries, retail and wholesale trade, construction, and high-technology manufacturing. Slow growth at all levels is forecast for government employment, but employment declines are forecast for agricultural processing industries (City of Sacramento, Department of Planning and Development 1987).

Based on this pattern of economic diversification, population projections for the next fifteen years predict an increase of nearly 49 percent in the current metropolitan area population. Paralleling robust regional economic growth in the next fifteen years, the city's population is expected to increase by 40 percent, from 327,000 to 458,000. Downtown Sacramento is the urban core of the metropolitan area. It serves as the regional office and is a commercial, governmental, and cultural center. Over 66,000 workers are employed in the central city, mostly in governmental and service-related positions (City of Sacramento, Department of Planning and Development, 1987). Downtown Sacramento's development and activity levels are among the most intense in the metropolitan area. Unlike the economies of many Mid-western cities currently experiencing industrial decine, Sacramento's economy is undergoing structural changes that include net *growth* in manufacturing activities (particularly the manufacture of electronics and electrical equipment), despite job loss in the older, agriculturally related, manufacturing sector. Many high-technology manufacturing firms have located in the Sacramento County areas of Roseville and Folsom, as well as along the Highway 50 corridor. When the North Natomas and Airport-Meadowview's Huntington Park areas are developed, it is expected that high-technology firms will locate in these areas as well.

The Social Construction of Urban Development:
North Natomas

Because of an abundance of agricultural land surrounding Sacramento, combined with ample contiguous vacant land within the boundaries of the city, the North Natomas and South Natomas areas of Sacramento have the greatest potential for future growth. According to the *1986 to 2006 General Plan for Sacramento,* North Natomas "is especially ripe for development." Planning projections suggest the potential of providing more new jobs than any other area in the city and assert that "nearly one-third of the city's projected employment growth will be found in North Natomas" (City of Sacramento, Department of Planning and Development 1987:14).

Because of the proximity to major freeways, and to the downtown central business district and Sacramento Metropolitan Airport, as well as the ready availability of land, both the North and South Natomas areas have been the object of intensive development activities. McCuen & Steele, KCS, Pacific Scene, Oates Enterprises, Centennial Development Company, RJB, Hoffman, and Lukenbill Enterprises are among the leading development corporations that have absorbed substantial acreage for commercial development in recent years. North Natomas has become the site of the most symbolically charged confrontation over the meaning and direction of urban development in the history of Sacramento. Therefore, this study will focus on the political struggle over the future of Natomas. The fight reveals the process by which material and ideological struggles between pro- and anti-growth forces create sharply contradictory meanings of urban culture and the quality of city life.

North Natomas comprises 9,320 acres located within both the city and the county of Sacramento. Including drainageways, roadways, and land parcels, there are 7,778 acres within the city and 1,577 acres within the county (City of Sacramento 1986). Its general boundaries include all territory north of Interstate 80 south of Elkhorn Road and west of the Natomas East Main Drainage Canal. North Natomas has been designated by the *General Plan* to be Sacramento's major growth area for new housing and employment. At peak development, termed "full buildout" by planners, the community is projected to account for a 35 percent increase in new housing (33,000 dwelling units) and a 30 percent increase in new jobs in the city (67,000 new jobs). Much of the area is earmarked for the expansion of high-technology electronics and research-oriented industries.

At present, there has not yet been substantial development of North Natomas. The current predominant land use is still agricultural. The area includes 660 acres of developed and undeveloped industrial land, most of which is located in the county. Low-density residential uses currently total an additional 260 acres within the city. Ownership patterns in North Natomas reflect the prevailing agricultural structure of California: a high percentage of the area held by a few landowners. The public-private partnership proposes to transform the area by centering future urbanization efforts on the magnet of a 200-acre sports standium–arena complex and a $43 million major league baseball stadium built on speculation. In antici-pation of $500 million in projected returns to development, major devel-opers have purchased all the available large landholdings surrounding the sports complex (*Sacramento Bee,* January 18, 1988:A1).

In addition to the relatively low cost of its undeveloped land, North Natomas enjoys transportation advantages that have attracted developers and investors. Interstate 5 and Interstate 80 provide regional access to the area. Numerous other roads provide extensive local and internal circula-tion. Although this transportation infrastructure offers significant benefits to developers, North Natomas is mired in drainage problems. The area is quite flat and crossed by numerous canals that are essential for drainage because of the area's clay soil and high water table. As a result, the cost to extend other infrastructure to North Natomas is likely to be quite high. Nevertheless, because of the huge potential for profits anticipated by the growth coalition, developers have offered to provide a variety of capital improvements at no cost to the city as a form of developer-initiated "link-age" policy. Although "linked development policies" have typically been initiated by community groups (cf. Smith 1988b), the developers have often been the driving force behind linkage in Sacramento. They claim that their proposals will mitigate several identified adverse environmental impacts in North Natomas.

The *North Natomas Community Plan* prepared by the city (City of Sacramento 1986) asserts that there will be an operating surplus gener-ated at "full buildout" of North Natomas. According to the partnership's development plan, private-sector developers will provide all necessary capital improvements *within* the North Natomas area and the city of Sacramento will provide traditional maintenance and operation services to the North Natomas area after capital improvements are installed and development occurs. Not surprisingly, this plan does not address the question of who will pay the spillover costs outside the area caused by the intensified population growth of Sacramento envisaged by the plan (e.g., traffic congestion, air pollution, and the additional burden to roads, sew-ers, and school enrollments).

The spillover effects are likely to be exacerbated by the parallel growth of the adjacent South Natomas area. The population of South Natomas doubled between 1970 and 1980, increased to 21,000 in 1985, and is pro-jected to climb to 35,000 by 1995. According to the *1986 to 2006 General Plan for Sacramento,* South Natomas has a "holding capacity" of an addi-tional 9,680 housing units, nearly 10 percent of the city's projected new housing. South Natomas has a projected "buildout" of 1.7 million square feet of retail space, 4.8 million square feet of office space, and .41 million square feet of "employee intensive" (i.e., business park) uses. At "full buildout" an additional 25,900 jobs are projected for South Natomas, an increase of nearly 700 percent over the existing 3,500 jobs in the community, and 12 percent of the entire city's projected employment (City of Sacramento, Department of Planning and Development 1987:16). South Natomas also has a high concentration of Hispanics who face the prospect of being either inconvenienced by negative externalities of rapid growth or displaced in the process.

The Environmental Impact Report and the Community Plan

In December 1983 and January 1984, the city of Sacramento received five applications to convert agricultural land within the North Natomas area to urban use. Such a conversion was not consistent with the provisions of the city's 1974 *General Plan* or the growth policy adopted by the City Council in 1982. Historically, city and county planning and zoning policies have emphasized the preservation of agricultural land for at least the next twenty years. Despite these policies, the City Council adopted the recommendations contained in a 1984 staff report to conduct various planning studies for the development of the North Natomas area.

The stated purpose of the *North Natomas Community Plan* was to enable the City Council to determine whether the urban development of the North Natomas area was feasible. The highlight was to be a detailed community planning and infrastructure study, done in conjunction with Sacramento County, that would ascertain market demand, constraints, and costs associated with the urbanization of North Natomas. Background studies included the examination of land use demand, transportation, water, sewer and drainage, environmental conditions, and current jurisdictional plans and policies affecting the project area.

Politically, the planning staff assigned to complete the study faced the formidable task of coming to terms with a largely skeptical assessment of the environmental impact of developing North Natomas prepared by Nichols & Berman, McDonal and Associates, and Omni-Means, Ltd., under technical assistance contracts with the city. The California Environmental Quality Act of 1970 (CEQA) requires state and local government agencies to prepare such environmental impact reports on public and private projects that may have a significant effect on the environment. It is patterned after the National Environmental Policy Act of 1969 (NEPA), which applies only to federal actions. The two acts are similar in that they force full disclosure of the environmental consequences of a proposed action and require that agencies' decision-making processes include a continuing and systematic consideration of environmental factors. Fifteen states have adopted similar requirements, but California's is the oldest and most extensive of the state environmental impact programs.

The greatest impact of CEQA has been on private projects permitted by cities and counties. In many localities, environmental impact reports clearly influence decisions about such permits. Since California has left much of the detail of how the law is implemented to cities, counties, and special districts, there are now hundreds of separate administrative procedures at the local level for managing environmental impact analysis (City of Sacramento, Office of Planning and Research 1986; Trzyna and Jokela 1974).

It is uncommon for permits to be denied because of an unfavorable environmental impact report, but modification of projects as a result of these reports is common. The intention of CEQA was to discourage "bad" projects from being initiated and to encourage developers to design their projects with environmental factors in mind from the start. The cost of environmental review is significant but is borne largely by the developers. Despite the fact that these costs are quite small in relation to total project costs, they are generally passed on to the consumer (e.g., an increase in the price of housing).

The environmental impact report prepared for North Natomas indicated that any plan for urban development would cause significant adverse environmental impacts. Interestingly, the report notes that several of these impacts, such as the conversion of agricultural land and the disruption of vegetation and wildlife, cannot be fully mitigated. The *North Natomas Community Plan*, prepared by the city's Office of Planning and Research as a response to the report, claims that many of the other adverse impacts identified in that report can be mitigated if the city "carefully but aggressively requires the implementation of the mitigation measures contained in [the] plan" (City of Sacramento 1986:1). Mitigation measures are replete throughout the plan, specifically addressing ways to lessen the impacts of North Natomas development both within the community and throughout the region.

The report states that in thirty years, an additional 500,000 people will be living in the city of Sacramento, which could mean water shortages, garbage surpluses, jammed roads, dirty air, and classrooms that are bursting at the seams. Interestingly, the three-inch-thick document lists "the potential adverse effects" of the projected growth in twenty-nine pages. In contrast the benefits, listed in one page of the document, include 419,777 new jobs (mostly in North and South Natomas) and a general claim of urban revitalization.

The identified adverse environmental impacts of development are extensive. Sacramento's air is among the most polluted in the nation; Sacramento ranks in the top ten cities for carbon monoxide and ozone contamination. This automobile-dependent, sunbelt city has limited mass transit that, when combined with a booming population, will only exacerbate the air pollution problem.

Air pollution is not the only problem resulting from increased automobile use. It is estimated that by the mid-1990s, much of Sacramento will suffer from severe traffic congestion on both highways and surface roads. This will result from developments approved after money for new roads has been depleted. To blame are the scores of residential subdivisions, shopping centers, and industrial parks approved over the past decade by the Sacramento City Council and the Sacramento County Board of Supervisors without the addition of new roads to provide access to them. The projects were approved at a time when state funds for new highways had long since dwindled and local governments had lost their ability to increase property taxes because of Proposition 13. Adding new real property to the tax base was seen as a potential solution to the fiscal crisis imposed by this proposition, but the resulting growth has only compounded the problems of traffic congestion and air pollution.

The adverse effect of those projects was exacerbated by other local political decisions such as the abandonment of responsibility for 45.4 miles of freeway in the mid-1970s by the county Board of Supervisors. On a smaller scale, the supervisors also dropped 1986 plans to widen a portion of a major thoroughfare because of strong neighborhood opposition. Ironically, these decisions, intended to reduce costs and protect neighborhoods from traffic, have added to the level of pollution and congestion of existing roads and freeways. Clearly, the future cumulative impacts of these decisions will be compounded by the extent of development planned for Natomas.

Sacramento's new light rail system was originally presented by local political elites in 1987 as a method of relieving congestion. The system was projected to attract 30,500 annual riders. However, Regional Transit System officials estimate that 60 percent of the riders will be those already using other forms of public transportation. After its first year of operation, the highly touted light rail system has had virtually no effect on reducing automobile demand in the city (*Sacramento Bee*, February 15, 1987).

Environmental influences on the potential for development in Natomas go beyond automobile impacts. The environmental impact report points out that according to federal water engineers, a levee that protects North Natomas is the one most likely to fail during a major flood in the

Sacramento area (see also *Sacramento Bee*, March 27, 1987). But levee failure is not the only concern, as was discovered during the record floods in 1986 when the water level was so high that it almost poured over the North Natomas levee. Because of this risk, the natural floodwaters will have to be diverted from any development in the area, or the Federal Emergency Management Agency will remove the city from the federally subsidized flood insurance program, which it manages. The absence of this low-cost flood insurance could curtail development.

Other issues integrally tied to Natomas development are water quality, limitations of water rights law, garbage disposal, sewage treatment, the costs of providing distribution facilities, and the costs and availability of energy supply. The environmental impact report prepared for the city suggests passing some of the costs of these impacts on to the citizenry; it proposes mitigation measures such as expanding recycling efforts and litter control programs. The public is asked to accept alterations in land use value to accommodate impacts of the exchange values gained by the public-private partnership.

Aware of these social costs as early as 1978, the federal Environmental Protection Agency granted the Sacramento Regional Sanitation District $40 million to build a South Natomas sewer system on the condition that there be no development of 19,000 adjacent North Natomas acres until 1999. Faced with the pressure by the growth coalition for development of North Natomas, the EPA demanded $4 million, plus $2.2 million in interest, to repay a portion of the sewer grant if the growth coatlition's city-approved sports arena were connected to the South Natomas sewer system. Undeterred by this penalty, the pro-growth Sacramento Sports Association has said it will pay the fee for Sacramento County if the EPA does assess the penalties. However, the association insists that the district guarantee that all other North Natomas developers will be forced to absorb part of the penalty if it is assessed. The magnitude of the penalty assessed by the EPA is inadequate to deter development in view of the huge profits.

The development of North Natomas could also leave school districts in the area up to $100 million short of what they need to provide adequate clasroom space. This is because of state legislation passed in reaction to Proposition 13 that allows the city to impose a development fee for new development but restricts the amount of the fee and limits it to a one-time assessment. In North Natomas, the maximum fee allowed would generate about $61.6 million. This is far less than the projected $159.8 million cost of constructing eighteen schools in the area that will be needed as a result of the anticipated new growth. Consequently, the city has proposed several local "linkage" policies to developers that include donating the land for the schools needed and/or signing development agreements that prohibit construction of residential projects until school funding issues are resolved with the affected district. (For further discussion of the political consequences of linked development policies, see Smith 1988b; Reed 1988.)

The Major Actors

Who are the major actors in the struggle over North Natomas? What do they expect to win or lose from this development? What is the meaning of "development" to the contending parties? What are their assumptions? How are the key actors connected to each other?

The Developers

The network linkages between the developers and their organizations have allowed them to greatly increase their economic and political power as they form common plans and strategies. Gregg Lukenbill, a young Sacramento native, is one of the most influential actors with regard to development in the Sacramento area, particularly Natomas. He and his company, Lukenbill Enterprises, own all or part of the parcels, a total of 1,700 acres, recently rezoned for commercial use. From his perspective, the community plan for development of North Natomas has been completed, and the next step is subdividing the land. "Development" includes a sports complex that has extensive financial backing from national and international sources of capital, including a large loan from the Allied Bank of Texas and a $25 million commitment to support the project from the Atlantic Richfield Corporation. The purpose of this complex is to house the Sacramento Kings basketball team and a future major league baseball team. Luckenbill is also a part owner of the Kings, a principal in the Sacramento Sports Association, and a prominent business leader in Sacramento. With over $16 million in landholdings, Lukenbill has been portrayed by the press as both savior of Sacramento and money-hungry scoundrel. His personal style and self-image are conveyed by his typical garb of plaid shirt and jeans. He casts himself as a "hometown boy just out to do good things for his community."

Lukenbill has worked hard to publically distance himself from other developers, maintaining that most developers "are the kind of people that [Sacramento] needs to be afraid of. They just want to go in there and build out their 95,000 square feet of office space and then hit the road to another city where they can work the same scam" (*Sacramento Bee*, September 27, 1987). Luckenbill insists that speculative involvement is not one of his motives and that he is "in it for the long haul." He considers his vision of major league sports, a twenty-four-hour downtown, and continued growth as a "gift" he can bring to Sacramento. He also sees himself as unfairly persecuted for his efforts: "A sad commentary on this town . . . those who seek to do something positive for the community are forced to pay so exorbitant a price" (*Sacramento Bee*, September 27, 1987). In pursuit of his cultivated style of freewheeling but beneficent capitalism, Lukenbill has repeatedly assured the community that no public moneys will be (or have been) used to finance the development of North Natomas. Ironically, this self-proclaimed local entrepeneur image contradicts his actual dependency on both local government loan guarantees and outside finance capital.

Another leading force in the growth coalition is the prominent and influential developer Richard Benvenuti, member of a well-known family of builders. He controls thousands of acres of land, concentrated in the fastest developing portions of Sacramento: Natomas, Roseville, Rancho Cordova, and downtown. His holdings are valued at more than $100 million, including the value of the prime land beneath the Kings arena, which anchors the Natomas development (*Sacramento Bee*, January 18, 1988). Benvenuti estimates that he has "turned over" $50 million to $100 million worth of land each year from 1982 to 1987. In North Natomas his holdings include 20–25 percent of the 3,000 partially developed acres.

In addition to land speculation, Benvenuti has interests in a number of related businesses including Whitney Properties, B-B Builders, RJB III, Orange Tree Business Park, RT Venture, Fabri Construction Company, RT Venture II, Sacramento Capitals University Business Center, RJB Company, and RJB Interests. Many of these businesses are joint ventures with other members of his family: Joseph, his father, and Gary, his brother.

The Sacramento Sports Association

The Sacramento Sports Association (SSA) is the developer holding company that owns the Sacramento Kings basketball team. The SSA also owns 435 acres in North Natomas between the airport and downtown that will be the site of homes, businesses, and a new, multipurpose sports stadium that was completed in late 1988. The stadium was designed to include a large indoor arena and an outdoor stadium designed to seat 65,000. Fifty percent of the SSA is owned by Joseph Benvenuti, the rest is owned by Gregg Lukenbill, Frank Lukenbill, Robert Cook, Steve Clippa, and Frank McCormack.

The SSA has blurred the subject of the costs and benefits of development of North Natomas by using a "pro-sports" versus "anti-sports" smokescreen. The development's opposition, which initially included the mayor, has been labeled "anti-sports," an unpopular label in this sports-loving community. This gambit has divided public opinion. As Michael Eaton, president of the Environmental Council of Sacramento, has said: "I'd much rather be fighting a chemical plant or an oil refinery than a sports complex, because then we'd have 95 percent of the public on our side instead of maybe 50 percent" (*Sacramento Bee*, March 29, 1987). To further their sports image, Gregg Lukenbill, Joseph Benvenuti, and developer Angelo Tsakopoulos have actively courted several baseball franchises. They have also approached the Los Angeles Raiders of the National Football League about moving to Sacramento if owner Al Davis is unable to resolve his dispute with Los Angeles Memorial Coliseum officials.

Finance Capital

The Sacramento Savings and Loan and two subsidiaries of the Bell National Corporation are the most active financial institutions in the development of North Natomas. Sacramento has been the base of operations for Sacramento Savings for 112 years. The two subsidiaries, Bell Savings and Equireal, are more recent investors in the area. The Capital Bank and the Bank of America also hold liens on property in North Natomas. Property assets of Sacramento Savings located in North Natomas include twenty land parcels with a total full assessed value of $11,104,137. This represents approximately one-fifth of the 9,000 acres slated for development in North Natomas. Both Sacramento Savings and Bell National cultivate many connections and interlock with other corporate influentials, including the Benvenuti brothers, Gregg Lukenbill, and the Sacramento Sports Association. All the major developers in North Natomas have financed their land projects through these financial institutions.

The ideology legitimating the investments of Sacramento Savings is set out in its 1986 annual report. The report refers to the bank's "long-term conservative investment practices." In contrast, Bell in 1982 declared "a change to lending for real estate investment shorter term loans at varying interest rates" and pointed out that undeveloped land is "sometimes rezoned and with offsite improvements can be developed for resale to other investors." Although they operate with two apparently different legitimations, both follow similar practices of purchasing agricultural land and holding it until zoning changes dramatically increase land value. Neither of the two financial institutions incorporates community concerns into its philosophy. Their investment policies, whether identified as "conservative" or as explicitly aimed at increasing short-term profit, have the same effect. Both policies sharply focus on profit gained through economic growth and land development.

In addition to the investments of these local and regional institutions of finance capital, $28.5 million in North Natomas has come from the Allied Bank of Houston. The Atlantic Richfield Company has agreed to provide an additional $25 million to underwrite the construction of a sports complex named the ARCO Arena.

The City Council

The structure of the local government can have important implications for its degree of power and, more specifically, where in local government power lies. Local governments vary in their scope of responsibility, their degree of autonomy from other political jurisdictions, the relative power of the mayor or the council, and the extent to which they are partisan or reformist. Sacramento's government has a broad scope of responsibilities that include almost all local services, such as police, fire, and sanitation, as well as social services, welfare programs, community development, job training, planning and zoning, education, and parks and recreation. The mayor shares appointment and budget-making powers with the City Council and thus has little more power than any council member. The council, which is elected by district, operates on a part-time basis and sets general policy; a full-time professional city manager supervises the various departments and runs the city on a day-to-day basis. As a consequence, Sacramento's part-time city government is oriented less toward the representation of diverse community interests than toward ensuring efficiently managed public services.

The City Council is a nonpartisan, reformist body whose members think of Sacramento as a system of problems that can be resolved through the application of technical or managerial skills, as opposed to a partisan body that is dominated by a cohesive political group or party. Reform governments typically are less concerned with accommodating diverse social groups than with responding to petitions from individual citizens. In practice, most reform governments are highly influenced by business interests (Rubin and Rubin 1986).

The Environmental Council of Sacramento

Throughout its sixteen-year history, the Environmental Council of Sacramento (ECOS) and its sixteen member groups (the American Lung Association, the Audubon Society, the California Native Plant Society,

Californians for Population Stabilization, the Capitol Bicycle Commuters Association, the League of Women Voters, the Modern Transit Society of Sacramento, the Natomas Community Association, the Orangevale Action Committee, Planned Parenthood, the Sacramento Old City Association, the Sacramento Toxics Alliance, Sacramento Valley Bicycle Advocates, the Save the American River Association, the Sierra Club, and Zero Population Growth) have spearheaded local volunteer efforts on behalf of effective land use planning, slow growth, coordinated transportation decisions, and clean air. A great deal of the strength of this coalition is due to the strong network of social relations it has established.

The council has raised air pollution issues for years to a largely unresponsive City Council and Board of Supervisors. Specifically, ECOS has asked that the Air Quality Plan be updated (rather than ignored) ever since the beginning of the North Natomas planning process and has reminded the City Council that development approvals in the absence of a new plan would be in violation of federal law. Its decision to file suit in court represented an escalation of political strategy after milder actions had failed.

From the council's perspective, the North Natomas plan simply does not provide the air quality protections that have been claimed for it. It sees the mitigation program, drafted late in the planning process by a consultant to the Sacramento Sports Association, as a step in the right direction but argues that there are unanswered questions about the effectiveness and enforceability of the program. More important, the members of ECOS believe that North Natomas should have been planned from the ground up as a transit-oriented community that has the compact development and densities needed to make mass transit work. They contend that vague, undocumented claims that North Natomas development will be "better than" development elsewhere are not a sufficient guarantee.

The leaders of ECOS assume that the eventual urbanization of North Natomas is a foregone conclusion given the political-economic and ideological resources of the growth coalition. However, they maintain that development of that area must be done in a manner that does not undercut efforts to achieve clean air and reasonable traffic flows. They point out that the council does not have the resources, obligation, or authority to enforce air pollution laws and plans throughout the region. That responsibility, they say, rests squarely with those elected to public office. They see North Natomas as too large an opportunity and too big a threat to ignore. Mike Eaton, council president, maintains that by approving the North Natomas development, city officials "built the biggest lightning rod and now they're saying, 'Why is lightning striking here?'" (*Sacramento Bee*, March 29, 1987).

The Politics of Collective Action: The Case of ECOS

Discontinuities between individual and group interests in the Environmental Council of Sacramento are mediated by a small group of individuals. President Mike Eaton is an articulate, charismatic young man with an extensive background in environmental politics. It is this background that lends "environmental credibility" to the pursuit of community use values. Research on group cohesion suggests that credibility is the single most important characteristic of a leader, for it determines attitude coalescence in a group and the ability to influence decision-makers (cf. Baron 1986; Burns 1978; Wilson 1973). In addition to qualities that produce observable results, such as expertise, symbolic and interpretive factors such as perceived motives have been found to be major components of credibility. Social actions taken by community organizations that are presented as serving a wider public good are typically viewed as "honest motives" (Rubin and Rubin 1986).

Eaton justifies his own political activism on behalf of a better quality of life in several ways that enhance the interpretive credibility of his organization. He warns northern Californians that his motives spring from firsthand experience with the social costs of growth. He has argued that "growing up in Southern California in the 60's certainly rang alarm bells for anyone who cared about clean air, traffic, and landscape. We could see the carpet of urbanization being rolled out, with all the negatives." Eaton adds to his credibility among mainstream local political elites by maintaining that he is a politician and not a protester. He contends that a Sierra Club lobbyist in Sacramento was his "guru" and that the "main attribute of a good lobbyist is the ability to suffer fools gladly." Yet his appeal to his own constituency depends on his ability to employ traditional populist rhetoric to bolster the members' commitment to slow, "collectively managed" growth. For example, with respect to the Natomas development, he has stated that he would "rather be fighting a chemical plant or an oil refinery than a sports complex, because then we'd have 95 percent of the public on our side instead of maybe 50 percent" (*Sacramento Bee*, March 27, 1987). Thus he agrees with many critics that land development in North Natomas was "bought" by the promise of bringing "big league" sports to Sacramento (see the following discussion of linkage). Eaton's background and ability to instill confidence are critical factors in defining the collective ideology of the organization. Members may be asked to forgo their primary interests in favor of the "mission" of ECOS.

But leadership qualities are not a sufficient explanation for member willingness to defer individual interests in favor of a collective good. Jeffrey Henig suggests that objective interests may be distinct from perceived, subjective interests, and that "the *discovery* and *interpretation* of real interests is an integral part of the mobilization process" (Henig 1982: 48, emphasis added). Although a person's initial decision to participate may result from a shared interest in the policy goal of preserving air quality in the community, the process of developing and sustaining a shared ideology may focus members' attention on other broader, partially expressive interests such as political empowerment. This shared ideology, initially adopted for instrumental reasons, soon becomes an end in itself; it may be a powerful asset for controlling dissent and assuring continued mobilization efforts when rational choice explanations would dictate withdrawal from the group. In fact, in groups where the focus of use values is at the community level, internal dissent is often discredited as pursuit of self-interest.

Yet without the shared ideology of political self-empowerment, an elite's abilities to exploit inequalities in material resource allocation (e.g., time, money, information) may deflate efforts to mobilize. Henig (1982: 67) notes: "City officials have the power to control information, its content, generation and release and authority to define the alternatives against which interests and conditions must be assessed." Power and authority to channel information flows express themselves in ways that vary from very rudimentary to extremely problematic, but community groups can, with the proper mix of skills and timing, break through these structural and institutional barriers.

Control of information flows goes beyond the rudimentary difficulties of assuring that group members are able to attend City Council meetings scheduled during working hours. Active concealment of information from public view often serves the traditional "public-private partnership" interest of quick implementation of development plans, as in the case of North Natomas. To acquire the North Natomas Development Agreements, which had already been released to the North Natomas landowners, applicants, and their attorneys, ECOS was forced to invoke the California Public Records Act (*Deering's California Government Code* 1979). Once the development agreements were released, their status changed from a preliminary draft to a matter of public record, thus making them subject to the government code.

Since timing is a critical part of political effectiveness, early access to information can be crucial to the success of a mobilization strategy. But access to information often requires institutional sophistication on the part of group members. This sophistication, once displayed, may add to group legitimacy as perceived by decision-makers. It is clear that a sophisticated knowledge of the land use planning process is not a commodity that is distributed equally among various community interest groups.

In the Natomas case, ECOS members were able to utilize their skills to discover weaknesses in the fabric of governmental decision-making. Clear understanding of the California Environmental Quality Act enabled the council to apply pressure in this dispute. Specifically, ECOS contended that the environmental impact report for the North Natomas development was inadequate. Logan and Molotch (1987:166) state that "if project opponents have the time, money and skill to read through lengthy materials, EIR's [environmental impact reports] can be put to significant use. Indeed, linked to other environmentalist strategies, the EIR seems to have eliminated certain major projects." Although the council was not able to "eliminate" the North Natomas project it was able to use CEQA to put pressure on the North Natomas growth coalition and obtain concessions from developers.

The Environmental Council has maintained that the North Natomas development would create a community of 60,000 residents. Coupled with the community of South Natomas, the two ares alone would constitute the twenty-fifth largest city in California. The council has pointed out that this addition to the state's seventh largest city would worsen traffic congestion, inhibit the revitalization of downtown Sacramento, promote land speculation in the region (in direct opposition to the growth coalition's exchange value focus), and force farmers out of business. Along with a number of its member organizations, it filed a lawsuit contending that state law required the city to more fully analyze the major traffic and air pollution impacts of the *North Natomas Community Plan* and its economic impact upon the downtown area of Sacramento and other neighborhoods, and to incorporate measures in the plan that would mitigate those impacts.

The attempt by ECOS to link development in North Natomas with its projected regional effects expands the base of support needed by use value advocates with an areawide focus. This base is crucial in a system where citizen representation in public-private partnership decisions is limited. Growth advocates often attempt to avoid these linkages by manipulating public perception. In North Natomas, community amenities were linked to the overall project. The Sacramento Sports Association paved the way by offering the amenity of professional sports. Clearly, it is advantageous for the growth coalition to emphasize these types of amenities. They are a perceptual tool that was useful in securing the support of City Council members and diverting community opposition and attention. More important, the amenity of the sports complex is a powerful mystification intended to create the perception that extensive "exactions" in the form of community use values have been levied for the right to develop, while masking the exchange value dimension of the transaction. This perception has reduced community willingness to push for future mitigating measures and, therefore, has had the effect of sidetracking action concerning many of the real costs of development. In this case, public perception that the social costs of growth can be compensated by a "big league" sports facility has outweighed the demand that these costs be mitigated (see Smith 1988b).

In disputes with community groups over how much land should be developed in North Natomas, the Sacramento Sports Association has repeatedly asserted that any restrictions would preclude building the sports arena complex and keeping the Sacramento Kings professional basketball team in Sacramento. Leading anti-growth activist Heather Fargo of the Natomas Community Association maintains that use value advocates were characterized as being "anti-sports [and] therefore anti-Sacramento and [even] anti-American. It was an incredibly effective wedge for the developers" (*Sacramento Bee*, December 28, 1986). In this way, pro-growth intersts were able to emphasize one community-felt need (professional sports in Sacramento) and delay or avoid serious discussion of broader community needs and interests.

As a result of concerns regarding impacts of the further development of Natomas, a number of lawsuits have been filed by ECOS and its allies seeking to alter the course of development. The litigation has been effective in stalling and confounding development. Even a number of legally unsuccessful suits have been politically successful in delaying further development of North Natomas along lines favored by the growth coalition. These delaying suits have included charges that the City Council violated open-meeting laws when members of the council met privately with developer Gregg Lukenbill in Melarkey's Restaurant and at City Hall; that the City Council underestimated traffic, pollution, housing, and cumulative impacts and, therefore improperly approved North Natomas plans; and that the City Council illegally obtained a one-year extension of its *General Plan* to give itself immunity for North and South Natomas decisions. In addition, a nonlitigious attempt to restrict North Natomas development died in September 1986 when a group calling itself the Save Open Space Committee failed to qualify an initiative for the 1987 city ballot.

A related lawsuit filed by the Natomas Community Association in November 1986 has been even more successful in delaying action in South
Natomas. The association charged that the council illegally approved
South Natomas development plans without adequately assessing environmental, financial, and other impacts. Superior Court Judge James T. Ford
ruled that the Sacramento City Council violated environmental law in approving the *South Natomas Community Plan*. The decision forced the
council to reconsider South Natomas plans calling for 6.4 million square
feet of offices, 1.7 million square feet of commercial space, and 25,000
housing units. Specifically, Ford ruled that cumulative traffic, pollution,
and other impacts of planned development in North Natomas were not
adequately considered before the 4,900-acre *South Natomas Community
Plan* was adopted in January 1986. He asserted that the council also violated the California Environmental Quality Act by failing to adopt adequate findings, which must describe whether environmental impacts are
significant and what can be done about them.

The strategy of opponents of growth has included both legal challenges
to general plans and development agreements, and specific challenges to
each proposed project in North Natomas. In a suit brought by the Environmental Council of Sacramento in March 1987 in pursuit of this strategy, the charge was that development agreements between the city and
developers in connection with North Natomas were improper. This challenge included opposition to the City Council's finding that an environmental impact report was not needed to approve development
agreements and detailed street planning. The Environmental Council
contended that the negative declaration that found an environmental impact report was unnecessary was flawed, that the city failed to study potential adverse environmental impacts of such concentrated land use, and
that the new land uses are inconsistent with the *Sacramento General
Plan*. The council asked that an environmental impact report be required,
that the development agreement be invalidated, and that an injunction be
issued to prevent the City Council from granting any more permits or undertaking new construction. A restraining order named the "real parties
in interest" as Lukenbill Enterprises, the Sacramento Sports Association,
and Richard, Joseph and Nancy Benvenuti, developers. Opponents of development in North Natomas publicly vowed to switch the subject of
court fights from general plans to the sports complex and other specific
projects if they were unsuccessful in these initial efforts.

The Natomas growth coalition has questioned the source of funding for
the anti-growth lawsuits, suggesting that developers of land along Highway 50, worried that new growth would affect their property, are serving
as the financiers. The Environmental Council's legal expenses have

totaled tens of thousands of dollars, but it has sidestepped direct questions regarding the source of its funding saying, "We have no developer funding. They [the supporters of development] just can't believe hundreds of people support this." Council representatives have said that nobody has contributed more than $1,000 (*Sacramento Bee*, December 28, 1986).

The ability of community groups to develop a perceived power in the community is a direct function of their ability to litigate, and ECOS had the skills and resources to pursue this avenue. But litigation itself does not ensure that use values will be fully considered in public-private partnership decisions. Early in the litigation, the attorney for the development interests dismissed the council's efforts, stating that "North Natomas is basically a political issue. . . . The [city] council has decided what it wants to do, and I find it difficult to believe litigation will turn that around" (*Sacramento Bee*, December 28, 1986). As the litigation progressed, supporters of the Natomas development stepped up their claims that the lawsuits were politically motivated and that other developers, with landholdings in a separate area of town, were funding the council's litigation efforts.

This was part of the ECOS "limited pie" strategy, which suggests that land use decisions, increasingly constrained by the difficulty of mitigating environmental problems, will pit developers against developers in their pursuit of exchange values. Logan and Molotch (1987:223) recognize this possibility and contend that "the ability of the environmental movements to break the unanimity of groups ordinarily in support of exchange values is one of their key strengths. Particularly effective are instances in which coalitions include either rich and powerful neighborhood groups or rentiers seeking to preserve a particular development strategy." The presence of these elite elements, and the constituent participation of the affluent generally, should not obscure the usual thrust of these movements: to enhance the use values of the public at large, particularly those of the less affluent populations. The strength of environmentalism clearly lies in the structural conditions that give it a strong potential for cross-class appeal. This "limited pie" strategy was particularly important in Sacramento becaues of the "unanimity" of local and national/international financial institutions regarding the exchange value of the North Natomas area.

Thus, ECOS has created the perception of power. It has demonstrated the ability to understand and employ complex environmental law, and it has created and sustained the illusion that it has the resources to continue litigation as needed. This is critical since the expense of continued litigation is often utilized by growth advocates to deplete the resources of community opposition. But sustained litigation efforts can work for both sides of the exchange—use value conflict.

As litigation continued, pressure was shifted from ECOS to the developers. Due to the uncertainty of the Natomas project, the Allied Bank of Texas considered backing out of its agreement to lend Gregg Luckenbill $28.5 million to build the sports arena. Walter Slipe, Sacramento city manager, maintained that the ECOS lawsuits were enough to make Allied sensitive to potential risk in North Natomas (*Sacramento Bee*, January 17, 1988). From Allied's perspective, the lawsuits would delay construction and boost costs to a point that the initial amount it was lending might not be enough to finish the Natomas project.

To reduce its perceived risk, Allied demanded protection of its investment before allowing the developer to draw against the loan. In the classic mode of public-private partnership, the city manager and the city treasurer made available $8 million from the City Employees Pension Fund to serve as collateral in case the potential cost overruns threatened completion of the Natomas project (*Sacramento Bee*, December 31, 1987). Interestingly, this arrangement was supposedly estabished without the knowledge of any City Council member (*Sacramento Bee*, January 12, 1988) and after repeated assertions by Luckenbill, in pursuit of his free-wheeling capitalist image, that the sports complex project was a private-sector project that required no government subsidies.

Luckenbill maintained that secrecy was necessary because he did not want "the message to get out that environmental lawsuits could kill major projects in Sacramento" (*Sacramento Bee*, January 17, 1988). Once again, the tenor of his statement suggests that people working to protect use values are somehow out of touch with the "real" needs of the city and that it is often necessary to negotiate agreements outside the existing public forum for decision-making. Unfortunately, pro-growth advocates often have this "secret ear" of decision-makers, which is an avenue unavailable to most community groups.

As a result of continued litigation and increased pressure from lenders, a compromise agreement has been reached that includes the following use value concessions by the public-private partnership:

1. An upgraded citywide automobile trip reduction ordinance as part of an air pollution mitigation program (a cost paid by the automobile-dependent public)
2. A commitment to roadway infrastructure design consistent with traffic management programs in the *North Natomas Community Plan*
3. A commitment by the city to adopt Housing Trust Fund and Transportation System Management Ordinances within six months

4. A binding commitment to maintain (or improve) the housing-to-jobs ratio in North Natomas, even if housing near the Sacramento Metropolitan Airport cannot be built due to noise

5. Construction of a cross-levee that would increase flood protection for existing homes in South Natomas and act as a deterrent to development of agricultural lands north of it

This last point is crucial since the final word on Natomas has yet to be written. Due to recent redrawing of federal flood maps by the Federal Emergency Management Agency, all of the Natomas area has been placed within a hundred-year floodplain. If the agency adopts the maps, no new houses can be built below the designated flood levels, and existing housing and commercial buidings must have flood insurance before they can be sold or refinanced. Failure to enforce building restrictions would result in withdrawal of agency-supplied flood insurance, which would effectively preclude financing of any construction in the area (*Sacramento Bee*, January 18, 1988).

The specter of a major flood once again pits land speculators in North Natomas against one another. Because of the cost of building levees, the location decided upon will be the northernmost boundary for development in Sacramento at least until the year 2000. The Sacramento Sports Association and Gregg Lukenbill favor construction of the levee at Elkhorn Boulevard, the southernmost of three alternatives and the one requiring the least time to develop. It is their hope that enough of the project can be completed in time to comply with the federal building restrictions. However, other landowners to the north oppose this alternative on the grounds that it would restrict the future development and profitability of their holdings. As a result, they have threatened to file suit against the City Council if it approves the settlement with ECOS. In response, Gregg Lukenbill charges that "trying to blow up the settlement over the location of the levee is fairly underhanded and unethical. Look, they've been riding our coattails for years and it's been a free ride for them. They've had nothing but total benefits. [The City Council] shouldn't let a few greedy developers stop them from approving the levee if it can reduce floor hazards" (*Sacramento Bee*, January 22, 1988). Thus, the final word on North Natomas seems destined to be mired in flooding problems. This is ironic since the classic limiting factor in the development of most sunbelt cities is lack of water.

Conclusion

Human agency is a force in cities. Local action by community organizations and grass roots movements is a central form of the agency of popular classes. However, views on why community organizations form and how they become effective differ widely. Henig (1982:40) suggests that "depending upon whom you talk to, establishing a collective response among individuals with a shared interest is either an automatic, nearly inevitable reaction or a difficult task demanding intelligence, leadership, strategy, and luck. Not surprisingly, the difference in viewpoint is often aligned with different attitudes toward the merits of group activity. Politicians, planners, and developers have often portrayed community mobilization in opposition to their plans as a knee-jerk reaction, an unthinking thorn in the side of progress."

A number of competing theoretical perspectives seek to explain citizen interest group activity. Henig (1982) provides a useful work in this area that will guide the following discussion. The key difference is in the way each explains the evolution from the emergence of citizen interests to the more complex exertion of group influence over government policy. For example, in the conventional pluralist view, governmental policy is depicted as an inevitable result of a process that takes into account all legitimate interests of the diverse factions of the citizenry (cf. Dahl 1961). However, the key word here is "legitimate," and the view does not take into consideration either elite or popular perceptions as to what constitutes a legitimate interest. This concept is critical since the view assumes that decision-makers are necessarily aware of all interests in the community due to the likelihood that any group of citizens may suddenly mobilize.

The Environmental Council has been able to utilize the concept of coalition implicit in its organizational structure to achieve a perceived reputation for power in the dispute over the Natomas land development. The leaders of ECOS are quick to point out that its actions have the complete commitment of its sixteen member organizations. Thus it is able to confront decision-makers with a clear claim to represent a collective interest. If legitimacy, as perceived by a decision-maker, is in part a function of the number of constituent pieces represented, then the implicit influence inherent in the council's organizational structure should exceed that of a group with an equal number of members but acting as a single entity.

Yet to explain the influence exerted by ECOS on the Natomas land use decision as simply a function of organizational structure is to avoid the more important issue which is the friction between the ideology of group members, the goals of the group, and the structure of the political arena. We agree with Galaskiewicz (1979) that the rules of the game and the institutions established to govern the competition among political groups are ideological forms that work for or against the interests of certain actors. It is not uncommon for community groups to encounter demographic, organizational, technological, economic, and political structures that offer resistance to the pursuit of use values.

Challenges to the presumption of a frictionless transition to action and effectiveness can be based on the simple fact that there is often tension between the interests of the collective and the interests of the individuals who make up the collective (Henig, 1982). Group membership is typically initiated because of shared ideology. Continued group membership reinforces this ideology, and the network of interactions among members acts to create a collective ideology for the group. Members are convinced of the effectiveness of collective political activity by a recounting of past successes of collective intervention. In addition, longevity is a factor since it is indicative of political success, and these successes can be effectively utilized in recruiting new members and guaranteeing the continued contribution of existing members. This point is critical since actors will opt for alternative modes of political expression or simply choose to withdraw from the political arena unless goals are realized.

Because of limited resources, the collective ideology that results from the network of interactions among members is often only peripherally related to individual interests. This is particularly true of coalition organizations such as ECOS, whose member groups may have more in common with each other ideologically (e.g., the Planned Parenthood Association and Zero Population Growth, or the Capitol Bicycle Commuters Association and the Sacramento Valley Bicycle Advocates) than they do with the specific political activities and general goals of the organization. However, in its negotiations with the Sacramento City Council, ECOS has been able to create the perception of a coalition solidified around a single issue.

The ability of ECOS to mobilize groups with overlapping but not necessarily identical goals is a reflection of the way the groups conceptualize use value. In this case a strong central ideology based on community use values (e.g., air quality, clean water, toxic waste removal) provides the unifying themes for the collective. Interestingly, these are use values that represent a public good, a situation where benefits are captured at the community level and not solely by the group members. Logan and Molotch (1987) note a recent shift in community organizing strategy away from a focus on neighborhood preservation and toward a focus on environmental activism. Perhaps such a shift reflects a need to solidify the divergent interests of various community groups into a stronger, centralized, citywide movement—particularly in the Western states, Logan and Molotch maintain, where cities like Sacramento have less precise ethnic, racial, and class divisions bounded by neighborhoods. This is attributed to the West's lesser degree of trade unionism, class consciousness, and ethnic neighborhood homogeneity, which allows people "to develop a large-scale concern for places beyond (but not excluding) the immediate neighborhood" (Logan and Molotch 1987). The result is an expanded politics of place centered on common control over such "place resources" as health, aesthetics, air quality, traffic impact, and life-style. Politics of place in sunbelt cities is especially pronounced among young urban professionals, who use their organizational skills in local politics to resist the social and physical costs of increasingly rapid growth (Smith 1988a).

The struggle over North Natomas is fraught with ironies and contradictions that reveal much about the subtle interplay among political, economic, and cultural forces that shape the further trajectory of growth in Sacramento. The expected economic return from the current urbanization of North Natomas is so great that developers rather than community groups have taken the initiative in proposing linkage policies. Their linkage plans have been designed to symbolically convey their willingness to compensate for the negative side effects of development, but such plans have the covert benefit of diffusing opposition to their development proposals. These compensatory gestures are further enhanced by the cultural style of freewheeling cowboy "entrepreneurship" pursued by Sacramento's most visible developer. However, this image has served to mask his actual dependence on both outside finance capital and local government loan guarantees.

The "partnership" between private developers and local public officials in Sacramento has met the active resistance of a citywide coalition of anti-growth-oriented community organizations. Ironically, the ability of the coalition to remain mobilized throughout the struggle over North Natomas has been facilitated by a past successful grass roots struggle against the widening of a major thoroughfare in a particular neighborhood, an action that made the citywide problem of traffic congestion perceptibly worse. The absence of traditional bases for community mobilization (e.g., race, ethnicity, and class) in undeveloped North Natomas has not deterred the mobilization effort. Instead, the objective contradictions presented in the decentralized pattern of past growth in the sunbelt city of Sacramento have set the stage for an expanded politics of place. This new focus has centered on communitywide use values such as clean air, environmental amenities, carefully planned land use, transportation policies, and democratically responsive political institutions.

In waging this type of political struggle, *both* pro- and anti-growth coalitions have claimed to represent communitywide interests, including the interests of the poor. Thus, attempts to influence the meaning of development often emphasize additional jobs, safer working conditions, better mass transit, and a stronger political voice. However, in Sacramento, "the poor" are neither self-organized on the basis of race, class, ethnicity or residential propinquity nor actively represented in the decision-making process of the "partnership" or ECOS. Thus, unless the council develops a mechanism for actually incorporating the interests of Sacramento's growing low-income and new immigrant populations, its claim to represent communitywide interests by virtue of its agenda is no more credible than the partnership's claim that the benefits of new jobs created by growth are bound to trickle down to the poor. Interestingly, ECOS has the potential for becoming a broad-based, cross-cultural group that advocates use value over exchange value, but without this incorporating mechanism, it will remain a coalition dominated by middle-strata constituency groups pursuing an arguably middle-class agenda. The fact that the council has agreed to a legal settlement of the North Natomas question that pays the organizations' court costs but leaves unresolved the specter of serious flooding raises the thorny question of goal displacement and underlines the material resource constraints of a political strategy that relies on law and the courts as a political resource. If the flooding question remains unresolved, a final irony may be the resurgence, in the "new" North Natomas district, of an "old" Sacramento architectural style—Victorian housing built with the main floor six to eight feet above ground level to cope with the city's frequent and serious floods.

That Sacramento will continue to grow is a certainty. Whether the city changes from "cowtown" to vital urban center or becomes yet another example of the sunbelt pattern of decentralized, metropolitan sprawl is still an open question. The answer to that question depends on the actual social and environmental costs of developing North Natomas, how they are mitigated, and who pays for them.

Note

In addition to the sources listed in the References, this research includes active participant observation by one of the authors of the activities of the Environmental Council of Sacramento (ECOS) and the Sacramento Old City Association, as well as tape-recorded, open-ended interviews with the following key actors: Gregg Luckenbill, developer; David Mogavero, past president of the association and current president of ECOS; Steven Sanders, environmental activist and current president of the association; Healther Fargo, past president of the Natomas Community Association; and Sacramento City Council members Joe Serna and David Shore.

References

Alinsky, Saul. 1971. *Rules for Radicals.* New York: Random House.

Baron, Robert A. 1986. *Behavior in Organizations.* Newton, Mass.: Allyn and Bacon.

Burns, James M. 1978. *Leadership.* New York: Harper and Row.

Catanese, Anthony J. 1984. *The Politics of Planning and Development.* Beverly Hills: Sage.

City of Sacramento. 1986. *North Natomas Community Plan* (May).

————. Department of Planning and Development and Attorney's Office. 1987. *The 1986 to 2006 General Plan for Sacramento* (July).

————. Office of Economic Development. 1987. *Economic Base Analysis* (May).

————. Office of Planning and Research. 1986. *California Environmental Quality Act: Statuses and Guidelines, 1986.*

————. Environmental Council. 1986. "North Natomas Community Plan and EIR Lawsuit Filed Today." Press release (June 13).

Cockburn, C. 1979. *The Local State.* London: Pluto.

Dahl, Robert 1961. *Who Governs?* New Haven, Conn.: Yale University Press.

Deering's California Government Code. 1979. Section 6250. San Francisco: Bancroft-Whitney.

Galaskiewicz, Joseph. 1979. *Exchange Networks and Community Politics.* Beverly Hills: Sage.

Gittell, Marilyn. 1980. *Limits to Citizen Participation: The Decline of Community Organizations.* Beverly Hills: Sage.

Gottdiener, M. 1987. *The Decline of Urban Politics: Political Theory and the Crisis of the Local State.* Beverly Hills: Sage.

Henig, Jeffrey R. 1982. *Neighborhood Mobilization: Redevelopment and Response.* New Brunswick, N.J.: Rutgers University Press.

Logan, John R., and Harvey L. Molotch. 1987. *Urban Fortunes: The Political Economy of Place.* Berkeley: University of California Press.

Reed, Adolph, Jr. 1988. "The Black Urban Regime: Structural Origins and Constraints," *Comparative Urban and Community Research* 1:138–189.

Rubin, Herbert J., and Irene Rubin. 1986. *Community Organizing and Development.* Columbus: Merrill.

Sacramento Bee. 1986. "Natomas Questions Go to Court" (December 28):A1.

————. 1987a. "Getting There Getting Tougher." Forum section (February 15):6.

————. 1987b. "Trying to Slow Growth, Not Traffic, to a Crawl" (March 27).

————. 1987c. "Watery Peril for North Natomas" (March 27).

————. 1987d. "Capital Officials Talking Tougher in Clean-Air Fight" (March 29).

————. 1987e. "Gregg Lukenbill's Sacramento: All Together Now?" Forum section (September 27):6.

————. 1987f. "Secret City Pension Deal Aided Arena" (December 31):A1.

————. 1988a. "Council Raps Slipe's Knuckles" (January 12):B1.

————. 1988b. "The Real Game Here: I've Got A Secret," Forum section (January 17):1.

————. 1988c. "Lives, Dollars at Stake in Natomas" (January 18):A1.

————. 1988d. "Natomas Pact Encounters New Threat" (January 22):B1.

————. 1988e. "More Than Just a Government Town: Sacramento Diversifying Its Economy" (March 6):D1.

Sacramento Chamber of Commerce. 1987. *Introducing Sacramento*.

Smith, Michael Peter. 1988a. *City, State, and Market*. New York: Basil Blackwell.

————. 1988b. "The Uses of Linked Development Policies in U.S. Cities." In *Regenerating the Cities: The U.K. Crisis and the American Experience*, ed. Michael Parkinson, Bernard Foley, and Dennis Judd. Manchester: Manchester University Press.

Trainor, Richard. 1987. "Raising Sacramento." *Sacramento Magazine* 13 (no. 10): 49–67.

Trzyna, Thaddeus C., and Arthur W. Jokela. 1974. *The California Environmental Quality Act*. Claremont: Center for California Public Affairs.

Wilson, James Q., ed. 1973. *Political Organizations*. New York: Basic Books.

15. In Search of Equal Partnerships: Prospects for Progressive Urban Policy in the 1990s

The much celebrated public-private partnership approach to the revitalization of U.S. cities has turned out to be a grossly unequal partnership with inequitable outcomes. The underlying strategy of the public-private partnership in the cities surveyed in this book has been to revive downtown commercial centers but little, if any, serious attention has been paid to the benefits that might flow to the less fortunate urban residents or to their neighborhoods. Most of the mayors, corporate leaders, newspaper editors, and other elites in these cities suffer from a common syndrome—the "edifice complex," which equates progress with the construction of high-rise office towers, sports stadiums, convention centers, and cultural megapalaces, but ignores the basic needs of most city residents. This is urban renewal by another name, but the game is essentially the same.

This may sound like a harsh judgment, but it is one that is warranted by the evidence of these case studies and other recent literature on urban development and restructuring (MacDonald 1984; Peterson 1985; Adams and Duncan 1988). Marc Levine appropriately concludes in Chapter 2 that "the corporate center approach appears flawed because it ignores such issues as the quality of jobs created and the linkage between development in one sector and development needs in another, while relying on the 'trickle down' effect rather than public targeting to encourage economic development in the most distressed urban neighborhoods."

Yet, as Levine, Gregory Squires, and other authors of this volume point out, in some cities since the late 1970s, progressive or populist mayors, as well as grass roots political reform movements, have opposed the corporate center approach, challenged local growth coalitions for political hegemony, and achieved some degree of success in articulating and, in a few cases, implementing new pro-people, pro-neighborhood policies.

In Cleveland, maverick Dennis Kucinich was elected on a populist platform. However, the possibility that the Kucinich administration might become a model for a new, progressive urban populism was soon dashed by a combination of united opposition to his efforts from Cleveland's most powerful business interests and, equally important, by Kucinich's failure to built an alliance with neighborhood organizations across racial lines. There is evidence to suggest that it was Kucinich's lack of political skills, as much as the strength of his opponents, that resulted in the rapid decline of his administration's popularity and then to his loss of the mayoral office (Swanstrom 1985).

Dennis Keating, Norman Krumholz, and John Metzger reinforce this perspective in their analysis of Cleveland (Chapter 7). They do note a few positive political developments in post-Kucinich Cleveland. Most significant, in their view, is the growing strength of neighborhood-based community development corporations, which have succeeded in recent years in winning financial support from both private foundations and the city government. Community development corporations in Cleveland have joined in public-private partnership efforts, at least as junior partners, focusing primarily on housing and small-scale economic development. These authors conclude, however, that "Although neighborhood-based development groups have received considerable assistance from the city and from private corporations and foundations, this assistance has not been commensurate with that provided for major downtown development projects. The political influence of neighborhood nonprofit development groups is not nearly equal to that of their for-profit counterparts, which exert much more influence at City Hall."

Mayor Richard Caliguri in Pittsburgh has turned out to be a more adroit politician than Cleveland's Kucinich. Alberta Sbragia, in Chapter 6, explains that Caliguri decided to include the city's neighborhood movements (at least those in white neighborhoods) in his political coalition. Caliguri's administration has allocated a majority of the federal funds received by the city to the neighborhoods and encouraged the creation of CDCs. Sbragia argues that "organization is the key variable explaining both why neighborhood groups . . . are now such legitimate actors in the politics of redevelopment and why they have received significant amounts of public money."

Organization has clearly been lacking in Pittsburgh's black neighborhoods—which are fragmented geographically and politically—and in the region's labor movement. Such once powerful unions as the United Steelworkers have been severely hampered by internal political strife, as well as battered by the transformation of the region's manufacturing economy to one dominated by high-technology industry, health, and education. Sbragia notes that Caliguri has supported the idea of creating a Tri-State Steel Authority—a special-purpose agency to revitalize the area's decimated steel towns—but little progress has been made (or can be expected) given the weak political position of the labor movement, both in the state and nationally.

Sbragia notes the concern of some Pittsburgh activists that by focusing on local economic development projects, "we've lost the ability to be good organizers." Absorption of neighborhood groups in "the gravy train" appears to have reduced political advocacy, as well as efforts to build a citywide biracial progressive movement. Perhaps Caliguri, whatever his motives, has succeeded in co-opting Pittsburgh's white activist community; perhaps it was the best choice available to them in the Reagan years.

Political and economic prospects are bleaker in Detroit. As June Marming Thomas says in Chapter 8, "Racial and income segregation have cut off the city from its [suburban] neighbors." Massive renewal projects such as Poletown and downtown megaprojects like the Renaissance Center have not stemmed the city's economic decline. An ambitious attempt to build a biracial progressive political movement, the Detroit Alliance for a Rational Economy (DARE), succeeded for time in establishing a political presence in the city that included electing one of its leaders, black lawyer Ken Cockrel, to the City Council. But DARE was disbanded in the mid-1980s. Many of its policy analysts have gone to work for Governor James Blanchard and are tackling economic issues in a regional and state context. Mayor Coleman Young, a mainstream Democrat, has a lease on City Hall as long as he wants it (Georgakas and Surkin 1975).

In Chicago, the election of the progressive black Mayor Harold Washington raised hopes that a major U.S. city might take significant new policy directions. The Washington administration adopted a citywide development plan, *Chicago Works Together*. Former Cleveland city planner Norm Krumholz spoke optimistically of this plan: "The Chicago Development plan of 1984 is the strongest indication thus far that American cities are willing to try to harness economic development for their disadvantaged residents. It is virtually certain to be the forerunner of similar plans, especially in cities where the political power of blacks and hispanics is on the rise" (Keating and Krumholz 1985).

The plan, as Larry Bennett delineates it in Chapter 9, recognizes that choices must be made and priorities set. It emphasizes increased public participation, job creation and retention, increased technical assistance to community economic development organizations, and increased job placement of city residents. It encompasses both sectoral and area strategies.

However, the Washington administration was not able to implement most of the plan. The city government was severely hampered by battles with the remnant of the Daley machine, resistance from the bureaucracy, a lack of financial resources caused in part by cutbacks in federal programs, and problems of the city's segregated education system. Of course, Washington's sudden death raises questions about the future of progressive politics in Chicago.

In New York, as Susan Fainstein and Norman Fainstein note in Chapter 4, there has been considerable neighborhood opposition to Mayor Edward Koch's pro-development policies. Activists have won some victories, such as stopping the Westway superhighway project. Rent controls have been maintained because of strong support from local unions and tenant activities. Community planning boards in the city's fifty-nine planning districts have allowed some citizen participation in making development decisions, which has reduced the negative impacts of some development on neighborhoods.

Fainstein and Fainstein conclude that "the elements of a new electoral coalition do exist among those who are extremely disaffected by the housing situation, members of racial minority groups, and progressive business leaders who are distressed by the city's deteriorating infrastructure and educational system." It remains to be seen whether there is a political leader who can combine these elements into a new majority.

The two runoff candidates in Boston's last mayoral race were a white populist, Ray Flynn, and a black civil rights activist, Mel King. Flynn, the winner, has attempted to run a nonracist, progressive, pro-neighborhood administration. He has brought into the government progressive policy experts and activists from Mass Fair Share and other citizen groups. As Peter Dreier describes in Chapter 3, the Flynn administration has made serious attempts to link downtown development to the needs of the city's neighborhoods, particularly in the area of affordable housing.

A New Urban Populism?

What is to be made of these signs of progressive activism? It is fair to say that from the mid-1970s to the present, activists in a variety of cities have had a not insubstantial impact on urban politics. In almost every major U.S. city, there is at least one progressive activist on the City Council—and in some cities, both large and middle-sized, either liberal (center-left) or progressive (left-center) coalitions have won the mayor's office and sometimes majority control of the city government. Neighborhood-based movements, such as Communities Organized to Promote Service (COPS) in San Antonio and United Neighborhood Organizations (UNO) in Los Angeles, have sprung up in many middle-sized and large cities and have forced even center and center-right urban governments to respond to their concerns. This combination of the entry of the 1960s activists into the urban electoral arena and the rise of new community organizations constitutes what might be termed a new urban populism. This is a national occurrence rooted in specific locales; it has no central headquarters and no national leader. It is extraparty in that it functions outside the old urban Democratic machines, and in some cities it has replaced them; yet the voting base includes much that remained of the old New Deal Democratic coalition. Leadership is often not organization-based, but is asserted by individuals who combine vision and energy with populist styles. In varying forms and strengths, elements of this new urban populism can be seen in Detroit, Cleveland, Boston, Chicago, Portland, Seattle, San Antonio, San Francisco, Santa Monica, West Hollywood, Burlington, St. Paul, Minneapolis, Hartford, Baltimore, Washington, D.C., and a number of university towns such as Davis, Chico, Santa Cruz, and Berkeley in California; Eugene, Oregon; Austin, Texas; Ann Arbor, Michigan; and Cambridge, Massachusetts (Boyte 1983; 1985; Clavel 1985).

The new urban populism is based on a vision of the city as a place where people should be given priority over buildings, cars, and businesses—and as a place where citizens have basic rights as residents of the city whether or not they own property. The ideology of these urban populists' efforts is an informal one, based loosely on the humanist writings of Lewis Mumford and Jane Jacobs and on the ideas of participatory and economic democracy that emerged from the movements of the 1960s. Three policy themes can be found in almost all cities with urban populist movements. The first is *balanced economic growth*. Progressive public officials and community activists want economic growth to be growth with equity, so that the largest number of people share in economic development, and that when social or environmental *costs* are involved, they are also shared or substantially mitigated by those people or institutions who benefit. This is in contrast to the old-style urban renewal–generated growth, in which some groups, usually the poor or minorities, paid the costs of economic development and the more affluent citizens reaped the benefits. Such a policy is a challenge to the terms of most current public-private partnerships.

The second is *citizen participation*, and the belief that residents of a city have a democratic right to participate in decisions about the physical and social development of both their neighborhood and the city center, and that it is the *responsibility* of urban governments to encourage, support, and promote the exercise of this right.

The third is the concept of *human scale*, of a built environment that encourages the social interaction of people and promotes face-to-face communication in comfortable and pleasant public places in the city. All of these themes have been discussed in planning documents, speeches, manifestos, and newspaper articles and some have been incorporated in the day-to-day practice of governing cities.

Urban populist movements strive to conserve and strengthen *all* of the neighborhoods in a city by pursuing the goal of promoting an active and secure community life. Public funds are expended for community development projects, neighborhood groups and organizations participate in the planning and implementation of projects and service delivery, and private development is regulated to mitigate the adverse effects on neighborhoods. Crime prevention is often community-based, with citizens participating through Neighborhood Watch programs and other collective preventive efforts.

In St. Paul, Minnesota, the city government, through its Neighborhood Partnership program, makes matching grants to neighborhood organizations for community improvement projects. The city government has also divided the city into districts with local Planning Councils that are responsible for developing neighborhood plans. In Portland, Oregon, the Office of Neighborhood Associations, a unit of the city government, provides financial and technical assistance to democratic neighborhood groups and helps them establish community crime prevention programs and carry out other projects. In San Antonio, the city's first Latino mayor, Henry Cisneros, responded to the demands of the militant neighborhood-based community organization COPS by redirecting millions of dollars to community improvement projects in the poorer Mexican-American areas of the city. In Santa Monica, California, the city government elected by a progressive political coalition, Santa Monicans for Renters Rights, provided public funds to democratic neighborhood organizations for staff salaries and for neighborhood improvement projects. A 1985 city plan requires the preservation of "neighborhood-serving" commercial uses. The city has provided funds to establish a nonprofit Community Corporation, which assists neighborhood organizations in the purchase and construction of cooperatively owned housing projects.

Urban populist movements try to use municipal powers to make the downtown a place where people of all races and classes can interact in a safe and pleasant manner. This means sponsoring and planning *mixed-use* projects that include shops, offices, and housing in the same physical location; building new public facilities such as aquariums, zoos, or theaters to attract city residents and suburban residents back downtown; and rehabilitating old structures such as railroad stations and post offices for new uses such as shops and restaurants. And it means requiring building designs that are *pedestrian oriented* and public places that encourage pedestrian use. In Seattle, for example, the old buildings in the Pioneer Square area have been preserved and renovated rather than razed, and the historic Pike Place Market had been saved from destruction by a citizens initiative movement. The city's "Magic Carpet" program provides free bus service in the downtown area. In Portland, innovative traffic management and the construction of a new light-rail trolley line have made the downtown a "walking place." Numerous old buildings have been renovated for new uses. New public squares and parks have been built and a freeway along the river has been closed and turned into a riverfront park. San Antonio has turned its riverfront into a pedestrian River Walk that mixes shops, stores, hotels, and offices. In Santa Monica, the city plan requires that the ground floor of all new downtown commercial buildings have space for shops and eating places. The city has also renovated its old downtown parking structures by turning their ground floor into rentable space for shops. All urban populist movements encourage and support the building of new, affordable housing in the central core. In St. Paul, the city assists in the creation of special loft housing for artists, and in Portland, buildings have been rehabilitated as single residency occupancy housing for poor, often homeless, individuals.

Many of the urban populist–influenced governments have "linked-development" policies under which developers of office buildings or other commercial projects must also provide housing, social services, or cultural facilities as a part of the right to develop in the city. The populist administration of Mayor Ray Flynn in Boston has announced such a policy, as has the city of San Francisco. In Santa Monica, a major office development was required to provide a child care center and a public park on site, and to build one hundred units of rental housing in a nearby neighborhood. The management of all new office developments in Santa Monica is required to pay into a housing trust fund and to provide funds for parks or other green open space.

Urban populist movements also sponsor projects, both in the city center and in the neighborhoods, that animate the city—increasing human activity there by getting people out of their homes (away from their television sets) and out of their cars. In Portland, an association of artisans and the city sponsor an outdoor Saturday Market where crafts people sell their products and art work. Every year in Portland there is "Art Quake"—a citywide arts and theater festival. During the summer, a city fair is held in the riverfront park; the city assists neighborhood groups that want to hold block parties by temporarily closing streets to traffic. In Santa Monica, since 1981 the city government has organized a weekly Farmers Market on a downtown city street, where small farmers park their trucks and sell fresh fruits and vegetables directly to consumers. The city also sponsors arts and crafts festivals on the downtown pedestrian shopping street, and free outdoor summer concerts on the city's historic ocean pier. In Seattle, Mayor Charles Royer has initiated a program called "Kidsplace" to increase children's use of the city by making it known to them, and by making it a safer place—both physically and socially—for them to explore. Many urban populist politicians encourage walking and bike riding as alternative means of transportation for enjoying and experiencing the city. Some city governments have added bike lanes to city streets, required new buildings to have bike racks, and built special bike paths in city parks and along rivers, lakes, and ocean fronts. City governments have also promoted public art by providing funds for outdoor murals, sculpture, and street theater. Urban populist movements attempt to increase citizens' participation in local government by providing new structures for participation, resources to aid in participation, and information about the choices the city faces. In Santa Monica, the city government subsidizes the broadcasting of City Council meetings by a local public radio station and publishes a monthly newsletter that is mailed to all households in the city. The city Planning Commission requires that developers meet with representatives of neighborhood organizations before major projects that affect the neighborhood are approved. The commission now notifies all tenants of new building projects; in the past the city notified only property owners. In San Antonio, Mayor Cisneros regularly appoints representatives of the neighborhood-based organization Cops to city task forces. In Portland, as part of a public participation process, the city holds workshops and hearings to set goals for the future development of the central city. In Davis, California, the City Council has awarded the cable television franchise to a cooperatively owned company; subscribers to the cable service democratically elect the company's board. Davis has begun a participatory planning process called Davis 2000 to determine the direction of its future growth. Davis and other cities also promote cooperative housing.

Most of the urban populist–influenced cities have established public boards and commissions to deal with the problems of racial minorities, women, senior citizens, funding for the arts, and other issues, and have appointed community activists to these governmental bodies. Some cities, such as Berkeley and Santa Monica, have changed the date of municipal elections from April of odd years to November of even years so that they coincide with state and presidential elections, when voter turnout is highest.

The leadership style of the mayors in these cities is frequently "populist." The mayors are seen in public a great deal, hold community meetings and public hearings on policy issues, present themselves as being accessible to the average citizen, and as having a "moderate" personal life-style. Leaders attempt to communicate directly with citizens, either in person or via the mass media, rather than through formal political organizations.

The new economic development policies adopted by most urban populist–oriented cities differ significantly from the traditional policy of attracting large companies from outside the city by offering them tax breaks and other subsidies. These new policies reflect the philosophy of the "home-grown economy"—that cities should stimulate the growth and expansion of *existing* businesses (especially middle-sized ones) and assist in the creation of *new* small businesses. To promote a home-grown economy, some cities are taking a careful inventory of *city assets* such as waterfront property, universities, historical buildings, geographic locale, and potential tourist attractions, and developing *strategic plans* for economic development, to be carried out by public action with the government acting as an entrepreneur, and by public-private partnerships in which the city shares in the risk and the profit of new business ventures. To implement strategic plans, cities have created new corporate bodies and staffed them with *public entrepreneurs*, not bureaucrats. The experience of Louisville, described in Chapter 11, is just one example.

In St. Paul a local foundation, at the request of Mayor George Latimer, funded the Lowertown Redevelopment Corporation, which has developed and is implementing a plan to turn an aging section of the downtown area into an "urban village" consisting of new shops, restaurants, offices, housing, and artist studios. The St. Paul Port Authority acts as a development bank and provides funds for construction of major industrial parks and shopping developments, and to finance strategic planning for St. Paul's waterfront property along the Mississippi River. In San Antonio, Mayor Cisneros personally wrote a strategic plan for the expansion of biotechnology and medical firms in the region, and he lobbied the state legislature to open an engineering school at the San Antonio branch of the University of Texas so that Mexican-Americans could study to become engineers. In Burlington, Vermont, Mayor Bernard Sanders established a Commission on Local Ownership that is promoting the expansion of local businesses and the creation of new, worker-owned businesses. In Santa Monica, the city established two new nonprofit development corporations: the Santa Monica Pier Restoration Corporation, to direct the renovation of businesses and public facilities on the city-owned pier, and the Third Street Mall Development Corporation, to revive the city's aging pedestrian shopping street. St. Paul, Chicago, and other cities have established *small business incubator* facilities that provide space and technical assistance to local entrepreneurs wishing to start their own businesses. Most of these cities have also entered into joint ventures with private firms in which the city shares in future profits in exchange for direct assistance or subsidies. These cities are also requiring large corporations to sign "first source hiring" agreements in which the companies agree to offer new jobs first to city residents, particularly those unemployed in the inner city. These cities are trying, within financial and other practical limits, to be entrepreneurial—to be masters of their own economic destinies, rather than more passive actors.

The Need for a National Urban Policy

There are, of course, deep-seated problems of race and class in most U.S. cities that local governments cannot resolve by acting alone. Boston and Chicago are cases in point.

Boston has a populist mayor, Ray Flynn, who has adopted many of the policies discussed in this chapter, but the city he governs has a legacy of class and racial division. The quality of education provided by the school system is abysmally low—for both whites and blacks—and the city does not have the financial means to pay for the necessary rebuilding and upgrading. Blue-collar jobs have left the city and the Boston region's new growth industries are in high-technology industries and services. There is a mismatch of urban residents' skills and training that the city itself cannot remedy. Chicago had a black populist mayor, Harold Washington, who, like Flynn, tried to adopt pro-neighborhood progressive policies and innovative economic development plans, but this city too has deep racial divisions, a dilapidated and failing school system, and thousands of uneducated unemployed. In both cities, as in most major U.S. cities, there is a shortage of affordable housing for the white and black working class. The Reagan administration has reduced support for low- and moderate-income housing, job training, aid to impoverished local school systems, and urban mass transit systems. The Reagan administration's real urban policy has consisted of a dramatic increase in military spending that has resulted in the allocation of public funds to suburban regions, particularly in the West and Southwest.

In the absence of a Democratic administration in Washington, D.C., the outlook for many older Mid-western and Eastern cities is bleak. The question remains whether the new urban populist movements can set an example of approaches to public policy and to politics that can be followed nationally by a Democrat, when one is able to win the presidency.

A Democratic administration in Washington could use a revived and refunded Department of Housing and Urban Development to spread the vision and policies of urban populism to other cities around the country. Such an administration would also provide substantial funds for programs in housing, mass transit, and job training for such cities as Boston, Chicago, and other older cities with large, poor inner-city populations. These older cities cannot be rebuilt at the same time that a military buildup is funded. The growing federal deficit and trade imbalance will not allow both guns and butter for urban areas. Choices will have to be made. The challenge is to reformulate the relationship of the federal government to the nation's cities.

The Reagan administration's neglect of urban problems and its advocacy of the "free enterprise" city has only made life in the central cities more miserable. Urban neighborhoods continue to decay, while the suburbs boom and the elite and commuters enjoy life downtown in high-rise complexes. A continuation of these policies will bring cities that resemble the megacities in the futuristic film *Blade Runner*, in which the minority poor live mean, violent lives, the white suburbanites having fled to other planets.

The decentralization of industry and population that is the result of earlier government policies, and of economic and technological change, cannot be reversed. Entry-level jobs for the unskilled are no longer available in manufacturing, where job growth has been relatively stable, although many jobs have left the cities. The growth of new jobs in the advanced service sector has taken place in the suburbs and in the cities; yet at neither location have city residents benefited. There is a mismatch of skills and of location that cannot be easily overcome. The movement to the suburbs cannot be reversed, not even by a "natural" back-to-the-city movement. It might be possible to stabilize the loss of population in some central cities, but it will be difficult. Perhaps some young families can be persuaded to stay in the cities. However, racial differences cannot be wished away. Although progress has been made in civil rights and in public attitudes about race relations, further progress seems to be at a standstill.

A progressive national urban policy should be designed to assist both people and places, but not indiscriminately. People who need help, and claim it as a right of citizenship, should be allowed opportunities and given resources to enable them to help themselves—and this might mean moving to the suburbs or to regional cities in search of economic opportunity and a new start. Relocation assistance and job training should be provided, and there should be strong enforcement of antidiscrimination laws in housing. It is foolish for Americans to abandon their cities, and it will not serve them to continue subsidizing the development of the "dual city" with its extremes of wealth and poverty; help should be conditioned. Cities that do not need federal aid should not automatically receive it through overly broad revenue-sharing and Community Development Block Grant (CDBG) formulas. Distressed cities should receive targeted aid only if they are willing to help themselves. This means a much greater reliance on matching grants, and on federal monitoring that measures both the equity and efficiency outcomes. The Department of Housing and Urban Development needs to be given a new mission: to recast the idea of a public-private partnership into that of the Social Compact. The new urban policy should be based on a collaboration between local and state governments, community groups, and business with the federal government providing resources and setting national standards. Federal aid from HUD to distressed cities should be conditioned on the negotiation of a Social Compact that would include:

- *An asset-based strategy for economic development.* Each city would be required to make an inventory of its resources—poorly used and vacant land, convertible buildings, waterfront property, educational and nonprofit institutions, infrastructure, capital pledged by local banks and insurance companies—and submit a plan detailed in a document similar to *Chicago Works Together* or St. Paul's "home-grown economy" for developing these resources to promote balanced growth.
- *Pledges of private-sector support from business, labor, foundations, and educational institutions.*
- Involvement of citizens in neighborhood needs assessment.
- Commitments from the state government for assistance. In some cases, this might require the creation of metropolitan tax districts to create a broader tax base.
- A plan for joint federal and local monitoring of goals and a timetable for results.
- A plan for improving the city's schools, possibly similar to the Boston Compact, in which jobs are promised as incentives for improved school performance.

What this might mean, in practice, is that before a city could receive a federal grant, for example, it would first have to demonstrate how the grant would fit into its overall strategy for economic development and how the money would help meet specified hiring or community development goals. Also, HUD would issue much clearer standards for jobs created for residents per dollar of subsidy. In the CDBG program, stricter targeting standards might apply, such as using the median income for the city rather than the Standard Metropolitan Statistical Area (SMSA). HUD would review and monitor jointly with the city all negotiated hiring agreements. Cities that offered tax abatements without clear and strictly specified benefits would not be eligible for HUD grants. Most HUD and CDBG grants would be loans or matching grants that would require the recipient city to demonstrate a local financial commitment to the projects proposed for assistance. State governments would be put on notice that they too had a responsibility to cities in partnership with the federal government. Assistance from HUD would be predicated on state assistance and implementation of state programs for economic development.

Under this new approach of negotiating Social Compacts with distressed cities to promote growth with equity, HUD would gather case studies and data about existing city and state programs and would share knowledge about what seems to work in one city with many other cities; it would incorporate this new social knowledge into the Social Compacts that it arranges. In this way, Americans would learn from one another. The idea of the Social Compact is to have the federal government play a leadership role in redefining the concept of public-private partnership, so that it becomes a more equal partnership rather than a smokescreen for subsidizing private development.

Requiring such city strategic planning might sound overly bureaucratic, but the fact is that many states *already* require cities to include up-to-date land use, traffic, housing, and other plans as part of the city's general plan. Consequently, much of the data is already available. What needs to be done is to link these plans to a *strategy* and to plan for implementation of projects in the context of that strategy. The thrust of the Social Compact is not so much planning as it is having the federal government provide leadership and incentives to urban communities so that genuine community-labor-government-business partnerships can be formed to revitalize their cities. The point is to learn from the innovative policies just mentioned and to utilize the existence of new community organizations, new city partnerships, and new state initiatives in economic development to construct a truly progressive federalism based on the idea of *equal* partnerships.

The following paragraphs detail how this new community-based partnership approach might work in some key areas of urban need.

A Community-Based Housing Supply Program

The laying of the political groundwork for a new national housing policy is already under way. Senator Alan Cranston (D-Calif.), chairman of the Senate Subcommittee on Housing, is committed to introducing a new national housing bill. Cranston held hearings in 1987 and 1988 attended by housing experts and community housing groups from around the country. He has asked developer James Rouse, whose Enterprise Foundation is dedicated to promoting low-income housing, to head a task force on housing policy, and he has contracted with professors at the Massachusetts Institute of Technology to produce a number of research papers on housing. The content of the Cranston bill is yet to be determined; many community housing advocates have begun to argue for a new approach based on a community housing supply program.

This program would rely heavily on a community-based, nonprofit housing delivery system to expand the long-term supply of low- and moderate-income housing. It would build on the experience of the numerous local housing partnerships and programs mentioned in the previous section of this chapter. Leading advocates of this new partnership include the National Low Income Housing Coalition and Mayor Ray Flynn's housing staff at the Boston Redevelopment Authority. Both envision a new National Housing Partnership program under which the federal government would provide matching funds to assist locally based nonprofit housing initiatives. Federal dollars would be matched by local governments, businesses, private foundations, the United Way, churches, and state government housing agencies. Money would be available for seed grants to enable local nonprofit housing groups to start up or to expand their development efforts. Capital grants would be provided to community-based partnerships for the construction of housing. (Direct capital grants reduce the long-term debt that escalates the cost of housing.) A new national housing agency in HUD would oversee the program of seed and capital grants.

Of course, while this bill goes through the legislative process and until the new community-based housing supply agency begins to produce housing, some immediate steps will be needed to deal with the homeless emergency and with the preservation of existing public and federally assisted housing. The Homeless Relief Bill, passed by Congress and signed by the president in 1987, provided some immediate relief for 1988—$425 million for emergency shelter, food, and health care. The next step is for a new administration to give priority to the Homeless Persons Survival Act, a bill filed by Senators Albert Gore (D-Tenn.) and Daniel Moynihan

(D-N.Y.) in the Senate, and by Representative Mickey Leland (D-Texas) and a host of cosponsors in the House. This is the best and most comprehensive bill to address the short-range needs of the homeless. It deals not only with housing but with funds for mental health, nutrition, education, social services for homeless children, and other aspects of the homeless situation.

The other immediate problem is preservation of existing public and subsidized housing. A moratorium should be imposed on the prepayment of HUD-financed mortgages by owners of apartment buildings that rent to low- and moderate-income persons. A number of these buildings are reaching the twenty-year mark when HUD provision of assisted rents will run out, and many of the buildings could then be converted to market-rate condominiums, resulting in massive evictions of low- and moderate-income families. A new incentive program is needed for the preservation of existing subsidized housing, particularly by conversion to tenant-purchase cooperatives—a program that has been effective at the local level in the city of Santa Monica, where the rent control law gives tenants the right to purchase the building in which they life if a fair price can be negotiated. The city's community housing corporation provides financial and technical assistance to low-income tenants who wish to purchase their buildings as limited-equity cooperatives. Adequate funding will still have to be provided for the country's existing 1.2 million public housing units. This includes funds for rehabilitation and for greater tenant involvement in management of their buildings (Schwartz et al. 1988).

A Strategic Mass Transit Policy

The Federal Mass Transportation Act of 1987 extends federal mass transit assistance through 1991. The bill was passed over the objections of President Reagan. Seventy percent of the federal mass transit subsidy payment for operating expenses goes to eight large urban systems: New York, Boston, Chicago, Philadelphia, Cleveland, San Francisco-Oakland, Detroit, and Washington, D.C. Maintaining this support for these systems is a necessity. Although only 3 percent of all urban trips are made by mass transit, over 70 percent of the riders of mass transit have incomes under $20,000. Forty percent of the ridership has an income less than $10,000. Sixty percent are females and 40 percent belong to minorities. Most existing mass transit systems clearly serve a low- and moderate-income group that cannot afford other means of transit. Given the low ridership of new fixed rail systems (as in Miami), and given the continued dispersal of population and business outside central cities, it does not make sense for the federal government to fund any new heavy rail systems. Instead, the Urban Mass Transit Administration should be made a part of HUD, and it should work with cities to develop transit programs that fit in with the cities' economic development and housing plans. Cities should be encouraged to consider construction of light rail systems, linked to downtown transit malls and to a regional bus system that would more easily transport city residents to suburban job locations. Light rail systems cost $5–$20 million per mile, compared with $50–$60 million per mile for heavy rail systems. New housing projects and industrial parks might be laid out along transit lines (Vuchic 1986).

Elements of new city and regional transit agreements would also include limiting the number of autos in downtown areas through discriminatory pricing mechanisms and restrictions on the area devoted to parking; creation of pedestrian streets and walkways in downtowns; required Traffic Systems Management programs similar to that adopted by Los Angeles for the Olympics.

Knowledge about people in cities and about the potential for walking and biking could be enhanced by HUD and UMTA involvement in the annual pedestrian conference that has been organized and sponsored since 1981 by the city of Boulder, Colorado. These conferences have brought together transit planners and urban design experts from many U.S. cities and from foreign countries to discuss how to make cities more walkable and less subject to the tyranny of the auto.

Both HUD and UMTA could require all urban transit systems that receive federal operating and capital subsidies to adopt traffic management programs, and require at least some to adopt pedestrian programs. Cities that used federal aid to expand existing fixed or light rail systems would be required to exploit the development potential of new stations—the new commercial activity and the enhanced location value—by linking new jobs and businesses to the employment needs of residents and building, where feasible, affordable housing near the transit line. The goal would be to promote more coordinated development, and to have a more balanced transit system—one that is multimodal, promotes access to the metropolitan region for all who live in it, and reduces environmental pollution.

The Urban Education Compact

Aid to urban school systems should be conditioned on the establishment of local compacts, modeled after the Boston Compact, which specify a sharing of responsibility for the improvement of the schools and provision of a link to jobs and job training for graduates of central city schools. The Social Compact agreement for economic development already outlined should include this educational component.

Federal assistance for court-ordered desegregation must be maintained. It should focus on early education and on the establishment of a variety of innovative and quality magnet schools. In addition, both HUD and the Department of Education should meet with the governors of states seeking federal aid to education to encourage the establishment of suburb-city tax sharing or alternate methods of financing improvements in urban schools.

In addition, cities with a substantial illiterate adult population should be encouraged to use school facilities for adult education programs. All cities should be encouraged to use upgraded school facilities for educational enrichment programs scheduled before and after school; for community education; and for the delivery of community services such as health and nutrition programs. Maximum use of the public educational infrastructure makes economic and social sense in terms of a return on past and future investment of public funds.

Welfare Reform, Job Training, and Relocation Assistance

There appears to be bipartisan agreement, both in Congress and around the nation, that the major component of the welfare system, Aid to Families with Dependent Children (AFDC), should be transformed into a program of education, training, day care, and work. (Congress passed a bill for moderate welfare reform along these lines in late 1988.)

Welfare and urban policy are critically related. A federal minimum benefit—a national standard for a decent level of assistance—would allow for the possibility of greater mobility for those on welfare and would introduce a much needed element of equity into the social safety net. Such mobility is to be encouraged, so that recipients have at least some chance of moving to areas of better economic opportunity without possibly receiving a lower set of benefits. But work training programs do not create permanent jobs. There must be jobs in the economy for those who have received training that developed new skills and work habits. One major reason for the success of the Massachusetts Education and Training welfare reform program is the state's low level of unemployment and high demand for entry-level workers.

These are all also matters of concern to the working poor, who make up the overwhelming majority of those who rely on the social welfare and unemployment systems for *temporary* help when in trouble because of job loss, medical problems, or other misfortune. *Less than 10 percent* of all welfare recipients are dependent on welfare for more than eight years. Sixty-six percent of all first-time adult AFDC recipients worked in the two years before going on welfare—and the most common reason that a woman with children applies for AFDC is that she becomes divorced or separated (Ellwood 1988).

Reforming the welfare system will not solve the much larger problems of the geographical separation of the urban poor and working class and available jobs, and the mismatch between the skills possessed by these people and those required by the economy. Reforming the welfare system does not help displaced workers in older industrial cities. Both groups need retraining assistance and, in some cases, relocation assistance. One step in the right direction would be the establishment of a computerized national job bank, and perhaps a national employment service linked to worker retraining such as the one that has operated successfully in Sweden.

Ultimately, urban policy must be seen not simply as a handout for poor people of color in central cities, but as an integrated part of an overall set of economic policies aimed at promoting growth *and* equity. This analysis has suggested the content of new, more equal partnerships for the nation's cities. Whether such partnerships can be achieved politically remains to be seen.

References

Adams, Terry K., and Greg Duncan. 1988. *The Persistence of Urban Poverty and Its Demographic and Behavioral Correlates.* Ann Arbor: Survey Research Center, University of Michigan.

Boyte, Harry. 1983. *The Backyard Revolution.* Philadelphia: Temple University Press.

————. 1985. *Community Is Possible.* New York: Harper and Row.

Clavel, Pierre. 1985. *The Progressive City.* New Brunswick, N.J.: Rutgers University Press.

Ellwood, David T. 1988. *Poor Support and Poverty in the American Family.* New York: Basic Books.

Georgakas, Dan, and Marvin Surkin. 1975. *Detroit: I Do Mind Dying.* New York: St. Martin's Press.

Keating, Dennis, and Norman Krumholz. 1985. "The Chicago Development Plan." *Journal of the American Planning Association* 51 (Summer):395–396.

MacDonald, Michael. 1984. *America's Cities: A Report on the Myth of the Urban Renaissance.* New York: Simon and Schuster.

Peterson, Paul, ed. 1985. *The New Urban Reality.* Washington, D.C.: Brookings Institution.

Schwartz, David D., Richard C. Ferlanto, and Daniel N. Hoffman. 1988. *A New Housing Policy for America: Recapturing the American Dream*. Philadelphia: Temple University Press.

Swanstrom, Todd. 1985. *The Crisis of Growth Politics*. Philadelphia: Temple University Press.

Vuchic, Vukan. 1986. "Urban Transit: A Public Asset of National Significance." *Urban Resources* 161 (Fall).